THE ESSENTIAL BIBLE

DICTIONARY

NORMAN HILLYER

Designed by Peter Wyart,
Three's Company

Worldwide co-edition organized and
produced by
Angus Hudson Ltd,
Concorde House,
Grenville Place, Mill Hill,
London NW7 3SA, England
Tel: +44 20 8959 3668
Fax: +44 20 8959 3678
coed@angushudson.com

ISBN 0 8024 2476 7

Printed in Singapore

1 2 3 4 5 6 7 8 9 06 05 04 03 02 01

Picture acknowledgments

Photographs
Tim Dowley: pp. 8, 15, 19, 29, 30, 37,
38, 40, 60, 63, 90, 94, 95, 115, 122, 130,
145, 160, 166, 172, 216, 231
Peter Wyart: pp. 3, 42, 64, 75, 96, 117,
127, 139, 150, 154, 173, 185, 192, 198,
203, 205, 236, 241

Illustrations
Frank Baber: pp. 70, 200
Peter Dennis: pp. 14 middle, 52, 53
Jeremy Gower: pp. 228 top, 229 top
Alan Harris: p. 104
James Macdonald: pp. 46, 49, 50, 80,
92-93, 123, 142, 167, 168, 170-171,
187, 194, 204, 220, 223, 226, 239
Alan Parry: pp. 1, 55 bottom, 71, 72,
131, 151, 156, 183, 228-229 bottom
Richard Scott: pp. 15 top, 54, 73, 150
top, 214, 240, 245
Pam Stephens: pp. 14 top, bottom, 15
bottom, 16, 17, 76 top, 105

Moody Press, a ministry of the Moody
Bible Institute, is designed for education,
evangelization, and edification. If we
may assist you in knowing more about
Christ and the Christian life, please write
us without obligation:

Moody Press
c/o MLM
Chicago, Illinois 60610, USA

THE ESSENTIAL BIBLE

DICTIONARY

NORMAN HILLYER

MOODY PRESS
CHICAGO

Preface

This Pocket Dictionary is based on the New International Version of the Bible (NIV), although reference is also made to a number of words familiar from the Authorized (King James) Version (AV/KJV).

The 2448 entries average only about 33 words each, so the work can claim to be concise. Readers will find that the Bible verses quoted will often provide further details on the topic consulted. Some puzzling expressions are explained (as in the entries for Double; Wings). The meaning of a term is mentioned in *italics*, when this is of some significance.

Compilers of dictionaries on any subject must gratefully build on the labours of those who have gone before. That leaves their successors freer to consult more recent literature. In the present case, this has involved Bible commentaries, scholarly journals and works on archaeology and the life and times of biblical days. The aim has been to make the result-ing volume as helpful, up-to-date and reliable as possible, while remaining a quick reference for the busy reader.

To our regret today, making clear the identity of flora, fauna, gems and even colours was not of great concern to ancient writers. Compare modern translations and our uncertainties about the original meanings are soon exposed; but the more likely guesses are given here.

Two books by experts in their field have proved invaluable: G. S. Cansdale, *Animals of Bible Lands* (Paternoster Press, 1970); F. Nigel Hepper, *Illustrated Encyclopedia of Bible Plants* (Inter-Varsity Press/Baker Book House, 1992).

My warm appreciation goes to the partners of Three's Company, Tim Dowley and Peter Wyart, for their skills in creating this book.
Norman Hillyer

Abbreviations

BIBLICAL BOOKS

Chron.	Chronicles
Col.	Colossians
Cor.	Corinthians
Dan.	Daniel
Deut.	Deuteronomy
Eccles.	Ecclesiastes
Eph.	Ephesians
Exod.	Exodus
Ezek.	Ezekiel
Gal.	Galatians
Gen.	Genesis
Hab.	Habakkuk
Hag.	Haggai
Heb.	Hebrews
Hos.	Hosea
Isa.	Isaiah
Jer.	Jeremiah
Jon.	Jonah
Josh.	Joshua
Judg.	Judges
Lam.	Lamentations
Lev.	Leviticus
Macc.	Maccabees
Mal.	Malachi
Matt.	Matthew
Mic.	Micah
Nah.	Nahum
Neh.	Nehemiah
Num.	Numbers
Obad.	Obadiah
Pet.	Peter
Phil.	Philippians
Philem.	Philemon
Prov.	Proverbs
Ps.	Psalms
Rev.	Revelation
Rom.	Romans
Sam.	Samuel
Song of Sol.	Song of Solomon
Thess.	Thessalonians
Tim.	Timothy
Zech.	Zechariah
Zeph.	Zephaniah

OTHER ABBREVIATIONS

AV/KJV	*Authorized (King James) Version*
JB	*Jerusalem Bible*
NEB	*New English Bible*
NIV	*New International Version*
NT	New Testament
OT	Old Testament
RSV	*Revised Standard Version*

CROSS REFERENCE TO COLOUR FEATURES

ACACIA *See* Trees p. 172.

A

AARON. Brother of Moses and Miriam (Exod. 6:20; Num. 26:59) and first high priest (Exod. 28–29; Lev. 8).

AARON'S STAFF. God appointed Aaron and the tribe of Levi to be Israel's priests (Num. 16), confirming their status by the miraculous budding and fruiting of Aaron's staff (Num. 17). The staff was preserved as a permanent reminder (Num. 17:10; Heb. 9:4).

ABADDON (or **APOLLYON**) (*Destruction*). 1. Place of the lost dead in Sheol (Job 28:22).
   2. Satanic angel of the bottomless pit (Rev. 9:11).

ABARIM (*Regions Beyond,* i.e. beyond the Dead Sea, as seen from Judah). Mountain range, including Mt. Nebo (Deut. 32:49).

ABBA (Aramaic). Child's familiar name for *father* (Mark 14:36; Rom. 8:15).

ABDON. Last minor judge (Judg. 12:13–15); from Pirathon, SW of Nablus.

ABEL. Shepherd son of Adam and Eve, murdered by his jealous brother Cain (Gen. 4; Heb. 11:4; 1 John 3:12). The first martyr (Luke 11:51) and an exemplar of righteousness (Matt. 23:35).

ABEL BETH MAACAH. Town, N of Lake Huleh, where Sheba took refuge from Joab (2 Sam. 20:15). Captured by Syrians (1 Kings 15:20) and Assyrians (2 Kings 15:29).

ABEL MEHOLAH. Town in Jordan valley, S of Beth Shan (Judg. 7:22). Birthplace of Elisha (1 Kings 19:16).

ABIATHAR. Alone escaped Saul's massacre of priests at Nob. Joined David (1 Sam. 22:20–23) and with Zadok courageously served him during Absalom's rebellion (2 Sam. 15:24–36; 17:15). Deposed by Solomon for supporting Adonijah's attempt to seize the throne (1 Kings 1–2).

ABIEZER. Name of Gideon's clan (Judg. 6:11), part of the tribe of Manasseh (Josh. 17:2). Responded to Gideon's call to fight Midianites (Judg. 6:34).

ABIGAIL. Wife of Nabal (1 Sam. 25:3). Dissuaded David from avenging her husband's insult, and on Nabal's death married him (1 Sam. 25:42). Shared his adventures at Gath and Ziklag (1 Sam. 27:3; 30:5). Bore him a son at Hebron (2 Sam. 3:3).

ABIHU. *See* Nadab.

ABIJAH. King of Judah (913–910 BC), who condemned Israel's apostasy before defeating their larger forces (2 Chron. 13).

ABILENE. Tetrarchy (fourth part of a region) of Lysanias (Luke 3:1), NW of Damascus.

ABIMELECH. 1. Dynastic name of Philistine kings of Gerar who made treaties with Abraham (Gen. 20–21) and Isaac (Gen. 26).

Acre, biblical Acco

2. Son of Gideon (Judg. 8:31). After Gideon's death, slew his 70 brothers and was made king at Shechem. Crushed a revolt at Shechem, but was killed attacking Thebez (Judg. 9).

ABIRAM. 1. With his brother Dathan and a Levite, Korah, met a dramatic death after rebelling against Moses (Num. 16).
2. Eldest son of Hiel. Died after his father rebuilt Jericho (870 BC), fulfilling an ancient curse (1 Kings 16:34; Josh. 6:26).

ABISHAG. Lovely girl of Shunem who nursed the aged David (1 Kings 1:1–4). After David's death, his eldest son Adonijah wanted to marry her (1 Kings 2:17–22) but King Solomon denied him, fearing a rival.

ABISHAI. Son of David's stepsister Zeruiah (2 Sam. 17:25), brother of Joab and Asahel (2 Sam. 2:18), and deputy army chief (2 Sam. 18:2). David prevented him from rashly slaying the sleeping king Saul (1 Sam. 26:7–9). Saved David's life (2 Sam. 21:17).

ABNER. Saul's cousin and commander in chief (1 Sam. 14:50). Supported Ish-Bosheth's claim to succeed Saul (2 Sam. 2:8), but later went over to David (2 Sam. 3). Murdered by Joab to avenge his brother Asahel's death (2 Sam. 3:27).

ABOMINATION OF DESOLATION. Expresses notion of desecration resulting in devastation. Foretold in Dan. 9:27; 11:31; 12:11). Applied to altar of Zeus erected in Jerusalem Temple (168 BC) by Antiochus Epiphanes (1 Macc. 1:54, 59; 2 Macc. 6:2). A sign of the last days (Mark 13:14; 2 Thess. 2:3–4; Rev. 17:5).

ABRAHAM (*Father of Multitudes*). Born at Ur of the Chaldees; after marrying Sarai, moved to Haran (Gen. 11:27–32) and then to Canaan, which God pledged to give to him and his descendants (Gen. 12). Although Abraham and Sarai were aged, God promised him a great family (Gen. 15; 17). Abraham's faith, severely tested by God's order to sacrifice Isaac (Gen. 22; Heb. 11:8–12), illustrates a right relationship with God (Rom. 4).

ABRAHAM'S SIDE ('bosom', AV/KJV). Jewish synonym for Paradise, used by Jesus to depict the bliss of the righteous dead (Luke 16:22).

ABRAM. Original name of Abraham (Gen. 17:5).

ABSALOM. Handsome son of king David and Maacah (2 Sam. 3:3; 14:25–27). Killed Amnon for raping his sister Tamar and was banished by David (2 Sam. 13). On his return he led a rebellion that seriously threatened David's rule (2 Sam. 15). His death in battle caused David great grief (2 Sam. 18).

ABYSS. Place of punishment for demons (Luke 8:31; Rev. 9:11; 20:3).

ACACIA *See* Trees p. 172

ACCO. Only natural harbour S of Phoenicia in OT times (Judg. 1:31). Ptolemais in Acts 21:7.

ACCUSER. Legal term for prosecuting counsel (Job 31:35); applied to Moses (John 5:45) and to Satan (Rev. 12:10).

ACHAIA. Greece (Acts 18:12).

ACHAN. By stealing booty from Jericho, caused Israel's defeat at Ai (Josh. 7). Stoned and cremated in a valley consequently named Achor (*Trouble*).

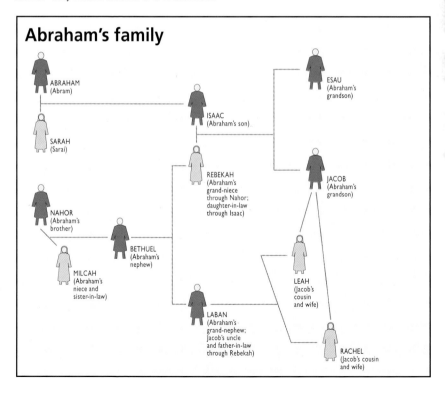

Abraham's family

- ABRAHAM (Abram)
- SARAH (Sarai)
- ISAAC (Abraham's son)
- ESAU (Abraham's grandson)
- REBEKAH (Abraham's grand-niece through Nahor; daughter-in-law through Isaac)
- JACOB (Abraham's grandson)
- NAHOR (Abraham's brother)
- MILCAH (Abraham's niece and sister-in-law)
- BETHUEL (Abraham's nephew)
- LABAN (Abraham's grand-nephew; Jacob's uncle and father-in-law through Rebekah)
- LEAH (Jacob's cousin and wife)
- RACHEL (Jacob's cousin and wife)

ACHISH. Philistine king of Gath, who harboured David after his flight from Saul (1 Sam. 21:10; 27:3).

ACSAH. Daughter of Caleb, given in marriage to Othniel for capturing Kiriath Sepher (Josh. 15:16). As her dowry, Caleb gave her valuable springs in the Negev (Judg. 1:12–15).

ACSHAPH. City SE of Acco (Josh. 19:25). Its king killed fighting against Joshua (Josh. 11:1).

ACTS OF THE APOSTLES. Written by Luke as a sequel to his Gospel (Acts 1:1). Outlines the contribution of Peter and Paul to the extension of the church after Christ's ascension, from Jerusalem, the centre of Judaism, to Rome, the capital of the Gentile world (Acts 1:8).

ADAM (*Man*). Both a personal name and a generic term. The first man (Luke 3:38) was formed by God as the climax to creation (Gen. 1:26; 2:7). Disobedience led to the man's expulsion from Eden (Gen. 3). Died aged 930 (Gen. 5:5). Adam's union with Eve illustrates the permanence of marriage (Matt. 19:4–6). Paul draws contrasts between Christ and Adam (Rom. 5:12–15; 1 Cor. 15:22, 45).

ADAM. Town in the Jordan valley, N of Jericho. The temporary blocking of the river, probably by collapsing limestone cliffs (most recently in 1927), enabled the Israelites to cross opposite Jericho (Josh. 3:16).

ADMAH. One of the cities of the plain (Gen. 14:2) destroyed with Sodom and Gomorrah (Deut. 29:23; Hos. 11:8). Now submerged under the Dead Sea.

ADONI-BEZEK. King of Bezek, captured by the forces of Judah and Simeon, and incapacitated (Judg. 1:5–7).

ADONIJAH. Son of David who tried to usurp the kingdom (1 Kings 1). The proclamation of Solomon as king panicked the rebels into surrender. Although pardoned by Solomon, Adonijah's later action was interpreted as treason and he was executed (1 Kings 2:22–25).

ADONIRAM (or Adoram). Superintendent of forced labour under David (2 Sam. 20:24), Solomon (1 Kings 4:6; 5:14), and Rehoboam. Stoned to death by rebels, setting off Jeroboam's revolt against Rehoboam (1 Kings 12:18).

ADONI-ZEDEK. Amorite king of Jerusalem. Overthrown by Joshua (Josh. 10:1–27).

ADOPTION. Legal term applied by Paul to converts' change of status to membership of God's family (Rom. 8:15–17, 23; Gal. 4:5–7).

ADRAMMELECH and **SHAREZER.** Sons of Sennacherib, king of Assyria, who murdered their father in 681 BC (2 Kings 19:37; Isa. 37:38).

ADRAMMELECH and **ANAMMELECH.** Deities worshipped by child sacrifice by settlers from the Syrian city of Sepharvaim brought to Samaria by the Assyrians (2 Kings 17:31).

ADRAMYTTIUM. Seaport of Mysia, on NW coast of Roman province of Asia (modern Turkey) (Acts 27:2).

ADRIEL. Saul's eldest daughter, promised to David for killing Goliath (1 Sam. 18:19; 2 Sam. 21:8).

Coin of Agrippa II

ADULLAM. Canaanite city (Josh. 12:15). David hid from Saul in a nearby cave (1 Sam. 22:1).

ADULTERY. Illicit sexual relations forbidden (Exod. 20:14) under pain of death (Deut. 22:22). Jesus condemned even the desire (Matt. 5:28). Bars entry into God's kingdom (1 Cor. 6:9), but is not beyond forgiveness (John 8:3–11). Figuratively, describes unfaithfulness by God's people (Hos. 2—3; 9:1; Matt. 12:39; 16:4; James 4:4; Rev. 2:22).

ADUMMIM. Steep pass between Jericho and Jerusalem (Josh. 15:7; 18:17); traditionally on the Good Samaritan's route (Luke 10:30).

AENEAS. Paralytic healed by Peter at Lydda (Acts 9:33).

AENON (*Springs*). Place near Salim, W of Jordan, where John the Baptist baptised (John 3:23).

AGABUS. Christian prophet of Jerusalem, whose prediction of famine was fulfilled about AD 46, in the reign of Claudius (Acts 11:28). Foretold Paul's imprisonment (Acts 21:10).

AGAG. King of Amalek, spared by Saul contrary to God's order, but executed by Samuel (1 Sam. 15).

AGAGITE. Not a discreditable allusion to Agag (Esther 3:1) but a reference to Haman's home of Agazi.

AGATE. Precious stone on the high priest's breastpiece (Exod. 28:19; 39:12). Used to beautify New Jerusalem (Isa. 54:12; chalcedony in Rev. 21:19).

AGRIPPA I (9 BC–AD 44). Son of Aristobulus and grandson of Herod the Great; in Acts 12 called Herod the king. Ruled over Judea and Samaria, AD 41–44.

AGRIPPA II (AD 27–100). Son of above; ruled over Iturea, Trachonitis and Lysanias. Twitted Paul with trying to convert him (Acts 25:13—26:32).

AHAB. King of Israel (874–853 BC). Married Jezebel of Sidon and built a temple for her god Baal (1 Kings 16:32). Consequently he had to contend with the prophet Elijah (1 Kings 17—22). Incited by Jezebel, Ahab seized Naboth's vineyard (1 Kings 21), and earned Elijah's sentence of doom. Misled by false prophets, Ahab was killed fighting the Syrians at Ramoth Gilead (1 Kings 22).

AHASUERUS. *See* Xerxes.

AHAZ. Succeeded his father Jotham as king of Judah (732–716 BC). Attacked by Israel and Syria, Ahaz refused Isaiah's appeal for trust in God (Isa. 7) and turned to Assyria for help (2 Kings 16:7), resulting in a century of vassalage for Judah (2 Kings 16:10–18; 2 Chron. 28:24).

AHAZIAH. 1. Succeeded his father Ahab as king of Israel (853–852 BC; 1 Kings 22:40). Denounced by Elijah for resorting to Baal-Zebub, god of Ekron (2 Kings 1:1–18).
2. Younger son of Jehoram, king of Judah. His brief reign (841 BC) condemned as evil (2 Chron. 22:3–9). Slain by Jehu (2 Kings 9:16–28).

AHIJAH. Prophet from Shiloh who tore up a new robe, symbolising the division of Solomon's kingdom (1 Kings 11:26–40). When Jeroboam led Israel into idolatry, Ahijah foretold his family's extinction and Israel's exile (1 Kings 14:6–16).

AHIKAM. Sent by Josiah to consult the prophetess Huldah (2 Kings 22:12). Protected Jeremiah when threatened with death (Jer. 26:24) as did his son Gedaliah, appointed governor of Judah by Nebuchadnezzar (2 Kings 25:22; Jer. 39:14).

AHIMAAZ. Zadok's son. During Absalom's rebellion ran secret messages to David (2 Sam. 15:27) and reported Absalom's defeat (2 Sam. 18:19–32).

AHIMELECH. High priest at Nob, slain by Saul for aiding David (1 Sam. 21—22).

AHINOAM. David's wife from Jezreel (1 Sam. 25:43). Captured at Ziklag by Amalekites, but rescued by David (1 Sam. 30). Bore David a son, Amnon, at Hebron (2 Sam. 3:2).

AHITHOPHEL. David's counsellor (2 Sam. 16:23) who conspired with Absalom. When his advice was rejected, he foresaw the collapse of the rebellion and hanged himself (2 Sam. 17).

AI. Town E of Bethel, burned by Joshua after his first attack failed due to Achan's sin (Josh. 7—8).

AIJALON. Levitical hill town guarding a strategic valley near Jerusalem. Originally allotted to Dan (Josh. 19:42; Judg. 1:35), occupied by Benjamites (1 Chron. 8:13), fortified by Rehoboam (2 Chron. 11:10), and captured by Philistines in the reign of Ahaz (2 Chron. 28:18).

AKELDAMA. Name of potter's field (Acts 1:19), bought as a cemetery for strangers with blood-money disowned by Judas Iscariot (Matt. 27:3–10; Zech. 11:12–13).

ALEXANDER. Common Greek name.
1. Son of Simon of Cyrene (Mark 15:21).
2. Member of the high-priestly family (Acts 4:6).
3. Would-be spokesman for Jews at Ephesus riot (Acts 19:33).
4. False teacher at Ephesus (1 Tim. 1:20).
5. Roman metalworker who troubled Paul (2 Tim. 4:14).

ALGUM *See* Trees p. 172.

ALIENS/STRANGERS. Having experienced Egyptian bondage, Israelites must treat non-Jews sympathetically (Exod. 23:9). In the NT a figure of speech for Christians in this world, away from their true home, heaven (1 Pet. 2:11).

ALLELUIA. *See* Hallelujah.

ALMIGHTY (*All-sufficient*). Divine title revealed to Abraham (Gen. 17:1).

ALMOND (*Watched for*). *See* Trees p. 172.

ALMUGWOOD. *See* Trees p. 172.

ALOES. *See* Herbs and spices p. 92.

ALPHA and **OMEGA.** First and last letters of Greek alphabet. As a title (Rev. 1:8; 22:13) alludes to divine involvement in the origin, preservation and ultimate end of all creation. *See* First and Last.

ALPHAEUS. 1. Father of Levi (Matthew), the tax collector (Mark 2:14).

2. Father of one of two apostles called James (Matt. 10:3; Acts 1:13).

ALTAR. *See* Tabernacle p. 214.

ALTAR OF BURNT OFFERING. *See* Tabernacle p. 214.

ALTAR OF INCENSE. *See* Tabernacle p. 214.

AMALEKITES. Nomadic Arabian tribe, descendants of Amalek (Gen 36:12). Chronic foes of Israelites, in days of Moses (Exod. 17:8), Gideon (Judg. 7:12), Samuel and Saul (1 Sam. 14:48), David (1 Sam. 27:8) and Hezekiah (1 Chron. 4:43).

AMASA. 1. Son of Ithra and David's sister Abigail. Led Absalom's rebel forces (2 Sam. 17:25); defeated by Joab (2 Sam. 18:7), but pardoned by David and appointed commander in chief (2 Sam. 19:13). Treacherously slain by Joab (2 Sam. 20:10).

2. Ephraimite prompted by the prophet Oded to secure the repatriation of Jewish prisoners of war from Pekah of Israel (2 Chron. 28:12).

AMAZIAH. 1. Succeeded his father Joash as king of Judah (796–767 BC). Overconfident after defeating Edom (2 Kings 14:7), he fatally attacked Jehoash of Israel (2 Kings 14:13).

2. Jeroboam II's priest who tried to silence the prophet Amos at Bethel (Amos 7:10).

AMBASSADOR. An envoy carrying a message (Isa. 57:9), not a modern state's resident representative. Used of Christ's representatives carrying his message of reconciliation (2 Cor. 5:20; Eph. 6:20).

AMEN. Term signifying agreement and acceptance (Deut. 27:15; Neh. 5:13; 1 Cor. 14:16). Jesus' unique formula 'I tell you the truth' (Matt. 5:18; 'verily' in AV/KJV) is literally 'Amen' and expresses messianic authority. Used as a divine title (Rev. 3:14).

AMETHYST. Precious stone on the high priest's breastpiece (Exod. 28:19; 39:12) and one foundation of the wall of New Jerusalem (Rev. 21:20).

AMMON, AMMONITES. Descendants of Ben-Ammi, Lot's younger son (Gen. 19:38), and so Israel's relatives (Deut. 2:19). They proved chronic enemies. Oppressed Israel (Judg. 3:13), but were defeated by Jephthah (Judg. 11) and Saul (1 Sam. 11:11), and punished by David for insulting his envoys (2 Sam. 10). Raided Judah in Jehoshaphat's day (2 Chron. 20) and assassinated Joash (2 Chron. 24:25), though were later

Domesticated animals

Donkey

Bull. Used in sacrifice (Lev. 4; 16:11-19); inadequate to remove sins (Heb. 10:4).

Camel. Valued desert animal (Gen. 37:25; Exod. 9:3). Proverbial for great size (Matt. 19:24). Hair used for rough but hard-wearing garments (Matt. 3:4).

Donkey. Valuable pack animal. Surefooted, content with poor fodder, able to cover 30 km (18 mi) a day and long-lived (25-40 years). As a royal mount, symbolised peace (Zech. 9:9; Mark 21:2).

Goat. Traditional sacrifice for expiation (Lev. 4:23; Heb. 10:4). Valued source of milk, and so for yoghurt and cheese (Prov. 27:27). In a mixed herd on the move, goats went ahead of sheep, hence the symbolism of goats for kings (Dan. 8:21). Goat hair woven into sackcloth for tents and rough clothing (Exod. 26:7; Heb. 11:37).

Heifer. Young cow, valued for ploughing (Judg. 14:18), threshing (Jer. 50:11) and milk (Isa. 7:21). Applied figuratively

Goat

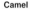
Camel

to beauty (Judg. 14:18), splendour (Jer. 46:20), stubbornness (Hos. 4:16), and being well trained (Hos. 10:11). The 'red' (golden) heifer was important in sacrifice: to ratify a covenant (Gen. 15:9), expiate a violent death (Deut. 21:1-9), or restore ritual cleanness (Num. 19; Heb. 9:13).

Horse. Valued in warfare (Job 39:19-25) for being sure-footed (Isa. 63:13), fearless (Jer. 8:6) and speedy (Jer.12:5). As an apocalyptic figure, associated with God's Spirit (Zech. 1:8), four seals in John's vision (Rev.6:2-8), and the triumphant Christ and his armies (Rev. 19:11)

Lamb. Principal animal of sacrifice (Exod. 29:38; Lev. 4:32; 12:6; 14:10; Num. 28:3), especially for Passover (Exod.

Horse and chariot

12; Mark 14:12). *See* Ram; Sheep.

Mule. Hybrid of a donkey stallion and a horse mare, combining surefootedness with strength. Crossbreeding forbidden by Lev. 19:19, so animals were imported (Ezek. 27:14).

Yoke of ox

Ox. Allowed for food (Deut. 14:4). Frequently offered in sacrifice (Num. 7). Used in ploughing (Amos 6:12), threshing (Deut. 25:4) and sometimes as a pack animal (1 Chron. 12:40). The wild ox (aurochs, Num. 23:22) died out about AD 1400.

Pig. Eats anything, from mice to roots; wild pig (boar) most at home in forest and marsh (Ps. 80:13). Listed as unclean food (Lev. 11:7; Deut. 14:8).

Ram. Male sheep, much used in sacrifices (Num. 7). Valued for food (Gen. 31:38) and wool (2 Kings 3:4). Figuratively, of the rich and powerful (Ezek. 34:17) and kings of Media and Persia (Dan. 8:3-7). *See* Shearing; Sheep.

Sheep. Greatly valued for wool (2 Kings 3:4), skins (Exod. 25:5), meat (1 Sam. 25:18), and as sacrificial animals (Exod. 20:24). Symbol of being leaderless (1 Kings 22:17) and helpless (Matt. 9:36). Associated with sin (Isa. 53:6), judgment (Matt. 25:32), God's people (Ps. 100:3; John 21:16) and Christ's concern (John 10). *See* Lamb; Ram; Shearing; Tail, fat; Wool.

Sheep at Beersheba market

Wild animals

Antelope. Arabian or desert oryx (Deut. 14:5; Isa. 51:20).

Bear. 1. The brown bear (1 Sam. 17:34-37). Unpredictable temper, stronger and a greater danger than a lion (2 Kings 2:24; Hos. 13:8; Amos 5:19).
2. The constellation Ursa Major (Job 9:9). The cubs of Job 38:32 are the seven main stars.

Behemoth. Hippopotamus (Job 40:15).

Dog. Semiwild mongrels which lurked outside the city walls, waiting for rubbish or dead bodies to be thrown out (Exod. 22:31; 2 Kings 9:36; Ps. 59:6). Pet house dogs were rare (Matt. 15:26). Figuratively used of Judaising intruders who disturbed the church (Phil. 3:2) and of those living unclean lives, whose proper place is therefore outside the heavenly city (Rev. 22:15).

Fox

Fox. The animals used to fire the Philistine harvest (Judg. 15:4) were probably jackals. Foxes are solitary, but jackals hunt in packs. Jesus' description of Herod Antipas (Luke 13:32) alludes to the rabbinic view of the fox as a creature of low cunning and of its insignificance compared with the lion.

Hind. Translating as 'deer' misses the spiritual significance of 'hinds' feet' in 2 Sam. 22:34; Ps. 18:33; Hab. 3:19. The female hind can climb higher and more securely than even her mate.

Hyena. Nocturnal carnivore with powerful jaws, useful as a scavenger. Places called Zeboim (*Hyenas*) (Deut. 29:23; 1 Sam. 13:18; Neh. 11:34), vouch for their numbers of old.

Ibex. 'Wild goat' in OT (Deut. 14:5; Ps. 104:18).

Jackal. The English word arose too late for early Bibles, which often translate as 'dragons' (Isa. 34:13; Jer. 51:37; Mic. 1:8; Mal. 1:3), almost always in a context of desolation.

Leopard. Spotted carnivore (Jer. 13:23), up to 1.5 metres (5 ft) long, taking prey by camouflage and stealth (Jer. 5:6; Hos. 13:7). Symbol of evil power (Dan. 7:6; Rev. 13:2).

Lion. Large tawny carnivore, prevalent in OT times but extinct in Palestine by 13th century AD. Hunted mainly

Scavenger dog

gazelle, but also threatened domestic animals (1 Sam. 17:34-37; Jer. 50:17; Amos 3:12); seldom attacked people (1 Kings 13:24-28). Noted for strength (Judg. 14:18), courage (2 Sam. 17:10), ferocity (Ps. 7:2), stealth (Ps. 10:9) and fearsome roar (1 Pet. 5:8). Its transformed nature characteristic of the messianic age (Ps. 91:13; Isa. 11:6-8). Depicted on thrones to proclaim royal might (1 Kings 10:19).

Wolf

Rat. The dangerous Black Rat carried bubonic plague, as Philistines (1 Sam. 6:4-5) and Assyrians (Isa. 37:36) discovered.

Rock badger. Translator's invention (Lev. 11:5, RSV), unknown to naturalists. Coney or Syrian hyrax is meant.

Serpent. Some 50 of 70 references to snakes allude to their being poisonous, and

Serpent

thus offer a ready picture of evil and danger, personal (Matt. 3:7), national (Isa. 14:29) or spiritual (Gen. 3:1; Isa. 27:1; Rev. 12:9). Gen. 49:17 refers to the desert viper hiding in the ground but striking if disturbed. Ps. 58:4-5 speaks of a popular myth: the cobra is charmed not by music but by the movement of the pipe being played (snakes are deaf). The bronze serpent affixed to wood (Num. 21:8-9) typifies Jesus' saving work on the cross (John 3:14-15; 12:31-33). See Nehushtan.

Viper. Figuratively applied by John the Baptist to scribes, Pharisees and Sadducees (fleeing from coming judgment like snakes from approaching fire: Matt. 3:7) and by Jesus (Matt. 12:34; 23:33); also by Paul, concerning the godless (Rom. 3:13). See Serpent.

Wild donkey. Onager (Job 39:5-6). Considered untamable (Gen. 16:12).

Wild goat. Nubian ibex (1 Sam. 24:2; Ps. 104:18).

Wild ox. Aurochs; curiously called 'unicorn' (*one-horned*) in AV/KJV, despite *horns* in Deut. 33:17. Strong (Num. 23:22), fierce (Ps. 22:21), powerfully horned (Ps. 92:10).

Wolf. Constant threat to livestock (John 10:12), but whose nature will be changed in the messianic age (Isa. 11:6; 65:25). Well describes Benjamin's character as a combative tribe (Gen. 49:27; Judg. 20) and Jewish leaders misusing their authority (Ezek. 22:27; Matt. 7:15).

forced to pay Judah tribute (2 Chron. 26:8; 27:5). Their constant antagonism denounced in the prophets (Jer. 49:1; Ezek. 25:1–7; Amos 1:13; Zeph. 2:8). Nehemiah protested against mixed marriages between Jews and Ammonites (Ezra 9:2; Neh. 13:23).

AMNON. Eldest son of David by Ahinoam (2 Sam. 3:2). Killed by Absalom for raping Tamar (2 Sam. 13).

AMON. 1. Son and successor of Manasseh as king of Judah (642–640 BC). His brief idolatrous reign was cut short by a palace revolution (2 Kings 21:18–26).

2. Governor of Samaria, ordered to secure the prophet Micaiah when Ahab embarked on the ill-fated battle of Ramoth Gilead (1 Kings 22:26).

3. Egyptian state god, based at Thebes (Jer. 46:25).

AMORITES. Highland descendants of Canaan (Gen. 10:16; Num. 13:29). Occupation of the Promised Land began with Joshua's overthrow of the Amorite kings Sihon and Og, who ruled most of Transjordan (Josh. 12). Their territory was allotted to Gad, Reuben and Manasseh (Num. 32:33). The Amorites were gradually absorbed (1 Kings 9:20), but their idolatry was remembered (1 Kings 21:26; 2 Kings 21:11).

AMOS. Shepherd and sycamore-fig farmer (Amos 7:14), called about 760 BC to prophesy (Amos 1:1).

AMOS (book). Foretells God's judgment upon Judah, Israel (Samaria), and surrounding nations (ch. 1—2), which in Israel's case (3—6) would be severe for despising her privileged position in God's plan (7:1— 9:10). The closing vers-

es promise the restoration of the Davidic kingdom (9:11–15).

AMOZ. Father of the prophet Isaiah (2 Kings 19:2; Isa. 1:1).

AMPHIPOLIS. Roman free town and commercial centre of Macedonia, on the river Strymon (Acts 17:1).

AMPLIATUS. Prominent Roman Christian greeted by Paul (Rom. 16:8). Common name among slaves and in catacombs.

AMRAM. Levite (Num. 3:19), father of Aaron, Moses (Exod. 6:20) and Miriam (Num. 26:59).

AMRAPHEL. King of Shinar (Gen. 14:1), whose attack on Sodom was beaten off by Abram.

ANAKITES/ANAKIM. Early giant hill people (Deut. 1:28), driven out by Joshua and Caleb (Josh. 11:21; 15:14).

ANANIAS. 1. Conspired with his wife Sapphira to cheat over the common fund (Acts 5:1–10).

2. Damascus Christian who ministered to the newly converted Saul of Tarsus (Acts 9:10).

3. High priest whose malpractice in examining Paul earned a colourful rebuke (Acts 23:2). Later led Paul's Jewish accusers before Felix at Caesarea (Acts 24:1).

ANATHOTH. Benjamite town, NE of Jerusalem (Josh. 21:18). Home of Abiathar (1 Kings 2:26), Jeremiah (Jer. 1:1), David's officer Abiezer (2 Sam. 23:27), and Jehu (1 Chron. 12:3).

ANCHOR. *See* Travel p. 229.

ANCIENT OF DAYS. Symbolic title for God presiding at the final Judgment (Dan. 7:9). The vision is of One supremely wise, pure and eternal.

ANDREW. Apostle (Matt. 10:2). From Bethsaida in Galilee (John 1:44), he moved to Capernaum (Mark 1:29) in a fishing partnership with Peter (Matt. 4:18). At first a disciple of John the Baptist (John 1:35–40). Good at introducing people to Jesus (John 1:42; 6:8; 12:21). Present at Jesus' ascension (Acts 1:13).

ANDRONICUS and **JUNIAS.** Leading Jewish Christians in Rome, who shared Paul's imprisonment (Rom. 16:7). *See* Junias.

ANGEL (*Messenger*). Created spiritual beings serving God (Gen. 28:12; Matt. 16:27; Heb. 1:7; 1 Pet. 3:22) and God's people (Gen. 24:7; Exod. 23:20; 1 Kings 19:5; Acts 5:19; Heb. 1:14). Fallen angels expelled from heaven (Matt. 25:41; Jude 6). *See* Archangel.

ANGEL OF THE LORD/OF GOD. Heavenly messenger. Sometimes identified with God (Gen. 31:11, 13; Exod. 3:2, 4; Zech. 3:1–2); or as Gabriel (Luke 1:19), God's agent of judgment (2 Sam. 24:16; Acts 12:23), deliverance (Exod. 14:19; Dan. 6:22; Acts 5:19), instruction (Gen. 24:7; Exod. 23:23;1 Kings 19:7; Matt. 2:13; Acts 8:26). Announced birth of Samson (Judg. 13:3), John the Baptist (Luke 1:11), and Jesus (Matt. 1:20).

ANGELS OF THE CHURCHES. Guardian angels of churches; or their personification (Rev. 1:20; ch. 2—3).

ANIMALS. Created by God, made subject to human beings (Gen. 1:20–26; Ps. 8:6) and named by Adam (Gen. 2:20); some preserved in Noah's ark (Gen. 7:2). The concern of divine laws (Exod. 22; Lev. 27:9; Deut. 5:14). *See* Domestic animals pp. 14-15; Wild animals pp. 16-17; Clean and unclean.

ANNA (Hannah in OT; *Grace*). Aged widow who recognised the infant Jesus as Messiah (Luke 2:36).

ANNALS OF THE KINGS. *See* Chronicles of the Kings.

ANNAS. High priest from AD 6. Deposed by Romans in AD 15, but Jews continued to recognise his authority (Luke 3:2). Greatly influential as his five sons and son-in-law Caiaphas all became high priests. Questioned Jesus prior to the trial before Caiaphas (John 18:13–24).

ANOINTING. Holy oil (Exod. 30:32) was used to signify people or objects being separated apart for God. Action associated with the Holy Spirit (1 Sam. 16:13; Isa. 61:1; Acts 10:38). *See* Oil.

Ruined aqueduct, Antioch of Pisidia

ANTELOPE. *See* Wild animals p. 16.

ANTICHRIST. Christ's final adversary (1 John 2:18; 4:3; 2 John 7).

ANTIOCH. 1. Antioch of Pisidia in Phrygia. Jewish settlers welcomed Paul (Acts 13:14), but enemies later secured his expulsion (Acts 13:50).

2. Antioch on the Orontes, 500 km (300 mi) N of Jerusalem, capital of Roman province of Syria. An early Christian centre (Acts 11) and birthplace of foreign missions (Acts 13). The church sent Paul and Barnabas to Jerusalem to obtain a ruling on admitting Gentile converts (Acts 15).

ANTIOCHUS EPIPHANES. Seleucid king of Syria from 175 BC. His attempts to stamp out Judaism provoked the successful Maccabean insurrection (1 & 2 Macc.).

ANTIPAS. 1. Otherwise Herod the tetrarch (Luke 3:1), who executed John the Baptist (Mark 6:14–28). Threatened Jesus (Luke 13:31–32) and vainly questioned him after his arrest (Luke 23:7). His steward's wife was a disciple (Luke 8:3).

2. Martyr of the church at Pergamum (Rev. 2:13).

ANTIPATRIS. City, formerly Aphek (Josh. 12:18), rebuilt by Herod the Great in honour of his father Antipater. Paul taken there for safety by the Romans, en route from Jerusalem to Caesarea (Acts 23:31).

APOCALYPSE. Alternative name for the last NT book (from the Greek word meaning '*revelation*'). *See* Revelation (book).

APOCRYPHA (*Hidden Things*). Twelve books accepted as canonical by the Roman Catholic Council of Trent (1545–1563), but approved by Protestants only for private edification: Tobit, Judith, Additions to Esther, Wisdom of Solomon, Ecclesiasticus (or Wisdom of Jesus ben Sira), Baruch, Letter of Jeremiah, Additions to Daniel, Susanna, Bel and the Dragon, 1 & 2 Maccabees.

APOLLOS. Eloquent Alexandrian Jew, deeply versed in OT and with some knowledge of Jesus. After further instruction by Priscilla and Aquila, powerfully preached Jesus as Messiah(Acts 18:24–28). One clique at Corinth even claimed his name (1 Cor. 1:12; 3:4–6).

APOLLYON. *See* Abaddon.

APOSTLE (*Sent*). Term applied to Jesus (Heb. 3:1) and to God's messengers to Israel (Luke 11:49), but mainly to the Twelve commissioned by Jesus (Matt. 10:2; Luke 6:13; Acts 1:13) and to Paul (Rom. 1:1). *See* Junias.

APPEAL TO CAESAR. Roman citizen's privilege of having his case transferred from a provincial court to the supreme tribunal in Rome (Acts 25:11).

APPIUS. Market town, 50 km (30 mi) from Rome, where Paul was met by Roman Christians (Acts 28:15).

AQUILA. *See* Priscilla.

AR. Capital of Moab, E of Dead Sea (Num. 21:15; Isa. 15:1).

ARABAH (*Wasteland*). Wilderness in general,

but especially the rift valley from Sea of Tiberias to Gulf of Aqaba.

ARABAH, SEA OF. *See* Dead Sea.

ARAM. OT name for Syria and N Mesopotamia.

ARAMAEANS. Natives of Aram, such as Laban (Gen. 25:20). The 'wandering Aramaean' of Deut. 26:5 refers to Jacob entering Egypt. *See* Syria.

ARAMAIC. Language of trade and diplomacy (2 Kings 18:26) from 9th century BC; commonly spoken in Palestine in NT times.

ARARAT. Mountainous district (Armenia) where Noah's ark grounded (Gen. 8:4). Refuge of Sennacherib's sons (Isa. 37:38).

ARAUNAH (*or* Ornan). Jebusite whose threshing floor David purchased for an altar to mark a plague's end (2 Sam. 24).

ARCHANGEL. Senior angel who signals the raising of the dead at Christ's second coming (1 Thess. 4:16). Several are named: Michael (Jude 9), Gabriel (Dan. 8:16 Luke 1:19) and Raphael (Tobit 7:15). Other Jewish literature adds Uriel, Raguel, Sariel and Remiel, making seven in all. *See* Angel; Angel of the Lord.

ARCHELAUS. Eldest son of Herod the Great by his Samaritan wife Malthrace. Succeeded his father in 4 BC, though without the title king (Matt. 2:22). Deposed by the Romans in AD 6 for his repressive rule.

ARCHERS. *See* War p. 240.

ARCHIPPUS. Fellow worker with Paul and Timothy (Col. 4:17; Philem. 2).

AREOPAGUS. Supreme court of Athens (Acts 17:19).

ARETAS. Dynasty name of Nabataean Arab kings. The last and best known was Aretas IV Philopatris (9 BC–AD 40). His daughter married Herod Antipas, who divorced her to marry Herodias (Mark 6:17). His governor tried to arrest Paul (2 Cor. 11:32).

ARIEL (*Altar-hearth*). Cryptic name for Jerusalem's Temple (Isa. 29:1–7).

ARIMATHEA. Hometown of Joseph, owner of Jesus' tomb (Matt. 27:57) Ramah in Samuel's day.

ARIOCH. 1. *See* Ellasar.
2. Officer who brought Daniel to Nebuchadnezzar to interpret the royal dream (Dan. 2:14).

ARISTARCHUS. Paul's Thessalonian companion, seized by Ephesian mob (Acts 19:29). With Paul in Jerusalem (Acts 20:4), Caesarea (Acts 27:2) and prison (Col. 4:10; Philem. 24).

ARK (Moses). Box of reedwork, used to house the infant Moses to outwit Pharaoh's extermination order (Exod. 1:22; 2:3).

ARK (Noah). Wooden vessel built to divine specification to preserve Noah, his family and some animals from the Flood (Gen. 6—9; Heb. 11:7; 1 Pet. 3:20).

ARK OF THE COVENANT.
See Tabernacle p. 215.

ARMAGEDDON (*Mountain of Megiddo*). Site of decisive battles, from Tuthmosis III (1468 BC) to Allenby (1917), and scene of final apocalyptic battle (Rev. 16:14). About 30 km (18 mi) from Haifa.

ARMOUR. *See* War p. 240.

ARMY. *See* War p. 240.

ARNON. Wadi forming boundary between Moab and Ammon (Judg. 11:18). Its crossing marked the beginning of Israel's conquest of land E of Jordan (Deut. 2:24).

AROER. 1. Town E of Dead Sea (Deut. 2:36), at limit of Hazael's conquests (2 Kings 10:33). David's ill-fated census began here (2 Sam. 24:5).
2. Town SE of Beersheba. Inhabitants shared David's spoils as compensation for Amalekite raids (1 Sam. 30:26–28).

ARPAD. Syrian city, NW of Aleppo. Assyrians boasted of its repeated capture (2 Kings 18:34; Isa. 37:13).

ARROWS. *See* War p. 240.

ARTAXERXES. King of Persia, 464–424 BC (Ezra 7:1; Neh. 2:1).

ARTEMIS. Greek goddess (Diana to Romans). Her Ephesus temple one of the seven wonders of the world. By tradition her image fell from the sky (probably a meteorite). When Paul's preaching threatened the trade in small votary shrines, the silversmiths rioted (Acts 19:23–41).

ASA. Reforming king of Judah, 911–870 BC (1 Kings 15—16). Deposed Maacah, influential

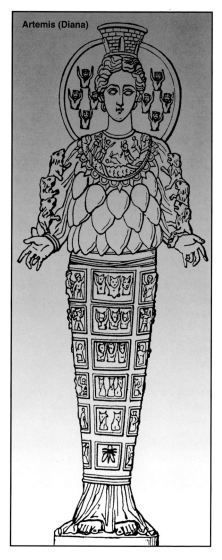

Artemis (Diana)

as queen-mother, for her pagan practices (2 Chron. 15:16). Trust in God brought victory over invading Cushites (2 Chron. 14:9–15), but faith later weakened and he suffered in warfare and sickness (2 Chron. 16).

ASAHEL. Son of David's sister Zeruiah, brother of Joab and Abishai (1 Chron. 2:16), and one of David's leading soldiers (2 Sam. 23:24). Used his fleetness of foot to overtake Abner at Gibeon, but lost his life in the ensuing fight (2 Sam. 2:18). Joab avenged his death (2 Sam. 3:27).

ASAPH. Musical Levite (1 Chron. 6:39; 15:17; 16:5). Author of Psalms (50; 73—83) used by Hezekiah in reviving Temple worship.

ASCENSION. The return of the resurrected Jesus to heaven (Mark 16:19; Luke 24:51; Acts 1:9). Foretold in Ps. 24:7; 68:18; John 14:2, 28; 16:5; 20:17.

ASCENTS, SONG OF. Pilgrim songs for festivals (Pss. 120—134).

ASHDOD (*Fortress*). Major Philistine city (Josh. 11:22; 1 Sam. 5:1). Azotus in Acts 8:40.

ASHER. Jacob's second son by Leah's maid Zilpah (Gen. 30:13). Descendants formed the tribe of Asher (Num. 26:44–47). Their prosperity (1 Chron. 7:30–40) foretold (Gen. 49:20). Contributed troops to David's army (1 Chron. 12:36), food to Solomon's household (1 Kings 4:16), and supported Hezekiah's revival of the Passover (2 Chron. 30:11). The aged Anna, who recognised the infant Jesus as Messiah, was of this tribe (Luke 2:36).

ASHERAH (*plural,* Asherim or Asheroth).

Canaanite goddess associated with Baal (Judg. 3:7). Name also applied to her groves (1 Kings 18:19), which the Israelites were told to destroy (Exod. 34:13).

ASHES. With sackcloth, symbol of mourning (Esther 4:1); with dust symbolised distress (Job 30:19) or worthlessness (Gen. 18:27).

ASHKELON. Philistine seaport, between Jaffa and Gaza (Judg. 1:18). Destroyed by Nebuchadnezzar in 604 BC.

ASHTAROTH. Capital city of Og, king of Bashan (Deut. 1:4), E of Sea of Galilee.

ASHTORETH. Canaanite goddess (1 Kings 11:5), whose depraved cult attracted the Israelites (Judg. 2:13).

ASHURBANIPAL. The last great Assyrian king (669–627 BC), son and successor of Esarhaddon. Released Manasseh from exile in Nineveh (2 Chron. 33:13). (Asnapper in Ezra 4:10, AV/KJV.)

ASIA. In the NT, the Roman province (western modern Asia Minor) included Mysia, Lydia and Phrygia, with Ephesus, Smyrna and Pergamum the main centres. *See* Seven churches.

ASIARCHS. Leading citizens chosen annually to administer cities of Roman province of Asia (Acts 19:31).

ASNAPPER. *See* Ashurbanipal.

ASSHUR. Hebrew term for Assyria (Num. 24:22; Ezek. 27:23).

ASSOS. Seaport of NW Asia Minor, opposite

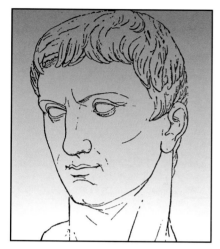

Caesar Augustus

island of Lesbos (Acts 20:13–14).

ASSYRIA. Country of upper Mesopotamia whose empire in 900–600 BC extended from the Persian Gulf to Palestine and Egypt. Kings mentioned in the OT are Tiglath-Pileser III (744–727), Shalmaneser V (726–722), Sargon II (721–705), Sennacherib (704–681), Esarhaddon (681–669), and Ashurbanipal (669–627). The empire abruptly collapsed under attacks from Babylonians and Scythians, the capital Nineveh falling in 612 BC (Nah. 3:7; Zeph. 2:13).

ATHALIAH. Daughter of Ahab, king of Judah, who married Jehoram, king of Israel, to seal an alliance (2 Kings 8:18). When in 841 BC Jehu slew her son Ahaziah, she seized power (2 Kings 11:1–3). Killed six years later when the priest Jehoiada proclaimed the surviving child Joash as king (2 Chron. 23).

ATHENS. Greek self-governing city of culture. Paul seized on the keen local interest in religion to proclaim Jesus (Acts 17:15–34).

ATONEMENT. The 'making at-one' of sinful human beings with a holy God through the life and death of Jesus (Rom. 3:21–26; 1 John 2:2). *See* Day of Atonement.

AUGUSTAN BAND. *See* Imperial Regiment.

AUGUSTUS. Additional name conferred on Caesar Octavian (63 BC–AD 14), who became first Roman emperor (23 BC). His decree sent Joseph and Mary to Bethlehem (Luke 2:1).

AVENGER OF BLOOD. Ancient custom authorised a victim's next of kin to avenge personal injury (2 Sam. 14:7). Moses limited punishment to the actual murderer to prevent decimation of clans through blood feuds (2 Kings 14:6). *See* Revenge.

AZARIAH (*The Lord is My Help*). Alternative name for king Uzziah (2 Kings 15:1–7). Original Hebrew name of Abednego (Dan. 1:7).

AZEKAH. Lowland city of Judah (Josh. 10:10). Defied Nebuchadnezzar (Jer. 34:7).

AZOTUS. Greek name of Ashdod (Acts 8:40).

B

BAASHA. King of Israel (909–885 BC). Seized the throne after murdering Jeroboam I's family, so fulfilling Ahijah's prophecy (1 Kings 14:6–18). Continually at war with Judah (1 Kings 15:16—16:7).

BABBLER. Scornful Greek slang term applied by Athenians to Paul (Acts 17:18). Literally '*seed-picker*', like a sparrow, picking up scraps.

BABEL. Hebrew name for Babylon, explained in Gen. 11:9 as being similar to Hebrew for 'confusion', a reference to God's imposing a language barrier in response to human pride in erecting the famous tower.

BAAL. Canaanite fertility god. The cult constantly infected Israel's worship, to the prophets' wrath (Num. 25:3; Jer. 7:9; Hos. 2:8; Zeph. 1:4).

BAAL PEOR. Moabite god, whose cult fatally attracted Israelites at Shittim (Num. 25:3; Deut. 4:3; Hos. 9:10).

BAAL-ZEBUB (Beelzebub in NT). Ekron god that Ahaziah king of Israel intended to consult (2 Kings 1:2–10).

BABYLON. Capital of Babylonia, founded by Nimrod (Gen. 10:10) on river Euphrates, S of Baghdad. Magnificently rebuilt by Nebuchadnezzar (Dan. 4:30); captured by Cyrus in 539 BC (Dan. 5:30). The place of Israel's exile (2 Kings 20:17). Name used metaphorically of Rome (1 Pet. 5:13; Rev. 14:8).

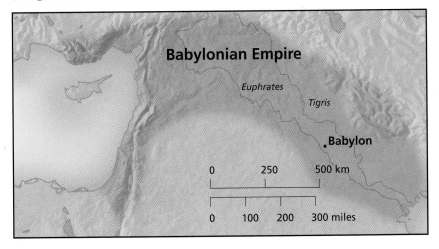

BABYLONIA. Modern S Iraq, also called Shinar (Gen. 11:2) and Chaldea (Ezek. 23:15).

BACKSLIDING. Apostasy, defection from faith (Jer. 2:19; Heb. 6:6); a sign of the last days (1 Tim. 4:1).

BAHURIM. Unidentified place near Jerusalem where Michal left her husband to become David's wife (2 Sam. 3:16). Home of Shimei (2 Sam. 16:5). Jonathan and Ahimaaz hid in the local well (2 Sam. 17:18).

BAKER. To Pharaoh, a valued skilled professional (Gen. 40:1). In humbler circles, baking usually a woman's chore (1 Sam. 8:13).

BALAAM. Prophet vainly bribed by king Balak of Moab to curse Israelites (Num. 22—24).

BALAK. Moabite king who tried to thwart God's will (Num. 22—24; Josh. 24:9).

BALANCE. Used commercially to weigh out silver before the advent of coinage (Gen. 23:16). Its honest use enjoined (Prov. 16:11); sharp practice evidently not uncommon (Lev. 19:35–36; Amos 8:5).

BALDNESS. Its association with disease (Lev. 13:40) sharpened the insult to Elisha (2 Kings 2:23). *See* Hair; Shaving.

BALM *See* Herbs and spices p. 92.

BANNER. *See* War p. 240.

BAPTISM. 1. Submission to John's baptism in water expressed repentance (Mark 1:4) and prepared for the ministry of Jesus (Matt. 3:3, 11). Jesus insisted on John's baptising him, thus identifying himself with sinful human beings (Matt. 3:13–17).
2. Christian baptism, administered in the name of Jesus (Acts 19:1–6), expressed repentance and faith (Acts 2:38) and entry into the church (Acts 2:41).

BAR-JESUS. Jewish trickster at the court of Sergius Paulus, Roman proconsul of Cyprus (Acts 13:6).

BARABBAS. Jewish revolutionary (Matt. 27:16–26).

BARAK. Rallied Israelites against the Canaanite general Sisera (Judges 4—5; Heb. 11:32).

BARBARIANS. Greeks' term for foreigners (Rom. 1:14; Col. 3:11), whose language to cultured Greek ears sounded like 'bar-bar'.

BAREFOOT. Sandals normally only worn outdoors. Walking barefoot in public signified poverty (Luke 15:22), mourning (2 Sam. 15:30) or enslavement (Isa. 20:3).

BARLEY. *See* Farming. p. 70.

BARN. *See* Farming. p. 70.

BARNABAS. Early Christian missionary, from a Jewish-Cypriot priestly family; cousin of John Mark (Acts 4:36; Col. 4:10). Courageously befriended Saul of Tarsus in Jerusalem (Acts 9:27), represented the Jerusalem church at Antioch where many Gentiles were being converted, and recognised this as work for Paul to take over (Acts 11:26). With Paul carried famine relief to Jerusalem (Gal. 2:1), where their mission to Gentiles was acknowledged (Gal. 2:9), although back in Antioch Barnabas temporarily succumbed to Judaising pressure (Gal. 2:13). With Paul evangelised Gentiles in Cyprus and Asia Minor (Acts 13—14). The Antioch church appointed Barnabas and Paul to go to Jerusalem for a ruling on circumcising Gentile converts (Acts 15). Parted from Paul over Mark (Acts 15:36–39).

BARRENNESS. Considered a divine curse (Deut. 7:14), bringing a childless wife grief and disgrace (1 Sam. 1:10; Luke 1:25).

BARSABBAS. 1. Surname of Joseph, a candidate to replace Judas Iscariot (Acts 1:23).
2. Surname of Judas, who with Silas accompanied Paul to Antioch to report the Jerusalem Council's decision on admitting Gentiles into the church (Acts 15:22).

BARTHOLOMEW. Apostle (Matt. 10:3; Acts 1:13), traditionally identified with Nathanael (John 1:45).

BARTIMAEUS. Blind beggar at Jericho whose persistence secured healing (Mark 10:46).

BARUCH. Jeremiah's devoted secretary (Jer. 36); exiled with him to Egypt (Jer. 43:6).

BARUCH (book; Apocrypha). Prayers and poems purporting to be by Jeremiah's secretary with the Jewish exiles in Babylon.

BARZILLAI. Wealthy long-standing supporter of David (2 Sam. 17:27; 19:31–39).

BASEMATH (*Fragrant*). Name of two of Esau's wives (Gen. 26:34; 36:3).

BASHAN. Og's fertile kingdom (Num. 21:33; Josh. 13:30), E of Jordan and N of Gilead, famous for oaks (Isa. 2:13), mountains (Ps. 68:15), lions (Deut. 33:22), and cattle (Deut. 32:14).

BASKET. *See* Domestic life p. 52.

BATHSHEBA. Uriah's wife, whom David stole (2 Sam. 11), thus earning God's condemnation (2 Sam. 12). In David's old age, she secured the succession for Solomon and thus her own status as queen-mother (1 Kings 1).

BATTERING RAM. *See* War p. 240.

BDELLIUM. Honey-coloured aromatic gum-resin, valued as a perfume (Gen. 2:12). Manna was similar in appearance (Num. 11:7).

BEANS (broad). *See* Foods p. 77.

BEAR. *See* Wild animals p. 16.

BEARD. Considered a handsome mark of Jewish virility (Ps. 133:2). Cutting, a sign of grief (Isa. 15:2). Mutilating another's beard, insulting (2 Sam. 10:4).

BEAST. Symbol of the final blasphemous power (Rev. 13), a composite picture of the four beasts of Dan. 7. He claims divine honours, but is destroyed at Christ's second coming (2 Thess. 2:8; Rev. 19:20).

BEAUTIFUL GATE. Popular name for the exquisite Nicanor Gate in the Temple, where a cripple was healed (Acts 3).

BED. *See* Domestic life. p. 52.

BEDROOM. *See* House p. 100.

BEE. *See* Insects p. 105.

BEELZEBUB. *See* Baal-Zebub.

BEER. (*Well*). 1. Israelite camp (Num. 21:16) near the river Arnon. Probably Beer Elim (Isa. 15:8).

2. Where Jotham fled from Abimelech after declaring his parable (Judg. 9). Probably Beeroth (2 Sam. 4:2).

BEER (drink). *See* Foods p. 77.

BEER LAHAI ROI. SW of Beersheba, where Hagar was divinely reassured (Gen. 16:14). Isaac settled there (Gen. 25:11).

BEEROTH. Hivite city, N of Jerusalem, whose inhabitants tricked Joshua into a treaty (Josh. 9:17).

BEERSHEBA (*Well of Seven*; Gen. 21:30). Ancient town, SW of Jerusalem, where in turn Abraham, Isaac and Jacob all settled (Gen. 22:19; 26:33; 28:10). 'From Dan to Beersheba' denotes the N and S extremes of the land.

BEGGING. Anyone unable to work depended upon almsgiving (Mark 10:46; Luke 16:3; John 9:8). Religious festivals attracted many beggars to Jerusalem to benefit from the pious (Luke 18:35; Acts 3:3).

BEHEMOTH. *See* Wild animals p. 16.

BEL (*Lord*). Another name for the chief Babylonian god Marduk (Jer. 51:44).

BEL AND THE DRAGON (Apocrypha). Two stories about Daniel, one describing his exposure of Bel's fraudulent priests and the other enlarging on his experience in the lions' den (Dan. 6).

BELIAL (*Worthless*). Synonym for Satan (2 Cor. 6:15).

BELSHAZZAR. Last ruler of Babylon, killed during its capture by Darius the Mede in 539 BC (Dan. 5).

BELT. *See* Dress p. 54.

BELTESHAZZAR. Daniel's Babylonian name (Dan. 1:7).

BEN-AMMI. *See* Ammon.

BEN-HADAD. Dynastic name of kings of Aram. 1. Son of Tabrimmon, whose help Asa king of Judah enlisted against Baashah king of Israel (1 Kings 15:18).

2. Contemporary of Ahab (1 Kings 20), assassinated by Hazael about 843 BC (2 Kings 8:7–15).

3. Hazael's son (796–770 BC), who continued his father's oppression of Israel (2 Kings 13; Amos 1:4).

BENAIAH. Outstanding captain of David's bodyguard (2 Sam. 20:20–23). Helped to thwart Adonijah's rebellion, backed Solomon as David's successor, and replaced Joab as commander in chief (1 Kings 1—2).

BENJAMIN. 1. Jacob's youngest son, called Ben-Oni (*Son of My Sorrow*) by his dying mother (Gen. 35:18). After Joseph was lost, he became his father's favourite (Gen. 42:4). Eventually this led to the family's reconciliation (Gen. 44).

2. Descendants of Benjamin, famous as left-handed stone slingers (Judg. 20:16). Tribe decimated following the affair of the Levite's concubine (Judg. 20—21). Loyalty to Saul's memory meant opposing David, as shown by Benjamites Shimei (2 Sam. 16) and Sheba (2 Sam. 19—20). But when Jerusalem became David's capital, Benjamin drew closer to Judah (1 Chron. 8:28), especially after the kingdom split (2 Chron. 11).

BERACAH (*Blessing*). Valley between Jerusalem and Hebron, where Jehoshaphat praised God for a remarkable bloodless victory (2 Chron. 20:26).

BEREA. City of S Macedonia, with a prosperous Jewish colony. Until Jewish opponents arrived, Paul's preaching met a good response (Acts 17:10–14).

BERNICE. Eldest daughter of Herod Agrippa I, born AD 28, and sister of Drusilla (Acts 25:13, 23; 26:30).

BERYL. Foundation gem of New Jerusalem's wall (Rev. 21:20). In OT the Hebrew word so translated is probably gold topaz (Exod. 28:17). Symbol of Tyre's prosperity (Ezek. 28:13).

BETH AVEN (*House of Iniquity*). Place E of Bethel near Ai (Josh. 7:2), NW of Michmash (1 Sam. 13:5), on the way to Aijalon (1 Sam. 14:23) and marking the boundary of Benjamin (Josh. 18:12). Ironic synonym for Bethel (*House of God*) in Hos. 4:15; 5:8; 10:5.

BETH HORON. Upper Beth Horon, 600 metres (2000 ft) above sea level, was NW of Jerusalem. In 3 km (2 mi) the steep pass dropped some 350 metres (1150 ft) to Lower Beth Horon. The twin towns (1 Chron. 7:24) controlled the Aijalon valley and marked the Benjamin-Ephraim boundary (Josh. 16:1–5).

BETH JESHIMOTH. Leading Moabite city, NE of Dead Sea (Num. 33:49).

BETH PEOR. City of Reuben (Josh. 13:20), E of Jordan (Deut. 3:29). Moses buried nearby (Deut. 34:6).

BETH SHAN. Fortified city at junction of Jezreel and Jordan valleys (Josh. 17:11), where Saul's body was dishonoured (1 Sam. 31:10).

BETH SHEMESH (*Sun Temple*). Town of Judah (Josh. 15:10), W of Jerusalem, where the ark of the covenant temporarily rested after the Philistines returned it (1 Sam. 6). Scene of Amaziah's defeat (2 Kings 14:11).

Theatre, Beth Shan

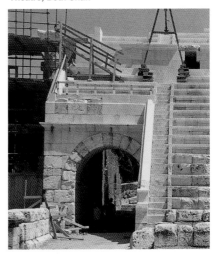

BETHANY. 1. Village on the Jericho road, 3 km (2 mi) from Jerusalem; home of Mary, Martha and Lazarus (John 11:1) and Simon the leper (Matt. 26:6) where Jesus was anointed. Jesus based here during his last week (Matt. 21:17).

2. Unidentified place E of Jordan where John baptised (John 1:28).

BETHEL (*House of God*). Place N of Jerusalem, near where Abraham sacrificed (Gen. 12:8), originally called Luz (Gen. 28:19). An ancient sanctuary (1 Sam. 7:16), chosen by Jeroboam to rival Jerusalem (1 Kings 12:26–29); in Elijah's day the centre of a school of prophets (2 Kings 2:2). Denounced for calf worship by Amos (3:14).

BETHESDA (*House of Double Outpourings*) or Bethzatha. Name of twin pools with five arcades in Jerusalem (John 5:2).

Bethlehem

BETHLEHEM. The city of David, 8 km (5 mi) S of Jerusalem, originally called Ephrath, the site of Rachel's tomb (Gen. 35:19). Home of Boaz (Ruth 2:4). Birthplace of Messiah (Mic. 5:2; Luke 2:4; John 7:42).

BETHPHAGE. Village on Mt. of Olives near Bethany (Luke 19:29).

BETHSAIDA. Town at N of Sea of Galilee. Home of Philip, Andrew and Peter (John 1:44). Denounced for unbelief, despite Jesus' miracles there (Matt. 11:21).

BETHZATHA. *See* Bethesda.

BETROTHAL. A couple's vows before witnesses with certain gifts made their commitment almost as binding as marriage itself. Dissolution required divorce (Matt. 1:19). Symbolised God's pledge of love for penitent Israel (Hos. 2:19).

BEULAH (*Married*). Symbolic name for Israel (Isa. 62:4), indicating its future fertility.

BEYOND THE RIVER. Persian province (Ezra 4:10, RSV; Trans-Euphrates in NIV).

BEZALEL (*In God's Shadow*). Gifted craftsman making the Tabernacle (Exod. 31:2; 36:1).

BIBLE. 1. *Name*: Derived from the Greek word for books .

2. *Divisions*: The Jewish (or Hebrew) Bible is the Old Testament, and divided into three sections: Law (Gen. to Deut.), *Prophets* (Josh., Judg., Sam., Kings, Isa., Jer., Ezek., Hos. to Mal.), and the *Writings* (Ps., Prov., Job, Song of Sol., Ruth, Lam., Eccles., Esther, Dan., Ezra-Neh., Chron.).

Books of the Bible

The Bible is made up of a "library" of sixty-six books, thirty-nine in the Old Testament, twenty-seven in the New. The writings of the **OLD TESTAMENT** first appeared as separate scrolls in Hebrew. The thirty-nine books of the Old Testament vary in authorship and style and can be divided into four major groupings:

History
Tracing the story of God's people from their entry into the Promised Land to the Exile.

Law
Sometimes called the Pentateuch, or "five scrolls."

Poetry and Wisdom
Full of proverbs, riddles, parables, warnings, and wise sayings.

Prophecy
God's prophets explained what had happened in the past, spoke out against evil in the present, and told what God would do in the future.

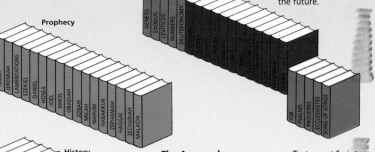

The Apocrypha

The Apocrypha (not illustrated) is a collection of books and additions to the Old Testament books written between 300 BC and AD 100. It was not accepted by the Jews as part of the Old Testament Scripture, and most Protestant denominations do not accept it as part of genuine Scripture. The books are interesting and valuable historical documents that range from historical narratives to pious fiction.

The twenty-seven books of the **NEW TESTAMENT** were written in Greek and can also be divided into different types of writing:

History

The four Gospels and the book of Acts are considered history. The Gospels, however, are also written to persuade readers to believe in Jesus, and portray Jesus as the Messiah.

Letters

These include Paul's letters to churches in various cities, his letters to individual Christians, and letters written by other apostles.

Revelation

This book opens with letters to seven churches in Asia Minor, but continues with vivid visions about the last days.

The Christian Bible comprises Old Testament (OT) and New Testament (NT), plus, for Roman Catholics, the Apocrypha. 'Testament' in its biblical sense means *covenant*.

Chapter divisions for the OT were first made about AD 1248 by Cardinal Hugo de Sancto Caro, and verse divisions by Rabbi Nathan about 1440. Robert Stephens divided the NT into verses in 1551; first included in the Geneva Bible (1560). Luke 20:37 shows how Bible references were made before these useful aids were introduced.

3. *Languages*. OT originally in Hebrew, except for a few Aramaic passages in Ezra and Daniel. NT written in Greek.

BILDAD. One of Job's three friends. His speeches occur in chapters 8, 18, and 25. A traditional moralist, he divides people into two classes, blameless or secretly wicked: God will prosper the one and destroy the other.

BILHAH. Slave girl given by Laban to Rachel on her marriage (Gen. 29:29). As Jacob's concubine, she bore Dan and Naphtali (Gen. 35:25).

BINDING AND LOOSING. Rabbinic expression to declare things forbidden or permitted. Authority given to Peter (Matt. 16:19) and to the disciples (Matt. 18:18). Exercised in Acts 5:1–11; 1 Cor. 5:3–5.

BIRDS. *See* p. 104.

BIRTHRIGHT. Eldest son's privilege of succeeding as head of the family (Gen. 25:31) with a double share of the property (Deut. 21:17) to finance the increased expenses involved.

BISHOP. AV/KJV term for church overseer (Phil. 1:1), equivalent to 'elder' (Titus 1:5–9).

BITHYNIA. Roman province in NW Asia Minor. Paul and Silas were forbidden to preach there (Acts 16:7); left to others (1 Pet. 1:1).

BITTER HERBS.
See Herbs and spices p. 92.

BITUMEN. Asphalt, occurring naturally in Babylonia (Gen. 11:3; 'slime' in AV/KJV) and near the Dead Sea (Gen. 14:10). Waterproofed Moses' basket (Exod. 2:3).

BLASPHEMY. Slandering God (Deut. 5:11), contempt for sacred places (Acts 6:13), and practising idolatry (Ezek. 20:27–39). Punishable by death (Lev. 24:16).

BLASPHEMY AGAINST THE HOLY SPIRIT. Ascribing the activities of Jesus to demonic inspiration (Mark 3:29).

BLASTUS. Personal servant of Herod Agrippa I, whose backing was secured, probably by bribery, by the people of Tyre and Sidon (Acts 12:20).

BLEMISH. Animals offered in sacrifice must be physically perfect (Exod. 12:5), as only the best is appropriate for God. 'Without blemish' describes the perfect sacrifice of Jesus (Heb. 9:14; 1 Pet. 1:19) and the perfect character of the glorified church (Eph. 5:27).

BLESSING. 1. God's bestowal of good, material (Gen. 22:17; Prov. 10:22; Heb. 6:7) and spiritual (Eph. 1:3).

2. Human response to God in praise and adoration (Ps. 103).

BLINDNESS. Sometimes considered a divine punishment (Deut. 28:28; John 9:2). Its healing a sign of Messiah (Matt. 11:5; Luke 4:18). Mark 8:22–25 describes not a partial failure but a double miracle. Those born blind liken human bodies to trees (trunk, boughs/arms, twigs/fingers), hence the man's first reaction. Jesus' second touch overcame the long learning period required by blind people enabled to see for the first time. Metaphor for lack of spiritual discernment (Matt. 23:16; John 9:41; 2 Pet. 1:9; Rev. 3:17).

BLOOD. The sacrificial shedding of blood (Lev. 17:11) is the basis of forgiveness (Heb. 9:22), foreshadowed in the Passover ceremony (Exod. 12:7) and fulfilled in the death of Jesus (John 1:29; 1 Pet. 1:19; Rev. 1:5).

BOANERGES (*Sons of Thunder*). Nickname of James and John (Mark 3:17), probably because of their temper (Luke 9:54).

BOAZ. 1. Prosperous Bethlehem farmer who married the widow Ruth under levirate law (*see* Brother-in-law's duty), and so became the great-grandfather of David (Ruth 2—4); Matt. 1:5).
   2. *See* Jachin and Boaz.

BODY. Used figuratively of believers (1 Cor. 12:27) and the local and universal church (Eph. 4:12; 5:23; Col. 1:18).

BODY, SPIRITUAL. The believer's resurrection body (1 Cor. 15:44), one suited to the heavenly realm. Possessed and controlled by the Spirit, like Jesus' glorified body (Rom. 8:11; 1 Pet. 3:18).

BOILS. The sixth plague may have been skin anthrax affecting the limbs (Exod. 9:9–11). Associated with leprosy in Lev. 13:18–23. Hezekiah was probably suffering from a carbuncle (Isa. 38:21).

BONDAGE. Used of Satan's grip upon a sick woman (Luke 13:16), sin (Acts 8:23), inevitable decay (Rom. 8:21); of God's peace as the tie uniting believers (Eph. 4:3).

BONES. As the body's framework, signifying health and strength (Job 20:11), and conversely when injured, indicating physical, spiritual or moral sickness (Job 2:5; Prov. 14:30; Ezek. 37). The unusual expression in Luke 24:39, omitting blood, implies the unique nature of the resurrection body.

BOOK OF THE ANNALS OF THE KINGS. Royal records, often used by biblical writers (1 Kings 11:41; 2 Chron. 16:11; Esther 2:23).

BOOK OF THE COVENANT. 1. The Deuteronomic law (2 Kings 23:2; 2 Chron. 34:30).
   2. *See* Covenant.

BOOK OF JASHAR. Collection of heroic songs, which has not survived (Josh. 10:13; 2 Sam. 1:18).

BOOK OF THE LAW. God's written directions, rather than legal enactments (Josh. 1:8). The book discovered in 622 BC during Temple repairs (2 Kings 22:8–10) was evidently part of Deuteronomy, judging by Josiah's reaction.

BOOK OF LIFE. Natural length of days (Exod. 32:32; Ps. 139:16), but usually refers to the list of believers, those who have spiritual life (Phil. 4:3; Rev. 3:5).

BOOK OF MOSES. The first five OT books (Gen. to Deut.). *See* Bible 2; Pentateuch.

BOOK OF THE WARS OF THE LORD. Ancient collection of songs celebrating Israel's early victories under God's leadership (Num. 21:14–15).

BOOTH. Impermanent hut of twigs and branches (Matt. 9:9).

> **BOOTHS, FEAST OF.** *See* Feasts and festivals p. 250.

BOTTLE. Modern translations avoid this word as suggesting glass. Goat-skin containers for carrying liquids, more convenient and lighter than pottery. Careful preservation essential (Jer. 48:12; Matt. 9:17).

BOTTOMLESS PIT. *See* Abyss.

BOUNDARY STONES. Marked ownership of land. To remove one amounted to robbing the owner of his property rights (Deut. 19:14).

> **BOW.** *See* War p. 240.

BOWELS. AV/KJV term for internal organs or viscera (2 Chron. 21:15; Acts 1:18). Figuratively, seat of deepest emotions (1 Kings 3:26; Phil. 1:8), as 'heart' today.

> **BOWL.** *See* Domestic life p. 52.

BOZRAH. Edomite capital city, SE of Dead Sea (Gen. 36:33; 1 Chron. 1:44). Its overthrow foretold (Jer. 49:13; Amos 1:12).

BRANCH. 1. Used of the golden lampstand (Menorah) in the Tabernacle, having a central stem and three branches on each side (Exod. 25:33).

2. Figuratively of Israel, likened to a tree (Ps. 80:10; Ezek. 17:23).

3. Term for Messiah, as a descendant of David (Isa.11:1; Jer. 23:5).

4. Describes the relationship of the believer to Jesus (John 15:5).

BRASS (AV/KJV). *See* Bronze.

> **BREAD.** *See* Foods p. 76.

BREAD, TO BREAK. 1. To have a meal, especially with others (Acts 2:46), or to care for physical needs in general (Isa. 58:7).

2. Breaking bread (Acts 20:7) is another name for the Lord's Supper (1 Cor. 11:20) or Eucharist (Thanksgiving) (Matt. 26:26).

BREAD OF GOD. Term claimed by Jesus (John 6:33); foreshadowed by God's gift of manna (Exod. 16).

Bottle – goat-skin container

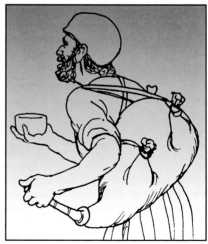

BREAD OF LIFE. One of the 'I am' titles used by Jesus (John 6:35), indicating the source and sustainer of spiritual life.

BREAD OF THE PRESENCE.
See Tabernacle p. 215.

BREASTPIECE. *See* Dress p. 55.

BREASTPLATE. *See* War p. 240.

BREATH. The vital element of physical life (Gen. 1:30), given by God (Gen. 2:7; Ezek. 37) and returned to him at death (Matt. 27:50).

BRIBERY. Giving or receiving money to pervert just dealing. Always condemned (Exod. 23:8; Isa. 5:23; Mic. 7:3).

BRICK. Rectangular baked shapes of clay (Gen. 11:3). The chemical reaction of straw (Exod. 5) made bricks extremely hard.

BRIDE. Veiled (Gen. 24:65), in her wedding finery (Song of Sol. 1:10), and crowned (Ezek. 16:12). Metaphorically applied to Israel in covenant relationship with God (Isa. 54:6; Jer. 2:2), to the church (2 Cor. 11:2) and to New Jerusalem (Rev. 21:9–10).

BRIDE PRICE. *See* Dowry.

BRIDEGROOM. Perfumed and garlanded (Song of Sol. 3:6, 11), his joy over his bride was proverbial (Isa. 62:5). Exempt from military service for a year (Deut. 20:7). Term applied to Messiah (Mark 2:19).

BRIERS. *See* Plants p. 170.

BRIGANDINE. *See* Coat of mail.

BRIMSTONE (AV/KJV). *See* Sulphur.

BRONZE. Alloy of copper and tin, fashioned into vessels (Lev. 6:28), *objets d'art* (Rev. 18:12), mirrors (1 Cor. 13:12), shackles (Jer. 39:7), armour (1 Sam. 17:5) and figures (Dan. 2:32; Rev. 9:20). Valued metal (Isa. 60:17), used in the Tabernacle (Exod. 27:3) and Temple (2 Kings 25:13).

Figuratively, of hardness (Jer. 6:28), brilliance (Dan. 10:6; Rev. 2:18), drought (Lev. 26:19; Deut. 28:23), stubbornness (Jer. 6:28), foreshadowing the crucifixion (Num. 21:9; John 3:14).

BROOK. Usually a wadi, dry in summer, is meant, not a permanent watercourse (1 Kings 17:7; Prov. 18:4).

BROOM. *See* Trees p. 172.

BROTHER. Applied not only to male children (Gen. 4:8; 1 Sam. 17:28), but by extension to members of tribe (2 Sam. 19:41) or nation (Lev. 10:6). Signifies those bound by covenant (Amos 1:9) and in particular fellow believers (Col. 1:2).

BROTHER-IN-LAW'S DUTY. Under levirate law, if a husband died childless, his brother was expected to marry the widow (Deut. 25:5–6; Matt. 22:24) to raise a family for the deceased. Levirate law thus gave widows economic and social protection and avoided breaking up estates (Jer. 32:7). 'Levirate' derives from Latin *levir*, 'husband's brother'.

BROTHERS OF JESUS. Named as James, Joseph, Jude and Simon (Matt. 13:55), they believed in Jesus only after the resurrection

(John 7:5; Acts 1:14). The risen Lord appeared to James (1 Cor. 15:7), afterwards a leader of the Jerusalem church (Gal. 1:19). Jesus counted any man who believed in him to be his brother, i.e. with the same heavenly Father (Mark 3:35).

BUCKLER. Small circular light shield *buckled* on the arm (2 Chron. 14:8; Jer. 46:3). Figuratively used of divine protection (Ps. 35:2; 91:4).

BULL. *See* Domesticated animals p. 14.

BULRUSH. Papyrus; used for Moses' ark (Exod. 2:3).

BURDEN. Anything which weighs down, literally (Exod. 23:5; 2 Kings 5:17) or metaphorically, in governing (Exod. 18:22), work (Num. 4:24; Matt. 20:12), responsibility (Num. 11:11), cares (Matt. 11:30), slavery (Exod. 1:11).

BURIAL. Because of the climate (John 11:39), burial was prompt, even for criminals (Deut. 21:23). The corpse, wrapped in linen (John 11:44), was carried on a bier (Luke 7:14), accompanied by lamentation (Mark 5:38; Acts 8:2) and flautists (Matt. 9:23). Lack of proper burial considered a misfortune (Ezek. 29:5). *See* Tomb.

BURNING BUSH. Scene of Moses' call to deliver Israel from Egyptian slavery (Exod. 3:3; Mark 12:26; Acts 7:30). Fire signifies God's presence (Judg. 13:20).

BURNT OFFERING. A sacrifice wholly burned, to atone for sins (Lev. 1:4). The victim had to be a ritually clean animal (Gen. 8:20) and without blemish (Lev. 1:3; Num. 28—29).

BUTLER (AV/KJV). *See* Cupbearer.

BYBLOS. *See* Gebal.

C

CAESAR. Roman emperors mentioned in the NT are Augustus, 27 BC–AD 14 (Luke 2:1), Tiberius, AD 14–37 (all other Gospel references), and Nero, AD 54–68 (in Acts, and Phil. 4:22).

CAESAREA. Mediterranean port built by Herod the Great to honour the Roman emperor Augustus (Acts 23:23).

CAESAREA PHILIPPI. City sited below Mt. Hermon, near where Peter acknowledged Jesus as Messiah (Matt. 16:13).

CAESAR'S HOUSEHOLD. Roman government officials, some of whom were Christians (Phil. 4:22).

CAIAPHAS. High priest (AD 18–36), son-in-law to Annas (John 18:13), his predecessor. In office at the time of Jesus' trial (John 11:49) and during the early persecutions (Acts 4:6).

CAIN. Adam and Eve's eldest son (Gen. 4). Murdered his brother Abel out of jealousy. Exiled to the land of Nod (*Wandering*), though protected by a divine mark from being killed himself. The nature of the mark is unknown. His character and fate recalled in Heb. 11:4; 1 John 3:12; Jude 11.

CAKE. *See* Foods p. 76.

CALAMUS. *See* Herbs and spices p. 92.

CALEB. One of Moses' spies sent to view the Promised Land (Num. 13:6). Joshua's loyal colleague, praised for his faith (Num. 14:6, 24). Outstanding warrior, still fighting at 85 (Josh. 14:6–15).

CALENDAR. Israel latterly used two calendars. One began in the autumn, based on agricultural seasons (Exod. 23:16; 34:22). The other, added after the exile, began in spring, reflecting Babylonian practice. *See* Feasts; Months; New Moon; Week.

Entrance to Roman theatre, Caesarea

CALF, GOLDEN. 1. Idolatrous image made by Aaron; destroyed by Moses (Exod. 32).

2. Jeroboam I of Israel set up golden calves at Bethel and Dan, to divert attention from the Jerusalem Temple(1 Kings 12:28).

CALL. Divine summons to heed a message (Exod. 3:4; 1 Sam. 3:4); to special work (Exod. 35:30–35; Matt. 10:1); to covenant relationship (Isa. 43:1); to discipleship (Matt. 4:21); to apostleship (Mark 3:13; Rom. 1:1); to preach (Acts 16:10); to holy living (1 Thess. 4:7); to eternal life (1 Tim. 6:12). The puzzling 'chosen' in the saying 'Many are called' (Matt. 22:14) means 'prove to be choice' (by their response).

CALVARY. *See* Golgotha.

CAMEL. *See* Domesticated animals p. 14.

CANA. Village N of Nazareth; scene of first miracle (John 2:1) and healing of nobleman's son (John 4:46). Home of Nathanael (John 21:2).

CANAAN. 1. Son of Ham (Gen. 9:18) and grandson of Noah,who cursed him for his unfilial behaviour (Gen. 9:25). Descendants listed in Gen. 10:15–19.

2. A Semitic people and their homeland, strictly the S Palestine coast (Num. 13:29; Deut. 1:7), though the term can apply to Palestine in general (Gen. 12:5; Num. 13:17).

CANAANITE (*Merchant*). Inhabitant of Canaan; more specifically, one trading there (Isa. 23:8; Ezek. 17:4).

CANAANITE GODS (Baal, Dagon, Asherah, Astarte) were a constant snare to the Israelites (Num. 25:3; 1 Kings 18:18; Jer. 11:13).

CANANAEAN. Aramaic surname of the apostle Simon (Matt. 10:4, RSV). The Greek form is 'Zealot' (Luke 6:15). *See* Simon 2.

CANDACE. Dynastic title for queens ruling Meroe (N Sudan). Her treasurer converted by Philip (Acts 8:27).

CAPERNAUM. Town by Sea of Galilee. Home of Peter and Andrew (Mark 1:29). Although Jesus' headquarters (Matt. 4:13), inhabitants were unresponsive (Luke 4:23; 10:15).

Remains of Capernaum synagogue

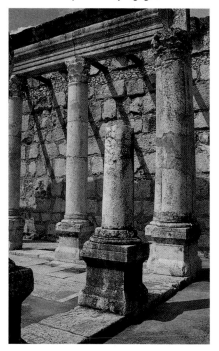

CAPHTOR. Crete; home of the Caphtorites (Deut. 2:23), 'Sea Peoples' that included the Philistines (Amos 9:7).

CAPITAL PUNISHMENT. Stoning was the Jewish punishment for blasphemy (Lev. 24:14) and adultery (John 8:5). The Romans used decapitation for Roman citizens and crucifixion for others (Luke 23:33).

CAPPADOCIA. Mountainous region in E Asia Minor, a Roman province from AD 17 (Acts 2:9; 1 Pet. 1:1).

CAPTAIN OF TEMPLE GUARD. Senior officer of local police force of Levites allowed by the Romans (Acts 5:24).

CAPTIVITY. See Exile.

CARCHEMISH (*City of Chemosh*). Syrian city at the main ford across the Euphrates, NE of Aleppo. Captured by Assyrians (Isa. 10:9), Egyptians (2 Chron. 35:20), and Babylonians (Jer. 46:2).

CARMEL. 1. Town in Judah (Josh. 15:55), S of Hebron. Home of Nabal and Abigail (1 Sam. 25).
   2. Range of hills, stretching from Bay of Acre, SE to Dothan. Scene of Elijah's challenge to Jezebel's god Baal (1 Kings 18:19).

CASSIA. *See* Herbs and spices p. 92.

CASTOR & POLLUX. Twin hero sons of Zeus and Leda, with reputed power over wind and waves. Ships were named after a patron deity to secure protection in storms (Acts 28:11).

CATHOLIC (*universal*) epistles. The seven let-ters of James, Peter, John and Jude, so called because they are addressed to the church at large.

CAUDA. Small island off SW Crete (Acts 27:16).

CEDAR. *See* Trees p. 172.

CENCHREA. Corinth's main port, on the isthmus of Greece (Acts 18:18; Rom. 16:1).

CENSER. Bowl for burning incense, of bronze (Num. 16:39) or gold (1 Kings 7:50).

CENSUS. In OT, for religious purposes (Exod. 30:12) or military service (Num. 26:2). In NT, for levying Roman taxes (Luke 2:1).

CENTURION. *See* War p. 240.

CEPHAS (Aramaic, *Loose stone*). Corresponds to the Greek name *Peter*, given by Jesus to the apostle Simon (John 1:42).

CHAFF. *See* Farming p. 70.

CHALDEA. Alternative name for Babylonia, modern S Iraq (Ezek. 23:15).

CHALDEAN. Language of Babylonia (Dan. 1:4).

CHAMBERLAIN. Confidential royal official (Esther 1:10; Acts 12:20).

CHARIOT. *See* Travel p. 228.

CHARMS. Their use condemned (Ezek. 13:20).

CHEBAR. Babylonian canal (Ezek. 1:1).

CHEDORLAOMER. King of Elam, who attacked Sodom and Gomorrah for rebelling against him (Gen. 14).

CHEEK. Suffering a blow on the cheek signified ignominy (Job 16:10), humiliation (1 Kings 22:24), defeat (Ps. 3:7), or meek acceptance (Matt. 5:39).

CHEMOSH. Moabite national god (Jer. 48:13) requiring child sacrifice (2 Kings 3:27).

CHERETHITES. Cretan settlers in Philistia (1 Sam. 30:14; Zeph. 2:5); with Pelethites formed David's bodyguard (2 Sam. 8:18), remaining loyal through the rebellions of Absalom (2 Sam. 15:18) and Sheba (2 Sam. 20:7).

CHERITH. Jordan tributary where Elijah was fed by ravens (1 Kings 17:3).

CHERUB (*plural,* cherubim). Spiritual beings guarding the tree of life (Gen. 3:24). In Ezekiel's vision they carry God's chariot-throne (Ezek. 10). *See* Ark of the covenant (p. 215, Tabernacle).

CHEWING THE CUD. Distinguishing characteristic of clean animals allowed for food (Lev. 11:3).

CHILDLESSNESS. Lack of children a grief (Hannah, 1 Sam. 1); sometimes viewed as a divine punishment (Gen. 20:18).

CHILDLIKENESS. Commended by Jesus to his followers (Matt.18:2–5). In Jewish society, children were without power or status and utterly dependent upon love.

CHIMHAM. Son of Barzillai who deputised for his aged father (2 Sam. 19:31–40).

CHINNERETH. Fortified city of Naphtali (Josh. 19:35), giving its name to the nearby Sea of Chinnereth (Num. 34:11); Sea of Galilee in NT.

CHIOS. Mountainous Aegean island (Acts 20:15).

CHLOE. Another name for the Greek goddess Demeter (Roman Ceres). 'Chloe's people' (1 Cor. 1:11) were probably devotees, whose form of religion would make them sympathetic to Paul's dislike of faction.

CHORAZIN. City NW of Capernaum on the Sea of Galilee. Its people unresponsive to Christ (Matt. 11:21).

CHRIST (*Anointed*). Greek form of Hebrew 'Messiah'.

Ruins at Chorazin

CHRISTIANS. Name first used at Antioch (Acts 11:26). Called Nazarenes by Jews (Acts 24:5).

CHRISTS, FALSE. Claimants to messiahship (Matt. 24:24), some coming from the desert, imitating Moses (Deut. 18:15; Matt. 24:26).

1 & 2 CHRONICLES. Two OT books narrating Israel's religious history up to the return from the Babylonian exile. Story continued in Ezra and Nehemiah.

CHRONICLES (Annals) **OF THE KINGS.** Not the OT books, but royal archives (frequently mentioned in 1 & 2 Kings).

CHRYSOLITE. Yellow topaz (Ezek. 1:16; Rev. 21:20).

CHRYSOPRASE. Golden-green gem (Rev. 21:20).

CHURCH. In the NT, not a building but the fellowship of Christians, locally (Acts 15:41), or universally (Eph. 5:23).

CHUZA. Steward of Herod Antipas. His wife Joanna helped to support Jesus and his disciples (Luke 8:3).

CILICIA. Roman province of SE Asia Minor, with a sizeable Jewish settlement (Acts 6:9) and Christian groups (Acts 15:23). Paul came from the capital, Tarsus (Acts 21:39).

CINNAMON. *See* Herbs and spices p. 92.

CIRCUMCISED. Synonym for Israelite, one who had undergone the rite of circumcision as a covenant sign, by contrast with pagans, the uncircumcised (Gal. 2:7–9; Col. 2:11).

CIRCUMCISION. Ancient custom of removing the foreskin (Gen. 17:10), symbolising covenant membership in a community. Carried out by Jews on the eighth day after birth (Lev. 12:3; Luke 1:59). Metaphorically describes loyalty to God (Deut. 10:16; Rom. 2:29). The early church refused to impose the rite on converted Gentiles (Acts 15) since faith in Jesus rendered it valueless (Rom. 3:30; Gal. 6:15). True circumcision was inward, and identified with conversion to Christ (Phil. 3:3; Col. 2:11).

CISTERN. Underground reservoir. Usually pear-shaped, with a narrow top, sealed to prevent accidents or theft (Exod. 21:33).

CITADEL. Strong point, a city's last refuge to be stormed (2 Sam. 12:26; 1 Kings 16:18).

CITIES OF THE PLAIN. Listed in Gen. 14:2. Overwhelmed (Gen. 19), according to archaeologists about 2000 BC, and now beneath the Dead Sea. The 'plain' is the fertile Jordan valley (Gen. 13:10).

CITIES OF REFUGE. Levitical cities to which anyone responsible for accidental homicide could flee (Num. 35). The purpose was to prevent interfamily blood feuds escalating.

CITY CLERK. *See* Town clerk.

CITY OF DAVID. Jerusalem (2 Sam. 5:9), but strictly only the citadel Zion (1 Kings 3:1). David's eventual capital, after Hebron (2 Sam. 5:5). Term also applied to Bethlehem (Luke 2:11), as David's birthplace (1 Sam. 16:1).

CITY OF GOD. Jerusalem (Ps. 87:2–3), a symbol of the city to come, New Jerusalem (Ps. 46:4, no rivers serve the earthly Jerusalem; Heb. 12:22). *See* Holy City.

CITY OF PALMS. Jericho (Judg. 1:16). Heat and abundant fresh water promote luxuriant growth.

CLAUDIUS. Roman emperor, AD 41–54. Banished Jews from Rome in AD 49 (Acts 18:2), according to Roman historian Suetonius for rioting about 'Chrestus'. *See* Agabus.

CLAUDIUS LYSIAS. Officer commanding the Roman garrison in Jerusalem. Arrested Paul (Acts 21:33) and sent him to Felix (Acts 23:24). Envied Paul his birthright citizenship (Acts 22:28).

CLEAN ANIMALS. Only ritually clean animals, those which chew the cud and have cloven hoofs (Lev. 11; Deut. 14), allowed for food. Now recognised as being on hygienic grounds.

CLEAN AND UNCLEAN. Terms applied to persons, animals, things and places which allowed or forbade the worshipper's approach to God (Lev. 10:10). Ceremonial defilement was caused by contact with a dead body (Num. 19:11) or infectious skin diseases (Lev. 13—14), by bodily functions (Lev. 12; 15), or through eating unclean animals (Lev. 11; Deut. 14). Provision for cleansing was defined in each case.

CLEMENT. Paul's colleague (Phil. 4:3). The name was very common.

CLEOPAS. One of the two disciples overtaken on the Emmaus road by the risen Christ (Luke 24:18).

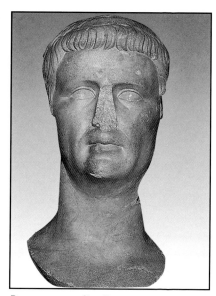

Roman emperor Claudius

CLOAK. *See* Dress p. 54.

CLOPAS. Husband (or father) of one of the women at the cross (John 19:25).

CLOTH. Usually of flax or wool, though not to be mixed (Lev. 19:19). Mixing would give rise to static electricity and prove uncomfortable to the wearer.

CLOUD. Cumulus clouds rising from the Mediterranean bring rain (1 Kings 18:44). High cirrus rainless clouds (Jude 12) generate the hot dry sirocco or khamsin winds from the desert (Isa. 25:5). The short-lived morning cloud (Hos. 6:4) symbolises the brevity of human life and prosperity (Job 7:9; 30:15). The glory cloud (Exod. 13:21) was a visible reminder of God's presence; associated with Christ's transfiguration (Matt. 17:5), ascension (Acts 1:9) and second coming (Rev. 1:7). *See* Wings.

COAL. Charcoal, not coal in the modern sense (2 Sam. 14:7; Isa. 47:14). The hot 'coals' of 1 Kings 19:6 and Isa. 6:6 were hot stones.

COAT OF MAIL. *See* War p. 241.

COAT OF MANY COLOURS. Variegated or long-sleeved robe (Gen. 37:3). Jacob's ostentatious display of favouritism towards Joseph.

COCKCROW. End of the third watch (3:00 AM), by Roman reckoning (Mark 13:35).

COFFIN. Stone sarcophagus (Gen. 50:26), not the modern box. Luke 7:14 refers to the usual bier (stretcher) carrying the body to burial.

COHORT. *See* War p. 241.

COINAGE. *See* Money p. 147.

COLLECTION FOR THE CHURCHES. Gentile believers' gift for impoverished Jewish Christians in Jerusalem (Rom. 15:26; 2 Cor. 8—9).

COLOSSE. City of Phrygia on the river Lycus (W Asia Minor), 16 km (10 mi) from Laodicea. Local Christians included Philemon (Philem. 1), his slave Onesimus (Col. 4:9; Philem. 10) and Epaphras (Col. 4:12).

COLOSSIANS. Written from prison (Col. 4:3) to a church Paul had not yet visited (Col. 2:1). He aimed to counteract a Jewish form of gnosticism some were propagating. Tychicus carried the letter (Col. 4:7) with those to Philemon and to the Ephesians (Eph. 6:21).

COLOURS. Jews were uninterested in colours as such; their language rather indicates distinctions between 'light' and 'dark'. So, for example, the field of John 4:35 is not the puzzling *'white* for harvest' but 'gleaming'.

COMFORTER. AV/KJV title for the Holy Spirit. 'Another Comforter' (John 14:16) means one of the same kind: the Spirit is to carry on Jesus' ministry (John 15:26; 16:7). *See* Counsellor; Holy Spirit.

COMMUNION. Sharing in common, especially regarding the body and blood of Jesus (1 Cor. 10:16), Christian fellowship (Acts 2:44) and the Holy Spirit (2 Cor. 13:14; Phil. 2:1).

CONCUBINE. Woman cohabiting with a man not her husband, a common practice (Gen. 16:2; 29:24; 2 Sam. 3:7). Mosaic law protected her (Exod. 21:7–11; Deut. 21:10–14). To lie with a king's concubine was interpreted as a threat to his throne (2 Sam. 16:21; 1 Kings 2:22).

CONIAH. Another name for Jehoiachin, king of Judah (Jer. 22:24; 37:1).

CONSCIENCE. Moral sense of right and wrong (Rom. 1:19). Needs enlightenment by God (Heb. 9:14), but can be hardened by human choice (1 Tim. 4:2; Titus 1:15). To defy the promptings of conscience wrecks faith (1 Tim. 1:19).

CONSCRIPTION. Forced labour imposed by king Solomon on his free subjects to undertake his massive building programme (1 Kings 5:13;

9:15), thus storing up resentment for the future (1 Kings 12:1–19).

CONSTELLATION. Group of stars whose arrangement suggests a figure; this prompted idolatrous worship (2 Kings 23:5). Constellations named include Great Bear (Ursa Major), Orion and Pleiades (Job 9:9; 38:31–32; Amos 5:8).

CONVERSATION. AV/KJV term for 'manner of life' (Ps. 37:14; 2 Cor. 1:12).

CONVERT. One who turns to God, and attends synagogue (Acts 2:11; 13:43) or through faith in Jesus joins the Christian fellowship (Rom. 16:5).

CONVOCATIONS (*called together*). Special religious occasions to which Israelites were summoned (Num. 10:2; Lev. 23:6). No laborious work was to be done (Num. 28:18).

COPPER. Deposits N of Gulf of Aqabah exploited by Solomon, who built the port of Ezion-Geber (Elath) for shipments (1 Kings 9:26). Refined in crucibles (Ezek. 24:11) and then poured into stone or clay moulds. Mixed with tin made bronze. *See* Cyprus.

COPPERSMITH. The term (2 Tim. 4:14) can mean a craftsman in any metal.

CORBAN (*brought near*). A gift brought to God. Jesus condemned neglect of parents on the specious excuse that the means for their support had been dedicated to God (Mark 7:11).

CORIANDER. *See* Herbs and spices p. 92.

CORINTH. Busy commercial city on the central isthmus of Greece. Paul's stay of 18 months (Acts 18) was unusually long for him.

1 & 2 CORINTHIANS. Paul sent several letters to the church at Corinth, of which we have the second (our 1 Cor., about AD 53) and fourth (our 2 Cor., about AD 55). He advises the church on problems raised by introducing Christianity into a pagan culture. Paul's first letter (1 Cor. 5:9) and third (2 Cor. 2:3; 7:8) have not survived.

CORNELIUS. Roman centurion at Caesarea, the first Gentile convert to Christianity (Acts 10).

CORNERSTONE. Foundation stone (Isa. 28:16; Jer. 51:26) or completing capstone (Ps. 118:22), which rabbis considered referred to Messiah. Fulfilment claimed by Jesus (Matt. 21:42). Symbolism used by Peter to explain Christ's rejection by the Jews (Acts 4:11; 1 Pet. 2:7).

CORNFIELD. The Pharisees' complaint (Matt. 12:1-2) was that plucking ears of corn on the Sabbath amounted to work (reaping). It earned Jesus' rebuke for their legalistic attitude which left no place for human need.

COS. Mountainous but fertile island off SW Asia Minor (Acts 21:1), famous for the medical school founded by Hippocrates about 400 BC.

COUNCIL, JEWISH. *See* Sanhedrin.

COUNSELLOR. Term applied to Messiah (Isa. 9:6) and to the Holy Spirit (John 14:16, 26; 15:26; 16:7; AV/KJV translates as 'Comforter'). The Greek word means 'one called alongside to help', often in a forensic sense ('Advocate' in 1 John 2:1, referring to Jesus).

COURIERS. *See* Travel p. 228.

COURT OF LAW. Courts met only when required, with one or more judges hearing witnesses for and against the accused. Jewish law required more than one witness, to discourage false accusations (Num. 35:30; Heb. 10:28). *See* Appeal to Caesar; Witness 1.

COURTYARD. Enclosure in a private house (2 Sam. 17:18), palace (1 Kings 7:8; John 18:15) or garden (Esther 1:5). The Tabernacle courtyard (outer court) was formed by curtains on poles, readily dismantled for travelling. Herod's Temple had four courtyards, in order of exclusiveness: Court of Gentiles, of Women, of Men (Israelites), and of Priests.

COVENANT. Agreement on future relationships. Most formal covenants in the Bible reflect Near Eastern treaties and are between unequal parties (God/humans; victors/vanquished) and involve obligations, promises, curses and blessings. God made covenants with Noah (Gen. 6:18), Abraham (Gen. 17), Israelites (Exod. 24), and David (2 Sam. 7). The covenant with Israel was sealed with the blood of sacrifice (Exod. 24:8; Zech. 9:11). Israel's inability to keep the divine covenant foreseen by Jeremiah, who spoke of a new covenant written in the heart (Jer. 31:31), a prophecy fulfilled in the sacrifice of Jesus (Matt. 26:28; 1 Cor. 11:25). *See* Bible 2; Book of the Covenant.

COVETOUSNESS. Forbidden (Exod. 20:17; Luke 12:15). Defined as idolatry (Col. 3:5). Achan stoned for the offence (Josh. 7:16–26).

COZBI. Midianite woman slain for enticing Israelites into idolatry (Num. 25:6, 15).

CREATION. God's action (Gen. 1:1; Rev. 4:11) by the Word (John 1:1–3), i.e. Jesus (John 1:14; Col. 1:16; Heb. 1:2). A new creation has been inaugurated (Gal. 6:15) with Jesus himself as the new Adam (1 Cor. 15:45; 2 Cor. 5:17).

CREATURES. 1. Animals as distinct from human beings (Gen. 2:19). Not to be worshipped, thereby usurping the place of the Creator (Rom. 1:25).
2. Celestial beings, seen in visions and described in the imagery of this world (Ezek. 1; Rev. 4:6).

CRESCENS. Paul's companion in his last imprisonment (2 Tim. 4:10).

CRESCENT. Moon-shaped pendant charm of gold (Judg. 8:26; Isa. 3:18).

CRETE. Narrow mountainous island, SE of Greece. OT Caphtor (Amos 9:7). Cretan Jews in Jerusalem at Pentecost (Acts 2:11). Titus commissioned to work there (Titus 1:5).

CRIMSON. Dye produced from the cochineal insect, which feeds on the holm oak. Isa. 1:18 refers to the virtual impossibility of removing the stain.

CRIPPLE. One named (Mephibosheth), cared for by David in memory of Jonathan (2 Sam. 9). The healing of cripples aroused excitement in Jerusalem (Acts 3:2; 4:9), and at Lystra (Acts 14:8) where a double miracle was involved, for the man walked without ever having learned to do so.

CRISPUS. Synagogue leader at Corinth (Acts 18:8), who responded to Paul's preaching (1 Cor. 1:14).

CROPS. *See* Farming p. 70.

CROSS. 1. Stake to which a condemned man was tied or impaled. The description of Christ's cross as a 'tree' (Acts 5:30; 1 Pet. 2:24) alludes to the curse attached to a dead body (Deut. 21:23; Gal. 3:13).

2. Figuratively applied to Christian preaching (1 Cor. 1:18), reconciliation (Eph. 2:16), humiliation (Phil. 2:8), discipleship (Matt. 10:38), and life in Christ (Gal. 2:20).

CROWN. Besides kings (1 Chron. 20:2) and queens (Esther 1:11), worn by the high priest (Exod. 29:6; Zech. 6:11). Christ's crown of thorns (John 19:2) mocked his royal claim. 'Joy and crown' (Phil. 4:1) means 'crowning joy'. Crowns of life (James 1:12; Rev. 2:10) or glory (1 Pet. 5:4) or righteousness (2 Tim. 4:8) refer not to their 'material' but to Christ's gift, not further specified.

CRUCIFIXION. Roman form of capital punishment for slaves and the worst criminals, though rarely for Roman citizens. The victim was flogged (Matt. 27:26), then made to carry the cross-beam to the place of execution outside the city (John 19:17). Stripped, doped (Matt. 27:34) and then nailed by hands and feet and left hanging just above ground level until dying several days later from exhaustion. Death sometimes hastened by the legs being broken (John 19:31). The charge was displayed (Mark 15:26).

CRUMBS. Well-to-do families wiped their greasy fingers with bread, then tossed it under the table for pet dogs (Matt. 15:27).

CRUSE. Small pottery flask for water (1 Sam. 26:11) or olive oil (1 Kings 17:12).

Position of the body during crucifixion

CUBIT. *See* Weights and measures 3.

CUCUMBER. *See* Foods p. 77.

CUMMIN. *See* Herbs and spices p. 92.

CUP. *See* Domestic life p. 52.

CUPBEARER. Royal wine taster, frequently an influential confidant of the king (Gen. 40:9–11; Neh. 1:11).

CURDS. *See* Foods p. 76.

CURSE. 1. Malediction to secure another's hurt (Num. 23:7; Rom. 12:14; James 3:9). Words spoken were deemed to possess inherent power to achieve their object.

2. Breaking God's law invokes the divine curse which brings about evil consequences (Gen. 4:11; Gal. 3:10).

3. Applied to Christ (Gal. 3:13) in Paul's interpretation of the cross.

CURTAIN. Tabernacle curtains were of linen and goat hair (Exod. 26). The curtain of the Temple ('sacred veil', Heb. 9:3) shutting off the holy of holies, measured 20 x 10 metres (60 x 30 ft); immensely heavy and impossible for human hands to split (Matt. 27:51).

CUSH. Nubia (N Sudan; Nah. 3:9), called Ethiopia by classical writers and modern translators, but not the modern state.

CUSHAN-RISHATHAIM. Mesopotamian king who subjugated Israel for 8 years, until their deliverance by the judge Othniel (Judg. 3:8–10).

CUSHION. The Greek word is literally 'a cushion for the head' (Mark 4:38); normally used by a rower to sit on.

CUSHITE. Behind criticism of Moses' marriage to a non-Israelite black woman was jealousy of his special relationship with God (Num. 12).

CUSTODIAN. Trusted male slave who took his master's son to school. Paul alludes to the practice (Gal. 3:24–25).

CUTHAH. Ancient city, NE of Babylon. Inhabitants deported by Sargon to Samaria; they took their god Nergal with them (2 Kings 17:24, 30).

CYMBALS. *See* Music p. 150.

CYPRESS. *See* Trees p. 172.

CYPRUS. Mediterranean island (OT Elishah). Home of Barnabas (Acts 4:36) and Mnason (Acts 21:16). Where Paul and Barnabas encountered the sorcerer Barjesus and the Roman proconsul Sergius Paulus (Acts 13). Cyprus gave its name to the metal copper, extensively mined on the island.

CYRENE. N African port whose large Jewish population (Acts 2:10) had a synagogue in Jerusalem when on pilgrimage (Acts 6:9). Home of the Simon who carried Jesus' cross (Matt. 27:32), missionaries to Antioch (Acts 11:20) and Lucius, a leader of the Antioch church (Acts 13:1).

CYRENIUS. *See* Quirinius.

CYRUS II ('the Great'). Persian king (559–530 BC) who conquered Babylon (539 BC). Allowed exiled Jews to return to Judah (2 Chron. 36:22; Ezra 1:1) and restore their Temple (Ezra 6:3). Daniel was in his service (Dan. 6:28; 10:1).

D

DAGON. Grain god worshipped by Philistines (Judg. 16:23;1 Sam. 5:5).

DALMANUTHA. Unidentified coastal district by the Sea of Galilee (Mark 8:10). Magadan in Matt. 15:39.

DALMATIA. Mountainous Roman province on Adriatic coast (2 Tim. 4:10). Illyricum in Rom. 15:19.

DAMARIS. Woman convert in Athens (Acts 17:34). Athenian women of high social rank usually kept in the background.

DAMASCUS. Capital of Syria (Isa. 7:8), astride trade routes (1 Kings 20:34) linking Egypt and Arabia with the East.

DAN. 1. Son of Jacob and Rachel's handmaid Bilhah (Gen. 35:25) and ancestor of one of the twelve tribes of Israel (Gen. 49:16). Danites first settled W of the Dead Sea (Josh. 19:40), but later under Amorite pressure (Judg. 1:34) some migrated N (Josh. 19:47).
2. Danite city, earlier called Laish (Judg. 18:29) or Leshem (Josh. 19:47). Northernmost Israelite settlement, hence the expression 'from Dan to Beersheba' (1 Sam. 3:20), meaning the whole land.

Philistine deity Dagon

DANIEL. 1. Man classed with Noah and Job for his godly wisdom (Ezek. 14:14, 20; 28:3). Not the OT prophet; appears as 'Danel' (about 1400 BC) in a non-biblical text.
2. Young Jewish noble, deported to Babylon in 597 BC (Dan. 1). Interpreter of dreams and visions (Dan. 2—12) and a leading official under Nebuchadnezzar, Belshazzar and Darius. His prophecy quoted by Jesus (Dan. 9:27; Matt. 24:15).

DANIEL (book). Tells the story of the prophet Daniel and his visions of the future. His prophecies form the background to Jesus' discourse on Olivet (Matt. 24—25; Luke 21), Paul's teaching on the Man of Lawlessness (2 Thess. 2), and the book of Revelation. The passage about the Son of Man (Dan. 7:13–14) is frequently quoted (Matt. 24:30; 26:64; Rev. 1:7, 13; 14:14).

DANIEL, ADDITIONS TO (Apocrypha). Passages added to Greek version of Dan. 3 (not in the Hebrew), purporting to give the words sung in Nebuchadnezzar's furnace by the three young men.

DARIC. *See* Money: Coinage p. 147.

DARIUS. 1. Darius the Mede (otherwise Cyrus II), son of Ahasuerus (Xerxes; Dan. 9:1), displaced Belshazzar as king of the Chaldeans in 559 BC when he was 62 (Dan. 5:30–31). Daniel was one of his district governors (Dan. 6:2).

2. Darius I (521–486 BC), king of Persia and Babylon (Hag. 1:1).

3. Darius II (423–408 BC), called Darius the Persian in Neh. 12:22.

DARKNESS. 1. Characteristic of evil (Luke 22:53), Satan (Acts 26:18; Rev. 16:10) and of unbelievers (Eph. 5:8); the destiny of wicked human beings (1 Sam. 2:9; Matt. 8:12; Jude 13) and fallen angels (2 Pet. 2:17).

2. Figuratively used of folly (Eccles. 2:13), hopelessness (Eccles. 5:17), hatred (1 John 2:9), distress (Isa. 8:22), terror (Gen. 15:12), lack of understanding (Job 38:19) or of the knowledge of God (Isa. 9:2). Without the light of Christ (John 1:5; 1 John 2:8), a person walks in darkness (1 John 1:6). Divine action is needed to dispel darkness (Gen. 1:4; Job 12:22; 2 Cor. 4:6). A sign of the last days (Joel 2:31; Acts 2:20).

DATHAN. With Abiram and Korah, rebelled against Moses and came to a dramatic end (Num. 16; Deut. 11:6; Ps. 106:17).

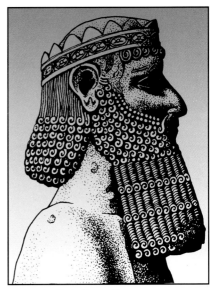

Darius the Mede (Cyrus II)

DAVID. King of Israel (1 Sam. 16 —1 Kings 2; 1 Chron. 2—29). Subjugated enemies, organised national worship and prepared for the building of the Temple. Musician (1 Sam. 18:10; Amos 6:5) and poet (2 Sam. 1:17; 23:1). Ancestor of Jesus (Matt. 1:17); prophesied Christ's coming and resurrection (Acts 1:16; 2:31). 'Son of David' a title of the expected Messiah (Matt. 12:23; Luke 20:41).

DAY OF ATONEMENT. Solemn annual fast (Lev. 16; Acts 27:9) reminding Jews that sacrifices were insufficient to atone for sin. Only on this day in the year the high priest entered the Most Holy Place and burned incense and sprinkled blood on the mercy seat to make atonement for the nation. *See* Scapegoat. The NT interprets the day's ritual as typifying the sacrificial work of Jesus (Heb. 9).

DAY OF THE LORD. The day when God breaks into history and, in popular expectation, establishes Israel as head over the nations (Acts 1:6). The prophets warned it meant judgment for all nations (Isa. 13:6; Jer. 46:10; Joel 3:14), including Israel (Zeph. 1). The NT sees it as the second coming of Christ (2 Thess. 2:2).

DAY OF PREPARATION. The day preceding a Sabbath or festival (Matt. 27:62).

DAY'S JOURNEY. *See* Travel p. 228.

DAYSMAN. *See* Umpire.

DEACON. The Greek word has the general meaning of waiting at table (Matt. 8:15). In 1 Tim. 3:8–13 a church appointment is meant.

DEACONESS. Title used of Phoebe, a member of the church at Cenchrea (Rom. 16:1). 1 Tim. 3:11 more probably refers to women deacons rather than wives of deacons. Deaconesses were needed to minister to their own sex, especially in baptism when candidates were unclothed.

DEAD SEA. Inland lake, fed by the Jordan; the lowest body of water in the world. With no outlet, water is lost only by evaporation. Consequently minerals are left, making the water five times saltier than the sea. No fish or vegetation can survive in it. In Ezekiel's vision a river of pure water flows from Jerusalem (which has no natural river) to bring life to the Dead Sea (Ezek. 47:8–12).

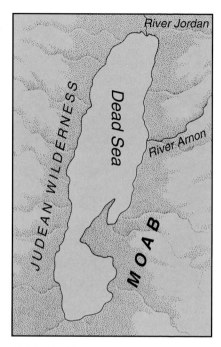

DEAD SEA SCROLLS. Popular name given to manuscripts found since 1947 in caves NW of the Dead Sea. All OT books (except Esther) are represented, including the earliest known copy of Isaiah, dated about 200 BC.

DEAFNESS. Its healing a messianic sign (Isa. 35:5; Matt. 11:5; Mark 7:37). Metaphorically describes the refusal to listen to God's word (Jer. 6:10; Acts 7:51).

DEATH. Universal (Job 30:23), the penalty for sin (Gen. 2:17; Rom. 5:12); in the power of Satan (Heb. 2:14) though subject to God's overruling (Job 2:6; Luke 12:5). By himself dying,

Christ destroyed death (Heb. 2:9; Rev. 1:18), thus stripping sin of its power (1 Cor. 15:54–56). His death for sinners (1 Cor. 15:3) reconciles them to God (Rom. 5:10) and removes fear of death (Heb. 2:15).

DEATH, SECOND. A Christian possesses Christ's life and so will not suffer the second death of unbelievers (Rev. 2:11; 20:6), the death of the soul (Matt. 10:28) in the lake of fire (Rev. 20:14).

DEBIR. Earlier called Kiriath Sepher (Judg. 1:11) or Kiriath Sannah (Josh. 15:49), near Hebron; captured by Joshua (Josh. 10:38).

DEBORAH. 1. Rebekah's nurse (Gen. 35:8).
2. Judge-prophetess (1125 BC) who ordered Barak to lead the Israelites against Sisera (Judg. 4). Deborah's victory song (Judg. 5) is one of the most ancient passages in the OT.

DEBT. *See* Money p. 146.

DECAPOLIS (*Ten Cities*). Federation of ten trading cities formed to safeguard the Greek way of life (Matt. 4:25). Included Gerasa (Luke 8:26) and Damascus (Acts 9:2). Pella gave refuge to Jerusalem Christians escaping from the Jewish-Roman war of AD 70 (Mark 13:14).

DECEIT. Characteristic of Satan (Rev. 20:10), and of the human heart apart from God (Jer. 17:9; 2 Tim. 3:13).

DELILAH. Philistine woman who ensnared Samson (Judg. 16).

DEMAS. Colleague of Paul (Col. 4:14; Philem. 24); later, out of self-interest, deserted him (2 Tim. 4:10).

DEMETRIUS. 1. Silversmith at Ephesus (Acts 19:24, 38) who instigated a riot because Paul's preaching threatened the trade in shrines for the goddess Diana (Artemis).
2. An outstanding Christian (3 John 12).

DEMON POSSESSION. The control of human beings by evil spirits, the effect of which might be seen in dumbness (Luke 11:14), blindness (Matt. 12:22), epilepsy (Matt. 17:18) or nudity (Luke 8:27).

DEMONS. Evil spiritual beings under Satan's control (Mark 3:22) and fearful of Christ's power (Luke 4:34; James 2:19). Idol worship is in reality demon worship (Deut. 32:17; 1 Cor. 10:20).

DEN OF ROBBERS. Pilgrims bringing foreign currency required money changers and sacrifices needed animals. Such commercial activities at festival times invited exploitation and led to noisy overcrowding in a Temple intended for God's worship. Jesus' scathing attack (Matt. 21:12–13) alludes to the religious leaders of Jeremiah's day who vainly assumed their vested interests in the Temple protected them from God's wrath (Jer. 7:11).

DENARIUS. *See* Money: Coinage p. 147.

DERBE. City of Lycaonia, NW of Tarsus (Acts 14:6; 16:1; Acts 20:4).

DEUTERONOMY. Moses reminds Israel of God's covenant (Deut. 1—11), laws applying in the Promised Land (12—26), and God's demand for obedience (27—30). Final blessing and appointment of Joshua (31—34).

DEVIL. *See* Satan.

Domestic life

Basket. Various sizes for bread (Gen. 40:16), figs (Jer. 24:1), trapping birds (Jer. 5:27). Different Greek words for basket indicate that the 5000 were Jews (Matt. 14:20) and the 4000 were Gentiles (Matt. 15:37). The latter kind of basket was large enough to hold Paul (Acts 9:25; 2 Cor. 11:33).

Bed. Until Roman times, raised beds on supports found only in richer houses (Amos 6:4). The paralytic's bed (Matt. 9:6) was a light pallet, easily rolled up.

Bowl. Household vessel, usually of pottery; of gold or silver in the Temple and in wealthy houses (1 Kings 10:21; 1 Chron. 28:17).

Cup. Drinking bowl of pottery or metal. At mealtimes a cup was shared, symbolising unity (Matt. 10:23). During the Passover meal several cups were passed round (Luke 22:17, 20), the third being the 'cup of blessing' (1 Cor. 10:16), for the final thanksgiving. The cup of salvation (Ps. 116:13) and cup of consolation (Jer. 16:7) signify what is offered (or imposed: Isa. 51:17).

Household gods. Small statues (teraphim) owned by the head of the household, hence Laban's concern at their loss (Gen. 31:35). Micaiah's grief at losing his (Judg. 18:14-26) suggests their importance.

Jar. Earthenware pitcher carried on head or shoulder, usually by women, brought water from the village well

Carrying water

(Gen. 24:14; John 4:28) to be emptied into much larger waterpots (Ruth 2:9; John 2:6). The cruse (1 Kings 17:10) was used for water (1 Kings 19:6), olive oil (1 Kings 17:12), wine (John 19:29) or perfume (Luke 7:37). Being porous, earthenware initially absorbs a little liquid; this reduces evaporation and keeps the contents cool. Easily broken, the pieces (sherds; Isa. 45:9), found in immense numbers,

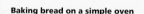

Baking bread on a simple oven

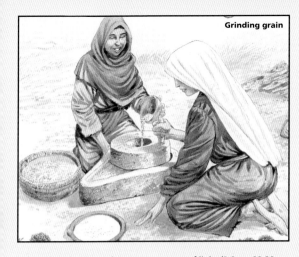

Grinding grain

help archaeologists to date sites. Dead Sea Scrolls hidden in jars with ceramic (heat-hardened) lids.

Lamp. Stone or pottery vessel holding olive oil (Exod. 25:6) and a flax wick. Found in abundance by archaeologists and invaluable for establishing dates of excavated sites. Symbolic of God's ability to discern (Prov. 20:27) and of divine precepts (Ps. 119:105). Also of a father's instruction (Prov. 6:23), of the permanence of the Davidic dynasty (1 Kings 11:36); negatively of destruction (Jer. 25:10). In the NT, symbolises inner light (Matt. 6:22), vigilance (Luke 12:35), witness (Matt. 5:14-16; John 5:35) and the prophetic message (2 Pet. 1:19). God is the ultimate source of light (2 Sam. 22:29; Rev. 22:5).

Loom. The simplest was four stakes in the ground forming a rectangle to hold lengthwise threads (warp) for crosswise threads (woof), as used by Delilah (Judg. 16:13-14). *See* Weaving.

Mat. Light mattress used as poor person's bed (2 Sam. 11:13; Matt. 9:2).

Mill. Rotating hand mill, essential for daily grinding (Deut. 24:6), comprising a fixed base stone (Job 41:24) and a top stone, joined by a wooden spindle; rotated by a handle near the edge of the top stone. The absence of the familiar sound of grinding spelt tragedy (Jer. 25:10; Rev. 18:22).

Mortar and pestle. Hand mill made from a hollowed stone or deep wooden bowl (mortar) and a stout wooden pole (pestle).Used to grind grain into flour (Num. 11:8; Luke 17:35) and herbs for seasoning and medicines.

Oil, olive. Used in medicine (Isa. 1:6; Luke 10:34) and cooking (Exod. 29:2) and for light (Exod. 25:6). Mixed with perfume, welcomed perspiring arrivals (Luke 7:46), and so a symbol of gladness (Isa. 61:3). In sacred anointing (Exod. 30:23-25) indicated 'setting aside' (as priests, Exod. 28:41; kings, 1 Sam. 10:1; prophets, 1 Kings 19:16). In healing (James 5:14), anointing signifies Christ 'setting aside' the sickness from the patient and bearing it himself (Matt. 8:17). It is not the oil which brings about healing but the prayer of faith (James 5:15). *See* Olive.

Oven. The simplest was a large shallow earthenware bowl set upside down over a fire (Lev. 2:4). Figuratively, of scorching drought (Lam. 5:10).

Pitcher. Earthenware jar for liquids (Exod. 25:29; Mark 7:4). Broken, symbolic of death (Eccles. 12:6).

Dress

Dress. The main garments were the tunic and belt (Exod. 12:11) and the cloak (2 Tim. 4:13). Heads were covered with material falling loosely over the shoulders or rolled like a turban (Exod. 28:4). Sandals (Acts 12:8), tied on with thongs (Mark 1:7), were worn only out of doors.

Belt. Kept cloak in place (Exod. 12:11). Made from rope, leather or rolled cloth. Implied in references to girding (Ps. 45:3).

Cloak. Rectangular outer garment of wool or linen, with an opening for the arms, worn like a cape (2 Tim. 4:13). At night served as a covering (Deut. 24:13). *See also* Robe.

Hair garment. Hard-wearing, if unfashionable, garment of prophets (2 Kings 1:8; Matt. 3:4).

Mantle. General word for outer cloak (1 Kings 19:13, AV/KJV). Served as a blanket at night (Exod. 22:27) or as emergency carrier (Exod. 12:34). Poetic term for complete cover (Ps. 65:13).

Necklace. Used as ornament (Num. 31:50) or to indicate royal appointment (Gen. 41:42). Figuratively speaks of pride (Ps. 73:6).

Nose ring. Personal adornment (Gen. 24:22). Extravagant use deplored as worldly (Isa. 3:21). Metaphorically, speaks of God's love (Ezek. 16:12).

Purse. The folds of a waistband serving to hold coins (Matt. 10:9).

Robe. Basic kimonolike garment (sometimes

Typical dress of a peasant man, peasant woman, child and wealthier man

translated 'tunic' or 'cloak'), of wool, linen or cotton. Usually made from two pieces of material joined horizontally at the waist, with openings for head and arms. Goat hair (sackcloth) worn at times of mourning. Jesus' seamless robe (John 19:23) was unusual enough for the soldiers to dice for it. *See* Cloak; Coat of many colours.

55

Sandals

Priest's costume

Ephod. Priestly waist dress of linen (1 Sam. 2:18; 2 Sam. 6:14) though, in the high priest's case, of costly embroidered material (Exod. 39) with bells and pomegranates attached (Exod. 28:31-35). Superstitious use could be made of it (Judg. 8:27; 17:5).

Breastpiece. The high priest's ornate pouch, decorated with twelve gems symbolising the twelve tribes of Israel (Exod. 28:15-21), and holding the Urim and Thummim (Exod. 28:30).

Sacred garments. Priestly dress, symbolising God's presence among his people (Exod. 28; Ps. 132:9). The adornment required of Christians is spiritual (1 Pet. 2:9; 5:5).

Turban. Headgear wrapped around the head (Ezek. 21:26; 24:17). Worn by the high priest (Exod. 28:4) with the sacred diadem attached (Exod. 29:6; Zech. 3:5).

Sackcloth. Crude garment of camel or goat hair (Isa. 50:3), covering the body from neck to ankles, as if for burial. Worn as a sign of mourning (Gen. 37:34), repentance (Matt. 11:21), protest (2 Sam. 21:10) or as an appeal for mercy (1 Kings 20:31). Could also be a prophet's garb (Isa. 20:2; Rev. 11:3).

Sandals. Soles attached to the feet with leather thongs (Gen. 14:23), removed indoors and in a holy place (Exod. 3:5). Indicated preparedness (Exod. 12:11; Eph. 6:15). Used to symbolise taking possession (Ps. 60:8), ownership (Josh. 1:3), transferring property (Ruth 4:7-8), or the refusal to fulfil levirate obligations (Deut. 25:9). *See* Barefoot.

Veil. Customarily covered a bride's face (Gen. 24:65; Song of Sol. 4:1). Metaphorically, explains Jewish inability to understand the gospel (2 Cor. 3:13-16; 4:3).

DEW. Sufficient in Palestine's rainless summer to maintain crops (Gen. 27:28; Isa. 18:4), and so a figure of blessing (Hos. 14:5; Mic. 5:7). Its absence was calamitous (1 Kings 17:1).

DIAMOND. Unknown in biblical times. In Exod. 28:18; 39:11, probably a white opaque stone is meant, and adamant in Jer. 17:1.

DIANA of the Ephesians. *See* Artemis.

DIDYMUS (*Twin*). Greek name for the apostle Thomas (John 11:16).

DILL. *See* Herbs and spices p. 93.

DINAH. Daughter of Jacob and Leah (Gen. 30:21) whose rape led to her brothers treacherously slaying Shechem's family (Gen. 34).

DIONESIUS THE AREOPAGITE. Member of Athens city council (*Areopagus*) (Acts 17:34).

DIOTREPHES. Demagogue who rejected John's authority, refused hospitality to travelling evangelists and excommunicated those who welcomed Christian visitors (3 John 9–10).

DISCIPLE (*Learner*). One who learns a leader's manner of life by following his teaching (Isa. 8:16; Matt. 5:1; Mark 2:18) and being in his company (Matt. 9:9; Mark 6:45; John 1:35).

DISCIPLE, BELOVED. Unnamed apostle in the Fourth Gospel, presumably John himself (John 19:26).

DIVINATION. Using supernatural means to gain insight into the unknown. Condemned (Lev. 19:26) as lies (Ezek. 13:6) and pagan (Deut. 18:10; 2 Kings 17:17).

DIVORCE. Apart from two situations (Exod. 22:16–17; Deut. 22:13–19), divorce was allowed under Mosaic law (Deut. 24:1–4) as a concession (Matt. 19:8). Jesus condemned divorce and remarriage (Mark 10:2–12) except for adultery (Matt. 19:9). The conversion of one of two pagan spouses could also lead to separation (1 Cor. 7:10–15).

DOEG. Edomite ordered by Saul to slay the priests at Nob (1 Sam. 21:7; 22:9–22).

DOG. *See* Wild animals p. 16.

DONKEY. *See* Domesticated animals p. 14.

DOOR. Metaphor for an opening for apostolic ministry (Acts 14:27; 1 Cor. 16:9; 2 Cor. 2:12; Col. 4:3) and the nearness of judgment (James 5:9). A title of Jesus (John 10:7, 9), indicating the believer's entrance into fullness of life.

DOORPOST. Blood sprinkled on Israelite doorposts at the first Passover (Exod. 12:22–23). *See* Ear.

DORCAS. Restored to life through Peter's prayer (Acts 9:36–41).

DOTHAN. Place N of Shechem, where lush pasture attracted Joseph's brothers (Gen. 37:17). The scene of an encouraging vision to Elisha's servant (2 Kings 6:11–23).

DOUBLE. Isa. 40:2 appears to mean double punishment, which is hardly 'comfort' (v. 1) or just (Gen. 18:25). The 'double' refers to the custom whereby a hopeless debtor publicly displayed the final demand, hoping some philanthropist would fold the note *double* and endorse it. The signature was as good as a modern cheque.

DOVE. *See* Birds p. 104.

DOVE'S DUNG. Popular Hebrew name for the plant 'Star of Bethlehem'. Its white and green flowers look like bird droppings. Bulbs highly priced at the siege of Samaria (2 Kings 6:25, AV/KJV).

DOWRY. Bridal gift of servants (Gen. 24:59), land (Judg. 1:15; 1 Kings 9:16), jewellery or clothes (Gen. 24:53).

DRAGON. Mythical figure representing God's enemy (Ps. 74:13; Ezek. 29:3; Rev. 12—13). *See* Bel and the Dragon (Apocrypha).

DRAWING WATER. Heavy menial task of slaves and women, imposed upon Gibeonites who tricked Joshua into a treaty (Josh. 9).

DREAM. Interpretations given directly to believers (Gen. 37:5–10), or through one of God's people (Gen. 41:25; Dan. 2). Five NT dreams concern the infancy of Jesus (Matt. 1—2); another was given to Pilate's wife (Matt. 27:19).

DRESS. *See* pp. 54-55.

DRESSER. Dressing sycamore-fig trees (Amos 7:14) involved tediously cutting the top of each fig to ensure its ripening pest free.

DRIED FRUIT. *See* Cake.

DRINK. Water was of course basic to life (Gen. 21:14), but wine provided the general drink (Isa. 55:1). Vinegar was wine made sour by fermentation; diluted, made a refreshing drink (Ruth 2:14; Mark 15:36).

DRINK OFFERING. Acknowledged God as the provider of basic sustenance (Exod. 29:38–42; Lev. 23:13).

DROPSY (oedema). Symptomatic of heart, kidney or liver disease. Dr Luke uses the Greek medical term (Luke 14:2).

DROSS. Scum separated from metals in smelting (Prov. 25:4). Used metaphorically of the wicked (Ps. 119:119) and backslidden Israel (Ezek. 22:18).

DROUGHT. Seen as a judgment (1 Kings 18; Hag. 1:11).

DRUNKENNESS. Condemned (Isa. 28:7; Rom. 13:13; 1 Pet. 4:3). Figuratively, of spiritual or mental confusion (Job 12:25; Isa. 51:17–23; Jer. 23:9).

DRUSILLA. Younger daughter of Herod Agrippa I and sister of Bernice and Agrippa II, born in AD 38. At 16, deserted her first husband (king of Emesa, Syria) to marry Felix, Roman governor of Judea (Acts 24:24).

DUMBNESS. *See* Mute.

DUNG GATE. Exit by which Jerusalem's rubbish was removed (Neh. 2:13).

DUNGHILL. Refuse dump (Ezra 6:11). Figuratively describes hopelessness (1 Sam. 2:8).

DURA. Open space near Babylon for Nebuchadnezzar's spectacular image (Dan. 3:1).

DUST. Used figuratively of multitudes (Gen. 13:16; Isa. 29:5), smallness (Deut. 9:21), poverty (1 Sam. 2:8), abasement (Gen. 18:27), and death Ps. 22:15). Dust on the head a sign of distress (Job 2:12) or contrition (Josh. 7:6). Signified the lowly origin of human beings (Gen. 2:7; 1 Cor. 15:47).

DWARF. Physical disability disqualifying from priestly office (Lev. 21:20).

DYEING. Scarlet dye produced from cochineal insects (Lev. 14:4), imperial purple from Mediterranean molluscs (Prov. 31:22; Luke 16:19; John 19:2); yellow and blue (Exod. 25:4) from plants.

EAGLE *See* Birds p. 104.

EAR. A Hebrew slave choosing to remain with his master had his ear pierced against the doorpost as a sign of permanently belonging (Exod. 21:6). Applying sacrificial blood to a priest's right ear, thumb and toe symbolised complete consecration (Lev. 8:23).

EARS OF CORN. Principally wheat (John 12:24) or barley (Exod. 9:31). Mosaic law (Deut. 23:25) allowed the poor to glean (Ruth 2:2). Later rabbinic law viewed this as work forbidden on the Sabbath, but Jesus disagreed (Matt. 12).

EARTH. God created a physical world (Gen. 1:1; Ps. 24:1) for human beings (Gen. 1:28), though subject to obeying his will (Deut. 28). The present earth will be replaced (Rev. 21:1).

EARTHQUAKES. Mentioned in connection with divine activity at the giving of the law on Mt. Sinai (Exod. 19:18), and in the days of Korah (Num. 16:31), Saul (1 Sam. 14:15), Elijah (1 Kings 19:11), Uzziah (760 BC, Amos 1:1; Zech. 14:5), Paul and Silas (Acts 16:26) and at the crucifixion (Matt. 27:54). A sign of judgment (Isa. 29:6; Ezek. 38:19) and of the last days (Joel 3:16; Matt. 24:7; Rev. 16:18).

EAST, MEN OF THE. Nomadic Arab tribes, descendants of Ishmael and chronic adversaries of Israel (Judg. 6:3).

EASTERN SEA. Another name for the Dead Sea.

EBAL (*Heap of Stones*). Barren mountain (overlooking Shechem) where six tribes pronounced a curse on disobedience and the other six tribes on nearby Mt Gerizim pronounced a blessing on obedience (Deut. 11:29; 27:13). The space between the two mountains forms a natural amphitheatre with remarkable acoustics. Site of stones inscribed with the divine law (Deut. 27:4) and of Joshua's altar to mark his victory at Ai (Josh. 8:30).

EBED-MELECH (*King's Servant*). Ethiopian official of Zedekiah. For rescuing Jeremiah (Jer. 38:7–13) his life was to be spared when the Babylonians attacked Jerusalem (Jer. 39:16–18).

EBENEZER. 1. Place S of Gilgal where the Philistines captured the ark of the covenant (1 Sam. 4).
2. Name (*Stone of Help*) of a monument erected between Mizpah and Jeshanah (Shen) to mark Samuel's victory over the Philistines, reversing an earlier defeat (1 Sam. 7:12).

EBER (*Emigrant*). Apart from the personal name, a poetic term for Israel (Num. 24:24).

EBONY. *See* Trees p. 173.

ECBATANA. Modern Hamadan, Iran, where Cyrus's decree authorising Temple's rebuilding was filed (Ezra 6:2).

ECCLESIASTES. OT Wisdom book, compiled about 200 BC, arguing that life's riddle is not to be solved through knowledge (Eccles. 1:13), possessions (2:4), hard work (2:18), sensual pleasures (3:13), oppression (4:1), religious profession (5:1) or folly (10:12). Whatever the puzzles of life, people must live with God always in mind (12:1, 13–14).

ECCLESIASTICUS (*Church Book*), or Wisdom of Jesus ben Sira (Apocrypha). Written about 180 BC by a Palestinian in Jerusalem, enjoining practical piety and morality through fear of the Lord and obedience to the law of Moses (1—23). Gives examples of famous men who followed these principles (24—50). Quotes from every OT book except Daniel.

EDEN (*Delight*). 1. Levite who promoted Hezekiah's reforms (2 Chron. 29:12; 31:15).
2. Place between Haran and the Euphrates, trading with Tyre (Ezek. 27:23). Captured by Assyrians (2 Kings 19:12).

EDEN, GARDEN OF. Abode of Adam and Eve (Gen. 2:8) before their expulsion (Gen. 3:23). Its beauty proverbial (Ezek. 36:35; Joel 2:3).

EDOM (*Red*). 1. First-born son of Isaac and twin brother of Jacob. Named Esau at birth, but called Edom after selling his birthright as eldest son for red pottage (Gen. 25:30).
2. Edomites generally (Num. 20:18; Amos 1:6). Chronic antagonists of Judah (Ps. 137:7) for which the prophets promised divine retribution (Jer. 49:7–22; Joel 3:19; Amos 9:12).
3. Territory S of Dead Sea occupied by Esau's descendants; formerly Seir (Gen. 32:3; Obad. 1).

EDREI. 1. Amorite city, S of Damascus, scene

of Israel's victory over Og king of Bashan (Deut. 1:4).

2. Town allotted to Naphtali (Josh. 19:37).

EGLON. 1. Moabite king, remarkable for obesity, whose assassination by Ehud led to Israel's liberation (Judg. 3:12–30).

2. City near Lachish, occupied by Judah (Josh. 10).

EGYPT. Mainly desert except where watered by the Nile. Lower Egypt (Jer. 44:1) is the delta area, N of Cairo; Upper Egypt (Isa. 11:11) is the Nile Valley, from Cairo to Aswan. The pyramids date from 2650 BC. The foreign Hyksos occupied the land about 1700 BC but retained the native ruling title of pharaoh. The Joseph stories (Gen. 37—50) belong to this period. About 1560 the Egyptians expelled the Hyksos and now all foreigners were suspect (Exod. 1:8). The next 500 years restored Egypt's glories and expanded her empire to the Euphrates. Then decline set in and Hebrew prophets constantly warned Israel not to rely on Egyptian help (Isa. 30:2; Jer. 2:18; Ezek. 30:6).

EGYPTIAN, THE. Unnamed leader of the Assassins (*Sicarii, Dagger Men*) who arrived in Jerusalem claiming to be a great prophet. Evaded capture when Felix defeated his band. The Roman officer Claudius Lysias at first thought Paul was the man (Acts 21:38).

EHUD. Left-handed Benjamite, second judge of Israel, who liberated Israel by assassinating Eglon king of Moab (Judg. 3:15–30).

EIGHTH DAY. Significant as the day of male circumcision (Luke 1:59), and of the climax of the Feast of Tabernacles (Num. 29:35; John 7:37).

The sphinx, Egypt

EKRON. One of the five main Philistine cities. The ark of the covenant was captured (1 Sam. 4:11) and lodged there for a while (1 Sam. 5:10). The local god was Baal-Zebub (2 Kings 1:2).

ELAH. Valley in the Shephelah where David overcame Goliath (1 Sam. 21:9).

ELAM (*Highlands*). Mountainous country E of Babylonia, with its capital at Susa (Shushan). After their usual practice, the Assyrians deported some Elamites to Samaria and some Israelites to Elam (Isa. 11:11). Elamite Jews were visiting Jerusalem at Pentecost (Acts 2:9).

ELATH. Edomite port on the Gulf of Aqabah, near Ezion Geber (Deut. 2:8).

ELDAD and **MEDAD.** Two of the seventy elders whom Moses summoned to the Tabernacle. They remained in the camp, however, yet were still endued with the spirit of prophecy (Num. 11:26–27).

ELDER. One vested with authority on grounds of age or experience (Exod. 3:16; Num. 22:4). Influential locally (Ruth 4:2) and nationally (1 Sam. 8:4). By NT times their civic authority was extended to include religious power (Matt. 15:2; Acts 4:5). The church made similar appointments (Acts 14:23; 1 Tim. 4:14; Titus 1:5; 1 Pet. 5:1). The 24 elders of the book of Revelation may refer to the 12 tribes of Israel plus the 12 apostles, or to the 24 divisions of the priesthood (1 Chron. 24).

ELEALEH. Reubenite city near Heshbon (Num. 32:3).

ELEAZAR (*God has Helped*). Aaron's third son (Exod. 6:23) who succeeded his father as high priest (Num. 20:25–28). His descendants ('sons of Aaron') provided almost all the high priests down to Maccabean times.

ELECTION. God's choice of an individual or group to fulfil a particular purpose (Rom. 9:11; 2 Tim. 2:10; 2 Pet. 1:10).

ELECT LADY. Either an individual or a local church (2 John 1, 13).

ELEMENTAL SPIRITS. Demonic forces, holding people in bondage until Christ broke their power (Gal. 4:3).

ELHANAN. Son of Jair, who slew Goliath's brother Lahmi (1 Chron. 20:5; slips in copying Hebrew letters account for the erroneous version in 2 Sam. 21:19).

ELI. High priest, whose kindliness (to Hannah, 1 Sam. 1:17; to the boy Samuel, 1 Sam. 3) was exposed as weakness in failing to discipline his sons (1 Sam. 2:22–25; 3:13). The shock of their death in battle and the loss of the ark of the covenant killed him (1 Sam. 4:12–18).

ELIADA (*Known to God*). 1. Son of David, born in Jerusalem (2 Sam. 5:16; Beeliada in 1 Chron. 14:7).
2. Father of Rezon, a gang leader in Damascus (1 Kings 11:23).
3. Benjamite commander during Jehoshaphat's reign (2 Chron. 17:17).

ELIAKIM. Son of Josiah, king of Judah. The Egyptians deposed his brother Jehoahaz, made Eliakim king and changed his name to Jehoiakim (2 Kings 23:34; 2 Chron. 36:4).

ELIASHIB. High priest who helped to rebuild Jerusalem's wall (Neh. 3:1), but later joined Nehemiah's opponents (Neh. 13:4).

ELIEZER (*My God Helps*). Abraham's steward from Damascus, who prior to Ishmael's birth was Abraham's heir (Gen. 15:2).

ELIHU (*He is My God*). Younger than Job's three would-be comforters but wiser (Job 32—36). Popular pious name.

ELIJAH (*The Lord is My God*). Strenuously opposed Ahab and Ahaziah for the Baal worship of their reigns (1 Kings 17—21; 2 Kings 1). His translation to heaven without dying (2 Kings 2) led to the expectation of his return (Mal. 4:5–6;

Matt. 11:14); fulfilled in the coming of John the Baptist (Luke 1:17; Matt. 17:10–12). Elijah appeared with Jesus on the Mount of Transfiguration (Matt. 17:3). Jesus' cry (Matt. 27:46–49) was misunderstood as a call for Elijah.

ELIM (*Trees*). Stopping place during Israel's wilderness wanderings; abundant in fresh water and palm trees (Exod. 15:27; Num. 33:9–10).

ELIMELECH. Naomi's husband, driven by famine to emigrate to Moab, where he died (Ruth 1:2–3; 4:3, 9).

ELIPHAZ. 1. Edomite son of Esau and father of Amalek (Gen. 36:4, 12).
   2. The first of Job's friends to harangue him on his presumed errors (Job 4—5; 15; 22).

ELISHA (*God is Salvation*). 9th-century prophet of Israel, successor to Elijah (1 Kings 19:16–21). Ministered for 50 years, through the reigns of Ahab, Ahaziah, Jehoram, Jehu, Jehoahaz and Jehoash (1 Kings 19; 2 Kings 2—9; 13). His healing of Naaman is quoted by Jesus (Luke 4:27).

ELISHAH. OT name for Cyprus (Ezek. 27:7).

ELISHAMA (*God hears [prayer for child]*). Popular parental choice of name.

ELIZABETH. Wife of the priest Zechariah and mother of John the Baptist. Related to Mary the mother of Jesus (Luke 1:5–57).

ELKANAH (*God Redeemed*). Ephraimite husband of Peninnah and Hannah. The latter, after years of childlessness, became the mother of Samuel (1 Sam. 1:1 — 2.20).

ELLASAR. Babylonian sun-god city (Gen. 14:1).

ELNATHAN (*God Gave*). Father-in-law of Jehoiakim who sent him to Egypt to secure the prophet Uriah's extradition (Jer. 26:22). He urged the king in vain not to destroy Jeremiah's prophecy (Jer. 36:12, 25).

ELOI, ELOI, LAMA SABACHTHANI. Jesus' cry on the cross (in Aramaic, Mark 15:34; in Hebrew, Matt. 27:46), the words of Ps. 22:1; bystanders thought he was calling Elijah (Matt. 27:47), traditionally believed to rescue the righteous in distress.

ELYMAS (*Wise Man*). Another name for Bar-Jesus, a Jewish charlatan at the court of Sergius Paulus, Roman proconsul of Cyprus (Acts 13:8).

EMBALMING. Egyptian method of preserving corpses of important individuals (Gen. 50:2–3, 26).

EMBROIDERY. Bezalel and Oholiab were gifted in the art (Exod. 35:30–35). Its value reflected in the spoils of war (Judg. 5:30), sumptuous clothes (Josh. 7:21; Ezek. 16:10), trading (Ezek. 27:16) and even sails (Ezek. 27:7).

EMERALD. Precious stone in the high priest's breastpiece (Exod. 28:18) and a foundation gem in the wall of New Jerusalem (Rev. 21:19).

EMIM, EMITES (*Terrors*). Early inhabitants of Moab, whose great stature inspired fear (Gen. 14:5; Deut. 2:10–11).

EMMANUEL. *See* Immanuel.

The oasis of En Gedi

EMMAUS. Village near Jerusalem, destination of two disciples on the first Easter evening (Luke 24:13).

EMPEROR. Title assumed by Julius Caesar as ruler of the Roman empire and continued by his successors (Acts 25:21).

EN (*Spring*). Common prefix for place names, reflecting the vital importance of water.

EN GEDI (Hazazon Tamar). Lush subtropical oasis, W of the Dead Sea, noted for aromatic plants (Song of Sol. 1:14). David's refuge from Saul (1 Sam. 24:1), and scene of Jehoshaphat's bloodless victory (2 Chron. 20).

EN MISHPAT (*Spring of Judgment*). Another name for Kadesh Barnea (Gen. 14:7).

EN ROGEL. Well-watered place near Jerusalem, bordering Judah and Benjamin (Josh. 15:7;

18:16). Jonathan and Ahimaaz waited here for news of Absalom's rebellion (2 Sam. 17:17). Scene of Adonijah's feast when plotting to seize the kingdom (1 Kings 1:9).

ENDOR. Town, S of Mt Tabor, where Sisera and Jabin died (Ps. 83:10). Saul consulted a local medium before his last battle (1 Sam. 28:7).

ENOCH. 1. City named after a son of Cain (Gen. 4:17).
2. Father of Methuselah (Gen. 5:18, 21) and 7th patriarch from Adam (Jude 14). He lived unusually close to God (Gen. 5:22; Heb. 11:15) and like Elijah was translated to heaven without dying (Gen. 5:24).

ENOSH (*Mortal Man*). Son of Seth and grandson of Adam, in whose days people first used God's covenant name in prayer (Gen. 4:26; 5:6–11; Luke 3:38).

EPAPHRAS. Paul's colleague (Col. 4:12; Philem. 23), who founded the churches at Colosse, Hierapolis and Laodicea. His news when Paul was imprisoned in Rome prompted the apostle to write his letter to the Colossians (Col. 1:7).

EPAPHRODITUS (*Charming*). Macedonian Christian who brought Paul an encouraging gift from the Philippian church. His strenuous efforts on Paul's behalf led to a serious illness (Phil. 2:25–30; 4:18).

EPHAH. *See* Weights and measures.

EPHESIANS. Paul's letter to the church at Ephesus, written about AD 61, and probably also intended for other churches in Asia Minor.

The great theatre, Ephesus

Declares God's eternal purpose through his church (Eph. 1—3) and the practical consequences for Christian living (Eph. 4—6).

EPHESUS. Major seaport in the Roman province of Asia; now 10 km (6 mi) from the sea, due to silting by the river Cayster. Site of the magnificent temple to the goddess Artemis (Diana) and an open-air theatre seating 25,000 people (Acts 19:27, 29). After a short visit in AD 52, Paul returned to make Ephesus his base for over two years (Acts 19:10; 1 Cor. 16:8). The local church is addressed in the first of the seven letters of Revelation (2:1–7).

EPHOD. *See* Dress p. 55.

EPHPHATHA (*Be opened!*). Aramaic word spoken by Jesus to heal a deaf man (Mark 7:34).

EPHRAIM (*Fruitful*). 1. Second son of Joseph and Asenath (Gen. 41:52). Though younger than his brother Manasseh, their dying grandfather Jacob indicated that Ephraim's descendants would outshine Manasseh's (Gen. 48).

2. Territory allocated to the tribe of Ephraim (Josh. 16).

3. Place E of Bethel, where Jesus retired after raising Lazarus (John 11:54).

EPHRAIM FOREST. NW of Shechem, where Absalom died (2 Sam. 18:6–15).

EPHRAIM, MOUNT. In the central range, W of Jordan, in territory allocated to the tribe of Ephraim (Jer. 4:15).

EPHRATH. Ancient name of Bethlehem in Judah, the scene of Rachel's burial (Gen. 35:19) and Naomi's home (Ruth 4:11).

EPHRON. Hittite who sold the cave of Machpelah to Abraham for Sarah's burial (Gen. 23:8; 49:30).

EPICUREANS. Philosophers who followed the teaching of Epicurus (341–270 BC), seeking happiness through tranquil detachment (Acts 17:18).

EPILEPSY. Twice healed by Jesus (Matt. 4:24; 17:15).

ER. Eldest son of Judah and his Canaanite wife; died because of some unspecified wickedness (Gen. 38:1–7).

ERASTUS. City treasurer of Corinth (Rom. 16:23). Perhaps the same man who worked with Timothy in Macedonia (2 Tim. 4:20), freeing Paul to continue in Asia Minor (Acts 19:22).

ESARHADDON. Son and successor of the Assyrian king Sennacherib (2 Kings 19:37). Reigned 681–669 BC.

ESAU (*Hairy*). The favourite of Isaac's twin sons. Although the elder, his inferiority to his brother Jacob was forecast at birth (Gen. 25:23) and by Isaac's dying blessing (Gen. 27:22–29). Ancestor of the Edomites (Gen. 36:9), whose chronic antagonism towards the Israelites constantly recurs (Num. 20:18; 1 Kings 11:14; Obad. 1–21).

ESHCOL (*Bunch of Grapes*). Valley N of Hebron, where the spies sent by Moses secured evidence of the fruitfulness of the area (Num. 13:23–24).

ESHTAOL. Lowland city, W of Jerusalem (Josh.

15:33; 19:41). Samson's burial place (Judg. 16:31). Nearby he had first experienced God's Spirit (Judg. 13:25). Danites emigrated to seek a more settled abode (Judg. 18:2, 11).

ESTHER (*Star*). Queen of Ahasuerus (Xerxes). Her Jewish name (Esther 2:7) was Hadassah (*Myrtle*).

ESTHER (book). Describes how a Jewess became the wife of a Persian king and risked her life to save her people from wholesale massacre. The feast of Purim was instituted to celebrate the Jews' deliverance (Esther 9:20–32).

ESTHER, ADDITIONS TO (Apocrypha). Some time before 114 BC a Jerusalemite named Lysimachus translated the Hebrew text of Esther into Greek and piously added 107 more verses mentioning the name of God, conspicuously absent from the OT book.

ETERNAL LIFE. The quality of life belonging to God (1 John 5:20) and his gift to believers in Jesus (John 3:15–16; Rom. 6:23).

ETHAN. Wise Ezrahite (1 Kings 4:31) who composed Ps. 89.

ETHBAAL. Sidonian king and father of Jezebel who married Ahab, king of Israel (1 Kings 16:31).

ETHIOPIA (*Burnt Face*). Not the modern state but part of Nubia, stretching from present-day Khartoum to Aswan; often called Cush, after the original settlers (Gen. 10:6). Ethiopian armies were defeated by Asa (2 Chron. 14:9–15), supported Hezekiah against Sennacherib (2 Kings 19:9), conquered Egypt (Nahum 3:9), and were beaten at Carchemish (605 BC; Jer. 46:2). Later became a Persian province (Esther 1:1).

ETHIOPIAN EUNUCH. Treasurer at the court of Candace, queen of Ethiopia (Acts 8:26–40).

EUNICE. Timothy's Jewish mother, renowned for her faith (Acts 16:1; 2 Tim. 1:5).

EUNUCH. Confidential court official, usually a castrate (Esther 2:3; Acts 8:27). Jesus used the term for one who renounces marriage for the sake of the kingdom of God (Matt. 19:12).

EUODIA and **SYNTYCHE.** Christian women at loggerheads in the church at Philippi (Phil. 4:2).

EUPHRATES. Largest river in SW Asia (the River, Deut.11:24), running 2000 km (1200 mi) from E Turkey to the Persian Gulf.

EUTYCHUS (*Fortunate*). Young man from Troas who fell from a window during Paul's lengthy sermon (Acts 20:7–12).

EVANGELIST. One called to proclaim the evangel, the good news about Jesus (Acts 21:8; 2 Tim. 4:5).

EVE (*Life*). The first woman, wife of Adam and mother of Cain, Abel and Seth (Gen. 3:20; 4:25). Used by the serpent to tempt Adam to eat forbidden fruit and so disobey God (2 Cor. 11:3).

EVIL. Malignant power or sinful action which causes pain, unhappiness or misery. Personified in Satan as the Evil One (Matt. 5:37; John 17:15; Eph. 6:16; 1 John 2:13). *See* Wickedness.

EVIL-MERODACH. Son of Nebuchadnezzar II.

On succeeding to the Babylonian throne in 562 BC, he freed Jehoiachin (2 Kings 25:27; Jer. 52:31).

EVIL SPIRITS. Unclean spirits (Matt. 10:1, AV/KJV) or demons (Matt. 8:31). Although part of Satan's kingdom (Matt. 12:24), they are ultimately under God's control (1 Sam. 16:14; Mark 5:13).

EXILE. Punishment for disobeying God (Deut. 28:41). Assyria deported the northern tribes (Israel/Samaria) in 732 and 722 BC (2 Kings 15:29; 17:6). A century later Nebuchadnezzar exiled to Babylon all but the poorest classes of Judah (2 Kings 24—25). Allowed to return 70 years later (Jer. 25:11–12; Dan. 9:2; Ezra; Neh.).

EXODUS (book). Recounts the events before and after the deliverance of Israel from Egypt under the leadership of Moses, including the plagues (Exod. 7—12), the institution of the Passover (12), the covenant at Sinai (19—31), and the construction of the Tabernacle (25—27; 35—40).

EXORCISM. Expelling an evil spirit by divine authority (Matt. 10:1; Mark 5:8).

EXPERT IN THE LAW. *See* Lawyer.

EXPIATION. Making amends for a wrong (Exod. 32:30; Num. 15:22–29; Heb. 9:22). In the NT, applied to the forgiveness brought about by Christ's sacrifice for sins (Rom. 3:25; Heb. 2:17; 1 John 2:2).

EXTORTION. Obtaining something by violence (Lev. 6:4) will ultimately meet its deserts (Ezek. 22:29; Hab. 2:6); refusing such action will reap its reward (Isa. 33:15).

EYE. Figuratively used of a common avenue of temptation (Matt. 5:29; 1 John 2:16), spiritual knowledge or ignorance (Gen. 3:7; Matt. 13:16), evangelism (Acts 26:18), God's care (Deut. 32:10), understanding (Mark 8:18).

EYE OF THE NEEDLE. Metaphor for something impossible (Matt. 19:24). The supposed allusion to a gate in Jerusalem's wall only large enough for an unloaded camel could not apply to Jesus' words: the gate is medieval.

EYE SALVE. Alludes to Phrygian powder, ground for the famous Laodicean medical school. Local Christians needed such treatment spiritually (Rev. 3:18).

EZEKIEL (*God Strengthens*). Deported to Babylon with other exiled Jews in 597 BC. His wife died the day before Nebuchadnezzar invested Jerusalem (Ezek. 24:2, 15–18). Five years later, commissioned as a prophet (Ezek. 1:2–3).

EZEKIEL (book). Prophecies to the exiled Jews in Babylon. Ezekiel proclaims judgment on sin (Ezek. 1—24), but assures people about the future (25—40) and gives details of the Temple and its services when they return to their homeland (41—48).

EZION GEBER. Stopping place during Israel's wilderness wanderings (Num. 33:35; Deut. 2:8). Later a major port at the head of the Gulf of Aqaba (Red Sea), developed by Solomon (1 Kings 9:26; 2 Chron. 8:17).

EZRA (*Help*). Priestly Jewish exile sent to Jerusalem by the Persian king Artaxerxes to establish the uniform observance of the Jewish law in the land (Ezra 7). After dealing with the problem of mixed marriages arising from the exile (Ezra 9—10), he returned to the Persian king. In 444 BC he was back in Jerusalem, publicly reading the law (Neh. 8). He is the founding figure of Judaism.

EZRA (book). Describes the Jews' return from exile and the rebuilding of the Temple (Ezra 1—6), despite local opposition; outlines Ezra's work in enforcing Jewish law (7—10). Originally Chronicles-Ezra-Nehemiah probably formed one book.

F

FACE. Signifies divine or human presence (Exod. 33:11;2 Sam. 14:24). To cover the face, a sign of mourning (2 Sam. 19:4), reverence (Exod. 3:6) or modesty (Gen. 24:65). To show the face is to accept (Num. 6:26); to hide or turn away the face is to reject (Ezek. 39:23).

FAIR HAVENS. Small bay of S Crete, unsuitable as a winter harbour (Acts 27:8).

FAITH. The motivation of believers (Heb. 11). Associated with forgiveness (Acts 15:9, Rom. 3:25); guidance (2 Cor. 5:7), healing (Matt. 9:22; James 5:15), justification (Rom. 3:26), loyalty (Luke 22:32), overcoming (1 John 5:4), prayer (James 1:6), preaching (Rom. 10:8), provision (Matt. 6:30), righteousness (Rom. 9:30), safety (Matt. 8:26), sanctification (Acts 26:18). *See* Trust.

FALL. Term applied to the consequences of Adam and Eve, created in God's image for fellowship with him, losing their divine destiny through disobedience (Gen. 3).

FAMINE. Natural calamity (Gen. 12:10, Ruth 1:1), sometimes seen as an act of God (Amos 4:6–7), to warn (1 Kings 17:1), punish (2 Sam. 24:13), or as a sign of the last days (Matt. 24:7).

FASTING. Abstinence from food and drink for a religious purpose (Ezra 8:21; Neh. 1:4; Luke 18:12).

FATE. Never viewed as blind chance but as being God-ordained (Job 20:29; Jer. 49:20), or self-inflicted (Jer. 50:15).

FATHER. In eastern understanding, the head of the family, a shepherd providing needs, and unquestioned ruler (implied in the 'mixed' metaphors of Luke 12:32, describing God). In the OT, God is said to be father of Israel (Deut. 32:6), but rarely of the individual (2 Sam. 7:14). Jesus never calls God the father of Israel, but always speaks of individual relationship (Matt. 6:9; 12:50).

FEAR. Apprehension of death (Heb. 2:15), loneliness (Isa. 41:10), public opinion (Mark 11:32), danger (Luke 8:24), or the supernatural (Luke 1:12). Forbidden (Matt. 6:25; Phil. 4:6), being needless (Matt. 10:31; 1 Pet. 5:7), for God is love (1 John 4:18). 'Fear and trembling' a catch-phrase of Paul's day (2 Cor. 7:15; Eph. 6:5; Phil. 2:12), not meaning cowering but, as contexts indicate, going all out to please.

FEAR OF GOD/OF THE LORD. Not dread, but awed reverence. Commanded (Deut. 10:12; 1 Pet. 1:17), being the basis of true religion (Eccles. 12:13; Luke 1:50; Acts 10:35), knowing God (Prov. 2:5), God's service (Josh. 24:14), godly living (Ps. 25:12), blessing (Ps. 31:19), a full life (Prov. 10:27), contentment (Prov. 15:16), wisdom (Prov. 1:7), true riches (Prov. 22:4), seeing evil for what it is (Prov. 8:13) and being able to avoid it (Prov. 16:6). Protects against fear of people (Matt. 10:28) and of death (Heb. 2:15). Characteristic of Messiah (Isa. 11:2); its absence a sign of godlessness (Rom. 3:18).

FEAR OF ISAAC. Divine title, meaning the God whom Isaac reverenced (Gen. 31:42, 53).

FEAST OF BOOTHS.
See Feasts and festivals p. 250.

FEAST OF DEDICATION.
See Feasts and festivals p. 250.

FEAST OF PASSOVER.
See Feasts and festivals p. 250.

FEAST OF PURIM, OR LOTS.
See Feasts and festivals p. 250.

FEAST OF TABERNACLES.
See Feasts and festivals p. 250.

FEAST OF UNLEAVENED BREAD.
See Feasts and festivals p. 250.

FEAST OF WEEKS.
See Feasts and festivals p. 250.

FEET WASHING. *See* Travel p. 228.

FELIX. Procurator of Judea (AD 52–59). In AD 55 he put down a riot instigated by an Egyptian messianic pretender (Acts 21:38). Hoping for a bribe, he kept Paul in prison for two years (Acts 24:26), though knowing he was innocent (Acts 23:29). Recalled by Nero in summer AD 59, he left Paul in gaol to gratify the Jews (Acts 24:27).

FELLOWSHIP. Believers sharing the life of God, spiritually and practically (Mal. 3:16; Acts 2:42).

FELLOWSHIP (or peace) **OFFERINGS**.

Thanksgiving or freewill offering (Lev. 7:11–21), the only sacrifice laymen could share.

FESTUS, Porcius. Successor to Felix as procurator of Judea (Acts 24:27). When Paul realised that his release would again be obstructed, he appealed over the head of the new procurator to the emperor at Rome (Acts 25:11).

FEVER. Conditions mentioned in Lev. 26:16 suggest gonorrheal blindness. Peter's mother-in-law (Matt. 8:14) was probably suffering from malaria, common in the Capernaum district.

FIELD. Figuratively, of preaching opportunities (John 4:35; 2 Cor. 10:13) and of the world in general (Matt. 13:38).

FIFTY YEARS OLD. When incredulous opponents declared Jesus was 'not yet fifty' (John 8:57), it would have been more natural to say 'forty' (concerning someone then about thirty). Probably alluding to the levitical age of retirement (Num. 4:3): 'You have not even reached the age of retirement from God's service, so how can you have seen Abraham?'

FIG. *See* Foods p. 77.

FINE LINEN. Flax spun (Prov. 31:13) into luxury material (Luke 16:19). Prescribed for priestly dress (Exod. 28:39) and for Tabernacle curtains (Exod. 26:1).

FINGER OF GOD. Symbol of divine action in confounding the Egyptian magicians (Exod. 8:19), and in inscribing the Ten Commandments (Exod. 31:18). Expelling demons (Luke 11:20) defined as the Spirit's action (Matt. 12:28).

Farming

Barley. Staple edible grain (Deut. 8:8), used by the poor for bread (Ruth 2:17; John 6:9).

Barn. Granary (Hag. 2:19) or storehouse (Deut. 28:8; Prov. 3:10). Often only a dry cistern in the ground, thickly covered with soil (Jer. 41:8), rather than a building (Luke 12:18). Metaphor for heaven (Matt. 13:30).

Oxen drag a threshing sledge

Chaff. Husks and broken straw blown away by the wind during the winnowing of grain (Job 21:18). Applied figuratively to the fate of wrongdoers (Jer. 13:24; Matt. 3:12).

Crops. Principal grain crops were wheat and barley. Secondary crops included lentils, beans, peas, onions, garlic and herbs.

Firstfruits. The earliest crops harvested, which were offered to God in thanksgiving (Deut. 26:1-11). The entire crop was God's, but the offering of firstfruits released the rest for the people to eat (Lev. 23:14). Figuratively applied to Israel in relation to the rest of the nations, ultimately to be restored to God (Jer. 2:3). Also applied to the risen Christ

(1 Cor. 15:20), to the gift of the Spirit to believers (Rom. 8:23), and to the first converts (Rom. 16:5; James 1:18).

Flax. The oldest of textile fibres (Josh. 2:6), used for making linen (Prov. 31:13). Its loss considered a divine judgment (Hos. 2:9).

Gleaning. Reapers had to leave corners of fields for the poor and landless (Deut. 24:19-22; Ruth 2). Figuratively applied to judgment (Isa. 17:5-6).

Grain. Main crops wheat (in the coastal plain, Jordan valley and Valley of Jezreel) and barley (on poorer soil, and needing a shorter growing season). The multiplication of seeds sown likened by Jesus to

spiritual fruitfulness (John 12:24).

Harvest. Citrus (February), flax (March), barley (April), grapes (June), olives (July), dates (August), seasonal figs (May, August, October).

Cutting grain with a sickle

Theme applied spiritually by Jesus (John 4:35) and others (Rom. 1:13; Heb. 12:11; James 3:8).

Ploughing. Earliest ploughshares were of pointed wood, which scarcely scratched baked soil, so the rainy season had to be seized (Prov. 20:4). The Philistine monopoly of iron (1 Sam. 13:20) restricted ploughing until David's day. The prohibition of Deut. 22:10 is against mismatching the animals' ability to pull (*see* Yoke).

Sheaf. The beginning of harvest was marked by dedicating to God the first cutting (of barley, the earliest crop), which was 'waved' before the Lord (Lev. 23:10-14) as an acknowledgment that food was God's gift. *See* Wave offering.

Sowing. Barley sown in November, followed by wheat. Millet, sesame, melons and vegetables planted in January.

Spelt. Coarse variety of wheat (Exod. 9:32; Isa. 28:25; Ezek. 4:9).

Threshing. Separating grain from harvested corn was done on the threshing floor, a hard flat space walled in with stones, located where it could catch the breeze for the winnowing process. Threshing small amounts done by beating grain with a stick (Ruth 2:17). For larger quantities, two oxen yoked together (Hos. 10:11) were tethered to a pole centred in the threshing floor and driven round and round, trampling on the grain. Or the oxen dragged threshing sledges, heavy planks toothed with flints or metal (Isa. 41:15; Amos 1:3). This not only freed the ears of corn but broke up the straw (making good

Ploughing with yoked oxen

fodder). Threshing floors valuable (2 Sam. 24:21) and a target for enemies (1 Sam. 23:1). The threshing floor a symbol of judgment (Isa. 21:10). *See* Winnowing.

Wheat. Pharaoh's dream of 'seven ears growing on one stalk' (Gen. 41:5) was the variety modern Egyptians call 'seven-headed wheat', after the branching habit of its ear. Seed sown in winter (Nov./Dec.). 'Wheat harvest' (April/June, depending on altitude) marked a major calendar division (Exod. 34:22). Ground into fine flour for sacrificial offerings (Lev. 2:1) and the sacred shewbread (Exod. 25:30). Made high quality bread; too expensive for most people, who used barley. As the choicest grain, symbolises believers at the final judgment (Matt. 3:12; 13:30).

Winnowing. After threshing (Ruth 3:2), shovel and fork ('fan' in Isa. 30:24, AV/KJV) were used to toss the grain. The breeze carried aside the chaff and straw (Isa. 41:16), allowing the heavier grains of wheat or barley to fall back at the farmer's feet. After sifting (Isa. 30:28; Amos 9:9), the grain was stored in jars, cisterns (Jer. 41:8) or granaries ('barns', Luke 12:18). Metaphor for judgment (Prov.

20:26; Jer. 51:2; Luke 3:17).

Yoke. In ploughing, a shaped piece of timber resting on the necks of oxen (Amos 6:12) or asses (Isa. 30:24), though not a combination of different animals (Deut. 22:10), thus avoiding unequal pull.

Winnowing with a fork

Figuratively, of servitude (1 Kings 12:1-11; Jer. 27-28) or of burdens (Matt. 11:29-30; Acts 15:10).

Farming year

MONTHS. Measured by the lunar cycle, from first sighting of new moon. As the lunar year is some 11 days shorter than the solar year, an extra month was inserted when required. Names for months often reflected the agricultural seasons.

First month, or Abib (*Ear,* of cereal), corresponding to March/April, month of Exodus and Passover (Exod. 13:4). After the exile called Nisan (Neh. 2:1). Barley and flax harvests, latter rains.

Second month, or Ziv (*Beauty*), April/May; early flowers.

Third month, or Sivan, May/June; early figs.

Fourth month, or Tammuz, June/July; grapes.

Fifth month, or Ab (*Green*), July/Aug.; olives.

Sixth month, or Elul, Aug./Sept.; dates, summer figs.

Seventh month, or Ethanim or Tishri, Sept./Oct.; early rains.

Eighth month, or Bul, Oct./Nov.; winter figs, ploughing.

Ninth month, or Chisleu (Kislev), Nov./Dec; sowing.

Tenth month, or Tebeth, Dec./Jan.; rains, snow on uplands.

Eleventh month, or Shebat, Jan./Feb.; almond blossom.

Twelfth month, or Adar (*Glory*), Feb./March; spring flowers, citrus fruit.

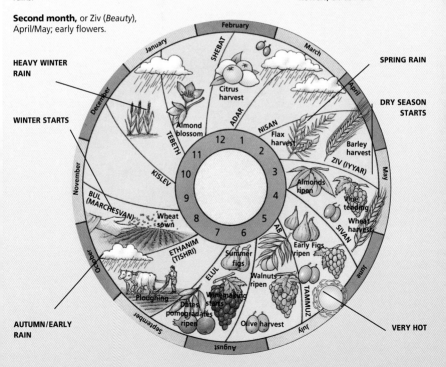

FINS AND SCALES. Under Mosaic food laws, fish lacking fins and scales were not to be eaten (Lev. 11:9–12; Deut. 14:9–10), a prohibition now recognised as wise on hygienic grounds.

FIRE. Often mentioned in connection with incense (Exod. 30:1) and sacrifices (Lev. 1:9), after its divine provision (Lev. 9:24; 2 Chron. 7:1); unauthorised offerings ('strange fire') were unacceptable (Lev. 10:1). Symbolised God's appearances (Exod. 3:2) and glory (Ezek. 1:13), guidance (Exod. 13:21), judgment (Isa. 66:15), or protection (2 Kings 6:17). Also used of the Holy Spirit (Matt. 3:11; Acts 2:3) and prophetic inspiration (Jer. 5:14; 23:29).

FIRMAMENT. The vault of heaven (Gen. 1:6; Ps. 19:1). The Hebrew word suggests reflected glory (Job 37:18).

FIRST AND LAST. Divine title, implying that what God initiates, he will perfectly complete (Isa. 44:6; Rev. 1:17; 22:13). *See* Alpha and Omega.

FIRST DAY OF THE WEEK (Sunday). Early Christian term for the day of Christ's resurrection (Matt. 28:1), which soon became the regular Christian day of worship (Acts 20:7; 1 Cor. 16:2), distinct from the Jewish Sabbath (Saturday).

FIRSTBORN. The firstborn male of Hebrew families and cattle belonged to the Lord (Exod. 13:2; Lev. 27:26). The eldest son's birthright included a double share of the estate (Deut. 21:17) to help with family costs when he succeeded his father as head of the household. The death of the firstborn was the final and decisive plague to fall upon Egypt (Exod. 12:29); but the Hebrew firstborn were preserved (Exod. 12:23).

After the Exodus, Hebrew children were redeemed by a payment of five shekels (Num. 18:16). Describes Christians as the firstfruits of Christ's redeeming work on the cross (Heb. 12:23). Applied to Christ himself (Rom. 8:29; Col. 1:15; Rev. 1:5) as one whose authority is as God's Son.

FIRSTFRUITS. *See* Farming p. 70.

FISH. *See* Foods p. 76.

FISHERMEN. At least seven apostles were fishermen: Peter, Andrew, James, John, Thomas, Nathanael, probably Philip (Matt. 4:18, 21; John 21:2). Fishermen's courage, skill, patience and loyal cooperation are qualities needed in Christ's followers (Matt. 4:19).

FISHING. *See* Net.

FLAMING DARTS. Arrows tipped with tow and pitch and set on fire. The shields alluded to in Eph. 6:16 were of wood covered with leather. On active service the leather was soaked in water to extinguish such darts.

FLAX. *See* Farming p. 70.

FLEECE. Sheep's wool, invaluable for clothing (Job 31:20). Used by Gideon to obtain a sign from God (Judg. 6:36–40). Fleeces formed a significant part of the tribute paid to Israel by Mesha, king of Moab (2 Kings 3:4).

FLESH. Term applied to kinship (Gen. 37:27), human frailty (Ps. 78:39), the marriage union (Gen. 2:24). Describes human self-centred, self-justifying existence, apart from God (AV/KJV of Rom. 8:1–13; Gal. 5:17). To devour another's

A fisherman on the Sea of Galilee today

flesh (Ps. 27:2) means to slander (injure with the mouth).

FLINT. Used for early cutting tools (Exod. 4:25). Describes resolute determination (Isa. 50:7), inflexibility (Ezek. 3:9) or stubbornness (Zech. 7:12).

FLOCK. Figuratively describes God's people (Isa. 40:11; John 10:16; 1 Pet. 5:2).

FLOOD. In general, storm water (Matt. 7:25); specifically, the deluge in the days of Noah (Gen. 7; 2 Pet. 2:5). The sudden and unexpected, like wadi flash floods after a downpour (Job 27:20; Dan. 9:26).

FLOWERS. Their brief spring display is likened to the brevity of human life (Job 14:2; James 1:10). *See* Lily.

FLUTE. *See* Music p. 150.

FOLLOW. Not necessarily to walk behind (John 21:20) but often to accompany (Ps. 23:6; Mark 5:37), or to join a leader (2 Sam. 20:11; Luke 5:27), implying obedience (1 Kings 18:21; John 12:26).

FOOD. *See* pp. 76-77.

FOOL. One guilty of unwise thought or behaviour (1 Sam. 26:21), often with the overtone of leaving God out of account (Ps. 14:1; Luke 12:20).

FOOT. Symbolised the defeat of an enemy (Josh. 10:24), possession (Josh. 1:3), supplication (1 Sam. 25:24), devotion (John 12:3), service (John 13:5), learning (Luke 10:39), or trouble (Ps. 94:18). Shaking the dust off one's feet indicates utter dissociation (Matt. 10:14; Acts 13:51).

FOOTSTOOL. Solomon's golden footrest (2 Chron. 9:18) is the only literal reference. Elsewhere the term symbolises submission or worship (Acts 7:49).

FORD. The only river crossing before the Romans built bridges (Josh. 2:7).

FOREFATHERS. A powerful sense of kinship reinforced Israel's belief that God's promises to Abraham, Isaac, Jacob and David continued to apply to their descendants (Lev. 26:42; Acts 3:25). But equally the sins of ancestors imperilled

Foods

'St Peter's fish'

Food. Bread was so much the staple that the word also means food in general (Matt. 6:11). Vegetables (Num. 11:5; Ezek. 4:9) and milk, yoghurt and cheese (Gen. 18:8; 2 Sam. 17:29) were also basic. Meat a luxury (1 Kings 4:23), but fish was plentiful in the Sea of Galilee (John 21:9). Figs and grapes eaten fresh or dried. Honey used for sweetening and salt for seasoning.

Meals. Little if anything eaten on rising. Light midday meal of bread, roast grain, olives, figs or other fruit (Gen. 43:16; Ruth 2:14). Main meal at sunset (Luke 17:7), when the family shared stew, vegetables and herbs from a common bowl. Meat rarely eaten by the poor, but fish was available from the Sea of Galilee. The fellowship aspect of mealtimes important among Christians (Acts 2:46; 20:7; 1 Cor. 11:33). *See* Lord's Supper.

Bread. Staple food, of barley, wheat or spelt; normally leavened with yeast, and baked on a griddle (Lev. 2:5) or in a clay oven (Hos. 7:4). Never cut, but broken by hand. Can mean food in general (Gen. 3:19) or material things in life (Deut. 8:3; Matt.

4:4). Unleavened bread used for quickness (Exod. 12:39).

Cake. Figs, dates and raisins, pressed into lumps made a nutritious food easy to carry (1 Sam. 30:12; 2 Sam. 6:19).

Curds. Milk fermented as yoghurt, often served with honey or wine (Gen. 18:8; Isa. 7:15).

Fish. Plentiful in Egypt (Num. 11:5), Tyre (Neh. 13:16), and the Sea of Galilee (Luke 5:6) where some 28 varieties are found. Eaten freshly cooked (John 21:9) or dried, salted or pickled (Matt. 14:17). An early Christian symbol (the letters of the Greek word for 'fish' made an acronym for 'Jesus Christ, God's Son, Saviour').

Honey. Wild honey abundant, in hollows of rocks and trees (Deut. 32:13; Judg. 14:8), and a precious food in the wilderness (Matt. 3:4). Term also used for a syrup made from grapes, dates or figs (Ezek. 3:3; Rev. 10:9). Sweetener (Exod. 16:31), acceptable as a gift (1 Kings 14:3).

A family shares from a common bowl

Figs

FRUIT

Fruit. Valuable food source safeguarded from premature picking (Lev. 19:23-25) and in times of war (Deut. 20:19). Frequent metaphor for maturity and fulfilment (2 Kings 19:30; Ps. 92:14; Matt. 3:8; Gal. 5:22). The twelve kinds of fruit on the tree of life (Rev. 22:2) symbolise constant abundant life.

Fig. Slow-growing tree; its destruction a national calamity (Joel 1:7) and seen as a judgment (Ps. 105:33). Figs eaten green in summer (Song of Sol. 2:13), pressed and dried for use later (1 Sam. 25:18). Symbol of peace and divine favour (1 Kings 4:25).

Raisins. Dried grapes (Num. 6:3), invaluable for storing; quick source of energy for workers or travellers (2 Sam. 6:19).

Olive. Berries harvested in November (Deut. 24:20) and crushed for the oil (Exod. 27:20). Eaten fresh or pickled, with bread. Its attractive timber prized for furniture (1 Kings 6:31-33). Symbolised virility (Ps. 52:8), fertility (Ps. 128:3), beauty (Jer. 11:16; Hos. 14:6), blessing (Deut. 7:13), peace (Gen. 8:11). *See* Oil.

Pomegranate. Shrublike tree, with scarlet blossom (Song of Sol. 7:12) producing apple-shaped fruit, whose juicy seeds make a refreshing wine (Song of Sol. 8:2). Also used medicinally, in tanning and as a red dye. Abundant in the Promised Land (Deut. 8:8); its failure brings despair (Joel 1:12).

VEGETABLES

Beans (broad). Sown in autumn, often between vines, and harvested after barley and wheat. Eaten raw or cooked (2 Sam. 17:28; Ezek. 4:9).

Cucumber. Missed by the Israelites after leaving Egypt (Num. 11:5). The 'lodge' in a cucumber field (Isa. 1:8, AV/KJV) was a rough hut on poles, to shelter a watchman guarding the growing plants. Abandoned after harvest, it soon presented a dreary picture of decay.

Lentils. Nutritious beans, stewed (Gen. 25:29-34; 2 Sam. 17:28) or eaten dried (Ezek. 4:9).

Pods. Carob or locust beans (Luke 15:16), abundant food for cattle and the poor in April/May.

Pottage. Vegetable stew (Gen. 25:29).

DRINK

Beer (drink). More accurately 'fermented drink', often made from dates. Israelites preferred wine, unlike Philistines, whose beer mugs are found in thousands by archaeologists.

Milk. Provided by cows (2 Sam. 17:29), goats (Prov. 27:27) and sheep (Deut. 32:14). Quickly turned sour in the warm climate, so most was used as yoghurt and cheese. Milk speaks of promoting life and growth, a sacrificed kid of death and disintegration: hence Exod. 23:19 prohibited the mingling of the two. Symbolic of plenty (Exod. 3:8), blessings (Isa. 55:1) and simple spiritual food (1 Pet. 2:2).

See also: Barley, Dove, Goat, Lamb, Manna, Oil, Olive, Ox, Partridge, Pigeon, Quail, Sheep, Wheat.

later generations (Exod. 20:5), a notion modified by Jeremiah (31:29–30) and Ezekiel (18).

FOREIGNERS. Visiting non-Israelites must be well treated (Exod. 22:21). Interest on loans could be charged to foreigners, but not to fellow Israelites (Deut. 23:20). God's people were often warned against pagan religions (Exod. 23:31–33) and forbidden to intermarry (Exod. 34:16; Neh. 13:26–27). Distinctions abolished in Christ (Eph. 2:13–17). *See* Sojourners; Stranger.

FORERUNNER. Royal official who prepared the road ahead of his king. The mission, if not the title, applied to John the Baptist (Mal. 4:5; Matt. 3:11).

FORGIVENESS. Re-establishing a broken relationship (Neh. 9:17; Mark 2:7), an undeserved act of grace on God's part for insolvent human beings (Matt. 18:23–35) through Jesus (Isa. 53:6; John 1:29). God's forgiveness is total (Jer. 31:34; 1 John 1:9), though conditional upon repentance (Mark 1:4) and our forgiving others (Matt. 6:15). *See* Sin, unforgivable.

FORTY. Number often associated with testing, or marking a development in biblical history: the flood (Gen. 7:4), the wilderness wanderings (Num. 32:13), surveying the Promised Land (Num. 13:25), the giving of the law (Deut. 9:9), punishment (Judg. 13:1), David's reign (2 Sam. 5:4), Elijah's recommissioning (1 Kings 19:8), the threat to Nineveh (Jon. 3:4), Jesus' wilderness temptations (Matt. 4:2), and the resurrection appearances (Acts 1:3).

FOUNDATION. As essential to faith as to a building (Isa. 28:16; Matt. 7:25).

FOX. *See* Wild animals p. 16.

FRANKINCENSE. Widely used for religious purposes (Lev. 2:1; Jer. 17:26), providing a lucrative trade (Isa. 60:6; Rev. 18:13). The gift to the infant Jesus (Matt. 2:11), while symbolising his priestly office, was a financial asset for the Holy Family when refugees (Matt. 2:14).

FREE. One not a slave (Col. 3:11), whether on account of birth (Gal. 4:22) or manumission (Deut. 32:36). Synonym for a Christian (1 Pet. 2:16) as one released from sin (John 8:34–36; Gal. 5:1) to serve Christ (1 Cor. 7:22).

FREEDMEN, SYNAGOGUE OF. Jerusalem synagogue favoured by descendants of freed slaves from the areas named in Acts 6:9.

FREEWILL OFFERINGS. Personal thank-offerings, additional to the set sacrifices (Lev. 22:23). Once generosity caused a strike (Exod. 36:2–6).

FRIEND OF THE BRIDEGROOM. Eastern equivalent of 'best man'. Figuratively describes the status of John the Baptist in relation to Jesus (John 3:29).

FRINGES. Tasselled border on an outer garment, intended as a reminder to keep God's commandments (Num. 15:38). Their ostentatious display earned Jesus' rebuke (Matt. 23:5).

FROGS. *See* Plagues of Egypt.

FRUIT. *See* Foods p. 77.

FULFILMENT. Applied to 1. Prophecy. Paramount for Jews (1 Kings 8:56) and the basis of Christian preaching (Acts 13:27), especially regarding Jesus the Christ (Messiah). *See* Matthew, Gospel of.

2. Law and Prophets (i.e. all the OT). Jesus came to bring out the full inner meaning of God's word (Matt. 5:17, 21–48; Gal. 6:2). Summed up in 'love' (Rom. 13:8; Gal. 5:14).

3. God's promises. What God says, he will do (1 Kings 8:56; Rom. 4:21; 2 Pet. 1:4).

4. Time. Jesus came at God's appointed moment in history (Gal. 4:4; Eph. 1:10), as did the Holy Spirit (Acts 2:1).

5. Vows. Promises made to God must be carried through (Num. 30:2; Eccles. 5:4).

FULLER. Professional launderer who bleached cloth from oil and grease preparatory to dyeing. At the transfiguration, Jesus' clothes are described as more dazzling than any fuller could achieve (Mark 9:3).

FULLER'S FIELD. Set outside a residential area, near a good water supply. After laundering, garments were spread out in the sun to dry (2 Kings 18:17; Isa. 7:3; 36:2).

FULLER'S SOAP. Natron (nitre) mixed with white clay or alkaline ash (Mal. 3:2).

FURNACE. The 'burning fiery furnace' of Dan. 3 was probably a brick kiln. An 'iron furnace' (Deut. 4:20; Rev. 1:15) was a crucible for smelting metal. Figuratively, hell-fire (Matt. 13:42; Rev. 9:2).

G

GAAL. Bandit leader who seized Shechem (Judg. 9:22–49).

GABBATHA. Decorative pavement outside Herod the Great's palace in Jerusalem (John 19:13).

GABRIEL (*God's Mighty One*). Archangel commissioned to deliver historic messages from God (Dan. 8:16; Luke 1:19).

GAD 1. Seventh son of Jacob (Gen. 30:10) whose descendants formed the tribe of Gad (Gadites). They settled E of Jordan (Num. 32). Their huge altar was misunderstood as idolatrous (Josh. 22:10–34).

2. Prophet who advised David (1 Sam. 22:5), organised music in Solomon's Temple and compiled a history of David's reign (1 Chron. 29:25, 29).

GADARENES. Inhabitants of Gadara, SE of Sea of Galilee (Matt. 8:28).

GAIUS. Common Latin name. 1. Macedonian companion of Paul, caught up in a riot at Ephesus (Acts 19:29).

2. Others mentioned in Acts 20:4; 1 Cor. 1:14; 3 John 1.

GALATIA. Roman province (from 25 BC) in N Asia Minor, named after invaders from Gaul (France) in 3rd century BC (Acts 16:6; Gal. 1:2; 1 Pet 1:1).

GALATIANS. An urgent letter to the churches of Galatia (Gal. 1:2), written by Paul about AD 49, to warn local Christians against teachers wanting to drag them back into Jewish practices (Gal. 1:6; 2:12; 4:10; 5:2). Christians are to live by faith in Jesus (3:11) and produce spiritual fruit (5:22).

GALILEE. Upland region in N Palestine, W of the Jordan (Josh. 20:7; 21:32).

GALL. *See* Plants p. 170.

GALLIO. Brother of Seneca the philosopher, and proconsul of Achaia in AD 52–53 (Acts 18:12). Executed by Nero in AD 65.

GALLOWS. Occurs nine times in Esther, as a translation of Hebrew for 'tree'. The Persian practice was to impale criminals (Esther 7:9).

GAMALIEL. Liberal Pharisee who advised the Sanhedrin not to take precipitate action against the apostles (Acts 5:34). Held in high repute (Acts 22:3).

GATE, CITY. Usually of wood covered with metal (Ps. 107:16) with iron bars (1 Sam. 23:7). Extra protection was given to the main gate by constructing a second wall in front of it with its own gate. This left a shady 'square' between the two walls (Esther 2:21) where citizens could meet (Ruth 4:1–4; 2 Chron. 32:6; Ps. 69:12).

GATEKEEPER. Official responsible for the city's safety (2 Kings 7:10). Levite gatekeepers concerned with Temple business (Neh. 13:5).

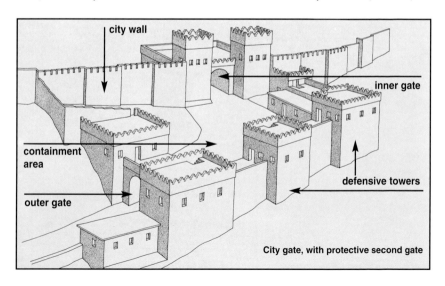

City gate, with protective second gate

GATH. Major Philistine city (Josh. 13:3); suffered for harbouring Israel's ark of the covenant (1 Sam. 5:9). Provided refuge for David from Saul (1 Sam. 21:10; 27:2). Men of Gath (Gittites) formed part of king David's bodyguard (2 Sam. 15:18).

GATH HEPHER. Jonah's birthplace (2 Kings 14:25); NE of Nazareth.

GAZA. Southernmost of the five major Philistine cities. Scene of one of Samson's exploits (Judg. 16:1) and of his end (Judg. 16:21–31). The city suffered bubonic plague when the Philistines lodged Israel's ark of the covenant in Dagon's temple (1 Sam. 6:17).

GEBA. Benjamite city (Josh. 18:24), N of Jerusalem, near Jonathan's daring attack on the Philistines (1 Sam. 14:5).

GEBAL. Phoenician port (Greek Byblos), N of Beirut. Provided stonemasons for Solomon's Temple (1 Kings 5:18) and ships' caulkers for Tyre (Ezek. 27:9).

GEDALIAH. Appointed by Nebuchadnezzar as governor of Judah in 587 BC. At Mizpah gave Jeremiah and other refugees political asylum. Assassinated by Ishmael (Jer. 40:6 —41:3).

GEHAZI. Elisha's servant. Suggested how to repay the Shunnamite woman's kindness (2 Kings 4:14); failed to revive her dead lad (2 Kings 4:31; 8:4). Struck with leprosy for cheating Naaman (2 Kings 5).

GEMARIAH. 1. Delivered Jeremiah's letter to Jewish exiles in Babylon (Jer. 29:3).
2. Royal secretary; unable to prevent Jehoiakim from burning Jeremiah's scroll (Jer. 36:10–12, 25).

GEMATRIA. Use of numbers for letters to interpret Scripture. The only clear biblical example is the number of the beast (Rev. 13:18); most manuscripts read 666, some 616. Probably Nero Caesar is intended, variant spellings of which produce either 666 or 616.

GENEALOGIES. 1. The principal OT family trees are those of Adam-Noah (Gen. 5); Cain (Gen. 4:17–22); Noah (Gen. 10); Shem (Gen. 11:10–26); Lot (Gen. 19:37–38); Abraham (Gen. 25:1–4); Nahor (Gen. 22:20–24); Ishmael (Gen. 25:12–18); Esau (Gen. 36); Israel (Gen. 46).
2. Important for determining place of residence after the conquest of Canaan (Num. 1; 26:52–56); transfer of property (Ruth 3:9–13; 4:1–11); royal succession in Judah (1 Kings 11:36; 15:4); priestly prerogatives after the exile (Ezra 2:62); the Roman enrolment under Augustus (Luke 2:3). Messiah was expected to come from the royal line of David (Matt. 12:23; 22:42; John 7:42).

GENEALOGY OF JESUS. Listed in Matt. 1:1–17 (from David) and Luke 3:23–38 (from Adam). The inclusion of women (Tamar, Rahab, Ruth, Bathsheba) in Jewish genealogies was contrary to custom. These particular names suggest the overruling of foreign or undesirable connections for divine purposes.

GENERATION. Can refer to a period of time (Exod. 3:15; Isa. 51:9), genealogies (Gen. 5; Num. 1), class of people (Deut. 32:5), or characteristics of an age (Deut. 1:35; Matt. 12:39). In Ps. 24:6 the other meaning, 'that which is generated', is meant (i.e. 'blessing', verse 5).

GENESIS (*Beginning*). Describes the creation of heaven and earth (Gen. 1), human origins and fall (2—3), population increase (4—5), the Flood judgment (6—9), and the rise of nations (10—11). The rest of the book narrates the lives of Abraham (12—23), Isaac (24—26), Jacob (27—36) and Joseph (37—50).

GENNESARET. Another name for the Sea of Galilee (Luke 5:1) and of the fertile plain to the NW (Matt. 14:34).

GENTILES. Jews' name for non-Jews (Neh. 5:8; Acts 10:28). Jesus' ministry was not intended for Gentiles (Matt. 10:5), though some pressed through to blessing (Matt. 8:10; 15:28). The conversion of Cornelius (Acts 10:45; 11:18) convinced the church that before God there is no difference between Jew and Gentile (Rom. 1:16; Col. 3:11; Rev. 7:9).

GERA. Fourth son of Benjamin (Gen. 46:21). His descendants included the judge Ehud (Judg. 3:15) and Shimei (2 Sam. 16:5).

GERAR. Canaanite city SE of Gaza (Gen. 10:19), where Abraham (Gen. 20:1) and Isaac (Gen. 26:1) lived for a time. The scene of Asa's great victory over the Ethiopian Zerah about 900 BC (2 Chron. 14:13).

GERASENES. Inhabitants of Gerasa, SE of the Sea of Galilee (Mark 5:1; Luke 8:26, 37). The same occasion in Matthew (8:28) refers to Gadara, which is much nearer and so more likely to be correct.

GERIZIM. One of two mountains overlooking Shechem and known as the mount of blessing (Deut. 11:29; 27:12; Josh. 8:33). Jotham addressed the Shechemites from a ledge halfway up (Judg. 9:7), where acoustics are remarkable. The sacred mountain of the Samaritans (John 4:20).

GERSHOM. Eldest son of Moses and Zipporah (Exod. 2:22); his descendants were Kohathite Levites (1 Chron. 23:14–15).

GERSHON. Eldest of Levi's three sons (Gen. 46:11). His descendants (Gershonites) were responsible for the care of the Tabernacle (Num. 4:21–28).

GESHEM. Arab who with Sanballat and Tobiah repeatedly opposed Nehemiah (Neh. 2:19; 6:1–6).

GESHUR. Small Aramaean kingdom, N of Bashan (Deut. 3:13–14). David married Maacah, the king of Geshur's daughter and mother of Absalom (2 Sam. 3:3).

GETHSEMANE (*Oil-press*). The garden (John 18:1) on the Mt. of Olives (Luke 22:39), where Jesus agonised in prayer (Matt. 26:36) before his arrest.

GEZER. Important Canaanite city on the Jerusalem-Joppa road. Withstood the Israelites (Josh. 16:10; Judg. 1:29), but not the later Egyptians. A pharaoh gave it to his daughter on her marrying Solomon (1 Kings 9:15–17).

GIBBETHON. Where Nadab died (1 Kings 15:27). Omri proclaimed king of Israel (885 BC; 1 Kings 16:17).

GIBEAH. Benjamite city, N of Jerusalem (Josh. 18:28). Suffered for gross immorality (Judg.

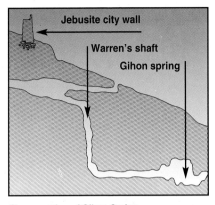

Jebusite city wall

Warren's shaft

Gihon spring

Cross section of Gihon Spring

19—20). Birthplace of Saul (1 Sam. 10:26) and his capital (1 Sam. 13:15).

GIBEON. Important city, NW of Jerusalem. Joshua enslaved its inhabitants for deceiving him into agreeing a treaty (Josh. 9). Joshua held to his promise by going to Gibeon's aid when attacked by Amorites (Josh. 10). The scene of Solomon's dream (1 Kings 3:5). After the exile, Gibeonites helped rebuild the Temple (Neh. 3:7).

GIDEON. Judge (nicknamed Jerub-Baal, Judg. 6:32) who delivered Israel from the Midianites (Judg. 6—8). His faith was remembered (Heb. 11:32).

GIFTS OF THE SPIRIT. Supernatural abilities endowed on believers by the Holy Spirit for God's service (1 Cor. 12—14). Foretold by Joel (2:28), promised by Jesus (Acts 1:4) and bestowed on the day of Pentecost (Acts 2).

GIHON. 1. River of the Garden of Eden (Gen. 2:13).

2. Spring in the Kidron Valley outside the E wall of Jerusalem. Scene of Solomon's coronation (1 Kings 1:45). When Jerusalem was threatened by a siege, Hezekiah cut an underground channel from Gihon to the Pool of Siloam within the city (2 Kings 20:20). *See* Siloam.

GILBOA. Range of mountains between the plain of Jezreel and the Jordan, W of Beth-Shan. The scene of Saul's final defeat (1 Sam. 31:8; 2 Sam. 1).

GILEAD. Hilly woodland (Song of Sol. 4:1), N of Dead Sea and E of Jordan. Famous for medicinal plants (Gen. 37:25; Jer. 46:11) and pasture (Num. 32:1).

GILGAL. 1. Israel's first camp near Jericho after invading Canaan (Josh. 4:19–24). Scene of circumcision, Passover, a theophany, and the Gibeonite treaty (Josh. 5:2, 10, 13—15; 9:6). Sacrifice offered there by Samuel and, misguidedly, by Saul (1 Sam. 10:8; 13:7–14). But later local worship was condemned as unacceptable (Hos. 4:15; Amos 4:4).

2. Highland town of Ephraim between Shiloh and Bethel, visited by Elijah and Elisha (2 Kings 2:1; 4:38).

GITTITES. *See* Gath.

GIVING. Valuable spiritual practice (Mal. 3:10; Luke 6:38; 12:33–34); to be done privately (Matt. 6:3), in response to God's blessing (Deut. 16:17; Matt. 10:8), generously (Rom. 12:8), systematically (1 Cor. 16:2), joyfully (2 Cor. 9:7) and according to ability (Ezra 2:69; Acts 11:29; 2 Cor. 8:12).

GLEANING *See* Farming p. 70.

GLORIFY. To praise divine character and action (Ps. 34:3; Dan. 4:37; John 12:28; 1 Pet. 2:12). Used figuratively of death (John 12:16).

GLORY. Characteristic of God's presence (Exod. 16:10; Luke 9:31–32) and power (Ps. 29:3). The plural 'glories' refers to angels (AV/KJV of 2 Pet. 2:10; Jude 8).

GNAT. *See* Insects p. 105.

GOAD. Pointed pole for urging on oxen in ploughing. Useful weapon (Judg. 3:31). Acts 26:14 alludes to a Greek proverb about fighting a god.

GOAT. *See* Domesticated animals p. 14.

GOATSKIN. Impregnated with fat and sewn up to make containers for water or wine (Gen. 21:14; Matt. 9:17).

GOD. Supreme Being, whose nature is self-disclosed as creator (Gen. 1:1), eternal (Isa. 40:28), giver (James 1:17), holy (Isa. 6:3), immutable (Ps. 102:27), judge (Gen. 18:25), life giver (John 5:26), love (1 John 4:16), omnipotent (Matt. 19:26), omnipresent (Ps. 139:7), omniscient (Heb. 4:13), self-existing (Exod. 3:14), sovereign (Dan. 4:35), spirit (John 4:24), transcendent and immanent (Isa. 57:15), wisdom (Dan. 2:20).

GOD, names of. Revealed in Scripture as an aid to faith (Ps. 9:10). *See individual names.*

GOD OF THIS WORLD. Satan (John 12:31; 2 Cor. 4:4; 1 John 5:19).

GODFEARERS. Gentiles attracted to Judaism but uncommitted by circumcision (Acts 10:2).

GODS, FALSE. Pagan objects, vainly worshipped to appease antagonistic spirits or to secure their help (Jer. 11:12). Themselves lifeless (Deut. 4:28; Isa. 4:9–18), but used by evil powers (1 Cor. 10:20–21). Forbidden to God's people (Exod. 20:3; Deut. 13).

GOG and **MAGOG.** Types of world rulers (Ezek. 38—39). They and their master Satan will be destroyed (Rev. 20:8).

GOLD. Lavishly employed in Tabernacle (Exod. 25) and Temple (1 Kings 6). One of the gifts to the infant Jesus (Matt. 2:11), useful for the family's immediate support. Its value not to be compared with faith (1 Pet. 1:7), knowing God (Ps. 19:10) or wisdom (Job 28:15).

GOLDEN CALF. 1. Image made by Aaron and the Israelites while Moses was on Mt. Sinai (Exod. 32).
2. Images set up at Bethel and Dan by Jeroboam I after the division of the kingdom, to deflect Israelites from the attractions of the Jerusalem Temple (1 Kings 12:26–33).

GOLGOTHA. Scene of Jesus' crucifixion (Matt. 27:33), explained as meaning 'The Place of the Skull', probably on account of the many executions there; or because the site suggested a skull's shape, hence 'Calvary' (from Latin for 'skull') in Luke 23:33.

GOLIATH. Philistine giant slain by David (1 Sam. 17). *See* Elhanan.

GOMER. Prostitute whom Hosea was told to

marry (Hos. 1:2–3) and later buy back from slavery (Hos. 3:1–2), an experience symbolising Israel's unfaithfulness, exile and return.

GOMORRAH. City destroyed by fire for its wickedness (Gen. 19:23–29), and now beneath the Dead Sea. The catastrophe is frequently recalled.

GOPHER WOOD. Cypress; its tough timber used for Noah's ark (Gen. 6:14).

GOSHEN. Pasture land of E Nile Delta allotted to Jacob's family (Gen. 45:10).

GOSPEL (*Good News*). Content of Christian preaching (Mark 1:1). The Greek word originally meant the reward given to a messenger bringing news of victory.

GOSPELS. Life and ministry of Jesus as told in the books of Matthew, Mark, Luke and John. These are the four canonical Gospels, those in the Christian 'canon', the list of accepted works.

GOSSIP. Frequent references suggest it was common. The evil consequences (Prov. 11:13) are condemned (Lev. 19:16; 2 Cor. 12:20).

GOURDS. Bitter fruits of colocynth (wild vine), which can be a violent purgative (2 Kings 4:39–41).

GOVERNOR. Official appointed to rule in the sovereign's name (Gen. 42:6; 1 Kings 4:19; Jer. 40:11). In NT, administrator of a Roman province (Matt. 27:2; Luke 2:2; Acts 23:24).

GRACE. That which God gives. Favourite Pauline term (some 100 times); applied to God's favour (Luke 2:40), forgiveness (Eph. 1:7) and spiritual gifts (Rom. 12:6). The Greek word also means 'thanks' (Col. 3:16); so, to 'say grace' is to 'give thanks'.

GRAIN. *See* Farming p. 70.

GRAIN OFFERING. Sacrifice of flour or baked cakes or plain grain, with oil, frankincense and salt (Lev. 2:1–16), accompanied by wine (Lev. 23:13). The poor could make a cereal offering instead of a burnt offering (Lev. 5:11).

GRAIN SHIP. *See* Travel p. 229.

GRASS. Springs up after rain, but soon disappears under hot sun (1 Kings 18:5; Ps. 129:6). Symbolised the brevity of human life (Ps. 90:5–6; 1 Pet. 1:24).

GRASSHOPPER. *See* Insects p. 105.

GRAVE. Normally in a limestone cave (Gen. 25:9) or shallow hole. Whitewashed (Luke 11:44) to warn passersby, because dead bodies conveyed ritual impurity (Num. 19:16; *see* Burial). General term for death (Gen. 37:35); even personified (Hos. 13:14). Metaphorically of mouth-related sins (Rom. 3:13).

GREAT SEA. Mediterranean (Josh. 1:4).

GREAVES. *See* War p. 241.

GREED. Covetousness, associated with impurity (Eph. 5:3) and money (Ezek. 33:31). It suggests a life without God (Rom. 1:29), that is, idolatry (Col. 3:5).

GREEK. Main language of the Hellenistic and Roman worlds from 333 BC to AD 500. *See* Bible.

GREEKS. In the NT, people of Greek language and culture, irrespective of country (Rom. 1:14). When contrasted with Jews (John 7:35), the term refers to Gentiles, that is, pagans. In Christ the distinction is abolished (Gal. 3:28).

GREETINGS. *See* Travel p. 228.

GRINDERS. Teeth (Eccles. 12:3).

GRINDING. Usually women's work (Job 31:10; Matt. 24:41), an added insult to Samson (Judg. 16:21).

GRUMBLING. Expressing discontent, at root a lack of trust in God (Exod. 16:8; 1 Cor. 10:10).

GUARD. Trustworthy men responsible for protection, military, civil or ecclesiastical (Gen. 37:36; Josh. 6:7; Judg. 7:19). For his bodyguard, David chose foreigners (2 Sam. 20:23 with 23:23); their personal loyalty would be to the king, not to politicians. Security officers in the Temple (Luke 22:52; Acts 5:24) were Levites.

GUARDIAN. In the Roman world, a personal slave-attendant who took a boy to school, heard his lessons and generally looked after him, until he came of age (at 14 in Roman law) (Gal. 4:2).

GUEST ROOM. Many of the better houses in Jerusalem had a large upper room (on the roof), needed for the crowds of pilgrims at festivals (Mark 14:14).

GUIDANCE. Promised to those who obey God (Ps. 32:8; Isa. 42:16; John 16:13). To be sought

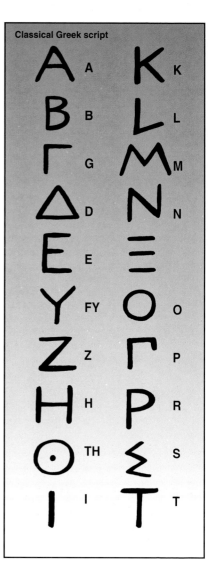

Classical Greek script

from God (Ps. 25:5; James 1:5), but never through spiritism (Lev. 19:31; 1 Chron. 10:13; Isa. 8:19).

GUIDES, BLIND. The Pharisees' 'blindness' (Matt. 23:16) symbolised spiritual darkness (Isa. 6:9).

GUILT. The consequence of breaking the divine law (James 2:10), that is, the law of love to God (Num. 15:31) or to one's neighbour (Num. 5:6). Conviction of guilt is the work of the Holy Spirit (John 16:8).

GUILT OFFERING. The guilt or trespass offering concerned sins that required restitution (Lev. 5:14—6:7).

HABAKKUK. Late 7th-century BC prophet who foretold the rise of the Babylonians (= Chaldeans, Hab. 1:6).

HABAKKUK (book). The prophet's debate with a God who fails to check wickedness in Judah, yet then reveals he will use the pagan Babylonians of all people to execute judgment (Hab. 1—2). The book ends with the prophet's declaration of trust (Hab. 3).

HABOR. Tributary of the Euphrates (2 Kings 17:6).

HADAD. 1. Canaanite storm god (Baal). Identified with Rimmon (2 Kings 5:18; Zech. 12:11).
2. Edomite prince who fled to Egypt to escape Joab, and later made trouble for Solomon (1 Kings 11:14–22, 25).

HADADEZER. Son of Rehob, king of Zobah, E of Hamath. Overpowered by David, despite help from Syria (2 Sam. 8:3–6).

HADES. Place of the dead (Rev. 20:13). The glorified Christ is in control (Rev. 1:18). The 'gates' of Hades (Matt. 16:18) refers to the power of death (gates being essential to a city's defences).

HAGAR. Sarah's Egyptian servant, who gives Abraham a son, Ishmael (Gen. 16), the future father of Arabian tribes (Gen. 25:12). For Paul, Hagar represents the servitude of the Sinai covenant, whereas Sarah symbolises the freedom of Abraham's true descendants (Gal. 4:24–26).

HAGGAI. Contemporary of Zechariah (Ezra 5:1). Urges Zerubbabel, governor of Jerusalem, and Jeshua, the high priest, to rebuild the Temple (Hag. 1); predicts future prosperity if the people give God priority (Hag. 2).

HAGRITES. Arabian tribe in Transjordan, descendants of Hagar, the mother of Ishmael (Ps. 83:6).

HAIL. Decimated Amorites fighting Joshua (Josh. 10:11). Hail often mentioned as a punishment for the wicked (Isa. 28:2, 17; Hag. 2:17; Rev. 16:21). *See* Plagues.

HAIR. OT Hebrews considered long hair manly (2 Sam. 14:26). Fashions change: deplored in NT men but admired in women (1 Cor. 11:14–15), though not the time it consumed (1 Pet. 3:3). Shaving off the hair symbolised mourning or the completion of a vow (Num. 6:18; Acts 18:18). Hair hanging loose a sign of ritual uncleanness (Lev. 13:45; Num. 5:18), ignored by the woman anointing Jesus: it was her only towel (Luke 7:44). Black hair a sign of youthful vigour (Song of Sol. 5:11); grey hair honoured (Prov. 16:31); white hair sometimes associated with the divine presence (Dan. 7:9; Rev. 1:14). *See* Baldness; Shaving.

HAIR GARMENT. *See* Dress p. 54.

HALF-SHEKEL. *See* Money p. 147.

HALF-TRIBE. The reference is always to Manasseh. Reuben, Gad and half of Manasseh, were allowed to settle E of Jordan (Num. 32), on condition that first they helped the other tribes to conquer the Promised Land (W of Jordan).

HALLEL (*Praise*). Psalms 113—118, sung at the major festivals of Passover (Mark 14:26), Tabernacles, Pentecost and Hanukkah.

HALLELUJAH (Hebrew, *Praise the Lord*). Call to worship, especially in most of Psalms 104—150. Alleluia in Greek (Rev. 19:1, AV/KJV).

HALLOWED. That which is set aside to God as holy: Sabbath (Exod. 20:11), Temple (Ps. 5:7), altar (Lev. 16:18–19), gifts (Num. 18:29), the Year of Jubilee (Lev. 25:10). In Jewish thought, 'name' represents the whole person, so 'hallowed be thy name' (Matt. 6:9) means 'recognise God as holy by living rightly'.

HAM. 1. Noah's second son (Gen. 5:32; 7:13). Ancestor of many peoples S of the Near East (Gen. 10).
    2. Poetic reference to Egypt (Ps. 105:23).

HAMAN. Persian prime minister under Xerxes (Esther 3:1) who plotted to destroy the Jews (Esther 3:6). Executed on his own gallows (Esther 7:10).

HAMATH. Royal Hittite city on the Orontes, between Aleppo and Damascus (Gen. 10:18). Destroyed by Assyrians (2 Kings 18:34), who deported its inhabitants to Samaria to replace Israelites (2 Kings 17:24–32).

HAMOR. Hivite prince whose son Shechem violated Jacob's daughter Dinah, provoking violent reprisals (Gen. 34). Acts 7:16 mentions an incident not in the OT.

HAMSTRING. Render horses useless by cutting knee tendon (Josh. 11:6).

HANAMEL. Owner of field Jeremiah bought in faith during the siege of Jerusalem (Jer. 32:7–12).

HANANEL. Tower in N Jerusalem (Neh. 3:1; 12:39; Jer. 31:38; Zech. 14:10).

HANANI. Imprisoned for rebuking Asa for seeking help from Egypt and not God (2 Chron. 16:7).

HANANIAH. 1. Gibeonite who falsely prophesied the end of the exile (Jer. 28:1–17).
2. Hebrew name of Shadrach (Dan. 1:7).

HAND. 1. God's hand symbolises his sovereign power (Josh. 4:24). Conveys strength (Ps. 89:21) and ability (Jer. 1:9), and brings blessing (2 Chron. 30:12; 1 Pet. 5:6) and security for his people (John 10:28), but punishment on those who oppose him (Exod. 7:5; Acts 13:11).
2. The right hand signifies honour (Acts 2:34) and fellowship (Gal. 2:9); the left hand the reverse (Matt. 25:33).
3. The laying on of hands consecrates offerings (Lev. 1:4), sets apart for God's service (Num. 8:10; Acts 6:6), conveys blessing (Acts 8:17) and healing (Acts 28:8). Hands lifted up (to God) in prayer and praise (Ps. 28:2; 1 Tim. 2:8). Washing hands signifies innocence (Ps. 26:6; Matt. 27:24).

HANGING. Strangulation applies only to suicides (Ahithophel, 2 Sam. 17:23; Judas, Matt. 27:5). In the book of Esther, 'hanging' probably means 'impaling', the usual Persian method of execution.

HANGINGS. Linen curtains or drapes for the Tabernacle (Exod. 27:9–15).

HANNAH (= Anna in NT). Elkanah's favourite wife; mother of Samuel (1 Sam. 1). Her song of thanksgiving has many parallels with Mary's Magnificat (Luke 1:46–55).

HANUKKAH. *See* Feast of Dedication p. 150.

HANUN. Son and successor of Nahash, king of Ammon. Insulted the messengers of David, who consequently invaded his country (2 Sam. 10).

HARAN. Mesopotamian commercial city (Ezek. 27:23), E of Carchemish. Site of famous temples to the moon-god Sin (Deut. 4:19). Abraham's home for a while (Acts 7:4), before emigrating (Gen. 12:1). Home of Isaac's wife Rebekah (Gen. 24). Jacob's refuge from Esau (Gen. 27:43).

HARBONA. Royal eunuch who introduced Esther to king Xerxes (Esther 1:10). Suggested Haman should be executed on his own gallows for molesting the queen (Esther 7:9).

HAROD. Copious spring at the foot of Mt. Gilboa where Gideon tested his troops' quality (Judg. 7).

HARP. *See* Music p. 150.

HARVEST. *See* Farming pp. 70-73.

HASMONAEANS. Family and dynasty of the Maccabees. The name derives from a priestly ancestor, Simeon (1 Macc. 2:1). *See* Maccabees.

HATRED. Satanic in origin and on a par with murder (John 8:44 with 1 John 3:15). But not necessarily involving antagonism. The Semitic mind commonly associates opposites without distinguishing shades of meaning. 'To hate' can simply mean 'to love less' (Gen. 29:31; Luke 14:26; John 12:25). The words quoted by Jesus, 'love your neighbor and hate your enemy' (Matt. 5:43), are not in the OT. The Dead Sea Scrolls reveal it was a popular saying of the day.

HAY. Figuratively describes worthless work (1 Cor. 3:12).

HAZAEL. King of Syria from about 843 BC (2 Kings 8:15). Elijah had revealed he would succeed to the throne (1 Kings 19:15–17) but be both powerful and cruel (2 Kings 8:7–14). Repelled Ahaziah and Jehoram at Ramoth Gilead

Ruins of ancient Hazor

(2 Kings 8:28–29) and repeatedly defeated Israel (2 Kings 10:32; 13:3–7, 22–25). Attacked Jerusalem, but was bought off by Joash of Judah (2 Kings 12:18).

HAZOR. Ancient Canaanite royal city, SW of Lake Huleh, captured by Joshua (Josh. 11:10–13). Fortified by Solomon (1 Kings 9:15), but later lost to Tiglath-Pileser III who deported the inhabitants to Assyria (2 Kings 15:29). Excavations suggest a population of 40,000.

HEAD. Used figuratively for uppermost, from its position in the human body (Dan. 2:38; 1 Cor. 11:3); foremost, as in animals (Joel 2:11); or for seat of authority, as containing the brain controlling thoughts and actions (Eph. 4:15–16). Vital for life (Col. 2:19).

HEALING. OT examples: Gen. 20:17; Num. 12:13; 21:7; 2 Kings 5:14), include raising the dead (1 Kings 17:17–23; 2 Kings 4:32–35). The divine motive goes beyond making people physically better (Luke 18:42, where the Greek word means to save as well as to heal). Employed to attract attention to the gospel (Matt. 4:23–25; Acts 8:6–8); to demonstrate God's power (Mark 5:19); to reveal Jesus both as Messiah (Matt. 8:17; 11:2–5) and divine (Matt. 9:6); to dispossess Satan (Matt. 12:22–28); to encourage repentance (Mark 2:17); and as a response to faith (Matt. 8:5–13). *See* Blindness; Mute; Oil.

HEARING. Attending to God's words involves obedient response (Deut. 4:1) and promotes spiritual growth (Luke 8:15). Conversely, inattention leads to disobeying God (Matt. 7:26) and is at best unprofitable (Matt. 13:19). When God is said to hear, it means divine action will follow (1 John 5:14–15).

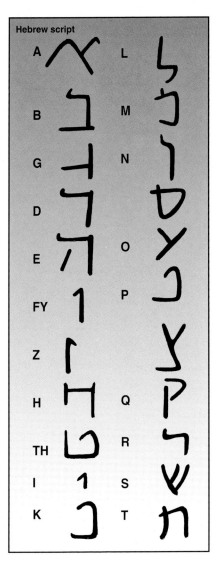

Hebrew script

A, B, G, D, E, FY, Z, H, TH, I, K, L, M, N, O, P, Q, R, S, T

HEART. Figuratively applied to conscience (Acts 2:37; Rom. 1:21), divine scrutiny (Mark 2:8), the spring of action (Luke 21:34; Acts 16:14), secret motivation (Isa. 29:13), and spiritual life (Mark 11:23–24; John 14:1; Rom. 5:5; Phil. 4:7).

HEAVEN. With the earth, describes all creation (Gen. 14:19), but specifically the sky (Gen. 27:39). God's home (Gen. 22:11) and thus the believer's security (Matt. 6:20; Phil. 3:20). After the exile, Jews said 'heaven' to avoid uttering the divine name; hence 'kingdom of heaven' not 'of God' in the most Jewish of Gospels (Matt. 3:2). Heaven, the scene of cosmic warfare (Rev. 12:7), will ultimately be destroyed (Isa. 51:6; 2 Pet. 3:10), but recreated (Rev. 21:1).

HEBER (*Companion*). Kenite whose wife Jael killed the Canaanite general Sisera (Judg. 4:17).

HEBRAIC JEWS. Palestinian Jewish Christians, normally speaking 'Hebrew' (Aramaic), not the Greek of Jews of the Diaspora (Acts 6:1).

HEBREW. Original language of OT, changing remarkably little over the 1000 years the biblical books cover. Written from right to left. Until 1000 BC only the 22 consonants were written. Readers added the appropriate vowels from knowing the language. From the Persian period (Cyrus, about 560 BC) Jews began to use the related international language Aramaic. By NT times, most Palestinian Jews spoke Aramaic. In synagogues the Scriptures were read in the sacred Hebrew, then translated into Aramaic for the congregation's benefit.

HEBREWS. Descendants of Abraham, as con-

Herbs and spices

Spices. Valued for seasoning food (Gen. 43:11), perfume (Exod. 30:34), deodorants (2 Chron. 16:14), cosmetics (Song of Sol. 5:1).

Aloes. OT term for modern eaglewood. Source of fragrant spice for perfuming clothes (Ps. 45:8) and beds (Prov. 7:17). Its bitter juice used in embalming (John 19:39).

Balm. Aromatic gum from Gilead, famed for healing properties (Jer. 46:11). Figuratively describes national relief (Jer. 8:22; 51:8).

Bitter herbs. Salad (Num. 11:5), eaten with the Passover lamb (Exod. 12:8; Num. 9:11), illustrating both Israel's hasty departure from Egypt (salad a food quickly prepared) and their bitter slavery.

Calamus. Ingredient of the holy anointing oil ('fragrant cane', Exod. 30:23), valued for its perfume (Song of Sol. 4:14; Ezek. 27:19).

Cassia. Aromatic herb used in the holy anointing oil (Exod. 30:24). Its fragrance prized (Ps. 45:8; Ezek. 27:19).

Cinnamon. Aromatic herb, highly valued for perfume and flavouring (Prov. 7:17; Song of Sol. 4:14; Rev. 18:13). An ingredient of the holy anointing oil (Exod. 30:23).

Coriander. Herb used in cooking and medicine. Compared with manna by Israelites (Num. 11:7).

Cummin (caraway or fennel in some translations). Nutmeg flower, a seasoning herb, especially on bread (Isa. 28:25). The dried fruits were lightly beaten (Isa. 28:27) to release

Cummin (Cyminum)

Cinnamon

Aloes

the black aromatic oily seeds. Jesus rebuked Pharisees for extending the Mosaic law on tithing to such small items, to the neglect of more important matters (Matt. 23:23).

Dill. Herb used for culinary and medicinal purposes (Matt. 23:23).

Mandrake. Perennial fragrant herb (Song of Sol. 7:13), alleged to have aphrodisiac properties (Gen. 30:14).

Mint. Horsemint or peppermint, which fastidious Pharisees insisted on tithing, to the neglect of more important matters (Matt. 23:23). Used in cooking,

medicine and as an air-freshener in synagogues.

Myrrh. Valuable balsam from red resin of S Arabia (Gen.

Rue

37:25), used in the holy anointing oil (Exod. 30:23). Prized for perfume (Ps. 45:8; Prov. 7:17). Brought to Jesus, as an infant (Matt. 2:11), at his crucifixion (Mark 15:23) and burial (John 19:39).

Nard. Expensive perfume from a Himalayan plant (Mark 14:3; John 12:3).

Rue. Perennial herb, valued by doctors and cooks (Luke 11:42).

Cave of Machpelah, Hebron

trasted with Egyptians (Gen. 39:14), Philistines (1 Sam. 4:6–9) or other foreigners (Exod. 21:2).

HEBREWS (NT book). Urges Jewish Christians not to fall back into Judaism. Expounds Christ's superiority over prophets (Heb. 1:1–4), angels (1:5 2:18), Moses (3), Joshua (4:1–13), the priestly office (4:14—10:18). The remaining chapters add practical exhortations to believers, with past examples of faith (11). Author unknown, despite many guesses. Paul not proposed as its author until the Synod of Carthage (AD 419).

HEBRON. Highest city in Palestine, formerly Kiriath Arba (Gen. 23:2), SSW of Jerusalem. Sometime home of Abraham (Gen. 13:18), Isaac

(Gen. 35:27) and Jacob (37:13–14). David made king of Judah there (2 Sam. 2:4). Absalom's base for his unsuccessful rebellion (2 Sam. 15:10).

HEDGE. Thorny bushes (Mic. 7:4) planted as a barrier (Hos. 2:6), especially to protect vineyards (Isa. 5:5). Symbol of God's protection (Job 1:10) or restriction (Job 3:23).

HEEL. Figuratively applied to Satan's limited success (Gen. 3:15) and to stealthy Danite tactics in war (Gen. 49:17). To lift up the heel (John 13:18, quoting Ps. 41:9) is to reject.

HEIFER. *See* Domesticated animals p. 14.

HELIOPOLIS (*City of the Sun*). Greek name for the Egyptian city of On, home of the priest Potiphera (Gen. 41:45). The famous sun-god temple destroyed by Nebuchadnezzar (Jer. 43:13; Ezek. 30:17). *See* Obelisks.

HELL. Fate of fallen angels (2 Pet. 2:4), in Jewish tradition those of Gen. 6:1–3. *See* Hades; Topheth.

HELLENISTS. Non-Greeks by nationality who regularly spoke Greek (Acts 6:1; 21:37) and adopted a Greek lifestyle.

HELMET. Figuratively applied to salvation (Isa. 59:17; Eph. 6:17; 1 Thess. 5:8) as necessary for spiritual strength.

HELPER. Purpose of woman's creation, as a man's partner (Gen. 2:18). Divine title (Ps. 10:14; Heb. 13:6). Personal service is on the list of spiritual gifts (1 Cor. 12:28).

HELPMEET. Word formed from Gen. 2:18

Snow-covered peaks of Mount Hermon

(AV/KJV), 'an help meet [suitable] for him' (a wife for Adam). The Hebrew term implies man's incompleteness without woman.

HEM. In Matt. 9:20 probably a tassel (Num. 15:38-40) on Jesus' outer garment, which proved the channel for healing a chronic haemorrhage. Popular belief held that clothes acquired their wearer's character (Acts 19:12; Jude 23). *See* Fringes; Tassel.

HENA. N Syrian city captured by Sennacherib (2 Kings 18:34; Isa. 37:13).

HEPHZIBAH (*My Delight is in Her*). 1. Mother of Manasseh, king of Judah (2 Kings 21:1).
2. Applied to transformed Zion (Isa. 62:4).

HERALD. The term usually means 'bringer of *good* news' (Isa. 40:9; 1 Tim. 2:7). Dan. 3:7 uses an Aramaic word for one publishing a royal decree.

HERBS. *See* Herbs and spices pp. 92-93.

HERDSMEN. Hired keepers of sheep, goats and other farm animals. The responsibilities for their welfare could lead to quarrels (Gen. 13:7; 26:20).

HERESY. Unorthodox teaching which could ruin spiritual life (2 Pet. 2:1).

HERMES. Greek god; called Mercury by Romans (Acts 14:12).

HERMOGENES. *See* Phygelus.

HERMON. Three-peaked mountain (3000 metres, 9000 ft), towering above Bashan and upper Jordan valley (Deut. 3:9) and snow-covered for many months. Once thickly forested (Ezek. 27:5) and harbouring lions and leopards (Song of Sol. 4:8). The N limit of Joshua's conquests (Josh. 11:3).

Herodion

HEROD AGRIPPA. *See* Agrippa I.

HEROD THE GREAT. Son of an Idumaean, Antipater, and an Arabian princess; king of Judah (Luke 1:5) and Samaria (ruled 37–4 BC). Violent dictator who executed rivals (Matt. 2:16). More peaceably, a great builder, including Caesarea. In 20 BC began renovating the Temple (John 2:20), a work not completed until AD 63. Marrying ten wives triggered succession problems.

HEROD THE TETRARCH. *See* Antipas.

HERODIANS. Jewish supporters of Herod Antipas. So hostile to Jesus that they allied with their usual antagonists, the Pharisees (Matt. 22:16).

HERODIAS. Granddaughter of Herod the Great. Deserted Herod Philip, her first husband (an uncle), and married another uncle, Herod Antipas. Engineered the death of John the Baptist (Matt. 14:3–12).

HESHBON. City E of Jericho, capital of the Amorite king Sihon (Num. 21:26); captured by Israelites (Num. 21:25). Region of pastures (Num. 32:1–3), vineyards (Isa. 16:8–10) and pools (Song of Sol. 7:4).

HETH. Ancestor of the Hittites (Gen. 10:15).

HEWERS. Excavators of rock, for a water cistern or well (Jer. 2:13). Term also used of Gibeonites made to be hewers of wood to provide Israelites with fuel, as punishment for their deceit (Josh. 9:21).

HEZEKIAH (*The Lord is My Strength*). King of Judah (2 Kings 18:5–6). Co-regent with Ahab, 729–716 BC; sole monarch, 716–686 BC. Brought water into Jerusalem (2 Kings 20:20) and fortified the city (2 Chron. 32:5); fostered literature (Prov. 25:1), but most noted for his religious reforms (2 Chron. 29:1–31:21). Successfully faced Assyrian threats (Isa. 36—38).

HIDDEKEL. Tigris river (AV/KJV of Gen. 2:14; Dan. 10:4).

HIDING PLACE. Palestine's limestone caves offered cover for fugitives (Josh. 10:17; 1 Sam. 23:19). Metaphor for God's protection (Ps. 32:7; Isa. 4:6).

HIEL. Rebuilt Jericho (1 Kings 16:34), vainly defying a curse (Josh. 6:26).

HIERAPOLIS. Local church (Col. 4:13) later led by the famous bishop Papias (AD 60–130), who reputedly knew the apostle John and Polycarp.

HIGH PLACE. Frequently a technical term for a Canaanite sanctuary on high ground (Num. 33:52), copied by Israelites (Amos 7:9).

HIGH PRIEST. Only Aaron (Exod. 28) and his descendants (Num. 25:10–13) could serve. Of such authority, the high priest's death was a national event (Num. 35:25). In NT times, appointed and deposed by the occupying Romans, but even out of office still recognised by Jews (as Annas and Caiaphas, Luke 3:2; John 18:13). Superseded by Christ as mediator of the new covenant (Heb. 4:14—5:10; 9:1–28).

HIGHWAY. *See* Travel p. 228.

HILKIAH (*The Lord is My Portion*). High priest who found the lost book of the law (2 Kings 22:3–8), prompting king Josiah's great religious reform.

HILLEL THE ELDER. Eminent rabbi (60 BC–AD 20), grandfather of Paul's teacher Gamaliel I (Acts 22:3). Favoured a more liberal interpretation of Scripture than the conservative Shammai. Both men attracted disciples, whose rivalry is behind the Pharisees' question about divorce (Matt. 19:3).

HIND. *See* Wild animals p. 16.

HIP. When Jacob's wrestling ended painfully, he still demanded blessing, that is, a share of his opponent's ability to overcome (Gen. 32:22–32).

HIRAM. King of Tyre. Provided building materials for David's palace (2 Sam. 5:11) and Solomon's Temple (1 Kings 5:6–10). Helped to crew Solomon's new merchant fleet (1 Kings 9:26–27) and made trade agreements with him (1 Kings 10:22).

HIRELING. Wage earner (Deut. 24:14), often as a day labourer in agriculture (Matt. 20:2) or for odd jobs (Deut. 24:14–15). More skilled workers too could be hired: goldsmith (Isa. 46:6), and masons, carpenters and other craftsmen (2 Chron. 24:12), mercenaries (2 Chron. 25:6) and even (unsuccessfully) a prophet (Neh. 13:2). The temporary nature of employment could mean being less conscientious (John 10:12).

HITTITES. Term applied to an ethnic group's great empire covering Asia Minor and the whole region of Syria (Josh. 1:4), which lasted from 1800 to 1200 BC.

HIVITES. Nation facing the Israelites invading Canaan (Exod. 3:8). Mentioned around Shechem (Gen.34:2), Gibeon (Josh. 9:7), Hermon (Josh. 11:3), and Lebanon (Judg. 3:3). Conscripted as building labourers for Solomon (1 Kings 9:20).

HOBAB. Moses' brother-in-law (Judg. 4:11), whose desert experience would be invaluable.

HOHAM. Amorite king of Hebron, allied with four other kings to punish Gibeon for making peace with Joshua. The subsequent battle of Beth-Horon led to the five kings being executed (Josh. 10).

HOLINESS. Uniquely applies to God (Hos. 11:9), and secondarily to what is associated with him: his people (Exod. 19:6; 1 Pet. 1:15), angels (Mark 8:38), prophets (Luke 1:70), day of rest (Gen. 2:3), locations (Exod. 3:5), Temple (Matt. 24:15), Scriptures (Rom. 1:2) and divine law (Rom. 7:12).

HOLY CITY. Jerusalem (Isa. 48:2; Matt. 27:53), as God's nominated abode (1 Kings 11:36). Term also applied to New Jerusalem (Rev. 21:2). *See* City of God.

HOLY GHOST. Term (for Holy Spirit) when AV/KJV was translated (1611). Some Anglo-Saxon Bibles have 'Holy *Guest*', appropriate for one who comes by invitation and remains only while welcome.

HOLY OF HOLIES *See* Tabernacle pp. 214-215.

HOLY ONE. Divine name, expressing God's essential attribute (Ps. 22:3); frequently all through Isaiah as 'the Holy One of Israel'.

HOLY PLACE. *See* Tabernacle pp. 214-215.

HOLY SPIRIT. God's presence in action. He appoints to ministry (Acts 20:28), assures of divine inheritance (Rom. 8:15–17), baptises (Acts 1:5), counsels (John 14:26), creates (Gen. 1:2), directs (Acts 13:2), empowers for service (Luke 24:49), equips (Exod. 31:3), gives life (Rom. 8:11), guides (Rom. 8:14), indwells (John 14:17), inspires (Num. 24:2), liberates (Rom. 8:2), prays (Rom. 8:26–27), is promised (Acts 2:33), prompts spiritual response (Ps. 51:10–12), regenerates (John 3:6), sanctifies (1 Pet. 1:2), strengthens (Rom. 8:26), teaches (Neh. 9:20), transforms (2 Cor. 3:18), unifies (Rom. 15:5). *See* Spiritual gifts; Wind 2.

HOMOSEXUALITY. Its practice consistently condemned (Gen. 19; Lev. 18:22; Rom. 1:24–27; 1 Cor. 6:9–10).

HONEY. *See* Foods p. 76.

HONOUR. Due to God (Ps. 29:2; John 5:23); also to the aged (Lev. 19:32), employers (1 Tim. 6:1), parents (Exod. 20:12; Matt. 15:4), rulers (1 Pet. 2:17), spouses (Heb. 13:4) and widows (1 Tim. 5:3). True honour is bestowed by God (1 Sam. 2:30).

HOOF. Animals with cloven hoof and that chew the cud were ritually clean (Lev. 11:3–8): oxen, sheep, goats, deer (Deut. 14:4–6).

HOOPOE. *See* Birds p. 104.

HOPE. In Scripture, not the feeble 'hope so' of everyday speech, but vibrant expectant trust in the living God (Ps. 25:3; Jer. 14:8). God's gift (2 Thess. 2:16) to believers through the gospel (Rom. 8:24; Col. 1:23; 1 Pet. 1:3). 'God of hope' (Rom. 15:13) means the one who inspires hope.

HOPHNI. *See* Phineas 2.

HOPHRA. Pharaoh (king) of Egypt; reigned 589–569 BC. Opposed Nebuchadnezzar besieging Jerusalem but had to retreat (Jer. 37:5–7). Assassinated (Jer. 44:30). Jeremiah derides him (Jer. 46:17).

HOR. Mountain on Edom border where Aaron died (Num. 20:22–29).

HORAM. King of Gezer, important Canaanite city on the Jerusalem-Joppa road (Josh. 10:33).

HOREB. The 'mountain of God' (1 Kings 19:8); alternative name for Sinai. Scene of Moses' call at the burning bush (Exod. 3), God's covenant with Israel (Deut. 5:2), and Elijah's recommissioning (1 Kings 19:1–19).

HORITES. Highlanders of Seir (Gen. 14:6), dispossessed by Edomites (Deut. 2:12).

HORMAH (*Destruction*). Canaanite town earlier called Zephath (Judg. 1:17). Scene of Israelite rout (Num. 14:40–45) for disobeying God, but later of an overwhelming victory (Num. 21:3).

HORN. Term can refer to an animal (Gen. 22:13), musical instrument (Exod. 19:13; Dan. 3:5), liquid container (1 Sam. 16:1), or part of an altar (Exod. 27:2). Symbolises strength (Zech. 1:18), dignity (Ps. 112:9), kingship, horns being uppermost on an animal (Dan. 7:24), or pride, carrying the head high (1 Sam. 2:1). Horn of salvation (2 Sam. 22:3; Luke 1:69) refers to the divine might to effect deliverance, from enemies or from sin.

HORNET. *See* Insects p. 105.

HORONITE. Term applied to Sanballat (Neh. 2:10), meaning a native of Beth Horon or Horonaim.

HORSE. *See* Domesticated animals p. 14.

HOSANNA (*O Save!*). Welcome to Jesus entering Jerusalem (Matt. 21:9), expressing the hope that he was Messiah. The cry derives from Ps. 118:25–26, sung during Passover season and so fresh in the crowd's mind.

HOSEA. Contemporary of Amos, both of them prophets to Israel (Ephraim) under Jeroboam II (Hos. 1:1).

HOSEA (book). Tells of Hosea's tragic married life (1—3) which patterns Israel's relationship with God. Israel's impending judgment for her unfaithfulness (4—13) need not be final, for the book ends with reassurance, if Israel turns back to God (14).

HOSHEA. Last king of Israel (2 Kings 15:30). Rebelling against Assyria led to his imprisonment (2 Kings 17:1–6; 18:9–11) and to the fall of Samaria (722 BC), bringing the N kingdom of Israel to an end.

HOSPITALITY. *See* Travel p. 228.

HOST OF HEAVEN. The stars, witnessing to God's splendour (Neh. 9:6) and control (Isa. 40:26), but tempting Israel to copy pagan cults (Deut. 4:19). Term also applies to angels (1 Kings 22:19; Luke 2:13), especially as the Lord's army (1 Sam. 17:45; Ps. 103:20–21).

HOSTILITY, DIVIDING WALL OF. The 'middle wall of partition' in the Temple (Eph. 2:14, AV/KJV), 1.5 metres (5 ft) high, symbolising the separation of Jew from Gentile. A notice in Hebrew, Greek and Latin warned Gentiles not to go beyond this barrier on pain of death (Acts 21:28).

HOUR. The third, sixth and ninth hours roughly correspond to 9 AM, noon and 3 PM (Matt. 20:3, 5). The eleventh hour (Matt. 20:6) has become proverbial for 'last opportunity'. The whole

House

House. Poorer families ate and slept in a single room, with niches for food and utensils. One third of the floor was on a higher level for the family. The rest sheltered domestic animals at night.

Bedroom. Poorer families lived in one room (Luke 11:7), shared at night with farm animals.

Window. Recessed narrow opening for air and light to enter (Ezek. 41:16) and for smoke to escape (Hos. 13:3). If high up, large enough to allow a person to go through (Josh. 2:15; 2 Kings 9:30-33; Acts 20:9; 2 Cor. 11:33). *See* Lattice.

Roof. The flat roof of a house, reached by an outside stairway (Luke 17:31), had to be safeguarded (Deut. 22:8) as it was much used, for

drying flax (Josh. 2:6), conversation (1 Sam. 9:25), relaxation (1 Sam. 11:2), privacy (Acts 10:9), an extra room (2 Sam. 16:22; 2 Kings 4:10), rough shelters at the Feast of Tabernacles (Neh. 8:16), and idolatrous worship (Jer. 19:13). The earthen roof, though beaten hard, allowed grass to sprout after rain (2 Kings 19:26). Flimsy enough to lead to the paralytic's healing (Mark 2:4).

Tiling. Not tiles in the modern sense, but the

usual roofing of rafters and rushes, plastered over with dried mud. Strong enough to be walked upon, yet easily removed (Luke 5:19).

Housetop. Flat roof, with a parapet (Deut. 22:8), reached by outside stone steps. Convenient for drying crops (Josh. 2:6) and privacy (Zeph. 1:5; Acts 10:9). Houses packed together in a city meant that in emergency it was possible to escape over the roofs (Matt. 24:17). After rain the mud roof lent itself briefly to grass (Isa. 37:27).

Key. Piece of wood with pegs corresponding to small holes in a wooden bolt on inside of door (Judg. 3:25). Symbol of authority (Isa. 22:22; Matt. 16:19; Rev. 1:18; 3:7) as that which permits the opening or locking of a door, literal or metaphorical.

Christian era is the 'last hour' (1 John 2:18). The 'hour of prayer' (Acts 3:1) reflects the Jewish practice of regular prayer three times a day (Ps. 55:17). 'Hour' can mean 'appointed time' (John 12:23). The half-hour of silence in heaven (Rev. 8:1) intensely dramatises the impending judgment. *See* Watches of the night.

HOUSE. 1. *See* pp. 100-101.
2. Descendants (2 Sam. 3:1).

HOUSEHOLD. Immediate family and relatives, slaves and concubines: the number could be large (Gen. 14:14; 46:26–27). The conduct of individuals within the unit affected others, for good or ill (Josh. 6:23; 7:24; Acts 16:31–34).

HOUSEHOLD, CAESAR'S. Slaves and freemen in the emperor's service in his palace in Rome. Some had become Christians (Phil. 4:22).

HOUSEHOLD GODS.
See Domestic life p. 52.

HOUSETOP. *See* House p. 101.

HULDAH. Jerusalem prophetess, consulted by king Josiah (2 Kings 22:14–20).

HUMILITY. Obeying God (Mic. 6:8) meets with his response (1 Kings 3:7–14; Isa. 57:15; Luke 18:14). Jesus gives the example (Matt. 11:29; John 13:15; Phil. 2:8). Even socially advisable (Luke 14:10).

HUNTING. Methods used included camouflaged pits (2 Sam. 23:20), nets (Job 18:8), snares (Ps. 124:7), traps (Amos 3:5) and the noose (Prov. 7:22). Food laws listed animals which might or might not be eaten (Lev. 11).

HUR. Held up Moses' hands during the battle against Amalekites (Exod. 17:10, 12) and supported Aaron during Moses' absence (Exod. 24:14).

HUSBAND. Unity between spouses is emphasised from the beginning (Gen. 2:24), and Paul's head-body analogy (Eph. 5:23) is similarly a symbol more of unity than of authority (Eph. 5:31). Ancient cultures taught husbands to rule their wives, but the NT stresses mutual love (Col. 3:19; 1 Pet. 3:7). The husband's death released his widow to remarry (Rom. 7:3). *See* Brother-in-law's duty.

HUSHAI. David's loyal and resourceful friend who helped to thwart Absalom's rebellion (2 Sam. 15:32–37; 16:16–18; 17:5–15).

HYENA. *See* Wild animals p. 16.

HYMENAEUS. Heretical teacher in Ephesus, excommunicated by Paul (1 Tim. 1:20; 2 Tim. 2:17).

HYMN. *See* Music p. 150.

HYPOCRISY. Ostentatious piety (Matt. 6:1–5; 23:13–29). The Greek word originally referred to playacting.

HYSSOP. *See* Plants p. 170.

I

I AM. Revealed divine name (Exod. 3:14), claimed by Jesus (John 6:35; 8:12, 28, 58; 9:5; 10:7, 11; 11:25; 13:19; 14:6; 15:1).

IBEX. *See* Wild animals p. 16.

IBZAN. Judged Israel for seven years (Judg. 12:8–10).

ICHABOD (*Where is the Glory?*). Born on the day Philistines captured the ark of the covenant (1 Sam. 4:19–22).

ICONIUM. Phrygian city where Barnabas and Paul's preaching (Acts 14:1–6) aroused antagonism (Acts 14:19; 2 Tim. 3:11).

IDOLATRY (*worship of images*). Prophets denounced images as worthless (Isa. 44:9–20) but luring into demon worship (Deut. 32:17; 1 Cor. 10:20). Anything that leads away from God amounts to idolatry (Eph. 5:5; 1 Pet. 4:3; 1 John 5:21).

IDOLS. Often shaped, signifying a god's particular quality: as a bull (2 Chron. 13:8) for power; a tree (Deut. 7:5) for life; a multi-breasted woman (Acts 19:24–35) for fertility. All pagan life embraced idol worship, so conversion to Christ risked ostracism from social life (1 Cor. 10:27–28) and loss of employment, as trades were organised into guilds involving pagan practices. *See* God's, false; Household gods.

IDUMEA. Greek name for Edom (Mark 3:8).

IJON. Store city of N Naphtali captured by Ben-Hadad of Syria to relieve Israelite pressure on Asa king of Judah (2 Chron. 16:4). Inhabitants deported to Assyria by Tiglath Pileser in 733 BC (2 Kings 15:29).

ILLYRICUM. Roman province of NW Macedonia from 27 BC (Rom. 15:19).

IMAGE OF GOD. Crowning distinction between human beings and animals (Gen. 1:26–27). Marred by the Fall, it requires renewal

Idols: image of Ishtar of Niineveh

Birds

Dove

Partridge

Raven

Dove. Member of the pigeon family, vegetarian and thus a 'clean' bird acceptable for food and sacrifice (Lev. 5:7; Matt. 21:12; Luke 2:24). Used by Noah to discover if flood waters had receded enough for leaves to grow (Gen. 8:8-12). Figuratively describes the Holy Spirit (Matt. 3:16) and the quality of innocence (Matt. 10:16).

Eagle. Hebrew and Greek terms also mean vulture (Matt. 24:28; Luke 17:37). Both birds are powerful (Exod. 19:4), swift (Jer. 49:22) and can fly high (Obad. 4).

Eagle

Hoopoe. The English word arose too late for AV/KJV, which calls the bird a 'heron' (Lev. 11:19). Scavenging for worms on manure heaps and being sacred to the Egyptians put it on Israel's unclean list (Deut. 14:18).

Ostrich. Well described in Job 39:13-18. For a short distance it can run at 80 km (50 mi) an hour.

Owl. Nocturnal and secretive bird of prey. On forbidden food lists (Lev. 11:16-18; Deut. 14:15-17). Symbolic of desolation (Ps. 102:6; Isa. 34:11; Zeph. 2:14).

Partridge. Seldom flies, but skips from cover to cover (1 Sam. 26:20).

Pigeon. Hardly distinguishable from doves. 'Clean' bird (being vegetarian) and when offered in sacrifice (Lev. 1:14; Luke 2:24) always described as 'young'.

Quail. Small migratory game bird (Exod. 16:13), which flies low and needs wind assistance (Num. 11:31).

Raven. Useful scavengers (looking for carcases, Gen. 8:7). Intelligent bird, used by God to feed Elijah (1 Kings 17:4).

Sparrow. House sparrow fits Ps. 84:3, but not Ps. 102:7 (AV/KJV), for sparrows are gregarious. Trapping sparrows for food (Matt. 10:29) was common.

Sparrows

Insects

Insects. The English word arose only in 1601, so is absent from earlier Bibles. Technically insects are invertebrates (without backbone) that fly. Species mentioned include ants, bees, crickets, fleas, flies, gnats, grasshoppers, hornets, locusts, moths, spiders.

Grasshopper

Bee. Canaan aptly described as flowing with milk and honey (Exod. 3:8) for myriads of wild bees lodge in rocks, hollow trees (Ps. 81:16) or any convenient hole (Judg. 14:8). Disturbing hives invited a furious attack (Deut. 1:44).

Gnat. Subject of third plague (Exod. 8). Matt. 23:24 refers to the finicky practice of drinking through a cloth to avoid swallowing an insect (regarded as ritually unclean).

Grasshopper. Eaten by the poor (Lev. 11:22). An invasion of grasshoppers taken as divine judgment (1 Kings 8:37). Symbolic of small size (Num. 13:33) and of great numbers (Ps. 105:34).

Hornet. The ability of this outsize wasp to inflict a vicious sting has been enlisted by modern armies. So Exod. 23:28, Deut. 7:20 and Josh.

24:12 are probably to be taken literally as the natural means God used.

Leech. Prov. 30:15 refers to the horse-leech; the 'two daughters' to its two-forked tongue, voraciously sucking blood.

Locust. The only insect allowed for human consumption (Lev. 11:22). Useful source of protein (Matt. 3:4), but the vast swarms (Jer. 51:14; Nah. 3:15) were notoriously destructive (Exod. 10:5; Joel 1:4). Joel 2:25 refers not to the reversal of time but to the replacement of labour's lost results.

Scorpion. Israelites faced its danger in the wilderness (Deut. 8:15), but most references are figurative. Rehoboam's threat (1 Kings 12:11) likened his intended treatment of Israelites to its vicious sting. Jesus' comment (Luke 11:12) alludes to its egg-shaped body.

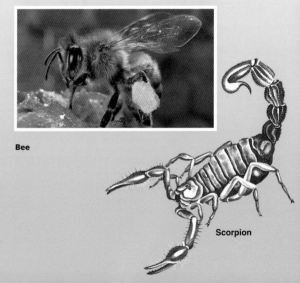

Bee

Scorpion

by Christ (Col. 3:10; 1 John 3:2). This divine stamp also declares God's ownership (Matt. 22:20–21) and the requirement to treat other human beings accordingly (Gen. 9:6; James 3:9).

IMITATION. Paul boldly offers himself as a pattern to follow because of his Christian practice (1 Cor. 4:15–17; Phil. 4:9; 2 Thess. 3:9). Other NT writers urge the same (Heb. 13:7), following Christ's own example (Matt. 11:29; John 13:15; 1 Pet. 2:21).

IMMANUEL/EMMANUEL (*God is with us*). Name for an unmarried woman's child, whose birth would be a special sign to Jerusalem (Isa. 7:14; 8:8). Prophecy applied to Jesus (Matt. 1:23).

IMMORALITY. Sexual deviance flouting divine standards (Exod. 20:14; Lev. 18:8, 22–23; 1 Cor. 6:18–20). A particular temptation to Israel when flirting with paganism (Num. 25:1; Deut. 23:17). *See* Homosexuality; Prostitution.

IMMORTALITY. Not subject to death. Attribute of God (1 Tim. 1:17) and of resurrected believers (1 Cor. 15:50–54). *See* Imperishable.

IMPARTIALITY. Characteristic of God (Deut. 10:17; Matt. 5:45; 1 Pet. 1:17); expected of judges (Lev. 19:15; Mal. 2:9) and believers (1 Tim. 5:21; James 3:17).

IMPEDIMENT. Term used of a deaf man who could hardly speak. Jesus' bizarre actions mimed what he was going to do: touching ears, spitting out impediment, looking upward and sighing to indicate prayer, before speaking the word of command (Mark 7:32–35). The healing a messianic sign (Isa. 35:6).

IMPERIAL REGIMENT. *See* War p. 241.

IMPERISHABLE. Not subject to decay: the quality ascribed to the believer's resurrection body (1 Cor. 15:42, 51–54), crown (1 Cor. 9:25), heavenly inheritance (1 Pet. 1:4), spiritual birth (1 Pet. 1:23). *See* Immortality.

IMPLANTED WORD. Divine seed (Matt. 13:23) received at conversion (James 1:21; 1 Pet. 1:23).

IMPORTUNITY. Shameless insistence (Luke 11:8).

IMPUTATION. Reckoning something to another. Applied to sin and to deliverance by Christ (Rom. 5:12–19; 2 Cor. 5:19–21; Gal. 3:13).

INCARNATION. Jesus' taking of human flesh (Latin, *carnis,* 'of flesh'), indicating he was both divine and human (John 1:1–18; 1 Tim. 3:16).

INCENSE. Aromatic resins and spices specially compounded (Exod. 30:34–36) and burned in divine worship (Exod. 30:7–9; Luke 1:10). Symbolises prayer (Ps. 141:2; Rev. 5:8). *See* Altar of incense.

INFANT. Rubbed with salt (Ezek. 16:4) to 'toughen the skin'; tightly wrapped in cloths (swaddling clothes; Luke 2:12), thought to keep limbs firm and straight.

INFINITE. Without limit as to time and space; strictly refers to God alone (Ps. 147:5), though by hyperbole applied to sins (Job 22:5) and national powers (Nahum 3:9).

INHERITANCE. On the human level, property willed on the father's death (Gen. 15:2; Matt.

21:38). The eldest son received a double portion (Deut. 21:17) since as the new head of the family he was now financially responsible. If there were no sons, daughters inherited (Num. 26:33). The Promised Land is Israel's inheritance by God's gift (Lev. 20:24) and Israel is God's inheritance (Jer. 10:16), that is, his property. In the NT the inheritance is narrowed down to Christ himself (Heb. 1:2). Believers are adopted into his family (Rom. 8:17) to receive a spiritual inheritance (Matt. 19:29; Acts 20:32; Col. 1:12; 1 Pet. 1:4).

INIQUITY. The Hebrew word emphasises the guilt of deliberate wrongdoing (Gen. 44:16) and the consequent penalty (Isa. 53:11) which Christ bore for us on the cross (Isa. 53:6; 1 Pet. 2:24).

INJUSTICE. Frequently charged against society (Deut. 24:17; 1 Sam. 8:3; Col. 4:1); failing to love one's neighbour (Rom. 13:10).

INK. Soot mixed with gum arabic and water, kept as a dried cake on which the scribe dipped his moistened pen. Easily washed off (Exod. 32:33).

INKHORN. Case holding reed pens and an ink container, fastened at the scribe's waist (Ezek. 9:2).

INN. *See* Travel p. 228.

INNOCENTS, MASSACRE OF. Herod the Great's slaughter of boys under two years (Matt. 2:16) is in keeping with his ruthlessness concerning rivals. The estimated population of Bethlehem suggests up to twenty children were involved.

INSECTS. *See* p. 105.

INSPIRATION. Applied to Scripture ('God-breathed', 2 Tim. 3:16; 2 Pet. 1:20–21), God's work (Exod. 35:30–35; Acts 13:2; Col. 1:29), prophets (2 Kings 17:13; Acts 11:27–28), spiritual gifts (1 Cor. 12–14), witness (Exod. 4:12; Matt. 10:19; 1 Cor. 10:13), enlightenment (Luke 2:27), hope (1 Thess. 1:3), joy (1 Thess. 1:6).

INSURRECTION. Rebellion against civil authority, not uncommon during the Roman occupation (Luke 23:19; Acts 5:36–37).

INTEGRITY. Upright and honest living (2 Kings 12:15; Ps. 7:8), commanded (Lev. 19:36; 1 Kings 9:4) and commended (Prov. 11:3), especially as a Christian witness (Titus 2:7).

INTENTION. Human plans and purposes, for good or ill, are not hidden from God (Heb. 4:12) and he can frustrate them (Gen. 50:20; 2 Sam. 7). No human power can thwart God's will (Jer. 23:20; Acts 12:11), although he will change his mind if sinners turn from evil (Jer. 18:7–10; Jon. 3:10). *See* Cities of refuge.

INTERCESSION. Praying on behalf of others (Exod. 32:11–13; 1 Chron. 6:14–42; Dan. 2:18). Practised by Jesus (Luke 22:32; Heb. 7:25). Urged on believers (1 Tim. 2:1).

INTEREST. *See* Money p. 146.

INTERMARRIAGE. Forbidden to Israelites, as it led to being lured into paganism (Deut. 7:3–4; Neh. 13:23–27). Christians warned not to marry unbelievers (1 Cor. 7:39).

INTERPRETATION. Ability to explain dreams (Gen. 40:16; Dan. 2:30), a divine gift (Gen. 40:8), as is the interpretation of tongues (1 Cor. 12:10).

INVOKING. Calling upon the divine name (2 Sam. 14:11; Isa.48:1; Acts 19:13). Invoking other supposed gods forbidden (Exod. 23:13; Josh. 23:7).

IOTA. *See* Jot and tittle.

IRON. Mined by Solomon near Ezion Geber (foretold, Deut. 8:9). Enemy chariots with iron fittings (Josh. 17:18; Judg. 4:3) often troubled the Israelites. The Philistine monopoly of iron (1 Sam. 13:19–22) makes David's triumphs all the more remarkable. Symbolises strength (Job 40:18), drought (Lev. 26:19; Deut. 28:23), stubbornness (Isa. 48:4), authoritative rule (Ps. 2:9; Rev. 2:27), the era of Rome (Dan. 2:40).

ISAAC (*He Laughed*). Son and heir promised to Abraham and Sarah in their old age (Gen. 17:19; 21:4). Grew up with his half-brother Ishmael, until Sarah made Abraham banish Hagar and her son (Gen. 21:8–14). Told by God to offer Isaac in sacrifice, Abraham's faith was severely tested but triumphant (Gen. 22; Heb. 11:17–18). At 40, Isaac married Rebekah (Gen. 24), and 20 years later fathered Esau and Jacob (Gen. 25:26). Famine drove him to emigrate to Gerar, where he prospered (Gen. 26). In old age, he prophetically blessed Jacob and Esau (Gen. 27; Heb. 11:20). Died aged 180 (Gen. 35:28); buried at Machpelah (Gen. 49:31). The 'child of promise' (Rom. 9:7–9; Gal. 4:28) appears in Scripture as a colourless character, but serves as the important middleman between Abraham and Jacob/Israel (Exod. 3:6).

ISAIAH (*The Lord Saves*). Eighth-century prophet to Judah (Isa. 1:1), based in Jerusalem (Isa. 7:1–3; 37:2), and the prophet most quoted in the NT. Called in 740 BC (Isa. 6:1), Jewish tradition claims he was martyred during Manasseh's reign (696–642 BC). His wife was a prophetess (Isa. 8:3); their two sons (Isa. 7:3; 8:1) were given symbolic names as a witness to Judah.

ISAIAH (book). Chapters 1—39, mostly in poetry, concern events during the prophet's ministry and his appeals to Judah to repent and trust God in the face of Assyrian threats. Chapters 40—66 speak of the restoration of the nation after exile in Babylon, with special passages ('Servant Songs') concerning Messiah (42:1–7; 49:1–9; 50:4–11; 52:13—53:12). Although many modern scholars deny the unity of the book, a number of factors support traditional authorship. Themes found throughout the book include notably the title 'Holy One of Israel' (rare outside Isaiah). Among the Dead Sea Scrolls is a complete copy of Isaiah (dated about 200 BC) with no break between chapters 39 and 40.

ISH-BOSHETH. Son and successor of Saul as king of Israel (2 Sam. 2:8–10; 4:1–12).

ISHMAEL (*God Hears*). Son of Abraham by Sarah's servant Hagar (Gen. 16:3–16). As a teenager he was sent away with his mother at Sarah's insistence (Gen. 21:9–21; Gal. 4:22–30). Ancestor of twelve Arabian tribes (Gen. 17:20; 25:12–16), chronic rivals of Israelites (Ps. 83:6).

ISRAEL. 1. The patriarch Jacob, renamed by God (Gen. 32:28).

2. The twelve tribes descended from Jacob's twelve sons (Gen. 49:28), and

3. their homeland (1 Sam. 13:19).

4. Politically the ten tribes of the north after the kingdom broke up (1 Kings 12:16), often identified with the most important of them, Ephraim (Hos. 11:8), or Samaria (2 Kings 18:34).

Twelve Tribes of Israel

DAN

Tyre

Dan (Laish)

Kedesh

ASHER

NAPHTALI

Golan

ZEBULUN

Sea of Chinnereth

MANASSEH

Shimron

Endor

Megiddo

ISSACHAR

Ramoth-gilead

MANASSEH

Jordan

Shechem

Succoth

Beth-dagon

EPHRAIM

Shiloh

GAD

DAN

Bethel

BENJAMIN

Gibeah

Jericho

Jebus (Jerusalem)

Heshbon

Bezer

JUDAH

REUBEN

Gaza

Hebron

Salt Sea

25   50 km

10   20   30 miles

— · — · Probable boundary of tribe of Israel

⟶ Migration of the tribe of Dan

◎ City of refuge

G R E A T   S E A

Beersheba

MOAB

SIMEON

5. The 'two houses of Israel' (Isa. 8:14) expresses a reluctance to accept the separation as permanent, as does 'the remnant of Israel' to describe Judah (Ezek. 9:8) following the fall of Samaria (722 BC).

6. Christ established his church on the model of the twelve tribes as the 'new Israel' (Matt. 19:28; Gal. 6:16; Rev. 21:12).

ISSACHAR. Fifth son of Jacob and Leah (Gen. 30:18), ancestor of one of the twelve tribes of Israel. Their territory (Josh. 19:17–23) was the rich plain of Jezreel.

ITALIAN REGIMENT. *See* War p. 241.

ITCH. Ringworm (Lev. 13:30–37). Mange (mite inflammation)is probably meant in Lev. 22:22 (AV/KJV) and scabies in Deut. 28:27.

ITHAMAR. Youngest of Aaron's four sons (Exod. 6:23), who exercised the priesthood with his brother Eleazar after the death of the other brothers, Nadab and Ahibu (1 Chron. 24:4).

ITTAI. Leader of Philistine troops from Gath who joined David (2 Sam. 15:17–22) and loyally supported him during his flight from Absalom (2 Sam. 18:2).

ITUREA. Region E of upper Jordan, belonging to Philip the tetrarch (Luke 3:1). Name derived from Jetur, ancestor of Arabian tribe descended from Ishmael (Gen. 25:15).

IVORY. Greatly valued (Ezek. 27:15) and subject to highly skilled carving and inlaid work. Used by kings (1 Kings 10:18) and the luxury trade (Amos 3:15; Rev. 18:12).

IVVAH. Syrian town, unable to withstand the Assyrians (2 Kings 19:13).

J

JAAZANIAH. Rechabite whose integrity provided an object lesson for disobedient Israelites (Jer. 35).

JABBOK. Jordan tributary, where Jacob wrestled with God (Gen. 32:22–23).

JABESH GILEAD. City of Gilead, E of Jordan. Destroyed for not supporting Mizpah decision to discipline Benjamin (Judg. 21:8), though 400 young women were spared and given to Benjamites to save tribe from extinction (Judg. 21:14). Saul (a Benjamite) rescued inhabitants from Ammonite threats (1 Sam. 11:1–11; 31:12; 2 Sam. 2:5–7).

JABIN. 1. Canaanite king of Hazor, defeated by Joshua (Josh. 11:1–10).
2. Another king of Hazor whose general Sisera oppressed Israel 20 years until slain by Jael (Judg. 4; Ps. 83:9).

JABNEH. Philistine coastal town (2 Chron. 26:6).

JACHIN (*He Establishes*) and **BOAZ** (*Strength*). Two tall decorated bronze pillars, freestanding before Solomon's Temple (1 Kings 7:15–22). Purpose uncertain.

JACKAL. *See* Wild animals p. 16.

JACOB (*Supplanter*). Twin brother of Esau, but born second (Gen. 25:21–26). Supplants Esau by buying his birthright (Gen. 25:29–34), then deceives his blind father Isaac into giving him the firstborn's blessing (Gen. 27:1–40; Heb. 11:20). Escaping from Esau, dreams of 'Jacob's ladder' (Gen. 27:41–28:20). Deceived by Laban into marrying Leah, but cheats Laban in return, grows wealthy at his expense (Gen. 29—30), then flees (Gen. 31—32). On the way to Canaan, wrestles with God, who changes his name to 'Israel' (Gen. 32:28). In old age Jacob/Israel settles in Egypt (Gen. 47) and adopts Joseph's two sons (Gen. 48:1–20; Heb. 11:21). His final blessing is upon all twelve sons (Gen. 49:1–27), whose descendants form the twelve tribes of Israel (Gen. 49:28). Dies in Egypt (Gen. 49:33); buried in Canaan (Gen. 50:1–14).

Rebekah's favourite (Gen. 25:28), he is chosen by God over his brother (Mal. 1:2–3; Rom. 9:13). His deviousness (Gen. 25:29–33; 27:18–24; 30:32–33; 32:4–5; 33:1–2) is made to serve God's wider plans, so that Jacob can be called 'our father' (Isa. 58:14; John 4:12).

JACOB'S LADDER. The subject of a fugitive's dream, assuring Jacob of undeserved divine care (Gen. 28:10–22). The local rock formations doubtless prompted Jacob to dream of a 'stairway'.

JACOB'S WELL. Located by John 4:5–6 in the Shechem area; given by Jacob (John 4:12) to Joseph (Gen. 48:21–22; Josh. 24:32). The immense amount of rubble in the well today confirms that the well is indeed 'deep' (John 4:11).

JAEL. Wife of Heber the Kenite, who lured the Canaanite general Sisera to his death (Judg. 4:17–22).

JAHAZ. Moabite town (Isa. 15:4; Jer. 48:34) where Israel defeated the Amorite king Sihon (Num. 21:23).

JAIR. Minor judge (Judg. 10:3).

JAIRUS. Synagogue ruler whose young daughter Jesus raised from the dead (Luke 8:49–56).

JAMBRES. *See* Jannes.

JAMES. 1. Son of Alphaeus, an apostle (Matt. 10:3), usually identified with James the younger (Mark 15:40).

2. The Lord's brother (Matt. 13:55). Accepted Jesus as Christ only after the resurrection (John 7:5; 1 Cor. 15:7); leader of the Jerusalem church (Acts 12:17; 15:13–21; Gal. 1:19).

3. Son of Zebedee (Matt. 4:21), the first apostle to be martyred (Acts 12:2). With brother John, their father, and Peter and Andrew, partners in fishing (Luke 5:10). One of the trio closest to Jesus (Matt. 17:1; Mark 26:37) who nicknamed him and John 'Sons of Thunder' (Mark 3:17; Luke 9:54).

4. Father of the apostle Jude (Luke 6:16).

JAMES (*letter*). Written by the Lord's brother, soon after AD 40, emphasising practical Christian conduct and common features with Judaism. Themes include faith and works (2:14–26), law (1:25; 2:8–13; 4:11–12), poor and rich (1:9–11; 2:1–7; 5:1–6), prayer (5:13–18), second coming (5:7–9), speech (3:1–12), submission to God (4:1–12), temptation (1:2–8, 12–15).

JANNES and **JAMBRES.** According to the Dead Sea Scrolls (on Exod. 7:11), magicians who vied with Moses (2 Tim. 3:8).

JANOAH. Town in Galilee, captured by the Assyrians (2 Kings 15:29).

JAPHETH. One of Noah's three sons (Gen. 5:32), saved from the flood (Gen. 7:13). His descendants (Gen. 10:2–4; 1 Chron. 1:5) are associated with Anatolia and the Aegean.

JAR. *See* Domestic life p. 52.

JARMUTH (*Height*). Leading Amorite city near Beth-Shemesh, with an estimated population of 2000 (Josh. 10:3–23).

JASHAR, BOOK OF. Lost collection of songs about national heroes (Josh. 10:13; 2 Sam. 1:18).

JASON. Jewish convert dragged before Thessalonica magistrates for harbouring Paul and Silas as alleged agitators. Released on giving security (Acts 17:5–9), though Paul and Silas had to depart (Acts 17:10).

JAVAN. Son of Japheth (Gen. 10:2); name applied to Mediterranean areas where his descendants settled, especially Greece (Ezek. 27:13, AV/KJV).

JAWBONE. Samson's weapon against the Philistines at a spot afterwards called Ramath-Lehi, '*Jawbone Hill*' (Judg. 15:15–18).

JAZER. Transjordanian town, near modern Amman, whose rich pastures attracted in turn Amorites, Israelites, Ammonites and Moabites (Num. 21:32; Josh. 13:25; Isa. 16:8; Jer. 48:32).

JEALOUSY. God tolerates no rivals (Exod. 20:5; Deut. 32:16). Human jealousy (Gen. 37:4; 1 Sam. 18:8; Acts 13:45) inevitably leads to sin (Gen. 37:20; 1 Sam. 18:11; Acts 13:50). A wife suspected of unfaithfulness could be subjected to trial by ordeal (Num. 5). Presumably her conscience influenced the result of drinking the 'water of bitterness'.

JEBUSITES. Tribe descended from Canaan (Gen. 10:16) and occupying Jerusalem (1 Chron. 11:4) and surrounding highlands (Num. 13:29).

JEDIDIAH (*Loved by the Lord*). God's name for the infant Solomon (2 Sam. 12:25).

JEDUTHUN. Levitical priest and head of a large family of musical prophets (1 Chron. 25:1–6; 2 Chron. 35:15).

JEHOAHAZ. 1. 11th king of Israel (874–798 BC); repeatedly troubled by Syria (2 Kings 13:1–9).

2. 17th king of Judah; reigned briefly (609 BC) before being exiled to Egypt by Pharaoh Necho (2 Kings 23:30–34). Also called Shallum (Jer. 22:11).

JEHOASH. Son and successor of Jehoahaz as 12th king of Israel (798–782 BC). Condemned for his godlessness (2 Kings 13:9–13). Captured Amaziah king of Judah and looted the Temple and palace (2 Kings 14:8–15).

JEHOIACHIN. Briefly king of Judah (597 BC; 2 Kings 24:8), also called Coniah (Jer. 22:24) and Jeconiah (Jer. 24:1). Deported to Babylon (2 Kings 24:12–15), but pardoned 37 years later by Nebuchadnezzar's successor (2 Kings 25:27–30).

JEHOIADA. Head of Jerusalem priests under Athaliah and Joash (2 Chron. 22:11). Plotted the deposition of Athaliah and the succession of young Joash (2 Chron. 23), whom he instructed in the law and prompted to repair the Temple (2 Kings 12). Died at 120 (2 Chron. 24:15–16).

JEHOIAKIM. Son of Josiah (1 Chron. 3:15) and 18th king of Judah (609–598 BC). Name changed from Eliakim by his Egyptian overlord (2 Kings 23:34–35). In 605 BC Jehoiakim became Nebuchadnezzar's vassal, but rashly rebelled in 602 (2 Kings 24:1) and in 598 met his death, aged 36 (2 Chron. 36:6; Jer. 22:18; 36:30).

JEHONANAB. *See* Jonadab 2; Rechabites.

JEHORAM. Confusingly, the name of two brothers-in-law, contemporary kings of Judah and Israel.

1. King of Israel (852–841 BC), after Ahaziah (1 Kings 22:50); also called Joram (2 Kings 1:17). Besieged Mesha king of Moab in Kir-Hareseth, but then withdrew in a panic (2 Kings 3:6–27). With Ahaziah king of Judah, attacked Hazael king of Aram, but was wounded at Ramoth Gilead (2 Kings 8:28–29). Returning to Jezreel to recover, assassinated there by Jehu (2 Kings 9:14–26).

2. King of Judah (848–841 BC), son and successor of Jehoshaphat (1 Kings 22:50) and husband of Ahab's daughter, Athaliah (2 Kings 8:18). Once securely king, massacred his six brothers. Suffered heavy defeats by Philistines and Arabs and finally was buried without honour (2 Chron. 21).

JEHOSHAPHAT. Son of Asa (1 Kings 22:41), 4th king of Judah (870–848 BC), praised for his faith (2 Chron. 17:3–9; 19:4–11). Unwisely sup-

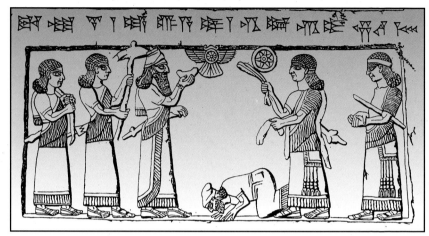

Obelisk relief of Jehu son of Omri

ported Ahab's attempt to recover Ramoth Gilead (2 Chron. 18), but won a remarkable victory over Moab and Ammon (2 Chron. 20:1–30). The '25 years' of his reign (2 Chron. 20:31) includes a co-regency of three years with Asa.

JEHOSHAPHAT, VALLEY OF. Symbolic location (Joel 3:2, 12) where God judges the nations. 'Jehoshaphat' (not a reference to the king of that name) is Hebrew for 'The Lord will judge'. *See* Valley of Decision.

JEHU. 1. Son of Hanani, who predicted the end of the house of Baasha king of Israel (1 Kings 16:1–7). Reprimanded king Jehoshaphat of Judah for supporting Ahab of Israel (2 Chron. 19:2). Wrote an account of Jehoshaphat's reign (2 Chron. 20:34).

2. Son of Jehoshaphat and 10th king of Israel (841–814 BC). Elisha sent a prophet to anoint him as king (2 Kings 9:1–13), thus completing

Elijah's commission (1 Kings 19:16–17). At Jezreel assassinated Jehoram of Israel, Ahaziah of Judah and Jezebel the queen (2 Kings 9:14–37). At Samaria wiped out the royal houses of Israel and Judah and slaughtered Baal's prophets (2 Kings 10).

JEHUDI. Son of Nethaniah who brought Jeremiah's scroll from Baruch and read it to a scornful king Jehoiakim (Jer. 36).

JEMIMAH (*Little Dove*). Job's first daughter after his restoration (Job 42:14).

JEPHTHAH. Judge and deliverer of Israel (Judg. 11:1–2:7). His rash vow if the Lord gave him victory involved his only daughter. Defeated Ephraimites fleeing over the Jordan fords were betrayed by their pronunciation when challenged by Jephthah's men.

JERAHMEEL. Jehoiakim's official who burned Jeremiah's scroll (Jer. 36:26).

JEREMIAH. Prophesied to Judah for 40 turbulent years (from 626 BC) through the reigns of Josiah, Jehoahaz, Jehoiakim, Jehoiachin and Zedekiah, until the fall of Jerusalem (587 BC). His sense of inadequacy was met with assurances of divine help (Jer. 1), despite antagonism and persecution (1:19; 11:19; 20:2; 26:8; 32:2; 33:1; 37—38; 43:2) and personal griefs (16:2; 20:14–18). Saved from exile to Babylon by being carried off to Egypt (43).

His unpopular messages from God made him a lonely man. He had some supporters: Ahikam (26:24), Gedaliah (39:14), Ebed-Melech (38:7–13), and his faithful secretary Baruch (32:12; 36; 45).

JEREMIAH (book). Contains the prophet's call (Jer. 1); God's warning messages for Jeremiah to proclaim (2—20); denunciation of kings and false prophets (21—24); Judah's 70-year exile (25—29); promise of restoration and a new covenant (30—33); warning not to flee to Egypt (40—44); message for Baruch (45); warnings to hostile nations (46—51).

JEREMIAH, LETTER OF (Apocrypha). Purports to be written by the prophet Jeremiah to Jews about to be exiled to Babylon. Ridicules the idols they will find there.

JERICHO. The world's lowest-lying city, 300 metres (900 ft) below sea level, in the Jordan Valley, N of the Dead Sea. City of Palm Trees (Deut. 34:3) where Eglon king of Moab was assassinated (Judg. 3:13–23). Home of Rahab (Josh. 2) before Joshua captured the city (Josh. 6). Unwisely rebuilt by Hiel of Bethel (Josh. 6:26;

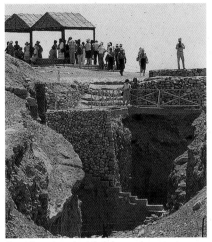
Remains of ancient Jericho

1 Kings 16:34). Scene of Jesus' healing the blind (Matt. 20:29; Mark 10:46) and home of Zacchaeus (Luke 19:1–9).

JEROBOAM. 1. Appointed overseer of forced labour by Solomon, but led a rebellion and had to flee to Egypt until Solomon's death (1 Kings 11:26–40). When the northern tribes rejected Rehoboam (1 Kings 12:1–15), Jeroboam became their king (1 Kings 12:20–25), reigning 931–910 BC. Erected sanctuaries at Bethel and Dan to dissuade northern tribes from going to the Jerusalem Temple (1 Kings 12:26–33). Denounced for misleading Israel (1 Kings 13:33; 14:20; 15:29–30; 2 Kings 13:6; 17:21–22).

2. Jeroboam II, son and successor of Joash as 13th king of Israel (2 Kings 13:13; 14:16). Condemned for injustice (Amos 5:11; 7:9–11; 8:4–6) during his long reign (793–743 BC).

JERUB-BAAL (*Let Baal Contend* [for himself]). Nickname of the judge Gideon (Judg. 6:32).

JERUEL. Wilderness SE of Tekoa, where the faith of king Jehoshaphat of Judah routed an alliance of Moab, Ammon and Edom (2 Chron. 20:16–26).

JERUSALEM. *See* pp. 118-119.

JERUSALEM COUNCIL. In AD 48, members of the Jerusalem church, led by James the Lord's brother, met representatives from Antioch, led by Paul and Barnabas, to determine how the now numerous Gentile converts should relate to the law of Moses, especially concerning circumcision (Acts 15).

JESHUA (*The Lord Saves*). High priest after the return from exile. Helped to rebuild the Temple and restore worship (Ezra 3). Contemporary with Haggai and Zechariah ('Joshua' in Hag. 1:1; Zech. 3:1–10).

JESHURUN (*Upright*). Poetic name for Israel (Deut. 32:15; 33:5, 26) and for God's Servant (Isa. 44:2).

JESSE. Grandson of Boaz and father of 8 sons, including David (Ruth 4:17; 1 Sam. 17:12). Mentioned in a messianic prophecy (Isa. 11:1, 10; Rom. 15:12) referring to the house of David.

JESUS (*Saviour*). Named by the angel (Matt. 1:21, 25). 'Jesus' is Greek equivalent of Hebrew 'Joshua'. Also known, from his background, as a Nazarene (Matt. 2:23; Mark 14:67) and a Galilean (Luke 23:6; foretold Isa. 9:1).

Born before Herod the Great's death in 4 BC at Bethlehem in Judea (Mic. 5:2; Matt. 2:1) of the Virgin Mary (Isa. 7:14; Matt. 1:18), though assumed to be Joseph's son (Matt. 13:55). Descended from David (Jer. 33:15; Matt. 1:17) of the tribe of Judah (Heb. 7:14). Circumcised and presented in the Temple (Luke 2:21–38). At 12 years (religious 'coming of age') taken to Jerusalem for his first Passover (Luke 2:41–50). Worked as a carpenter at Nazareth (Mark 6:3). At around 30 years (Luke 3:23), about AD 28 (Luke 3:1), baptised by his cousin John (Matt. 3:13–15), then faced Satan's attack in the desert (Matt. 4:1–11) before launching his public ministry, based on Capernaum (Matt. 4:13–17). Chose apostles (Matt. 4:18) and other messengers (Luke 10:1–17).

Proclaimed the good news of the kingdom of God (Isa. 61:1; Matt. 4:23), healed (Isa. 53:4; Matt. 8:17), raised the dead (Matt. 11:5), offered many signs to arouse faith (John 7:31), and taught (Matt. 7:29), often in parables (Matt. 13:13), all concentrating on the people of Israel (Matt. 15:21–28). Foretold his rejection by the Jewish leaders, and his death and resurrection (Matt. 16:21). Showed himself alive to his disciples over forty days (Acts 1:3), commissioned them to spread the good news to the world (Isa. 49:6; Matt. 28:19; Eph. 3:6), and finally went back to heaven with the promise of returning (Acts 1:11; 1 Thess. 4:14–17). *See* Brothers of Jesus; Christ; Son of God; Son of Man 2.

JESUS JUSTUS. *See* Justus 2.

JETHER. Gideon's eldest son who, because of his youth, dared not kill the Midianite kings (Judg. 8:20).

JETHRO. Also called Reuel (Exod. 2:18). Midianite priest who gave Moses his daughter Zipporah in marriage (Exod. 2:21; 4:18).

Following the Exodus from Egypt, advised Moses to delegate authority (Exod. 18:1–27).

JETUR. One of Ishmael's twelve sons (Gen. 25:15). His descendants fought against Israel (1 Chron. 5:19). Also the name of their country E of Jordan (= Greek Iturea in Luke 3:1).

JEWS. Originally, inhabitants of Judah (2 Kings 16:6). After the exile applied generally to Israelites (Ezra 4:12). In the NT, one who is not a Gentile (Gal. 2:14), Samaritan (John 4:22) or convert (Acts 6:5), distinctions done away in Christ (Gal. 3:28).

JEZEBEL. 1. Ahab's wife (1 Kings 16:31), an evil influence on her husband (1 Kings 21:25) and son Jehoram (2 Kings 9:22). Persecuted God's prophets and promoted Baalism (1 Kings 18:4, 19). Engineered Naboth's murder (1 Kings 21), but came to an ignominious end (2 Kings 9:30–37).
2. Symbolic name for a false prophetess, who like her OT namesake seduced God's people (Rev. 2:20).

JEZREEL. 1. Highland city of Judah (Josh. 15:56), E of Megiddo, where Ahab built a summer palace (1 Kings 21:1; 18:45–46). While recovering from wounds (2 Kings 8:29), Jehoram was assassinated by Jehu (2 Kings 9:22–24), who also ordered Jezebel's death (2 Kings 9:30–37) and wiped out the rest of Ahab's family (2 Kings 10:1–11). Home of Naboth (1 Kings 21:1).
2. Eldest son of the prophet Hosea (Hos. 1:4). The meaning of 'Jezreel' (*God Sows*) symbolises both the sowing of disaster and a reborn people (Hos. 1:5, 11).

Statue of Jesus the healer, Galilee

JEZREEL, PLAIN OF. Between Beth-Shan and Mt Carmel; scene of frequent battles.

JOAB. David's general (2 Sam. 8:16), renowned for many victories (2 Sam. 2:12–32; 10:6–14; 11:1–25; 12:26–29; 1 Kings 11:15–16; 1 Chron. 11:6). Remained loyal to David during Absalom's rebellion (2 Sam. 18:1–15). Reproached David for mourning Absalom's death (2 Sam. 19:1–8). Sided with Adonijah (1 Kings 1:7) and executed by Solomon (1 Kings 2:5, 28–34).

JOAH. Hezekiah's recorder (court herald). During the siege of Jerusalem (701 BC), involved in negotiations with the Assyrians (2 Kings 18:18).

JOANNA. Wife of Herod's steward Chuza; one of the wealthy women supporting Jesus (Luke

Jerusalem

Jerusalem. Captured by David about 1000 BC and made his capital (2 Sam. 5:5-9). By bringing the ark of the covenant into the city made Jerusalem also the religious centre, replacing Shiloh (2 Sam. 6:17-18; Ps. 122). Magnificently endowed by Herod the Great's works, including his rebuilding of the Temple (John 2:20). City destroyed in AD 70 (Mark 13:2).

God's chosen city (1 Kings 8:44; 2 Chron. 32:19), and so known as 'the city of God' (Ps. 46:4), 'the holy city' (Neh. 11:1), 'the city of the Lord' (Ps. 48:8), 'the city of the Great King' (Matt. 5:35), 'the Throne of the Lord' (Jer. 3:17). Also

called the City of David, strictly speaking meaning the old fortress (2 Sam. 5:7). Burial place of David (1 Kings 2:10), Solomon (1 Kings 11:43) and ten other kings. *See* Zion.

Jesus visited Jerusalem as an infant and as a boy of 12 (Luke 2:22, 42). Frequently there during his ministry, notably when cleansing the Temple (John 2:13-23) and to

complete his mission (Matt. 20:18-19). Scene where the first believers received the Spirit at Pentecost (Acts 2:5), suffered persecution (Acts 8:1; 9:2), and formed the mother church (Acts 15).

New Jerusalem is the heavenly city (Isa. 65:18-19; Rev. 3:12) and true home of believers (Heb. 12:22; Rev. 21).

The site of David's city of Jerusalem

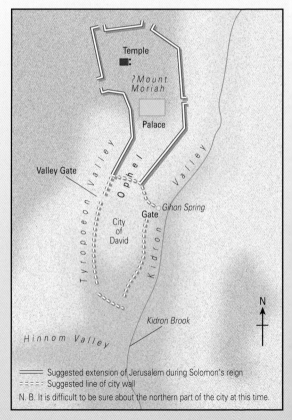

Temple
?Mount Moriah
Palace
Valley Gate
Tyropoeon Valley
Ophel
Kidron Valley
Gihon Spring
Gate
City of David
Kidron
Kidron Brook
Hinnom Valley

N

▬▬▬ Suggested extension of Jerusalem during Solomon's reign
= = = = Suggested line of city wall
N. B. It is difficult to be sure about the northern part of the city at this time.

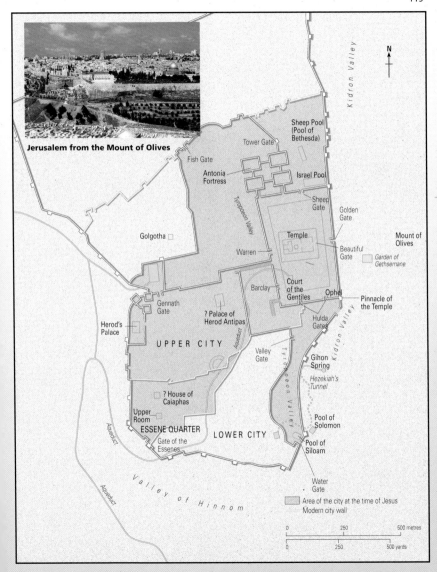

Jerusalem from the Mount of Olives

N

Kidron Valley

Sheep Pool
(Pool of
Bethesda)

Tower Gate

Fish Gate

Antonia
Fortress

Israel Pool

Sheep
Gate

Golden
Gate

Golgotha

Temple

Mount of
Olives

Warren

Beautiful
Gate

*Garden of
Gethsemane*

Tyropoeon Valley

Court
of the
Gentiles

Ophel

Barclay

Pinnacle of
the Temple

Gennath
Gate

? Palace of
Herod Antipas

Hulda
Gates

Herod's
Palace

Aqueduct

UPPER CITY

Valley
Gate

Gihon
Spring

*Hezekiah's
Tunnel*

Kidron Valley

Tyropoeon Valley

? House of
Caiaphas

Pool of
Solomon

Upper
Room

ESSENE QUARTER

LOWER CITY

Pool of
Siloam

Gate of the
Essenes

Aqueduct

Water
Gate

Aqueduct

V a l l e y   o f   H i n n o m

Area of the city at the time of Jesus

Modern city wall

0	250	500 metres
0	250	500 yards

8:3). Told the disbelieving apostles of the resurrection (Luke 24:10).

JOASH. 1. Father of Gideon, who roused the neighbours by destroying his father's Baal altar (Judg. 6).

2. Prison governor at Samaria ordered to imprison Micaiah for his unacceptable prophecies (1 Kings 22:26).

3. Ahaziah's baby son (also called Jehoash), hidden from Athaliah when she massacred the royal family. Six years later, Jehoiada the high priest led a coup, proclaimed Joash king of Judah, and Athaliah was killed (2 Kings 11). Later in his reign (835–796 BC), Joash rebuilt the Temple (2 Kings 12:5–16), but after Jehoiada's death allowed pagan practices to reappear (2 Chron. 24:17–22).

4. *See* Jehoash.

JOB. Outstandingly upright, wealthy and respected character of Uz in Edom, though a worrier (Job 1:1–5). Suddenly losing everything, he agonised over the mystery of God's love yet apparent hostility. James 5:11 commends Job's patient endurance.

JOB (book). The prose prologue (Job 1—2) describes Job's prosperous life being devastated by calamities. In a series of verse dialogues, he pours out his anguish, not so much about suffering as his bewilderment at God and his ways. Three well-meaning friends, Eliphaz, Bildad and Zophar (3—31), and then a fourth, Elihu (32–37), respond. In 38:1–42:6 God exposes Job's theology as far too narrow. In the prose epilogue God rebukes the friends and tells Job to pray for them. Then Job's health, wealth and family are restored (42:10–17). The book's author and date are alike unknown.

JOCHEBED. Daughter of Levi, born in Egypt, wife of Amram and mother of Moses, Aaron and Miriam (Exod. 6:20; Num. 26:59).

JOEL (*The Lord is God*). The best known of a dozen men of this name is one of the Minor Prophets, but his identity is a mystery. Even his father (Joel 1:1) is not mentioned elsewhere. His prophecy of Pentecost (Joel 2:28) is quoted in Acts 2:16.

JOEL (book). Vividly pictures a locust invasion (Joel 1:2–2:11) to warn Judah and Jerusalem of impending judgment if people fail to repent (2:12–17). But the Lord promises renewal (2:18–32). The Day of the Lord will bring judgment on the nations (3:1–16) and blessing for God's people (3:17–21).

JOHANAN (*The Lord Shows Favour*). Army captain who after the fall of Jerusalem (586 BC) supported Gedaliah, appointed governor by the Babylonians. Gedaliah fatally ignored his warning of Ishmael's assassination plot (Jer. 40:13–16). Johanan pursued Ishmael in vain (Jer. 41:11–18). Fearing Babylonian reprisals for Gedaliah's death, he rejected Jeremiah's advice and carried him off to Egypt with many of the people (Jer. 42—43).

JOHN (Gospel). The work of the apostle John, seeing deeper significance in Jesus' ministry (John 20:30–31), hence his description of miracles as signs (2:11). The Prologue (1:1–18) looks back to the pre-existence of the Word of God. After narrating Jesus' public ministry (1:19–12:50) and final private words to the disciples (13—17), describes Jesus' arrest, trial, crucifixion (18—19) and resurrection (20—21). *See* I am.

1 JOHN. Homily written by the apostle John as an eyewitness of Jesus' ministry (1 John 1:1–4) to encourage Christians against those who were now denying Christ (2:19, 22, 26). God is light (1:5) and love (4:8) and Jesus truly the Son of God (4:15; 5:1, 5). Spiritual knowledge is the privilege of all believers (2:20; 4:13) and is to be worked out in practical Christian living (2:3–6). Themes are repeatedly intertwined throughout.

2 JOHN. Brief letter addressed by the apostle to 'the elect lady and her children' (2 John 1), probably a symbolic reference to a church. John is warning them against false teachers (2 John 7–11).

3 JOHN. Personal note by the apostle, praising Gaius for his practical Christian life (3 John 1–8), warning him against the self-important Diotrephes (9–10) but commending Demetrius (12), men whose identity is otherwise unknown to us.

JOHN (*apostle*). Fisherman (Matt. 4:21) and apostle (Matt. 10:2); with Peter and James, Christ's closest companions (Mark 5:37; 9:2; 14:33). Entrusted with the care of Jesus' mother (John 19:26). Not named in his Gospel but called the 'beloved disciple' (John 13:23). *See* Boanerges.

JOHN THE BAPTIST. Born to Elizabeth and Zechariah in their old age (Luke 1:5–25, 57–80). Christ's herald (Mal. 3:1; Matt. 11:2–15). Fearless preacher (Matt. 3:1–12), soon silenced by Herod (Matt. 4:12; 11:2–14; 14:1–12).

JOHN MARK. *See* Mark, John.

JOIAKIM. High priest before the exile (Neh. 12:10, 12, 26).

JOIARIB. One of Ezra's messengers sent ahead from Babylon to ask Iddo, leader of a Jewish settlement, to find Levites and Temple servants to prepare for the exiles' return (Ezra 8:16–17).

JOKNEAM. Canaanite town guarding a pass between the Valley of Jezreel and the Sharon Plain (Josh. 12:22; 21:34).

JONADAB (or Jehonadab). 1. Son of David's brother Shemeah, who enabled Amnon to seduce Absalom's sister Tamar (2 Sam. 13:3–5, 32).
2. Son of Rechab, who helped Jehu to abolish Baalism in Samaria (2 Kings 10:15). Promoted Rechabites' nomadic life and abstinence from wine (Jer. 35:6–10).

JONAH. Prophet from Gath Hepher near Nazareth. Predicted that king Jeroboam II would restore Israel's old borders(2 Kings 14:25).

JONAH (book). Narrates a prophet's reluctance to allow Gentiles the chance to repent and so escape judgment. God shows him that no situation (Jon. 2:10) and no person (3:10; 4:10) is beyond his loving reach. Book quoted by Jesus (Matt. 12:39–41; 16:4).

JONATHAN (*The Lord Gave*). 1. Levite of Bethlehem, compelled to go with migrating Danites to serve in their sanctuary at Dan (Judg. 17—18).
2. Saul's son, whose lone attack on the Philistine outpost at Geba led to a great Israelite victory, nearly marred by the king's foolish order forbidding food (1 Sam. 14). Devoted friend of David (1 Sam. 18:1–4; 19:1–7; 20; 23:16–18). Killed at Gilboa (1 Sam. 31:2), greatly mourned

by David (2 Sam. 1). One surviving son, lame Mephibosheth (2 Sam. 9).

JOPPA. Modern Jaffa.

JORAM. *See* Jehoram 1.

JORDAN (*Descender*). Major river of Palestine, meandering over 220 km (138 mls) through a deep rift valley, while falling 900 metres (3000 ft) from Mt. Hermon through Lake Huleh and the Sea of Galilee to the Dead Sea, 390 metres (1300 ft) below sea level. Until Romans built bridges, crossing was restricted to fords (Judg. 3:28), impassable when river was in flood, except by divine intervention (Josh. 3:15–16). *See* Adam (place).

JOSEPH. 1. First son of Jacob and Rachel (Gen. 30:24). His dreams led to enslavement (Gen. 37) and prison (Gen. 39). His gift of interpreting dreams resulted in release and high office (Gen. 40—41). Famine brought his brothers and father to Egypt (Gen. 42—47). Jacob adopted Joseph's two sons (Gen. 49). Died at 110 (Gen. 50:26); buried in the Promised Land (Josh. 24:32).

2. The descendants (tribe) of the patriarch Joseph (Gen. 49:22), forming also, through his sons, the tribes of Ephraim and Manasseh (Num. 1:10).

3. Name sometimes applied to the northern kingdom (Ezek. 37:16).

JOSEPH OF ARIMATHEA. Wealthy member of the Sanhedrin and secret disciple (Matt. 27:57). Buried Jesus' body in his own tomb (Mark 15:43–46).

JOSEPH BARSABBAS. Candidate to succeed

River Jordan near the Sea of Galilee

Judas Iscariot (Acts 1:23).

JOSEPH OF NAZARETH. Descendant of David and husband of the Virgin Mary (Matt. 1:18). Assumed to be Jesus' father (Luke 4:22). By trade a carpenter (Matt. 13:55) in Nazareth (Luke 2:4). Not mentioned during Jesus' ministry, so had probably died by then.

JOSHUA (*The Lord Saves*). Moses' aide (Exod. 17:9–14; 24:13; 33:11; Num. 13:8, 16). The comparable Greek name is 'Jesus' (Heb. 4:8, AV/KJV).

JOSHUA (book). Describes Joshua's call to succeed Moses and lead the Israelites into the Promised Land (Josh. 1). Crosses Jordan (2—4), circumcises the Israelites (5), and captures Jericho (6) and Ai (7—8). Makes a treaty with

Gibeonites (9), captures many towns in Canaan (10-12), and allocates the land among the twelve tribes (13—22). Makes a final exhortation to the nation (23) and renews the covenant at Shechem (24).

JOSIAH. Son of Amon and Jedidah (2 Kings 22:1), who became the 16th king of Judah (640–609 BC) at the age of eight. Reforms he began in 628 BC (2 Chron. 34:1–7) were accelerated in 622 when workmen found the Book of the Law during Temple repairs (2 Chron. 34:14–33). Re-established the Passover (2 Chron. 35:1–19). His death at Megiddo fighting Pharaoh Necho halted reforms and Judah reverted to paganism, which soon led to exile. Mourned by Jeremiah (2 Chron. 35:25).

JOT and **TITTLE.** Jot is the smallest Greek letter (*iota,* transcribed '*i*' in English). Tittle is a tiny mark distinguishing certain Hebrew letters from one another. Jesus is saying (AV/KJV of Matt. 5:18; Luke 16:17) that nothing in Mosaic law is insignificant.

JOTHAM. 1. Youngest of 70 sons of Jerub-Baal (Gideon), who survived the massacre of his brothers by Abimelech and proclaims a fable against the institution of kingship (Judg. 9).
    2. Son of Uzziah (2 Kings 15:30) and 11th

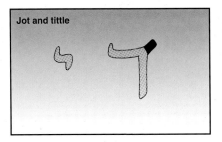

Jot and tittle

king of Judah (750–735 BC, including ten years co-regency with his leprous father, 2 Chron. 26:21). His faith led to successes against Ammon (2 Chron. 27).

JOY. For all its wars and wickedness, the OT uses an exuberant vocabulary of nearly 30 different Hebrew words for joy, especially towards God (Ps. 4:7; Hab. 3:18) and concerning the messianic age (Isa. 35). Fulfilled in Christ (John 8:56; 16:20–22), associated with the Holy Spirit (Acts 13:52; Gal. 5:22), and a mark of true discipleship (Phil. 4:4) even in suffering (Rom. 5:3; 1 Pet. 4:13).

JUBAL (*Trumpet*). Inventor of musical instruments (Gen. 4:21).

JUBILEE. *See* Year of Jubilee.

JUDAH (*Praised*). 1. Fourth son of Jacob and Leah (Gen. 29:35). Persuaded his brothers to sell Joseph into slavery instead of killing him (Gen. 37:26), but possessed a less savoury side (Gen. 38).
    2. Judah's descendants, forming the largest tribe (Num. 1:27). The royal house of Judah (Gen. 49:10) includes David (Jer. 21:11–12) and culminates in Jesus (Matt. 2:6; Heb. 7:14; Rev. 5:5).
    3. The kingdom of Judah, frequently distinguished from the north, Israel. Inhabitants exiled to Babylon (Jer. 52:27) for 70 years (Jer. 25:11–12; Dan. 9:2). By NT times called Judea.

JUDAISM. The Jewish way of life, dating from the Babylonian exile. By Paul's day (Gal. 1:13–14) included the 'traditions of the fathers', reinterpretations of Mosaic law to help Jews face conditions of their day (Mark 7:1–13).

JUDAS THE GALILEAN. Jewish freedom fighter (Acts 5:37) against the Romans about AD 6, heralding the rise of the Zealots.

JUDAS ISCARIOT. Apostle, notorious for betraying Jesus (Matt. 10:4), prompted by Satan (John 13:21–30) and greed (Matt. 26:14–15; John 12:4–6). Committed suicide (Matt. 27:1–5).

JUDAS SON OF JAMES. One of the Twelve (Luke 6:16; John 14:22); Thaddaeus in Matt. 10:3.

JUDAS MACCABAEUS. Exploits narrated in 1 Maccabees (Apocrypha). Third son the priest Mattathias (1 Macc. 2:4). Led a successful revolt against the Seleucid king Antiochus IV Epiphanes for desecrating the Temple in 167 BC (2:39–4:35). Marched on Jerusalem, purified the Temple and rededicated the altar (4:36–61), afterwards commemorated by the Feast of Hannukah or Dedication (John 10:22). Killed in battle (1 Macc. 9:1–18) in 161 BC. *See* Hasmonaeans.

JUDE (or Judas). Brother of Jesus (Mark 6:3) and author of the Letter of Jude; not an apostle (Jude 17).

JUDE (letter). Warns against immoral and heretical teachers infiltrating the church (Jude 4, 12, 16) and urges readers to stand firm in their faith (20–25). Fond of threesomes (verses 1, 2, 4, 5–7, 11, 12, 19), conspicuously absent from corresponding verses in 2 Peter.

JUDEA. Term for Judah from Roman times (Matt. 4:25).

JUDGE. Local courts of seven popularly elected judges (more in larger towns) were primarily for arbitration (Deut. 16:18; 2 Chron. 19:5), with harder cases going to higher courts (Deut. 17:8–11; 2 Chron. 19:8–10). The Book of Judges concerns individual political-military leaders in the turbulent period after the days of Joshua until Israel's first king. Samuel the last judge of this type (1 Sam. 7:15). God is supremely Judge of all (Gen. 18:25; Heb. 12:23), but has delegated the authority to Jesus (John 5:22, 27; Acts 17:31).

JUDGES (book). Traditionally attributed to Samuel. Describes Israel's periods of apostasy between the death of Joshua and the choice of Saul as king, the oppressed people's appeals to God and his sending deliverers (Judg. 2:16—16:31). The final chapters (17—21) tell of leaderless anarchy (21:25).

JUDGMENT, LAST. The first major event after Christ's second coming (Matt. 25:31–46). The judgment of believers is not for sin (2 Cor. 5:21; 1 John 1:7), which has been dealt with on the cross (Heb. 9:27–28; 1 Pet. 2:24), but a verdict on their Christian lives (1 Cor. 3:12–15; 1 Pet. 1:17).

JUDGMENT SEAT. Platform used as a judicial bench (John 19:13; Acts 18:12) or for official business (Acts 12:21). Metaphorically applied to unerring divine justice (Rom. 14:10; 2 Cor. 5:10).

JUDITH (Apocrypha). Describes how a beautiful Jewish widow enticed and murdered Nebuchadnezzar's general Holofernes, thus causing the besieging army to retreat. Written about 100 BC.

JULIUS. Centurion charged with bringing Paul from Caesarea to Rome (Acts 27:1). Disregarded Paul's warning about the crossing (Acts 27:11), but prevented the soldiers from killing the prisoners when the ship foundered (Acts 27:43).

JUNIAS. Greek literature provides 250 examples of the name, all feminine. In Rom. 16:7 perhaps the wife of Andronicus. Both are described as apostles before Paul. 'Apostle' thus applies to a larger group than the Twelve and includes a woman.

JUSTICE. Scrupulous fairness, characteristic of God (Gen. 18:25; Deut. 32:4; Ps. 45:6) and charged on human beings (Deut. 16:20; Isa. 56:1; Col. 4:1).

JUSTIFICATION. Right relationship with God (Hab. 2:4; Rom. 5:1) brought about by him (Rom. 4:1–8) in response to faith (Gen. 15:6; Gal. 3:6), not by following a code of practice (Rom. 5:1; Gal. 2:16; Phil. 3:4–9).

JUSTUS, JESUS. 1. Surname of a candidate to succeed Judas Iscariot (Acts 1:23).
2. Another Christian, with Paul when he writes to the church at Colosse (Col. 4:11).
3. Jewish sympathiser who welcomed Paul when the apostle broke with the synagogue at Corinth (Acts 18:7).

KABZEEL. Hometown of Benaiah (2 Sam. 23:20), in S Judah (Josh. 15:21), E of Beersheba.

KADESH BARNEA. Oasis in NE Sinai, on S border of Wilderness of Zin, where Miriam died (Num. 20:1). Israelite base when spies were first sent into Canaan (Num. 13:17, 26).

KADMONITES (*Easterners*). Early Canaanite tribe (Gen. 15:19), renowned for wisdom ('men of the East', 1 Kings 4:30).

KANAH. 1. Wadi along Ephraim-Manasseh border (Josh. 16:8), discharging into the Mediterranean, N of Jaffa.
2. Town of Lebanon foothills, SE of Tyre (Josh. 19:28).

KAREAH. Father of Johanan and Jonathan, who after Nebuchadnezzar captured Jerusalem joined Gedaliah at Mizpah (Jer. 40:8), but scorned Jeremiah's prophecy (Jer. 43:2–5).

KEBAR. *See* Chebar.

KEDAR (*Swarthy*). One of the twelve sons of Ishmael (Gen. 25:13), ancestor of a nomadic Arabian tribe in Transjordania (Ps. 120:5; Isa. 42:11), famed for bowmen (Isa. 21:17) and flocks (Isa. 60:7).

KEDEMAH (*Eastern*). Youngest son of Ishmael, ancestor of nomads of N Transjordania (Gen. 25:15), among the 'men of the East' famed for wisdom (1 Kings 4:30), but notorious for their antagonism towards Israel.

KEDEMOTH. Reubenite town (Josh. 13:18), N of the Arnon. Gave its name to the local desert (Deut. 2:26).

KEDESH. Cananite royal city, NW of Lakr Huleh, captured by Joshua (Josh. 12:22). Allocated to Naphtali (Josh. 19:37) and made a city of refuge (Josh. 20:7). Home of Barak (Judg. 4:6). In 734 BC taken by Tiglath Pileser III of Assyria (2 Kings 15:29).

KEILAH. Fortified lowland town of Judah. NW of Hebron (Josh. 15:44). David delivered it from a Philistine siege, but suspecting treachery retreated (1 Sam. 23:1–13).

KENAZ. Caleb's brother (Josh. 15:17) and father of the judge Othniel (Judg. 3:8–11).

KENITES (*Smiths*). Midianite tribe (Gen. 15:19) of S Judah whose friendly relationship with Israel (Num. 10:29; Judg. 4:11) was remembered (1 Sam. 15:6). Their faith led to the rise of the Rechabites (Jer. 35).

KENIZZITES. Tribe of S Canaan (Gen. 15:19) from whose ranks Caleb became a great supporter of Joshua (Num. 32:12; Josh. 14:6, 14).

KEREN-HAPPUCH (*cosmetic horn,* i.e. 'beautifier'). Job's third daughter after his restoration (Job 42:14).

KERETHITES. *See* Cherethites.

KERITH. *See* Cherith.

KETURAH. Abraham's concubine, mother of Arabian tribes (Gen. 25:1–6).

KEY. *See* House p. 101.

KEYS OF THE KINGDOM. Given by Jesus to Peter (Matt. 16:19), explained as the commission to bind or loose, an authority shared by all believers (Matt. 18:18; Acts 5:1–11; 13:8–11) and relating to the gospel, not to politics or a hierarchy.

KIDNEYS. Choice portion in sacrifices and always burned with the fat (Lev. 3:4; 1 Sam. 2:16). Figuratively, a person's inward being (Ps. 16:7; Jer. 12:20) and seat of emotions (Ps. 73:21); 'reins' in AV/KJV.

KIDRON (*Murky*). River and valley between Jerusalem and Mt. of Olives (2 Sam. 15:23; 1 Kings 2:37; John 18:1), for centuries a rubbish dump (2 Chron. 29:16; Jer. 31:40), and handy for burning pagan cult objects (1 Kings 15:13; 2 Kings 23:6).

KIMHAM. *See* Chimham.

KIN, NEXT OF. *See* Avenger of blood; Brother-in-law's duty.

KING. Israel looked to God as their king (Ps. 95:3) but political pressures (Judg. 17:6) brought a demand for a visible monarch (1 Sam. 8:5). As Samuel warned (1 Sam. 8:11–18), some Israelite kings became despots (2 Kings 21:1–18). Despite his shortcomings, David was looked back on as the ideal king (Isa. 9:7), a role perfectly fulfilled in Jesus (Jer. 23:5; Rev. 17:14).

KINGDOM. In biblical usage refers to royal rule and authority, not to a country.

KINGDOM OF GOD/HEAVEN. Leading Gospel theme, foreshadowed in the OT (Judg. 8:23; Ps. 93; Dan. 2:44; Matt. 11:11). Deferring to Jewish reluctance to mention the divine name, Matthew usually speaks of kingdom of heaven, not kingdom of God (compare Matt. 3:2; Mark 1:15; Luke 4:43). Major subject of Jesus' preaching (Matt. 4:17; 6:10; 7:21–23; 13:52) and of the apostles (Acts 8:12; 28:31; 1 Cor. 4:20).

1–2 KINGS. Narrates the history of 400 years of Israel's monarchy, from the death of David (965 BC) to the fall of Jerusalem and the final exile (586 BC). After Solomon's reign and his building of the Temple (1 Kings 1—11), the country is split. The affairs of the N kingdom of Israel (Samaria), from its establishment under Jeroboam I until the Assyrian conquest, and of the S kingdom of Judah, from Rehoboam to Ahaz (1 Kings 12—2 Kings 17) are followed by Judah's history from Hezekiah to the Babylonian exile (2 Kings 18—25). Each reign is dated, the king's achievements summarised and a spiritual assessment given.

KING'S GARDEN. Near the Pool of Siloam and irrigated by its waters (2 Kings 25:4).

KING'S HIGHWAY. International route from Gulf of Aqaba to Damascus (Num. 20:17). So called because it had royal protection as a diplomatic route. *See* Roads.

KING'S POOL. Pool of Siloam (Neh. 2:14).

KING'S VALLEY. Wide valley near Salem (Gen. 14:17), where Absalom erected a monument to

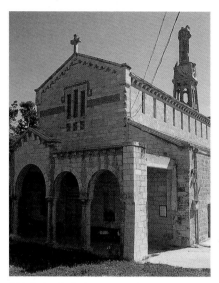

Kiriath Jearim today

himself (2 Sam. 18:18).

KINNERETH. *See* Sea of Galilee.

KIOS. *See* Chios.

KIR HARESETH. Heavily fortified Moabite capital, on a precipitous hill, E of Dead Sea. A serious siege persuaded king Mesha to sacrifice his son (2 Kings 3:25–27).

KIRIATH ARBA. Hebron (Judg. 1:10).

KIRIATH JEARIM (*Woodland Town*). Gibeonite capital (Josh. 9:17); Kiriath Baal in Josh. 15:60, indicating its earlier pagan associations. The ark of the covenant left here for 20 years (1 Sam. 7:1). Home of the prophet Uriah (Jer. 26:20).

KIRIATH SEPHER. Earlier name of Debir (Josh. 15:15).

KISH. Benjamite father of king Saul (1 Sam. 9:1–2) and ancestor of Mordecai (Esther 2:5).

KISHON. Wadi draining waters from the Plain of Esdraelon into the Mediterranean, N of Haifa. Scene of Sisera's defeat by Barak (Judg. 4:7) and Elisha's slaughter of the prophets of Baal (1 Kings 18:40).

KISS. Affectionate gesture within the family (Gen. 27:26; Luke 15:20) and between Christians (Acts 20:37; Rom. 16:16). Given to welcome (Luke 7:45), express romantic love (Song of Sol. 1:2), seduce (Prov. 7:13), or deceitfully to betray (2 Sam. 20:9; Luke 22:47). Used ceremonially in idol worship (1 Kings 19:18). *See* Greetings.

KITTIM. Cyprus (Num. 24:24; Jer. 2:10); settled by descendants of Javan (Gen. 10:4).

KNEES. Used as a symbol of adoption (Gen. 50:23; Job 3:12), entreaty (2 Kings 1:13), prayer (Dan. 6:10; Acts 20:36),reverence (Ps. 95:6), respect (Esther 3:2), worship (Isa. 45:23; Phil. 2:10). Weakened by fear (Dan. 5:6) or fasting (Ps. 109:24).

KNIVES. Earlier ones made of flint, which kept a sharper edge than bronze or iron. Used for circumcision (Josh. 5:2), pruning (Isa. 18:5), and in sacrifice (Gen. 22:6). Ritual self-mutilation (Lev. 19:28) condemned as pagan (1 Kings 18:28).

KNOP (AV/KJV). Knoblike decoration in Tabernacle (Exod. 25:31) and Temple (1 Kings 6:18).

KNOWLEDGE. In the Bible more usually concerned with experience (Gen. 3:7; 2 Chron. 1:10) than with intellect (Dan. 1:17; Acts 7:22); frequently related to God (Prov. 2:5; Jer. 9:24; Hos. 4:6; John 7:17), spiritual growth (John 8:32; 17:3) and discernment (Dan. 1:17; Matt. 12:25; Acts 14:9; 1 Cor. 12:8; 1 John 4:2). Euphemism for sexual intimacy (Gen. 4:1; Matt. 1:25, AV/KJV).

KOHATH. With his brothers Gershon and Merari, ancestors of the three divisions of Levites (Exod. 6:16–19). In the wilderness the Kohathites were responsible for the Tabernacle sanctuary (Num. 3:27–32; 4:1–20). Later prominent as Temple musicians (1 Chron. 6:33–48). Supported Jehoshaphat in his remarkable victory at En Gedi (2 Chron. 20:19) and helped Hezekiah to restore the Temple (2 Chron. 29:12).

KORAH. Notorious rebel against the authority of Moses and Aaron. With his supporters came to a dramatic end (Num. 16).

KORAZIN. *See* Chorazin.

L

LABAN. Son of Bethuel (Gen. 28:5) and Nahor (Gen. 29:5); Rebekah's brother (Gen. 24:29) and Jacob's uncle (Gen. 28:2). Tricked Jacob into marrying Leah before Rachel (Gen. 29:25, 28). But Jacob proved the wilier and enriched himself at Laban's expense (Gen. 30:25-43). Fled with family and wealth; Laban pursued him, but agreed to a pact (Gen. 31).

LABOUR, FORCED. Condition of peace for enemies surrendering to Israel (Deut. 20:11). By conscripting Israelites for his extravagant building works (1 Kings 5:13), Solomon stored up trouble for his successor (1 Kings 12:1-16).

LACHISH. Canaanite city, between Gaza and Jerusalem (Josh. 10:32). Captured by Sennacherib in 701 BC and made his base for attacking Jerusalem (2 Kings 18:14, 17).

LAKE OF FIRE. Doom of beast, false prophet (Rev. 19:20) and devil (Rev. 20:10); defined as the 'second death' (Rev. 20:14; 21:8), implying final separation from God (2 Thess. 1:9). The picture recalls the destruction of Sodom and Gomorrah (Gen. 19:24).

LAMB. *See* Domesticated animals p. 14.

LAMB OF GOD. Symbol for Christ (John 1:29, 35), used 28 times in Rev. (chapters 5-7; 12-15; 17; 19; 21-22), embracing the ideas of innocence, purity and sacrifice.

LAMECH. 1. Descendant of Cain and the first recorded polygamist; father of Jabal, Jubal and Tubal-Cain, forerunners respectively of nomads, musicians and smiths (Gen. 4:18-24).
2. Son of Methuselah and Noah's father; lived 777 years (Gen. 5:25-31).

LAMENESS. Disqualified a Levite from priestly service (Lev. 21:18) and an animal from being offered in sacrifice (Deut. 15:21). Healing the disability a messianic sign (Isa. 35:6; Matt. 11:5). Figuratively describes spiritual weakness (Heb. 12:13).

LAMENTATIONS (book). Traditionally attributed to Jeremiah (2 Chron. 25:35). Dirges describe Jerusalem's destruction and the exiles' despair (ch. 1), the Lord's disowning his rebellious people (2), Jeremiah's grief (3), Israel's former glory and present misery (4), and a final prayer for mercy (5).

LAMP. *See* Domestic life p. 53.

LAMPSTAND. Domestic use rarely mentioned (Dan. 5:5; Matt. 5:15). Seven-branched candelabrum (Menorah) in the Tabernacle (Exod. 25:31-40) and Temple (1 Kings 7:49). Symbolic of churches as centres of witness (Rev. 2:5).

LANDMARK. *See* Boundary stones.

LANDOWNER. Israelite families held land in tenancy, as from God (Gen. 13:15). So far as possible, land was inalienable (1 Kings 21:3). If

Ruins of ancient Laodicea

need compelled its sale, land must be restored to the original family every fifty years (Lev. 25). During NT times, much of Galilee was in the hands of foreign absentee landlords, the background to the parable of the tenants (Matt. 21:33).

LANGUAGES. *See* Aramaic; Greek; Hebrew; Latin; Tongues, speaking in.

LAODICEA. Phrygian city of Asia Minor. The church (Col. 2:1; 4:12–16) later earned rebuke from Christ (Rev. 3:14–22), his charges highlighted by the local situation: water was brought by aqueducts from Hierapolis (hot springs) and Colosse (cold); both supplies reached Laodicea lukewarm. White clothes spiritually needed by Christians contrasted with the local black wool which brought material wealth. Eye salve, famous at the Laodicean medical school, was

useless for spiritual sight. The door of fellowship with Christ (Rev. 3:20) was therefore shut – from the inside.

LAODICEANS, LETTER TO THE. Paul wrote more letters than the NT preserves (*see* 1 & 2 Corinthians), including one to the church at Laodicea (Col. 4:16).

LAPPING. To avoid misplaced boasts of prowess (Judg. 7:2), Gideon's army was reduced, first by releasing the fainthearted (Deut. 20:8; Judg. 7:3) and then by a test (Judg. 7:4). The 300 who did not kneel to drink from the stream (Judg. 7:5–7) demonstrated their watchfulness against surprise attack.

LASHES. The punishment of 40 lashes (Deut. 25:3) was in practice limited to 39 (2 Cor. 11:24) to avoid breaking the commandment.

LAST DAY. The day of general resurrection and judgment (John 6:39, 40, 44, 54; 11:24; 12:48). The 'last day of the feast' (John 7:37) was the eighth day of the Feast of Tabernacles, when the water libation was *not* poured out, adding significance to Jesus' claim to offer living water.

LAST DAYS. The time of Messiah's coming, foreseen by prophets (Isa. 2:2; Dan. 12:9; Mic. 4:1), fulfilled by Jesus and the Spirit (Acts 2:17; 1 Pet. 1:5, 20); marked by general godlessness (2 Tim. 3:1–5; 2 Pet. 3:3; Jude 18).

LAST TRUMPET. The final summons to God's people to gather (Isa. 27:13; Matt. 24:31; 1 Cor. 15:52; 1 Thess. 4:16). *See* Trumpet.

LATIN. Used by Romans for official business. With 'Hebrew' (strictly, Aramaic) and Greek, one of the three languages of NT times (John 19:20). About 27 Latin words (in Greek form) appear in the NT, including census, centurion, colony, legion, praetorium.

LATTICE. Wooden grill covering a window space (2 Kings 1:2; Prov. 7:6; Song of Sol. 2:9). Glass unavailable until Roman times. *See* Window.

LAVER. *See* Tabernacle p. 215.

LAW (Hebrew *Torah*). God's revelation to Israel to govern conduct, given through the first five OT books (Genesis to Deuteronomy, the 'law of Moses'). Disobeying the law (Deut. 27:26) meant rejecting God's authority. Jesus opposed legalistic interpretations of the law (Matt. 15:1–9) and drew out its deeper application (Matt. 5:17–48). He approved the essence of the law as love to God and neighbour (Matt. 22:37–40, quoting Deut. 6:5 and Lev. 19:18). *See* Book of the law.

LAW AND PROPHETS. Shorthand expression for the whole OT (Luke 16:16, 29). *See* Bible 2.

LAWGIVER. God alone is the true legislator and judge. Earthly courts act only on his authority (Isa. 33:22; James 4:12).

LAWLESSNESS. Disobeying God's commandments, his principles of right living, is sin (1 John 3:4). The 'man of lawlessness' (2 Thess. 2:3), not further identified, is doomed to destruction for doing Satan's work (2 Thess. 2:8–9).

LAWSUITS. Their multiplication a sign of national decadence (Hos. 10:4) and lack of spirituality (1 Cor. 6:1–8).

Illustration of a rabbi holding up the *Torah*

LAWYER. Jurist of Roman law (Acts 24:1; Titus 3:13). AV/KJV references are to scribes as experts in Jewish law.

LAYING ON OF HANDS. *See* Hand 3.

LAZARUS. 1. Brother of Martha and Mary of Bethany. Jesus raised him from the dead (John 11:1–44; 12:1–2), an action that divided opinion (John 11:45–53).

2. The only character in a parable given a name (Luke 16:19–31), doubtless because of its meaning (*God Helps*). The story underlines the perils of selfish luxury blinding eyes to the needs

of others, and after death the uselessness of former wealth and status and the impossibility of another chance to change one's mind. Earthly circumstances are not decisive in themselves, only attitudes towards them.

LEAD. Used in refining silver and gold (Jer. 6:29; Ezek. 22:18–20), some inscriptions (Job 19:24) and plummets for soundings at sea (Acts 27:28).

LEAH. Unattractive daughter of Laban (Gen. 29:16–17), whom Jacob was tricked into marrying (Gen. 29:29). Mother of Reuben, Simeon, Levi and Judah (Gen. 29:30–35) and of Issachar, Zebulun and Dinah (Gen. 30:16–21). Praised as one of the two women who 'built the house of Israel' (Ruth 4:11). Buried at Machpelah near Hebron (Gen. 49:31).

LEATHER. Animal skins treated by tanning. Used for garments (Lev. 13:48–59; Heb. 11:37), Tabernacle protection (Exod. 26:14) or containers for liquids (Gen. 21:14; Judg. 4:19; Matt. 9:17).

LEAVEN. *See* Yeast.

LEBANON (*White*). Mountain chain, 160 km (100 mi) long, parallel with the Palestine coast (Josh. 9:1), with peaks up to 3000 metres (nearly 10,000 ft). Named after its long-lasting snows (Jer. 18:14). Famed for cedar forests and timber trade (1 Kings 5:6).

LECTURE HALL. Hired by Paul when Jews stopped him preaching in the synagogue in Ephesus (Acts 19:9).

LEECH. *See* Insects p. 105.

LEES (AV/KJV). Sediment formed during maturing of wine. Removed by straining through a cloth (Isa. 25:6). Figuratively, of complacency (Jer. 48:11; Zeph. 1:12).

LEFT-HANDED. Ehud's ability surprised the unsuspecting king of Moab (Judg. 3:15). The advantage of the left-handed Benjamites (Judg. 20:16; 1 Chron. 12:2) was in rendering useless an adversary's shield on his left arm. Because Israelites took bearings by facing the rising sun, the left hand indicated N (AV/KJV of Gen. 14:15; Ezek. 16:46).

LEG. Legs of the crucified were broken to hasten death (John 19:31–33). Figuratively, of strength (Ps. 147:10; Rev. 10:1).

LEGION. *See* War p. 241.

LEHI (*Jawbone*). Town of Judah associated with Samson's weapon (Judg. 15:9–19).

LEMUEL (*Belonging to God*). Arabian king (Gen. 25:14), with a wise mother (Prov. 31:1–9).

LENDING. *See* Money p. 146.

LENTILS. *See* Foods p. 77.

LEOPARD. *See* Wild animals p. 16.

LEPROSY. Skin diseases (Lev. 13—14), requiring quarantine (even for a king, 2 Chron. 26:21). Biblical terms so translated may not always refer to true leprosy (Hansen's disease). Healing must be certified by a priest, the medical officer in Bible times (Lev. 14:1–32; Matt. 8:1–3).

LETTER, SMALLEST. *See* Jot and tittle.

LETTER WRITING. The form of NT letters followed the practice of the time: as in 1 Tim. 1:1–2, opening with the sender's name (Paul), authority (apostle), addressee's name (Timothy), prayerful greeting (grace, mercy, peace). At the end, a closing greeting (1 Tim. 6:21) and sometimes the sender's signature (2 Thess. 3:17) to authenticate the main contents, usually dictated to a scribe.

LEVI. 1. Third son of Jacob and Leah (Gen. 29:34). With Simeon, exacted vengeance upon Shechem for raping Dinah (Gen. 34). Their behaviour appalled Jacob (Gen. 49:5–7).

2. Earlier name of the apostle Matthew (Matt. 9:9; Mark 2:14).

LEVIATHAN. 1. Crocodile (Job 41).

2. Mythical seven-headed monster of the primeval chaos (Job 3:8; Isa. 27:1) and a symbol of evil (Ps. 74:14).

LEVITES. Descendants of Jacob's son Levi (1 Chron. 6), set apart to help in priestly duties, for which they received tithes instead of land (Num. 1:47–54; 18:21–32).

LEVITICUS. Details laws on holiness, sacrificial offerings (Lev. 1—7), Tabernacle service (8—10), ritual uncleanness (11—15), Day of Atonement (16), miscellaneous regulations (17—25), covenant promises and warnings against disobedience (26), redemption (27).

LIBNAH. Canaanite city near Lachish (Isa. 37:8); captured by Joshua (Josh. 10:29; 21:13).

LIBYA. Country W of Egypt. Libyan troops helped Shishak king of Egypt to invade Judah (2 Chron. 12:2–4; Lubim in AV/KJV). Home of Simon of Cyrene (Matt. 27:32) and of witnesses at Pentecost (Acts 2:10).

LIFE. God its source and giver (Job 27:3; Acts 17:25). Priceless (Lev. 24:17–18; Matt. 6:25). Although relatively brief (Ps. 90:10; James 4:14), its end not final for the believer (John 11:25). Its purpose, the service of God here (Josh. 24:15; Matt. 6:33; John 4:34) and hereafter (1 Thess. 4:13–17; Rev. 22).

LIGHT. God's creation (Gen. 1:3; 2 Cor. 4:6; Rev. 21:23) and a divine attribute (1 John 1:5), reflected in believers (Pss. 34:5; 2 Cor. 3:18). Available to all (John 1:9), but unacceptable to unbelievers (John 3:19). Figuratively, of God's word (Pss. 19:8; 119:105, 130; 2 Pet. 1:19) and of God's people (Luke 16:8; John 12:36; 1 Thess. 5:5).

LIGHT OF THE WORLD. Israel's commission (Isa. 49:6), now given to disciples (Matt. 5:14) because they are Christ's (John 8:12).

LIGHTNING. Natural references (Exod. 9:23; 2 Sam. 22:15; Ps. 135:7) relate to divine activity. Implies the divine presence (Exod. 19:16; Rev. 4:5) and describes the dazzling radiance of angels (Dan. 10:6; Matt. 28:3). The Seventy's joyful surprise on using Jesus' name is evidence of Satan's fall (Luke 10:18). 'Like lightning' alludes not to brightness but to sudden unexpectedness. 'Heaven' speaks of the exalted position of power, now lost forever by Satan (Isa. 14:12; John 12:31; Rev. 12:7–10).

LIKENESS. Representations of God forbidden (Exod. 20:4); no artistic likeness could express his limitless characteristics. Human likeness to God (Gen. 1:26; 5:1), marred by sin, is restored in Christ (1 Cor. 15:49; 2 Cor. 3:18).

LILY. *See* Plants p. 170.

LIMESTONE. Sedimentary rock formed from sea shells. Abundant in the central hills of Palestine, providing numerous caves (Gen. 19:30; Josh. 10:16; 1 Sam. 22:1), including those at Qumran, where the Dead Sea Scrolls were found.

LINEN. Luxury fabric, used especially for religious purposes (Exod. 25:4; Dan. 10:5; Matt. 27:59; Rev. 15:6). Woven from flax (Exod. 9:31; Josh. 2:6).

LINTEL. Wooden beam across top of doorposts (Exod. 12:22).

LION. *See* Wild animals p.16.

LION OF JUDAH. Messianic title of power (Rev. 5:5, alluding to Gen. 49:9–10).

LIVER. Usually mentioned with kidneys as a choice sacrifice (Exod. 29:13), being regarded as the location of life. Used in divination (Ezek. 21:21).

LO-AMMI (*Not My People*). Gomer's third child, like the second, Lo-Ruhamah, apparently the product of harlotry (Hos. 1:9).

LO-RUHAMAH (*Not Pitied*). Gomer's second child (Hos. 1:6), so named to reflect unfaithful Israel's threatened loss of God's tender mercy.

LOBE. Marked by blood as a sign of the priest's surrendering the organ of hearing to God's service (Lev. 8:23). A slave deciding to remain permanently in his master's service had his ear lobe pierced 'at the door', that is, in a public ceremony (Deut. 15:17).

LOCUST *See* Insects p. 105.

LOD. *See* Lydda.

LODGE. *See* Cucumber.

LOINS. As the site of reproductive organs, metaphor for physical descent (Gen. 35:11, av/kjv), strength and drive (Job 40:16) or secret designs (Jer. 11:20; 17:10; Rev. 2:23). Choice part of sacrificial animal, representing the worshipper's best offering (Lev. 3:4). To 'gird up the loins' is to tuck up outer dress to prepare for action (Exod. 12:11). *See* Reins.

LOIS. Timothy's maternal grandmother (2 Tim. 1:5).

LOOM. *See* Domestic life p. 53; and illustration, p. 245.

LORD. Most translations distinguish between three uses of the English word:
   1. lord (no capital), as a respectful address (Gen. 23:11);
   2. Lord (capital L), meaning master, without necessarily any religious overtones;
   3. Lord (all capitals), God's revealed name (Exod. 3:2).

LORD'S DAY. First day of the week (Rev. 1:10), commemorating the resurrection of Jesus (Matt. 28:1; Acts 20:7; 1 Cor. 16:2).

LORD'S PRAYER. Pattern prayer given by Jesus to his followers (Matt. 6:9–13; Luke 11:2–4).

LORD'S SUPPER. Farewell fellowship meal shared by Jesus with his disciples, to be re-enacted by believers as a reminder of Jesus' sacrifice (Matt.

26:17–29; 1 Cor. 11:20–34). *See* Bread, to break 2.

LORD'S TABLE. Paul's reference to the fellowship meal instituted by Jesus for his followers (1 Cor. 10:21), a contrast with the offerings table common to most pagan temples.

LOT. Son of Haran (Gen. 11:27). Emigrated to Canaan with uncle Abram (Gen. 12:5) before moving on to Sodom (Gen. 13). Rescued by Abram from raiders (Gen. 14:16) and by angels from Sodom (Gen. 19:16). Lot's involuntary incest led to the establishment of Moabites and Ammonites (Gen. 19:30–38). *See* Abraham.

LOTS, CASTING. Divination to discover God's choice, especially in allocating shares in the Promised Land (Josh. 18:6; Prov. 16:33). Marked stones or sticks gave a yes or no answer (Josh. 7:14–18; 1 Sam. 10:20–24; Acts 1:26). *See* Feast of Purim; Urim and Thummim.

LOT'S WIFE. Apparently overcome from sulphur fumes from Sodom's destruction (Gen. 19:26), her fate illustrates the consequence of disobedience and the unexpected suddenness of judgment (Luke 17:31–33; Heb. 10:38–39).

LOVE. God's love (1 John 4:16) describes the Father's relationship to the Son (John 5:20; 15:9) and to believers (John 14:21; 16:27), who in turn are bidden to love one another Heb. 13:1; 1 Pet. 2:17). The love of things is deplored (1 Tim. 6:10; Heb. 13:5), as is the failure to love God and his people (2 Tim. 3:2–4).

LUBIM. People of Libya (AV/KJV of 2 Chron. 12:3; Nah. 3:9).

LUCIUS. 1. Prophet-teacher serving the Antioch church (Acts 13:1–2), probably an early evangelist from Cyrene (Acts 11:20).

2. Jewish Christian of Corinth (Rom. 16:21).

LUKE. Gentile author of Third Gospel and Acts, about one quarter of NT. Doctor (Col. 4:14) and Paul's travelling companion (2 Tim. 4:11; Philem. 24), as indicated by the 'we' passages in Acts 16:10–17; 20:5–15; 21:1–18; 27:1–28:16. May be the 'brother' in 2 Cor. 8:18.

LUKE (Gospel). Written about AD 62 by the physician Luke. Relates the births of John the Baptist and Jesus (Luke 1—2), followed by Jesus' Galilean ministry (3:1–9:50), his final journey to Jerusalem (9:51–19:44), and his ministry, death and resurrection there (19:45–24:53). Luke's special interests include the Holy Spirit, joy, prayer, women, the disadvantaged.

LUST. Passionate desire, usually sexual (Prov. 6:25; Col. 3:5); metaphor for paganism (Ezek. 6:9).

LUZ. 1. Earlier name of Bethel, scene of Jacob's dream (Gen. 28:19).

2. Hittite city founded by man who betrayed the original Luz to the tribe of Joseph (Judg. 1:22–26).

LYCAONIA. Hilly region of Cilicia (NW Turkey), where Paul preached (Acts 14:6) and healed a cripple (Acts 14:8–18).

LYCIA. Mountainous coastal region of S Asia Minor. With Pamphylia formed a Roman province from AD 43 (Acts 27:5).

LYDDA. City SW of Joppa (1 Chron. 8:12), where Peter healed Aeneas (Acts 9:32–35).

LYDIA. 1. Coastal region of the Roman province of Asia. Provided mercenaries for Egypt (Isa. 66:19; Jer. 46:9) and Tyre (Ezek. 27:10).

2. Dealer at Philippi in purple cloth from Thyatira. Paul's first European convert (Acts 16:14–15).

LYING. Evident from the beginning: Satan (Gen. 3:4); Cain (Gen. 4:9); Abram (Gen. 12:10–20); Isaac (Gen. 26:7–9); Jacob (Gen. 27:24). Condemned (Exod. 20:16); taken seriously by the early church (Acts 5:1–11; 13:10; Eph. 4:29). Characteristic of false prophets (Isa. 9:15; Jer. 23:25) and of unbelievers (2 Thess. 2:9–12). Banished at the last (Rev. 20:10; 21:8; 22:15).

LYRE. *See* Music pp. 150-151.

LYSANIAS. Governor of Abilene (Luke 3:1). Mentioned in a local inscription dated between AD 14 and 29.

LYSIAS. Cognomen (family name) of the tribune Claudius (Acts 23:26; 24:22), acquired on becoming a Roman citizen.

LYSTRA. City of Lycaonia, SW of Iconium (NW Turkey). Roman colony from 25 BC. Paul's healing of a cripple aroused great enthusiasm, until Iconium Jews arrived (Acts 14:6–20; 2 Tim. 3:11). On a return visit, Paul enlisted Timothy (Acts 16:1–3).

M

MAASEIAH (*The Lord's Doing*). Favourite name with parents.

MACCABEES. Heroic Jewish family, who led the national revolt against the Seleucid king Antiochus IV Epiphanes. *See* Hasmonaeans; Judas Maccabaeus.

1 MACCABEES (Apocrypha). Written about 100 BC; narratesJewish history of 175–135 BC through the careers of Mattathias (1 Macc. 2), Judas Maccabaeus (3:1—9:22), Jonathan (9:23— 12:53), and Simon (13—16).

2 MACCABEES (Apocrypha). Another account of the Maccabaean Revolt, more concerned with its effect on the Temple; covers 180–161 BC.

MACEDONIA. Roman province of N Greece (Acts 16:9–14; 19:21–22; 20:1–6; 1 Tim. 1:3). Christians praised for their generosity (Rom. 15:26; 2 Cor. 8:1; 11:9).

MACHIR. Loyally protected Mephibosheth (2 Sam. 9:4–5); supported David with provisions (2 Sam. 17:27–29).

MACHPELAH. Field and cave, N of Hebron;

burial place for Sarah (Gen. 23:7–20), Abraham (Gen. 25:9), Rebekah, Isaac, Leah and Jacob (Gen. 49:29–33).

MAGADAN. Unidentified locality by the Sea of Galilee, visited by Jesus after feeding the Four Thousand (Matt. 15:39). Mark 8:10 has 'Dalmanutha', either an alternative name or a nearby place.

MAGI. Gentile astrologers, who interpreted a remarkable star as signifying the birth of a special Jewish king (Matt. 2:1).

MAGIC. Enlisting supernatural forces to secure information (divination) or marvellous results (sorcery). The practice widespread (Gen. 41:8; Dan. 1:20; Acts 8:11), but condemned (Ezek. 13:18–20; Rev. 21:8).

MAGOG. Said to be the country where Gog reigns (Ezek. 38:2; 39:6). With Gog, symbolises pagan nations allied against God's people (Rev. 20:8–9).

MAHANAIM. Gadite city in Gilead (Josh. 21:38) where Jacob camped before facing Esau (Gen. 32:2). David's base during Absalom's rebellion (2 Sam. 17:27).

MAHER-SHALAL-HASH-BEZ. (*Spoil Speeds, Prey Hastens*). Symbolic name given to Isaiah's third son to certify the prophecy of Assyria's imminent removal of Syria and Ephraim as threats to Judah (Isa. 8:1–4).

MAHLON AND CHILION (Kilion). Ephrathites from Bethlehem in Judah, sons of Elimelech and Naomi, and first husbands of Ruth and Orpah (Ruth 1:2–5; 4:9–10).

MAJESTY. God's greatness, glory and power (Exod. 15:7) and a divine title (Heb. 1:3; 2 Pet. 1:16), generating praise in his people (Pss. 8:1; 111:3) and terror among the godless (Isa. 2:10; 2 Thess. 1:9).

MAJOR PROPHETS. Five OT books (Isa., Jer., Lam., Ezek., Dan.), so called because of their comparative length, not greater importance.

MAKIR. *See* Machir.

MAKKEDAH. Canaanite royal city in the lowlands of Judah, captured by Joshua. Five local kings hiding in a cave were executed (Josh. 10).

MALACHI (*My Messenger*). Author of last OT book. Familiar with Temple conditions in Nehemiah's day, but nothing more is known about him.

MALACHI (book). Compiled as a dialogue between the Lord and his people. Graphically denounces slack religious life in Jerusalem (Mal. 1—2), but announces a coming messenger and a great outpouring of blessing (3—4).

MALCHUS. High priest's servant whose ear Peter cut off (John 18:10); healed by Jesus (Luke 22:51).

MALE. Ancient peoples preferred male children, to maintain the family line (1 Sam. 1:1), hence Pharaoh's attempt to restrict Hebrew families (Exod. 1:22). Inequality between the sexes abolished in Christ (Gal. 3:28). *See* Homosexuality.

MALKIJAH (*My King is the Lord*). Favourite name, given to about 12 men, including king Zedekiah's son into whose cistern Jeremiah was thrown (Jer. 38:6).

MALTA (Melita). Scene of Paul's shipwreck en route for Rome (Acts 27:43; 28:1), and of his healing local sick (Acts 28:8–9). No snakes on Malta today.

MAMMON. Aramaic and Greek term for property in general (Luke 16:9–13). People are stewards, not owners, of material wealth, which is to be used in the service of the true owner, God (1 Chron. 29:14).

MAMRE. 1. Amorite who helped Abram to rescue Lot (Gen. 14:13).
  2. Oak grove, the site of Abram's altar (Gen. 13:18), of God's promise of a son (Gen. 18:1–15), and from which Abram saw the smoke of Sodom's destruction (Gen. 19:27). Near Machpelah (Gen. 23:17).

MAN. Generic term for human beings (Gen. 1:27; Matt. 4:4) or meaning male not female (Gen. 2:23; Matt. 7:24). Both Hebrew and Greek make this clear by using different words. *See* Adam; Image of God.

MAN OF LAWLESSNESS. Embodiment of rebellion against God and his laws, but identity much debated. An individual claiming to usurp God (2 Thess. 2:4; *see* Dan. 11:36) and closely associated with Satan (2 Thess. 2:9). His end is assured (2 Thess. 2:3, 8).

MAN OF SIN. AV/KJV rendering of 2 Thess. 2:3 for 'man of lawlessness' in more recent translations, following earlier MSS not available in 17th century. The meaning is the same (1 John 3:4).

MANAEAN. Prophet-teacher in the church at Antioch, foster brother of Herod the tetrarch (Acts 13:1).

MANASSEH. 1. Joseph's firstborn son (Gen. 41:51), adopted by Jacob (Gen. 48:5). His descendants formed the tribe of Manasseh (Num. 1:34); their territory, on both sides of the Jordan (Josh. 13:29; 17:1–18), bore the same name (Judg. 6:35).
  2. Son of Hezekiah (Jer. 15:4) and king of Judah for 55 years (696–642 BC), a reign marked by bloodshed and apostasy (2 Kings 21:1–18), Deported to Babylon (then part of the Assyrian empire) but had a change of heart and was restored (2 Chron. 33:10–13).

MANASSEH, PRAYER OF (Apocrypha). Purports to give his prayer of repentance when in exile (2 Chron. 33:18).

MANDRAKE. *See* Herbs and spices p. 93.

MANGER. Feeding trough for cattle, often a hollowed-out limestone block (Job 39:9; Isa. 1:3; Luke 2:7). Term also applied to stable (Luke 13:15).

MANNA (*What is it?*). Breadlike food miraculously provided during Israel's wilderness years (Exod. 16:31). Symbolic of spiritual food now offered by Christ for life's journey (John 6:31–35).

MANOAH. Samson's father, a Danite of Zorah (Judg. 13:2; 16:31).

MANSION (*stop for travellers*). Archaic term (John 14:2, 23, AV/KJV) derived from Latin Vulgate.

MANTLE. *See* Dress p. 54.

MAON. Highland city, S of Hebron. Refuge for David and his men from Saul (1 Sam. 23:24). Home of surly Nabal (1 Sam. 25).

MARA (*Bitter*). Naomi's forlorn self-designation on returning to Bethlehem from Moab (Ruth 1:20).

MARAH (*Bitter*). First campsite after Israel crossed the Red Sea (Exod. 15:23), only to find the local water undrinkable.

MARANATHA (Aramaic, '*Come, our Lord!*'). Prayer for Jesus' return (1 Cor. 16:22).

MARDUK. Chief Babylonian god (Jer. 50:2), otherwise called Bel (Isa. 46:1; Jer. 51:44). *See* Bel and the dragon.

MARESHAH. Lowland town in Judah (Josh. 15:44; 2 Chron. 11:8); scene of Asa's victory over Zerah's Ethiopians (2 Chron. 14:9–15).

MARK (Gospel). Written by John Mark, Peter's associate, about AD 65, and probably the earliest Gospel. Narrates in vivid pen pictures the Galilean ministry of Jesus (Mark 1:1—6:29), his withdrawal from Galilee (6:30—9:32), and brief return (9:33–50), his ministry in Judea and Perea (10), Passion (11–15) and Resurrection (16).

MARK (symbol). Brand or tattoo on hand or forehead commonly symbolised devotion to a god and claimed that god's protection. The protective 'mark of Cain' (Gen. 4:15), and the 'mark of the beast' (Rev. 13:16) are alike undefined.

MARK, JOHN. Son of Mary (Acts 12:12) who accompanied cousin Barnabas (Col. 4:10) and Saul to Antioch (John in Acts 12:25) on the first missionary journey (Acts 13:5, 13). Later went to Cyprus with Barnabas (Acts 15:37–39). With Paul during the apostle's imprisonment in Rome (2 Tim. 4:11; Philem. 24) and later with Peter (1 Pet. 5:13).

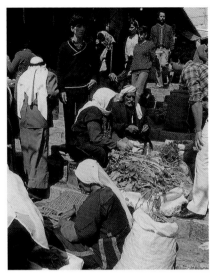

Market at Bethlehem

MARKETPLACE. Area inside city gate for selling goods (Amos 8:5) and services (Matt. 20:3), meeting people (Matt. 23:7; Mark 6:56; Acts 17:17), children's play (Matt. 11:16) and public business (Acts 16:19). Essential because 'streets' were narrow alleys.

MARRIAGE. Regarded as customary (no OT word for bachelor: Jer. 16:2 is exceptional, for a divine purpose. Usually arranged (Gen. 24). Mixed marriages forbidden to Israel (Deut. 7:3; 1 Kings 11:1–8; Ezra 9:12), as is marriage to an unbeliever (2 Cor. 6:14). The unique husband-wife relationship (Gen. 2:24; Matt. 19:4–6) symbolises God's covenant with his people (Isa. 54:5; Rev. 21:2). *See* Betrothal; Brother-in-law's duty; Dowry; Polygamy.

MARRIAGE OF THE LAMB. Fulfilment of OT expectation of God's intimate relationship with his people (Isa. 62:5; Jer. 3:14; Hos. 2:14–20). The NT applies the symbolism to Christ and his church (Eph. 5:25; Rev. 19:7).

MARS HILL. *See* Areopagus.

MARTHA (*Mistress*). Sister of Mary and Lazarus (John 11:1), close friends of Jesus at Bethany. As the elder sister, Martha took responsibility for entertaining (Luke 10:38–42). Responded to Jesus' teaching on resurrection (John 11:20–27).

MARTYR (*witness*). The NT normally retains the primary meaning of the Greek word (Acts 1:22), but the early church soon came to use the term to mean 'witness even to the point of death' (Rev. 2:13).

MARY (= OT Miriam). 1. While betrothed to Joseph, made pregnant by divine action (Isa. 7:14) and gave birth to the promised Messiah (Mic. 5:2–3; Matt. 1—2; Luke 1—2). Present at the beginning and end of Jesus' ministry (John 2:1; 19:25) and left in the care of the apostle John (John 19:27). With the disciples after the resurrection (Acts 1:14).

2. Sister of Martha and Lazarus at Bethany (John 11:1). Her devotion commended by Jesus (Luke 10:42). Anointed Jesus, anticipating his death (John 12:1–7).

3. Mother of James and Joses, among well-to-do women supporting Jesus (Luke 8:2). Present at the crucifixion (Matt. 27:56); early at the empty tomb (Mark 16:1), but disbelieved concerning the resurrection (Luke 24:9–11).

4. Mother of the evangelist Mark, in whose home disciples prayed for Peter in prison (Acts 12:12–17).

5. Hard-working Roman Christian greeted by Paul (Rom. 16:6).

MARY MAGDALENE. Delivered from seven demons (Mark 16:9). Supported Jesus (Luke 8:2). Present at the cross (Matt. 27:56), burial (Mark 15:40) and the empty tomb (Mark 16:1). The first to see the risen Christ (John 20:11–18).

MASCHIL/MASKIL. Heading of Ps. 32 and twelve other Psalms. Meaning unknown.

MASSAH (*Testing*). Spring on the Exodus route where Israel sorely tried God's patience (Exod. 17:7; Deut. 33:8).

MASTER. Different Greek words mean householder (Matt. 24:43), teacher (Matt. 23:8), 'one standing over' (Luke 5:5), or master of servants (Matt. 10:24), the last usually translated 'Lord' when referring to God or Christ (Matt. 3:3).

MASTER OF THE BANQUET. One appointed to regulate distribution of wine to prevent excess ruining a party (Ecclesiasticus 32:1; John 2:8).

MAT. *See* Domestic life p. 53.

MATTAN. Priest of Baal, killed with Athaliah (2 Chron. 23:17).

MATTANIAH (*The Lord's Gift*). Popular name with parents. Among those mentioned is Zedekiah (his original name, 2 Kings 24:17).

MATTHEW. Capernaum tax collector, called to be an apostle (Matt. 9:9); otherwise Levi (Luke 5:27).

MATTHEW (Gospel). Anonymous, but traditionally by the apostle; probably composed AD 60–70. The most Jewish of the Gospels, including many references to fulfilled prophecy (Matt. 1:22; 2:5, 15, 17, 23; 4:14; 8:17; 12:17; 21:4; 27:9). Chapters 1—2 cover the childhood of Jesus, followed by five sections of teaching, each ending with similar words (7:28; 11:1; 13:53; 19:1; 26:1). The book concludes with the Passion (26—27) and resurrection (28).

MATTHIAS. Chosen to replace Judas (Acts 1:23, 26).

MAZZAROTH. Probably signs of the zodiac; the Hebrew word (Job 38:32) is obscure.

MEAL. Wheat or barley grains ground for flour (Num. 15:20; Neh. 10:37).

MEAL OFFERING. *See* Grain offering.

MEALS. *See* Foods p. 76.

MEASURES. *See* Weights and measures p. 242.

MEASURING LINE. Used to decide allotments of land (Ps. 16:6) which were then marked by boundary stones (landmarks), not to be moved (Deut. 19:14). As symbolising all-inclusiveness, applied to divine justice (Isa. 28:17) or destruction (Isa. 34:11; Lam. 2:8).

MEAT MARKET. Paul's assurance that Christians need have no qualms about buying from a pagan market (1 Cor. 10:25) shows how free he now was from Jewish food restrictions.

MEDAD. *See* Eldad.

MEDES. Descendants of Japheth (Madai, Gen. 10:2). The conquerors of Babylon (Isa. 13:7; Jer. 51:28; Dan. 5:28).

MEDIA. Modern Azerbaijan and part of Kurdistan. Jewish settlers (Esther 1:3) present in Jerusalem at Pentecost (Acts 2:9).

MEDIATOR. Go-between bringing estranged parties together, as did Moses (Exod. 20:19; Num. 16:48) and Joab, for David and Absalom (2 Sam. 14). By the new covenant brought about by his perfect sacrifice, Christ is the mediator between human beings and God (1 Tim. 2:5; Heb. 8:6; 12:24).

MEDITATION. In the OT, not a silent practice (the Hebrew word means 'muttering'), as is clear from Josh. 1:8. Its object, to know God better through his word (Ps. 1:2) and works (Ps. 145:5). *See* Reading.

MEDIUM. Consulting a necromancer, one claiming to call up the spirits of the dead, was forbidden (Lev. 20:27; 1 Chron. 10:13).

MEEKNESS. Willingness to learn and carry out God's will (Num. 12:3) The only Beatitude quoted from the OT (Ps. 37:11; Matt. 5:5).

MEETING, TENT OF. Tent set outside the camp as a meeting place between God and his people (Exod. 33:7–11) before the construction of the Tabernacle, though the term is sometimes applied to the latter (Exod. 40:2).

MEGIDDO. Canaanite royal city, SE of Carmel, dominating the Plain of Jezreel. Captured by Israel (Josh. 12:21), but Manassites lost it (Judg. 1:27). Rebuilt by Solomon (1 Kings 4:12; 9:15).

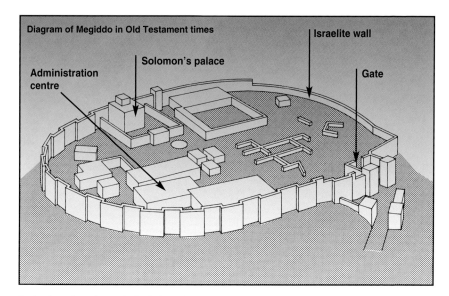

Diagram of Megiddo in Old Testament times

Administration centre

Solomon's palace

Israelite wall

Gate

Both Ahaziah and Josiah died there (2 Kings 9:27; 23:29). *See* Armageddon.

MELCHIZEDEK (*My King is Righteous*). Priest-king of Jerusalem who met Abram on his return from rescuing Lot (Gen. 14). Prefigured Christ (Ps. 110:4; Heb. 5:6).

MELITA. *See* Malta.

MEMPHIS (Noph in AV/KJV). Ancient capital of Lower Egypt, on the Nile S of Cairo; famous for pyramids. Site of numerous temples (Ezek. 30:13), a lure to Jewish refugees (Jer. 2:16; 44:1).

MENAHEM. King of Israel (752–742 BC) after assassinating Shallum. Vassal of the Assyrian king Tiglath-Pileser III (Pul, 2 Kings 15:14–22).

MENE, MENE, TEKEL, PARSIN. Words appearing on the wall during Belshazzar's feast, announcing the end of the Babylonian empire (Dan. 5:25–26). Everyone could read the words: mene, *numbered* or *mina* (a measure); tekel, *weighed* or *shekel;* peres (singular of parsin), *divided* or *Persia* or *half mina* or *half shekel*. But it needed Daniel to interpret their application. The U of Upharsin (AV/KJV) means 'and'.

MEPHIBOSHETH. Grandson of Saul, treated kindly by David for Jonathan's sake (2 Sam. 4:4; 9:6–13). His apparent disloyalty angered David (2 Sam. 16:1–4), who was later partly appeased by an explanation (2 Sam. 19:24–30).

MERAB. Saul's daughter, promised to David but given to Adriel of Meholah (1 Sam. 18:17, 19) by whom she had five sons (2 Sam. 21:8).

MERARI. Third son of Levi (Gen. 46:11), whose descendants (Merarites) form one of the three main classes of Levites.

MERATHAIM. Babylon (Jer. 50:21).

MERCY. Compassion towards the needy, characteristic of God (Deut. 4:31; Ps. 25:6; Mic. 7:18) and urged upon his people (Mic. 6:8; Matt. 5:7; Luke 6:36).

MERCY SEAT. Gold cover, supporting two cherub figures (Exod. 25:17–22), over the ark of the covenant. The place of God's meeting with Moses (Num. 7:89) and where blood was sprinkled on the Day of Atonement (Lev. 16; Heb. 9:3–5). Paul uses the Greek word in Rom. 3:25 ('propitiation', AV/KJV), implying that upon Christ Jesus, mercy seat of purest gold, rests the divine glory, for he is at once victim, priest and altar. *See* Ark of the covenant (p. 215).

MERIBAH (*Complaint*). Two campsites during Israel's wilderness wanderings (Exod. 17:7; Num. 10:13), both so called because people grumbled about lack of water. Moses suffered the backlash (Num. 27:14; Ps. 106:32–33).

MERODACH-BALADAN. Powerful king of Babylon, whose emissaries Hezekiah welcomed, to Isaiah's dismay (2 Kings 20:12–18; Isa. 39:1–7).

MESHA. King of Moab, who paid heavy tribute to Ahab. On Ahab's death, rebelled in vain against Jehoram. Besieged in his capital Kir Haraseth, he sacrificed his son on the city wall. Israel took fright and retreated (2 Kings 3:4–27).

MESHECH. Son of Japheth (Gen. 10:2). His barbarous descendants in Asia Minor (Ps. 120:5) traded in slaves as well as copper (Ezek. 27:13). Associated with northern hordes attacking Israel in the messianic age (Ezek. 38:3; 39:1).

MESHULLAM (*Replaced*). Popular name with parents following a lost child.

MESOPOTAMIA (*Between Rivers*). Land between Euphrates and Tigris (Gen. 24:10; Acts 7:2). Acts 2:9 may refer to descendants of Jewish exiles who stayed on in Babylonia.

MESSENGER. Swift courier on foot (2 Sam. 18:24) or on horseback (Esther 8:10; 'post' in AV/KJV), essential for early governments. Term also applied to prophets (Hag. 1:13), angels (Dan. 4:23) and specifically to John the Baptist (Mal. 3:1; Matt. 11:10).

METHUSELAH. The longest-lived patriarch, 969 years (Gen. 5:21–27).

MICAH (*Who is Like the Lord?*). 1. Ephraimite whose silver image became a snare to Danites who stole it (Judg. 17—18).

2. Prophet of Moresheth (Jer. 26:18), author of the OT book (Mic. 1:1), ministering some time between 740 and 686 BC.

MICAH (book). Foretells national destruction (Mic. 1) because of corrupt life (2) and leaders (3). The Lord's plan for Israel and Judah (4—5), though involving judgment (6), will bring final victory (7). Noted for the prophecy of Messiah's birth at Bethlehem (5:2) and for stressing obedience to God (6:6–8).

MICAIAH. Son of Imlah, who upset Ahab with his prophecies (1 Kings 22:8–28).

MICHAEL. Archangel guardian of Israel (Dan. 12:1); involved in spiritual warfare (Dan. 10:13, 21; Jude 9; Rev. 12:7). *See* Archangel.

MICHAL. Younger daughter of Saul, won by David as his wife (1 Sam. 14:49; 18:20–28). She saves his life (1 Sam. 19:11–17), but Saul spitefully gives her to another man (1 Sam. 25:44). Restored to David after Saul's death (2 Sam. 3:13–16), though scorn of David's dancing before the Lord led to her being cursed with childlessness (2 Sam. 6:16–23).

MICHMASH. Town N of Jerusalem (Isa. 10:28), near scene of Jonathan's triumph over the Philistines (1 Sam. 13:23 –14:14).

MIDDLE WALL OF PARTITION. Christ's destruction of the barrier separating Jew from Gentile (Eph. 2:14) alludes to the stone wall, 1.5 metres (5 ft) high, in the Court of the Gentiles. Its inscription in Hebrew, Greek and Latin forbade non-Jews going further into the Jerusalem Temple on pain of death.

MIDIAN. Son of Abraham, banished with Keturah's five other sons, seen as Isaac's rivals (Gen. 25:1–5). His nomad descendants (1 Chron. 1:32–33) inhabited desert country NW of the Gulf of Aqaba. Midianites carried Joseph into Egypt as a slave (Gen. 37:25–28, 36). Moses took refuge in Midian (Exod. 2:15), married a Midian priest's daughter (Exod. 2:21), and was there called by God to lead the Hebrews out of Egypt (Exod. 3:1–15; 4:18–19). For luring Israel into immorality and idolatry, Midianites suffered vengeance (Num. 31:1–12). Seven years of Midianite oppression were ended by Gideon (Judg. 7; Ps. 83:9).

MIGDOL. Frontier town of NE Egypt (Exod. 14:2). Home for some Jews in 7th century BC (Jer. 44:1). Its destruction foretold (Jer. 46:14). The expression 'from Migdol to Aswan (Syene)' indicates Egypt's N and S frontiers (Ezek. 29:10).

MIKTAM. Heading to Psalms 16 and 56—60. Meaning unknown.

MILCAH. 1. Daughter of Abram's brother Haran, wife of Nahor and mother of eight sons (Gen. 22:20–23).
2. One of Zelophehad's daughters who won the right to inherit (Num. 27:1–8).

MILCOM. The Ammonite god Molech (AV/KJV) of 1 Kings 11:5, 33; 2 Kings 23:13).

MILDEW. Fungus attacking grain (Deut. 28:22), clothing (Lev. 13:47) or a building (Lev. 14:34).

MILE. The Roman mile (Matt. 5:41), 1000 paces.

MILETUS. Flourishing commercial centre on W coast of Asia Minor (Acts 20:15, 17; 2 Tim. 4:20). Jewish settlement and site of a temple to Apollo. Local Christians warmly attached to Paul. Today the harbour is an inland lake due to silting by the river Maeander.

MILITARY SERVICE. *See* War p. 241.

MILK. *See* Foods p. 77.

MILL. *See* Domestic life p. 53.

MILLENNIUM (*1000 years*). Christ's first coming resulted in Satan's banishment from heaven (Rev. 12:9–17). His second coming means

The theatre at Miletus

Satan's banishment to the Abyss for 1000 years (Rev. 20:2–7), according to the divine, not the human, timetable (Ps. 90:4; 2 Pet. 3:8).

MILLO (*Mound*). Earthen platform to support a structure (Judg. 9:6, 20). In hilly Jerusalem, terraces formed by retaining walls filled with soil provided extra building space. Existing in David's day (2 Sam. 5:9); renovated by Solomon (1 Kings 9:15, 24; 11:27) and Hezekiah (2 Chron. 32:5).

MINING. Job 28:1–11 vividly describes the process.

MINISTRY. One giving personal service, usually meaning to God: by angels (Ps. 103:20; Matt. 4:11), Levites (Num. 16:9), priests (Joel 1:9). Those who serve Jesus (Matt. 27:55) are copying his example (Matt. 20:26–28). Evangelism is ministry (Acts 1:17; Rom. 11:13); so is church service in all its variety (1 Cor. 12; 1 Tim. 3).

MINOR PROPHETS. OT books from Hosea to Malachi, so called not for being less important but shorter than the Major Prophets (Isaiah to Daniel).

MINT. *See* Herbs and spices p. 93.

MIRACLE. Divine intervention to forward God's purposes (Josh. 4:23) and to witness to Jesus as Messiah (Matt. 11:2–5; John 2:11; Acts 4:10). *See* Healing; Signs and wonders.

MIRIAM (Mary in NT). Sister of Moses and Aaron (Num. 26:59), and a prophetess (Exod. 15:20–21). Stricken with leprosy for belittling Moses (Num. 12:1–15). Died at Kadesh (Num. 20:1).

MIRROR. Made of polished metal (Exod. 38:8), not glass. The reflection was indistinct (1 Cor. 13:12). Christians are to reflect their Lord (2 Cor. 3:18).

MIST. The rapid vanishing of mist before the rising sun symbolised God's ability to remove sins (Isa. 44:22), Judah's fickle love (Hos. 6:4), and the fate of idolators (Hos. 13:3) and false teachers (2 Pet. 2:17).

MITHREDATH. 1. Persian court treasurer who released the Temple vessels to Sheshbazzar (Ezra 1:8).
2. Persian official in Samaria who advised Artaxerxes to stop Jews rebuilding the Temple (Ezra 4:7).

MITYLENE. Town on Lesbos, off the W coast of Asia Minor (Acts 20:14).

Money

Debt. Could result in prison (Matt. 18:30) or slavery (2 Kings 4:1; Matt. 18:25). Figuratively describes the sinner's debt with God (Luke 7:42; 1 Pet. 1:18-19). *See* Interest; Pledge.

Interest. Not to be demanded of fellow Israelites but could be charged to foreigners (Deut. 23:19-20). Violating the prohibition resulted in poverty (Neh. 5:1-13).

Lending. Simple OT agricultural life needed loans only to tide over hard times, not for investment. No interest was to be charged to fellow Israelites, only to foreigners, and strict rules applied about pledges as security (Exod. 22:25-27). NT economy was more advanced and loans for investment could be made (Matt. 25:27). *See* Debt; Interest; Pledge.

Pledge. Security until payment is made (Gen. 38:17-20). Strictly regulated to protect the poor (Exod. 22:26).

Silver. Early measure of wealth (Gen. 13:2) and medium of exchange (Gen.

Coin of Pontius Pilate, A.D. 30

Coin of procurator Felix, AD 59

23:15); by NT times used as currency (Matt. 10:9; 27:3). Of less value than wisdom (Job 28:15); incapable of ransoming the soul (1 Pet. 1:18). Refining of silver figurative of purifying God's people (Zech. 13:9).

Tax. Apart from the atonement poll-tax (Exod. 30:11-16; Matt. 17:24), taxes came in with the monarchy –

as Samuel had warned (1 Sam. 8:10-18). Solomon's ambitious programmes demanded heavy burdens (1 Kings 5:13-17), which his successor Rehoboam foolishly increased (1 Kings 12:3-14). The NT accepts fair taxation as necessary (Matt. 22:17-21; Rom. 13:6-7). *See* Half-shekel.

Double shekel of Sidon.

Coinage

For centuries, payments were made by weighing out silver (Gen. 23:16) or by barter (Gen. 47:17; 1 Kings 5:10). First biblical mention is to the Persian *daric* (Ezra 2:69), introduced by Darius (521-486 BC). Greek and Roman monetary systems both operated in Palestine (Matt. 10:9). Greek coinage was based on the silver *drachma* (Luke 15:8). Two drachmas made a *didrachmon* (Matt. 17:24), four drachmas a *stater* (Matt. 17:27). The Roman money unit was the silver *denarius,* equivalent to a day's wages (Matt. 20:2). The widow's mite (Mark 12:42) was a bronze *lepta,* eight of which were worth an *as* ('farthing', Luke 12:6, AV/KJV).

Coin of Hygeia, Tiberias

Denarius. Basic Roman silver coin, the worth of a day's labour (Matt. 20:2; 22:19). Equivalent to Greek drachma (Luke 15:8).

Half-shekel. Annual atonement payment (Exod. 30:13-16), the basis of the Temple tax (Matt. 17:24). Paid by males from age twenty.

Shekel. Standard silver measure of weight (Gen. 20:16), which became a Jewish monetary unit in NT days; worth about four days' labour. The half-shekel poll-tax for all (Exod. 30:13-15) symbolised the common indebtedness of sinners to God, irrespective of rank or riches.

Top left: Coin of the Second Jewish Revolt, with the only known contemporary representation of Herod's Temple. Top right: Coin showing the Temple of Diana, Ephesus. Above: Coin of Nero.

Talent. Largest unit of measure, of about 30 kg (66 lbs) for weighing gold, silver, bronze and iron (1 Chron. 29:7). By NT times, the talent was a denomination of money, equivalent to about 6000 days' wages. The amounts mentioned in the parables (Matt. 18:24; 25:14-30) represent huge sums.

MIZPAH (*Watchtower*). 1. Benjamite town (Josh. 18:26), Israel's traditional assembly place (Judg. 20:1; 1 Sam. 7:5–12, 16; 10:17). Fortified by Asa (1 Kings 15:22). Governor Gedaliah assassinated there (Jer. 40—41).

2. Hometown of Jephthah (Judg. 10:17; 11:29), S of river Jabbok in N Gilead (Gen. 31:49).

3. Moabite town, a refuge for David's parents (1 Sam. 22:3).

MNASON. Early Cypriot convert (Acts 21:16).

MOAB. Name of Lot's son (Gen. 19:37), his descendants and their country, E of the Dead Sea. Moses was in Moab when instructed about Canaan (Num. 33:50—36:13). There he expounded the law (Deut. 1:5), renewed the covenant (Deut. 29—30), and viewed the Promised Land before his death (Deut. 34:1–6). Moabites often at odds with Israel (Num. 22—24; Judg. 3:12–30; 1 Sam. 14:47; 2 Chron. 20:1–23). Condemned by prophets (Isa. 15—16; Jer. 48; Ezek. 25:10–11; Amos 2:1–2; Mic. 6:5; Zeph. 2:8–9).

MOLECH. Ammonite god (1 Kings 11:5), denounced for the ritual practice of child-sacrifice (Lev. 18:21; Jer. 32:35).

MONEY. *See* pp. 146-147.

MONEY CHANGER. Converted pilgrims' coins into Temple currency to purchase sacrificial animals, wine and oil from stalls packing the Court of the Gentiles, and for payment of the half-shekel poll-tax (Exod. 30:11–16; Matt. 17:24). The commercial din made prayer impossible (Matt. 21:12–13).

MONTHS. *See* Farming year p. 73.

Moon-god

MOON. Phases signalled by trumpets (Num. 10:10; Ps. 81:3). The new moon marked the beginning of a new month and the day was designated a Sabbath (Isa. 1:13) with special sacrifices (Num. 28:11–15; Amos 8:5).

MOON-GOD. Widely worshipped, as archaeology reveals, especially at Ur and Harran, places associated with Abram's early days, and at Hazor. A fatal attraction to God's people (Deut. 4:19; 2 Kings 23:5; Col. 2:16).

MORDECAI. Esther's cousin and guardian (Esther 2:5–7), who uncovered a plot against king Ahasuerus (Esther 2:21–23). Refused to kowtow to the vizier Haman (Esther 3:2–6) who determined to exterminate all Jews. The plot failed and Mordecai succeeded him as vizier (Esther 5—7). The 'Day of Mordecai' (2 Macc. 15:36) was later equated with the Feast of Purim

(Esther 9:20–32).

MOREH, OAK OF. Sacred tree near Shechem where Abram built an altar (Gen. 12:6), Jacob buried idols (Gen. 35:4) and Joshua renewed the covenant (Josh. 24:26).

MORESHETH. Lowland Judah town near Gath (Jer. 26:18; Mic. 1:14).

MORIAH. Hill of Isaac's sacrifice (Gen. 22:2), identified with the site of the Temple (2 Chron. 3:1).

MORNING STAR (Venus). Identified with Jesus Christ (Num. 24:17; 2 Pet. 1:19; Rev. 2:28; 22:16), heralding the dawn of a new day.

MORTAR AND PESTLE.
See Domestic life p. 53.

MOSES. The greatest OT figure: Israel's liberator and lawgiver. The name is Egyptian for *son;* Hebrew wordplay associated it with his rescue from the Nile (Exod. 2:10).
Early life. Born into a Levite family (Exod. 2:1), but brought up as a prince (Exod. 2:5–10; Acts 7:22). When forty years old, kills an Egyptian in defending a Hebrew and has to flee to Midian, where he marries (Exod. 2:11–22). Forty years later, God calls him to deliver his people (Exod. 3:1–4:18).
Exodus. After many appeals to Pharaoh, reinforced by the plagues (Exod. 5—12), liberates his people (Exod. 13—14) and leads them for forty years in the wilderness (Exod. 15:22—18:27).
Law. God gives him detailed rules of moral and religious life for the nation (Exod. 19—40; Lev.; Num. 1—12; 15; 28—30) and instructions on life in the Promised Land (Num. 34—35; Deut. 7—31).

Final days. Praises God (Deut. 32) and blesses the tribes (Deut. 33). Dies aged 120 in sight of the Promised Land (Deut. 34).
Another Moses. Foretold (Deut. 18:15). Fulfilled in Jesus (Acts 3:20–22).

MOSES' SEAT. Stone seat on the synagogue platform near the sacred scrolls (Luke 4:20). Pharisees were the authorised teachers of the law of Moses (Matt. 23:2).

MOSES, SONG OF. Rev. 15:3 alludes to two great OT songs of Moses, exulting in divine deliverance (Exod. 15) and recounting God's mercies to his people (Deut. 32).

MOST HIGH. Divine title (Gen. 14:18–22; frequently in Psalms), expressing God's total supremacy (Ps. 91:9; Dan. 4:17; Mark 5:7).

MOST HOLY PLACE. *See* Holy of Holies.

MOTHER. Childlessness the greatest misfortune, but one God could overcome (1 Sam. 1). Used figuratively of God's love (Isa. 66:13) and of Christ's church (Gal. 4:21–31), and negatively of evil influence (Jer. 50:11–15; Rev. 17:5).

MOTHER-OF-PEARL. Included in mosaic pavement at the Susa palace of Ahasuerus (Esther 1:6).

MOTIVE. Unerringly known to God (1 Chron. 28:9; Matt. 22:18; 25:31–46; Luke 21:1–4).

MOUNTAIN OF GOD. Horeb (Exod. 3:1), otherwise called Sinai (Deut. 33:2).

MOUNTAINS. Dominating feature of Palestine. Ranges run N–S, influencing agriculture (Joel

Music

Musical instruments.
Identification hazardous, but included *Strings*: lyre (Gen. 4:21), the heart-shaped kinnor (1 Chron. 15:16), and several types of harp (1 Sam. 10:5; Ps. 71:22). *Wind instruments*: pipe (1 Kings 1:40; Matt. 9:23), horn (Josh. 6:4), trumpet (Num. 10:2), flute (Isa. 5:12). *Percussion*: cymbals (2 Sam. 6:5), bells (Exod. 28:33), drums (Exod. 15:20). Uncertainty about Nebuchadnezzar's Babylonian orchestra (Dan. 3:5) is evident from the variety of guesses in modern translations.

Cymbals. Bronze plates struck (2 Sam. 6:5).

Flute. Reed instrument, suitable for cheerful occasions (Isa. 5:12; Matt. 11:17) or sad (Jer. 48:36). Professional flautists were engaged for funerals (Matt. 9:23).

Harp. Not the modern instrument, but the lyre (Gen. 4:21; 1 Sam. 16:23).

Lyre. Stringed instrument (Gen. 4:21; Ps. 33:2) of wood (2 Sam. 6:5; 1 Kings 10:12).

Ram's horn. Used to hold oil (1 Sam. 16:1) or as a trumpet (Shofar; Josh. 6:4; Ps. 81:3).

Tambourine. Percussion instrument (Gen. 31:27; Exod. 15:20; Ps. 81:2). 'Timbrel' in AV/KJV.

Trumpet. Summoned Israelites to assemble (Num. 10:1; Joel 2:15) and to attend festivals (Lev. 25:8-12). Announced king's accession (1 Kings 1:39). Its piercing sound employed to call to arms (Judg. 6:33-35), give signals in battle (Josh. 6:16; Judg. 7:19; 2 Sam. 2:28) or warn of imminent danger (Jer. 4:5; Joel 2:1). Associated with divine activity (Exod. 19:16; Zech. 9:14; Matt. 24:31;1 Thess. 4:16; Rev. 8:7). *See* Last trumpet.

Hymn. The worship of God in religious song enjoined (Eph. 5:19; Col. 3:16) and practised (Acts 16:25; 1 Cor. 14:26), following Jesus' example (Matt. 26:30). Early Christian hymns may be behind such passages as Phil. 2:6-11; Col. 1:15-20; Heb. 1.

Songs, spiritual. Spirit-inspired songs (Eph. 5:19; Col. 3:16).

See also: Song of Ascents, Song of the Lamb, Song of Moses, Song of Solomon.

A Jewish rabbi blows a ram's horn trumpet

A lyre player

3:18), climate (Deut. 11:11), communications (Isa. 52:7), settlements (Exod. 15:17), worship (Deut. 12:2; John 4:21).

MOURNING. Included weeping (Luke 7:32), beating of breasts (Isa. 32:12; Luke 23:48), tearing clothes and wearing sackcloth (2 Sam. 3:31), fasting (1 Sam. 31:13; Matt. 9:15), hiring professional mourners (Jer. 9:17; Amos 5:16; Mark 5:38). Its absence a feature of New Jerusalem (Rev. 7:17; 21:4).

MOUSE. Vague general term for a rodent (Lev. 11:29). Bubonic plague spread by black rats is behind 1 Sam. 5:12; 6:4–5; Isa. 37:36.

MOUTH. Figuratively applied to divine authorisation (Num. 22:38; Jer. 1:9; Ezek. 3:27; thus mistakenly omitted as 'redundant' by some translations of Matt. 5:2), faith (Ps. 81:10), judgment (Isa. 11:4), death (Gen. 4:11), peril (2 Tim. 4:17), false doctrine (Rev. 14:5), speech (Pss. 10:7; 51:15; Prov. 15:2).

MULBERRY. *See* Trees p. 173.

MULE *See* Domestic animals p. 15.

MURDER. Deliberate homicide, attracting the death penalty (Num. 35:16–21), but only on corroborated testimony (Num. 35:30). *See* Cities of refuge.

MUSICAL INSTRUMENTS. *See* Music pp. 150-151.

MUSTARD. *See* Plants p. 170.

MUTE. Inability to speak (Ps. 38:13), the healing of which is a messianic sign (Isa. 35:6; Mark 7:37). Jesus' apparently bizarre actions in Mark 7:33–34 mimed to the deaf-mute what he was about to do: touching ears and tongue, spitting out the impediment, looking up to heaven and sighing (prayer).

MUTHLABBEN. Tune name or liturgical direction (Ps. 9, title). Meaning disputed.

MYRA. City of Lycia, SW Asia Minor. Its nearby port a staging post for the Alexandria-Rome grain fleet (Acts 27:5).

MYRRH. *See* Herbs and spices p. 93.

MYRTLE. *See* Plants p. 170.

MYSIA. Part of the Roman province of Asia from 129 BC, NW Turkey today (Acts 16:7–8; 20:5–13). Includes Adramyttium, Assos, Pergamum and Troas.

MYSTERY. In the Bible, a secret divinely revealed (Dan. 2:18), particularly concerning God's plan of salvation (Matt. 13:11; Rom. 16:25; 1 Cor. 2:7; Eph. 3:3; Rev. 10:7).

MYTH. In the NT, applied derogatorily to false stories (1 Tim. 1:4; 4:7; 2 Tim. 4:4; Titus 1:14).

N

NAAMAN. Syrian general cured by Elisha (2 Kings 5). Jesus mentions the incident to warn Jews of the consequences of unbelief (Luke 4:27).

NABAL (*Fool*). Wealthy sheep and goat farmer in Maon near Carmel, whose churlish behaviour would have led to violence but for his wife Abigail's intervention (1 Sam. 25).

NABOTH. Refused to sell the king his vineyard near Ahab's palace at Jezreel (1 Kings 21:1–16), since it was family property and so inalienable (Num. 36:7–9). Jezebel engineered Naboth's death (1 Kings 21:5–14), but on going to seize the property, Ahab was confronted by Elijah and warned of dire consequences (1 Kings 21:15–29; 2 Kings 9:21–37).

NADAB. Son and successor of Jeroboam I of Israel, assassinated by Baasha after a brief reign (910–908 BC). Denounced for his evil life (1 Kings 15:25–31).

NADAB and **ABIHU.** Two of Aaron's four sons (Exod. 6:23) who saw the divine glory on Mt. Sinai (Exod. 24:9). Consecrated as priests (Exod. 28:1–4), but that very day suffered dramatic retribution for sacrilege (Lev. 10:1–2).

NAHASH. Ammonite king whose defeat at Jabesh-Gilead established Saul as first king over Israel (1 Sam. 11).

NAHOR. Son of Terah and Abram's brother. Married his niece Milcah (Gen. 11:27, 29). His granddaughter Rebekah became Isaac's wife (Gen. 24).

NAHUM (book). Prophecy exulting over Nineveh's imminent fall on account of her savage cruelty and idolatry. Announces God's intention to destroy the Assyrian capital (Nah. 1); vividly describes the final onslaught of the Babylonians, Medes and Scythians in 612 BC (Nah. 2—3). Nineveh was never rebuilt.

NAILS. Prophets mocked idols that needed nails to keep them in place (Isa. 41:7; Jer. 10:4).

NAIN. Hill town SE of Nazareth, where Jesus raised a widow's dead son (Luke 7:11).

NAIOTH (*Dwellings*). District of Ramah, a refuge for David from Saul, and where Samuel headed a community of prophets (1 Sam. 19:18–24).

NAMES. Carefully chosen for their meaning (*examples in some entries*), often to indicate character, actual or hoped for. To 'call on the name' is to summon the aid of the one named to act according to character (Ps. 116:4).

NAMES, CHANGED. Indicate new destiny, character or relationship. Abram, *High Father* (empty name: childless at age 99); Abraham, *Father of a Multitude* (Gen. 17:5). Sarai, *Domineering*; Sarah, *Princess* (Gen. 17:15). Jacob, *Deceiver;* Israel, *Prince with God* (Gen.

32:28). Simon, *Heard* (i.e. born in answer to prayer); Peter, *Rock* (John 1:42).

NAOMI (*Sweet*). With her family driven by famine to Moab, where husband and sons-in-law die. Returns to Bethlehem with her daughter-in-law (Ruth 1). Encourages Ruth to marry Boaz, a kinsman (Ruth 2:1), and so preserve the inheritance within the family (Num. 27:8–11; Ruth 4:5). The marriage led to Naomi's becoming David's ancestor (Ruth 4:17–22).

NAPHTALI. Name of Jacob and Bilhah's son (Gen. 30:7), the tribe formed by his descendants and their territory (W of Sea of Chinnereth and Upper Jordan, Josh. 19:32–39). Jesus spent much of his ministry in the area, which included Gennesaret, Bethsaida, Capernaum and Chorazin (Matt. 4:15).

NAPKIN. Sweat cloth (Acts 19:12) or scarf to wrap around face of a corpse to keep mouth closed (John 11:44; 20:7). Used by the disloyal servant to hide money (Luke 19:20).

NARD. *See* Herbs and spices p. 93.

NATHAN (*Gift*). Prophet who informs David that his successor will build the Temple, although the Lord will build a house (dynasty) for him (2 Sam. 7). Rebuked David for his crimes against Uriah (2 Sam. 12). Instrumental in securing the succession for Solomon (1 Kings 1:8).

NATHANAEL (*God has Given*). Native of Cana and one of the first disciples (John 1:45–49; 21:2). Identified with the apostle Bartholomew because of his association with Philip (Matt. 10:3).

Church of the Annunciation, Nazareth

NAZARENE. Term applied to Jesus, because of his hometown of Nazareth (Matt. 2:23; Mark 14:67; 16:6), and thus to his followers (Acts 24:5).

NAZARETH. Galilean town (not mentioned in OT, Josephus or Talmud) on the road connecting Sepphoris, only 5 km (3 mi) away, with the Damascus-Egypt trade route, yet proverbially obscure (John 1:46). Home of Joseph and Mary (Matt. 2:23), and of Jesus for 30 years (Matt. 4:13; Luke 4:16).

NAZIRITES (*Consecrated*). Jewish men and women committed to God by a special vow, for a period or for life (Judg. 13:3–5; 16:17; 1 Sam.

1:11) and following the regulations in Num. 6:1–21.

NEAPOLIS. Seaport, SE of Philippi; base for Paul's Macedonian mission (Acts 16:11).

NEBAIOTH. Ishmael's firstborn son (Gen. 25:13) and ancestor of Arabian tribe renowned for sheep raising (Isa. 60:7).

NEBAT. Only mentioned as father of Jeroboam I (1 Kings 11:26), to distinguish his son from Jeroboam II.

NEBO (*Nabu*). 1. Babylonian god of wisdom and writing (Isa. 46:1), considered the son of Marduk (Bel). Names beginning with *Neb-* refer to this deity.
2. Mountain NE of Dead Sea, from which Moses last viewed the Promised Land (Deut. 32:49; 34:1).

NEBUCHADNEZZAR (*O Nebo, Preserve the Dynasty!*). Outstanding king of Babylon (reigned 605–562 BC), a great general and lavish builder; responsible for the Hanging Gardens of Babylon and many temples (53 unearthed). Invaded Judah, and after several rebellions captured Jerusalem on 16 March 597 (2 Kings 24—25). Jewish exiles (Jer. 25:11) included Daniel (Dan. 1—4).

NEBUZARADAN. Commander of Nebuchadnezzar's guard. In 587 BC destroyed Jerusalem and deported many Jews to Babylon (2 Kings 25; Jer. 52:26–30), but freed Jeremiah (Jer. 39:11–14).

NECK. Symbolised servitude (Deut. 28:48) or submission (Josh. 10:24; Jer. 27:2—28:14). *See* Stiff-necked.

NECKLACE. *See* Dress p. 54.

NECO. Pharaoh (610–595 BC) who vainly supported a failing Assyria against the rising Babylonians (2 Kings 23:29; 2 Chron. 35:20–24; Jer. 46:2).

NECROMANCY. Consulting the spirits of the dead about the future (1 Sam. 28:8), a practice forbidden (Deut. 18:10–12; Isa. 8:19).

NEEDLE, EYE OF THE. Ancient proverb for the impossible. A Jerusalem postern gate sometimes suggested is medieval.

NEGEB (*South*). Roughly SW of Dead Sea, often home for Patriarchs (Gen. 13:1; 24:62), Amalekites (Num. 13:29) and Canaanites (Num. 21:1). Beersheba the chief town under David (2 Sam. 24:7). Frequently the scene of battles (Josh. 10:40; Judg. 1:9; 1 Sam. 30:1; 2 Chron. 28:18; Jer. 13:19; Obad. 19–20).

NEHEMIAH (*The Lord Comforts*). Trusted official (Neh. 1:1) of the Persian king Artaxerxes (465–424 BC), who appointed him governor of Judea in 445 BC (Neh. 2:6). Despite local antagonism, rebuilt the wall of Jerusalem (Neh. 6:15), left his brother Hanani in charge (Neh. 7:2) and returned to Persia (433 BC). A second visit (Neh. 13:6) revealed the need for further reforms (Neh. 13:10–31).

NEHEMIAH (book). Based on Nehemiah's memoirs, tells of his determination to rebuild Jerusalem (Neh. 1:1–2:9), against fierce opposition (2:10, 19; 4:1–8; 6:1–14). Re-establishes religious life (8—10; 12) and removes abuses (13).

NEHUSHTA. Mother of Jehoiachin, king of Judah (2 Kings 24:8). Deported to Babylon (2 Kings 24:15; Jer. 22:24–27).

NEHUSHTAN (*Bit of Bronze*). Hezekiah's scornful description of Moses' bronze serpent (Num. 21:4–9) which people had now turned into an idol (2 Kings 18:4).

NEIGHBOUR. Anyone nearby, not necessarily next door. The NT often repeats the commandment to love one's neighbour (Lev. 19:18; Matt. 19:19; 22:39; Luke 10:27–36; Rom. 13:9; Gal. 5:14; James 2:8). Duty to neighbour frequently expounded (Exod. 20:16–17; 22:5–15; Lev. 19:13–18; Rom. 13:10; 15:1–2). 'Love your neighbor and hate your enemy' (Matt. 5:43) is not in the OT. Jesus refers to the contemporary view (echoed in the Dead Sea Scrolls).

NEPHILIM. Giants (Num. 13:33), descended from those mentioned in Gen. 6:1–4, apparently fallen angels who mated with women, an incident alluded to in 2 Pet. 2:4; Jude 6.

NERGAL. Popular Assyrian god worshipped by Cuthites who settled in Samaria (2 Kings 17:30).

NERO. Roman emperor (AD 54–68), when Paul appealed (Acts 25:11).

NET. Used to snare birds (Prov. 1:17), game (Isa. 51:20) and fish (Matt. 4:18). Fishermen used the circular casting net, 5 metres (15 ft) across, weighted at the edges. It was whirled around and skilfully dropped over a shoal in the shallows. The seine (dragnet) was 3 metres (9 ft) broad and very long, held upright by corks and weights, like a fence. The two ends were then brought together and hauled in. After use, nets

A fisherman casts his net

needed washing (Luke 5:2), drying (Ezek. 26:14) and mending (Matt. 4:21). Used figuratively for catching people (Ps. 57:6; Prov. 29:5; Ezek. 19:8; Hos. 5:1; Mic. 7:2), of human helplessness against God's power (Ezek. 32:3; Hab. 1:14–16) and of the kingdom of heaven (Matt. 13:47).

NETHER WORLD. Abode of the dead (Ezek. 31:14), the 'darkness' of 2 Pet. 2:4, 17; Jude 6, 13.

NETHINIMS. Temple servants (1 Chron. 9:2; Neh. 3:26; AV/KJV which simply transliterates the

Hebrew). Many had been exiles in Babylon (Ezra 2:58; 8:20).

NETOPHAH. Levite town (1 Chron. 9:16), SE of Bethlehem (Neh. 7:26).

NETTLES. *See* Plants p. 171.

NETWORK. 1. Bronze mesh under altar of burnt offering (Exod. 27:4), to facilitate airflow.

2. Interlacing bronze decoration on the two freestanding pillars (Jachin and Boaz) before Solomon's Temple (1 Kings 7:17); looted by Nebuchadnezzar (Jer. 52:22).

NEW MOON. Its first sighting from Jerusalem began a new month and was signalled by trumpets and hilltop torches to the rest of Israel. Day kept by a festival (Num. 28:11–15; Ezra 3:5; Col. 2:16). The 7th new moon, beginning the month of Tishri, which included the solemn Day of Atonement, was specially marked (Num. 29:1–6).

NICANOR. 1. General sent by Antiochus Epiphanes to put down the Maccabaean Revolt. His defeat and death (on 13 Adar 161 BC) celebrated by Jews as Nicanor Day (1 Macc. 7:49; 2 Macc. 15:36).

2. One of seven disciples appointed to relieve the apostles from 'serving tables' (Acts 6:5).

NICODEMUS. Challenged about spiritual rebirth (John 3). Later revealed his support for Jesus (John 7:50; 19:39).

NICOLAITANS. False teachers (Rev. 2:6, 15) charged with advocating pagan immorality, like Balaam (Num. 31:16; 2 Pet. 2:15). Apparently followers of an otherwise unknown Nicolas.

NICOLAS (Nicolaus). The only non-Jew of the Seven, appointed to distribute charity (Acts 6:5).

NICOPOLIS (*Victory City*). Paul's rendezvous with Titus (Titus 3:12), NW of Athens.

NIGER (Black). Teacher-prophet at Antioch (Acts 13:1).

NIGHT. Figuratively describes evil (Mic. 3:6; John 13:30). Its banishment a characteristic of heaven (Rev. 21:25; 22:5).

NILE. Annual flooding (Jer. 46:7; Amos 8:8) vital to Egyptian agriculture (Isa. 19:7). Prominent concerning Moses' early days (Exod. 2:1–10) and the plagues (Exod. 7—8).

NIMROD. Son of Cush, famous for hunting and military exploits; founded Nineveh (Gen. 10:8–12; 1 Chron. 1:10; Mic. 5:6).

NINEVEH. Ancient Mesopotamian city (Gen. 10:11) on E bank of Tigris. Assyrian capital in Sennacherib's day (2 Kings 19:36). Inhabitants surprised Jonah by responding to God's threat of judgment (Jon. 3:6; Matt. 12:41). The city's final destruction (612 BC) the subject of Zeph. 2:13–15 and the book of Nahum.

NISROCH. Assyrian god (2 Kings 19:37; Isa. 37:38).

NO (*Great City*). Thebes, capital of Upper Egypt (AV/KJV of Jer. 46:25; Ezek. 30:14–16; Nah. 3:8).

NOADIAH. 1. Levite exile who brought back silver and gold for the Temple (Ezra 8:33).

2. Prophetess confederate with Tobiah and Sanballat against Nehemiah (Neh. 6:14).

NOAH. Lamech's son (Gen. 5:29); his godliness (Gen. 6:9) led to his surviving the flood (Matt. 24:37–38) and being the subject of a divine covenant (Gen. 6—9; Isa. 54:9). Exemplar of faith (Heb. 11:7). His preaching (2 Pet. 2:5) not mentioned in OT but can be presumed.

NOB. Town of priests near Jerusalem (Isa. 10:32), where David was succoured by Ahimelech (1 Sam. 21:1–10), a gesture betrayed by Doeg the Edomite. Saul slew the inhabitants and only Abiathar escaped to join David (1 Sam. 22:9–20).

NOD (*Wandering*). Unidentified land E of Eden, where Cain was exiled (Gen. 4:14–16).

NOMADS. After settling in the Promised Land, Israel was reminded of spiritual lessons from their earlier nomadic life (Hos. 2:14–15; 12:9), the pilgrim life of God's people (Heb. 11:13—16; 1 Pet. 1:17; 2:11).

NORTH. *See* Left-handed.

NOSE RING. *See* Dress p. 54.

NUMBER SYMBOLISM. *One:* unity, completeness (Deut. 6:4; John 10:30). *Two:* unity (Exod. 32:15; Mark 6:7), witness (Num. 35:30; John 8:18; Rev. 11:3). *Three*: divinity (Matt. 28:19), divine acts (Exod. 19:11; Hos. 6:2; 1 Cor. 15:4). *Four:* completeness (Isa. 11:12; Jer. 49:36; Rev. 21:16). *Six:* humanity (Gen. 1:26–31; Exod. 20:9). *Seven* (3 + 4): wholeness (Gen. 2:2; 2 Kings 5:10). *Forty:* judgment (Gen. 7:4), testing (Deut. 8:2; Luke 4:2). *Triangular numbers* mentioned in Scripture: 120 (Acts 1:15), 153 (John 21:11), 276 (Acts 27:37). For 666, *see* Gematria. *See also* Seventy times seven.

NUMBERS (book). Although many numbers are quoted, the Hebrew title 'In the desert' more fittingly describes the contents. Narrates stages in Israel's wanderings, at Sinai (Num. 1:1–10:10); the journey to Kadesh (10:11–12:16), where rebellion delays progress (13:1–20:13); and finally on to Moab (20:14–32:42). Includes instructions regarding religious practice (5:1–10:10) and on life in the Promised Land ahead (27—30).

NURSE. Woman who breastfed a child (Gen. 21:7) or took care of one (Ruth 4:16, AV/KJV). Symbolic of nurture, care and protection (Num. 11:12; 1 Thess. 2:7, AV/KJV).

O

OAK. *See* Trees p. 173.

OBADIAH (*Servant of the Lord*). 1. Shielded the Lord's prophets from Jezebel (1 Kings 18:3–16).
2. Author of the OT book.

OBADIAH (book). Tells of Edom's punishment for taking advantage of Jerusalem's fall (587 BC).

OBED. Son of Boaz and Ruth (Ruth 4:17; Matt. 1:5).

OBED-EDOM. Philistine of Gath, greatly blessed for housing the ark of the covenant (2 Sam. 6:10–12).

OBEDIENCE. Both Hebrew and Greek words basically mean 'listen-and-respond to'. Essential for the godly life (Lev. 18:4; John 14:15). Applies to relationships with parents (Col. 3:20), church (Heb. 13:17) and the state (1 Pet. 2:13), though subject to the overriding authority of God (Acts 5:29).

OBELISKS. Symbol of the Egyptian sun god at Heliopolis (*See* On). Jer. 43:13 prophesies their destruction by Nebuchadnezzar.

ODED. Prophet in Samaria in the days of Pekah of Israel and Ahaz of Judah, who secured the release of prisoners of war (2 Chron. 28:6–15).

ODOUR, PLEASING. Figure of speech for divine acceptance (RSV of Gen. 8:21).

OG. Amorite king of Bashan, whose fertile territory was captured by Israel (Num. 21:33–35). His outsize bedstead displayed in Rabbah (Deut. 3:11).

OHOLAH. Allegorical name for faithless Samaria (Ezek. 23:4).

OHOLIAB. Divinely-inspired Danite craftsman, who helped to construct the Tabernacle (Exod. 31:6).

OHOLIBAH. Allegorical name for Jerusalem, acting the harlot(Ezek. 23:4).

OIL, OLIVE. *See* Domestic life, p. 53.

OLD AGE. Considered a mark of divine approval (Gen. 15:15; Isa. 46:4) and respected (Lev. 19:32) as wise (Job 32:9).

OLD MAN. Sinful human nature before renewal by Christ (Rom. 6:6; Eph. 4:22; Col. 3:9).

OLIVE. *See* Foods p. 77.

OLIVES, MT. OF (Olivet). Ridge overlooking E Jerusalem (Mark 13:3); in Jesus' day thickly covered with olive trees (Matt. 26:30). Location of Ezekiel's vision of divine glory (Ezek. 11:23) and of Jesus' ascension (Acts 1:12).

OMEGA. *See* Alpha.

The Old City of Jerusalem viewed from the Mount of Olives

OMRI. King of Israel, reigning 885–873 BC (1 Kings 16:16–28). *See* Samaria 1.

ON (*City of Pillars*). Egyptian centre of the sun-cult, N of Cairo. *See* Heliopolis; Obelisks.

ONAN. Met an untimely end for refusing to consummate his levirate marriage (Gen. 38:4, 8–10). *See* Brother-in-law's duty.

ONESIMUS (*Useful*). Philemon's runaway slave. Converted by Paul, he became a much-appreciated helper (Col. 4:9). Paul's letter to Philemon reveals the background.

ONESIPHORUS (*Profitable*). Succours Paul at Ephesus and Rome (2 Tim. 1:16–17; 4:19).

ONO. Town NW of Lydda (1 Chron. 8:12). Sanballat and Geshem tried to lure Nehemiah to meet them nearby (Neh. 6:2).

ONYX. Jewel in high priest's breastpiece (Exod. 25:7; 28:9–12). A foundation of the wall of New Jerusalem (Rev. 21:20).

OPHEL (*Swelling*). Spur jutting between Kidron and Tyropoen Valleys, fortified by David on capturing Jerusalem (2 Chron. 27:3; 33:14).

OPHIR. Renowned for finest gold (Gen. 10:29; 1 Chron. 29:4; Ps. 45:9; Isa. 13:12). Probably India, N of Bombay, location of commodities mentioned in 1 Kings 10:11; Job 28:16.

OPHRAH. 1. Benjamite town (Josh. 18:23), also called Ephron or Ephrain (2 Chron. 13:19), the Ephraim of 2 Sam. 13:23. NE of Jerusalem.

2. Gideon's home (Judg. 8:27), where his son Abimelech killed his own 70 brothers as possible rivals (Judg. 9:5).

ORAL TRADITION. Stories handed down by word of mouth, sometimes in song (Exod. 15:1; Num. 21:17; Deut. 31:30; Judg. 5:1). The western party game of whispering a message from person to person and expecting a mangled result at the end is baffling to the easterner, whose powerful memory has no difficulty in transmitting messages accurately.

ORION. Constellation (Job 9:9; 38:1; Amos 5:8), named after the mythical Greek hunter.

ORNAN. *See* Araunah.

ORPAH. Moabite wife of Chilion and Ruth's sister-in-law (Ruth 1:4, 14).

ORPHANS. God's special concern (Exod. 22:22; Ps. 68:5). They were to benefit from tithes (Deut. 14:29) and receive general support (James 1:27), especially in matters of justice (Deut. 24:17; Isa. 1:17).

OSNAPPAR. The Assyrian king Ashurbanipal (669–627 BC), who deported some peoples from Lower Mesopotamia to Samaria (Ezra 4:9–10, RSV; Asnapper in AV/KJV).

OSTRICH. *See* Birds p. 104.

OTHNIEL. Captured Kiriath-Sepher and won Caleb's daughter Achsah and important springs (Josh. 15:16–19). Rescued Israel from oppression by the Edomite king Cushan-Rishathaim (Judg. 3:8–11).

OVEN. *See* Domestic life p. 53.

OVERSEER. Literal meaning of the misleading term 'bishop' in AV/KJV (1 Tim. 3:1; 1 Pet. 2:25).

OWL. *See* Birds p. 104.

OX. *See* Domesticated animals p. 15.

OX GOAD. Long pointed rod, used to urge on oxen. Samson found one a useful weapon (Judg. 3:31). Occurs in a Greek proverb about the foolishness of fighting a god (Acts 26:14).

P

PADDAN ARAM. Mesopotamian homeland of Bethuel, Isaac's father-in-law (Gen. 25:20), where Jacob found a wife (Gen. 28:2–7).

PALESTINE. Name originally given by the Romans to Israel's Promised Land, by an irony derived from Israel's old enemy, the Philistines.

PALM TREE. *See* Trees p. 173.

PALSY. *See* Paralysis.

PAMPHYLIA. Fertile coastal plain of S Asia Minor, NW of Cyprus. Cities include Perga and Attalia (Acts 13:13; 14:25). Local Jews were in Jerusalem for Pentecost (Acts 2:10).

PAPHOS. Port of SW Cyprus and provincial capital (Acts 13:4–13).

PAPYRUS. *See* Plants p. 171.

PARABLE. Short story to convey a spiritual truth, usually with one main point of comparison. Distinctive feature of Jesus' teaching on the kingdom of God. Based on nature (Matt. 13:24–30) or everyday activities (Matt. 13:33, 47; Luke 10:30; 12:16).

PARADISE. From a Persian word meaning 'walled garden' (Eccles. 2:5; Song of Sol. 4:12). The comfort promised to the beggar Lazarus (Luke 23:43); the setting of Paul's heavenly vision (2 Cor. 12:4) and of the tree of life (Rev. 2:7, alluding to Gen. 2:9).

PARALYSIS. Its healing (Matt. 8:5–13; 9:1–8; 12:9–14; Acts 8:7) a messianic sign (Isa. 35:6).

PARAN. Wilderness in N Sinai; Ishmael's home (Gen. 21:21). Location of Israelite camp, from which spies were sent into Canaan (Num. 13:3). Mt. Paran (Deut. 33:2; Hab. 3:3) is poetic for Sinai.

PARAPET. Essential low wall guarding edge of flat roof (Deut. 22:8).

PARTHIANS. Inhabitants of a region SE of Caspian Sea. Local Jews (Acts 2:9) were descendants of Israelites exiled by Assyria in 8th and 7th centuries BC.

PARTRIDGE. *See* Birds p. 104.

PASHHUR. 1. Temple police chief, who punished Jeremiah for predicting Jerusalem's fall (Jer. 20:1–6).
  2. Priest son of Malkijah (1 Chron. 9:12) who consulted Jeremiah on behalf of king Zedekiah (Jer. 21:1) and then had the prophet dumped into a muddy cistern for demoralizing Jerusalem's defenders (Jer. 38:1–6).

PASSION. Term applied to the suffering and death of Jesus (Acts 1:3, AV/KJV).

PASSOVER. *See* Feast of Passover.

PASTOR. Endowment for local church leadership (Eph. 4:11) rather than to a definite office. Loyalty to Christ the Chief Shepherd is required (1 Pet. 2:25), self-sacrifice (John 10:11) and concern for the lost (Matt. 18:12–14).

PASTORAL EPISTLES. 1 & 2 Timothy and Titus, so called (from 1726) because they give advice to young Christian ministers.

PASTURE. Essential for agrarian life (Gen. 47:4; Num. 35:2–7). Its ruin symbolised desolation (Lam. 1:6; Ezek. 25:5). Spiritually, the blessing of believers (Ps. 37:3; John 10:9).

PATARA. Port of Lycia, SW Asia Minor, with an excellent harbour (Acts 21:1).

PATIENCE. Divine characteristic (Neh. 9:30; 1 Pet. 3:20), often translated 'longsuffering'. A fruit of the Spirit (Gal. 5:22), expressing love to others (1 Cor. 13:4) and trust in God (Ps. 40:1; James 5:7).

PATMOS. Small rocky Aegean island, SW of Ephesus (Rev. 1:9).

PATRIARCHS. Israel's founding fathers, usually meaning Abraham, Isaac, Jacob, Joseph and his brothers, although David is revered as one in Acts 2:29.

PAUL (*Small*). Roman name of Saul of Tarsus (Acts 13:9; 22:28). Once the persecutor of Christians, he was converted by a vision of Christ and appointed Apostle to the Gentiles (Acts 9:1–19). Made three great missionary journeys (Acts 13:1–14:28; 15:36–18:22; 18:23–21:14). Arrested in Jerusalem and after two years in prison in Caesarea (AD 58–60), he

appealed to Caesar and was sent to Rome (Acts 21:17—28:31). Martyred at Rome, about AD 65–67. Not all his letters have survived (*see* 1 & 2 Corinthians), but 13 (Rom.–Philem.) are included in the NT (*see* Hebrews, NT book).

PAVEMENT. Site of Pilate's judgment seat at the Praetorium (John 19:13).

PEACE. More than absence of war (Deut. 26:6). God's gift (Isa. 26:12; John 14:27; Gal. 5:22), to be prayed for (Num. 6:26; Rom. 1:7); a messianic sign (Isa. 9:6–7). The result of right relationship, with God (Rom. 5:1) and with others (1 Thess. 5:13), and so a common greeting (Dan. 10:19).

PEACE OFFERINGS. *See* Fellowship offerings.

PEACEMAKER. Not one who passively accepts a situation but confronts and resolves the difficulty (Matt. 5:9; 1 Pet. 3:11, quoting Ps. 34:14).

PEARL. The only gem formed by injury to an organism, a fact relevant to the gates of pearl (Rev. 21:21) providing the only entrance into the City of God (John 14:6). The gem's rarity value and beauty gives point to Matt. 7:6; 13:45.

PEKAH. Seized the throne of Israel by murdering Pekahiah (2 Kings 15:25–31).

PEKOD. Aramaean tribe dwelling E of the Tigris. Ezek. 23:23 foresees they will be one of God's instruments to punish Jerusalem (poetically called Oholibah, Ezek. 23:4).

PELATIAH. 1. Simeonite leader who drove out Amalekites from the hill country of Seir (1 Chron. 4:42).

2. Incited Jerusalem to rebel against Babylon. Fell dead on hearing his condemnation (Ezek. 11:1, 13).

PELETHITES. Members of David's bodyguard (2 Sam. 8:18), who proved loyal during the rebellions of both Absalom (2 Sam. 15:16–22) and Sheba (2 Sam. 20:7). Helped to secure Solomon's succession against Adonijah (1 Kings 1:38).

PELUSIUM. Greek name of Egyptian fortress, E of Nile delta. Destroyed by Nebuchadnezzar (Ezek. 30:15–16; Hebrew place name Sin in AV/KJV).

PENIEL (*Face of God*). Jacob's name for the pass where he wrestled with a mysterious 'man' (Gen. 32:30). Later fortified by a tower; destroyed by Gideon (Judg. 8:8–17), but rebuilt by Jeroboam I to defend his new capital of Shechem (1 Kings 12:25).

PENINNAH. Elkanah's second wife, who mocked Hannah's childlessness (1 Sam. 1:1–4).

PENTATEUCH (*Five-volumed [book]***).** First five OT books (Gen. to Deut.), the 'book of the law' (Neh. 8:3), 'book of Moses' (Neh. 13:1) or 'law of Moses' (Dan. 9:11).

PENTECOST (*Fiftieth*). Term for the 50th day after Passover, the OT Feast of Weeks (Exod. 34:22; Deut. 16:16). Birthday of the Christian church (Acts 2:1), when 120 disciples were baptised in the Holy Spirit. *See* Feast of Weeks, p. 250.

PEOPLE OF GOD. Divine title for Hebrews as the chosen race (Exod. 8—9; Acts 13:17). Applied to Christians (1 Pet. 2:10).

PEOR. Moabite mountain where Balak pressed Balaam to curse Israel (Num. 23:28). Location of Israel's idolatry (Num. 25:3; Ps. 106:28).

PERAEA. District NE of Dead Sea, part of Herod the Great's kingdom and of the tetrarchy of Herod Antipas. Most Jews travelled from Galilee to Judea through Peraea to avoid Samaria. Once Jesus conspicuously did not (John 4:4).

PERDITION. Eternal destruction (2 Pet. 3:7), fate of all evil forces opposing God (2 Thess. 2:3; Rev. 17:8, 11). Applied personally to Judas Iscariot (John 17:12).

PEREZ (*Bursting*). Twin brother of Zerah, sons of Tamar and Judah's incestuous union, so named because of the unusual violence of his birth (Gen. 38:28–30).

PERGA. Religious centre in Pamphylia (Acts 13:13; 14:25).

PERGAMUM. Ancient capital of Mysia; in the Roman province of Asia and a centre of emperor worship (Rev.1:11; 2:12).

PERIZZITES. Highland people (Josh. 17:15) near Shechem (Gen. 34:20) whom Israel met in Canaan (Gen. 13:7; Josh. 3:10).

PERJURY. Lying under oath; condemned (Lev.6:3) and will be judged (Mal. 3:5; 1 Tim. 1:10) for God is the God of truth (Ps. 31:5).

PERSECUTION. Opponents' malicious words (Ps. 69:26; Matt. 5:11) or actions, the inevitable lot of believers (John 15:20; 2 Tim. 3:11). In the early days, mob violence (Acts 14:19), and later

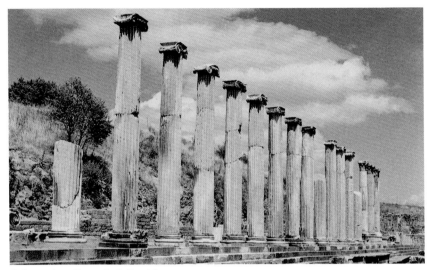

Columns from the ancient city of Pergamum

official policy (Heb. 10:33; 11:37; Rev. 2:10).

PERSEVERANCE. Steadfast persistence is to be a Christian characteristic (Gal. 6:9; James 1:3–4; 2 Pet. 1:6; Heb. 12:1), practised in prayer (Acts 1:14; Rom. 12:12; Col. 4:2), especially under trials (Rom. 5:3–4; James 1:12; 5:11; 1 Pet. 2:19).

PERSIA. Strongest under Cyrus the Great (559–530 BC); his empire extended to Egypt, Greece and India. Persian kings mentioned include Cyrus (2 Chron. 36:22), Darius (Ezra 4:5), Xerxes (Ahasuerus) (Esther 1:1), Artaxerxes (Ezra 4:7).

PETER (*Rock*). Fisherman (Matt. 4:18) of Bethsaida (John 1:44). Apostle (Matt. 10:2); renamed by Jesus (Mark 3:16). One of Jesus' inner circle (Matt. 7:1). Confessed faith in Christ (Matt. 16:16; John 6:69). By character, impulsive (Matt. 14:28), affectionate (John 13:9), presumptuous (Matt. 16:22), boastful (Matt. 26:33), penitent (Matt. 26:75; John 21:15–17), courageous (Acts 4:13), leader (Acts 1:15). Involved in miracles (Acts 3:7; 5:5, 10, 15; 9:34, 40) and powerful preaching (Acts 2:14–36; 3:12–26; 4:8–12; 5:29–32; 10:34–43). *See* Cephas.

1 PETER. Addressed to Christians in five Roman provinces (1:1) N of the Taurus mountains. Peter writes to encourage believers facing suffering and persecution for their faith (1:6; 2:12, 19–20; 3:13–17; 4:12–14; 5:8–10). The letter is soaked in the OT, referring to prophets and their messianic message (1:10–12), 'stone' imagery (2:4–8), people of God (2:9–10), Sarah and Abraham (3:6), Noah and the Flood (3:20). Many OT quotations (1:16, 24–25; 2:6, 7, 8, 22–25; 3:10–12, 14; 4:8, 18; 5:5, 7).

2 PETER. In his second letter (2 Pet. 3:1), Peter alludes to the prophecy of his death (1:14–15) and to seeing Jesus' transfiguration (1:16–18). He warns against libertines, men promising a freedom which amounts to moral licence and leads to sexual slavery (2:19). His opponents deny the lordship of Christ (2:1), final judgment (2:3, 9–10) and the second coming (3:4).

PETHOR. City on the Euphrates, S of Carchemish. Home of Balaam (Num. 22:5; Deut. 23:4).

PETRA (*Rock*). Nabataean capital, the biblical Sela (2 Kings 14:7).

PHARAOH. Title of Egyptian kings from 15th century BC. Considered divine and responsible for the people's welfare (Ezek. 29:3). Those named in OT are Shishak, So, Tirhakah, Neco, Hophra.

PHARISEES (*Separated Ones*). Lay sect who promoted oral additions to the law (Matt. 15:2), allegedly handed down by Moses with the written law. Usually receive a bad press in NT for their fastidiousness, to the neglect of more important matters (Luke 11:39–44).

PHILADELPHIA. 1. Decapolis city; OT Rabbah (Deut. 3:11); modern Amman.
2. Anatolian city (Rev. 1:11), benefiting much economically from pilgrims attending its many pagan temples. The Jewish community was at odds with local Christians (Rev. 3:7–13).

The Treasury, Petra

PHILEMON (Letter). Tactful note to a Christian of Colosse, converted by Paul (Philem. 19) and a sometime colleague (Philem. 1). The apostle urges Philemon to welcome back his runaway slave Onesimus, now a believer.

PHILETUS. Accused by Paul of heresy (2 Tim. 2:17).

PHILIP. 1. Called by Jesus (John 1:43) to be an apostle (Matt. 10:3). Lived in Bethsaida of Galilee, as did Peter and Andrew (John 1:44). Mentioned in connection with the feeding of the Five Thousand (John 6:5), Greek pilgrims (John

12:22) and his desire to see the Father (John 14:8).

2. One of the Seven chosen to dispense relief (Acts 6:5). Ministered in Samaria (Acts 8:5–13), then to an Ethiopian official (Acts 8:26–38), and between Azotus (Ashdod) and Caesarea (Acts 8:39–40), where he settled (Acts 21:8–9).

3. Son of Herod the Great and Mariamne. Married Herodias, mother of Salome, but she left him to live with Herod Antipas (Matt. 14:3).

4. Son of Herod the Great and Cleopatra of Jerusalem. Married Salome, daughter of Herodias. Unusually for a Herod, a good ruler (Luke 3:1), reigning from 4 BC to AD 34. The only Herod to mint coins bearing the emperor's likeness.

PHILIPPI. Commercial city, named after Philip II, father of Alexander the Great. Paul founded the local Christian community (Acts 16:12–40).

PHILIPPIANS (letter). Paul writes to thank Christians at Philippi for their support (Phil. 1:1–11; 4:1, 10–20) and warns against disunity (1:27; 2:2–4) and Jewish threats (1:28–30; 3:2).

PHILISTIA. Coastal region S of Carmel, locality of the five main Philistine cities (Josh. 13:3).

PHILISTINES. Sea peoples from Crete (Caphtor, Amos 9:7), who settled in the coastal region between Egypt and Gaza (Exod. 13:17). Abraham and Isaac on good terms with king Abimelech and his general Phicol (Gen. 20—21, 26), but later Philistines and Israel were enemies (Josh. 13:1–4; Judg. 3:1–4, 31). Samson married a Philistine wife, but it led to strife and his death (Judg. 13—16). Capturing the ark of the covenant caused the Philistines much trouble (1 Sam. 4—6). With chariots (1 Sam. 13:5) and a

Philistine priest

monopoly of iron (1 Sam. 13:19–22), they continued to harass Israel, until Saul (1 Sam. 13—31) and David (2 Sam. 5; 8; 21:15–22) overcame them. While a fugitive, David had forged a relationship with some Philistines (2 Sam. 15:18), who became loyal members of his bodyguard (1 Kings 1:38).

PHINEHAS (*Black*). 1. Grandson of Aaron (Exod. 6:25) who demonstrated his zeal for God (Num. 25:7–13; 31:6) and his diplomacy (Josh. 22:13–32).

2. Son of Eli. With his brother Hophni, priests at Shiloh (1 Sam. 1:3). Despised their office (1 Sam. 2:22–34) and were killed in battle (1 Sam. 4:11).

PHOEBE. Christian worker in Cenchraea (Corinth's port). Paul urges the Roman church to support her in some undefined commission (Rom. 16:1–2).

PHOENICIA. Coastal district of Canaan, from Mt. Carmel to the mouth of the Orontes. Home of a Gentile mother who secured her daughter's healing from Jesus (Matt. 15:21–28). Stephen's martyrdom led to the area being evangelised (Acts 11:19). Visited by Paul (Acts 15:3; 21:2).

PHOENIX. Harbour of S Crete (Acts 27:12).

PHRYGIA. Part of the Roman province of Asia from 103 BC. Local pilgrims were in Jerusalem for Pentecost (Acts 2:10). Visited by Paul (Acts 16:6; 18:23). Phrygian churches included those at Colosse, Hierapolis and Laodicea.

PHYGELUS and **HERMOGENES.** Among those who deserted Paul (2 Tim. 1:15). No reason is given.

Binding phylacteries

PHYLACTERIES (*means of protection*). Two 'boxes' of animal skin containing Bible verses (Exod. 13:1–10–16; Deut. 6:4–9; 11:13–21) written by hand on parchment, one attached to a Jew's left arm and the other to his forehead before morning prayers. Unknown among present-day Samaritans; but some found at Qumran include the Ten Commandments. Their use derives from pious interpretation of Exod. 13:9, 16; Deut. 6:8; 11:18. Jesus did not criticise their use, only their ostentatious display (Matt. 23:5).

PIG. *See* Domesticated animals p. 15.

PIGEON. *See* Birds p. 104.

PILATE, Pontius. Roman governor of Judea (AD 26–36) under Tiberius. Enraged Jews by bringing standards bearing the emperor's image into Jerusalem and by raiding Temple funds to finance a water supply for the city. Luke 13:1 may refer to the resulting riots. Recalled to Rome in AD 36 for massacring Samaritans. His conduct of Jesus' trial reveals his obstinacy (John 19:22), weakness (Matt. 27:18) and expediency (John 27:24).

PILLAR. Early pillars supporting buildings (Judg. 16:29) were of wood set in a stone base. Figuratively applied to wisdom (Prov. 9:1), mountains ('pillars of heaven', Job 26:11), foundation members of a church (Gal. 2:9), spiritual overcomers (Rev. 3:12). *See* Jachin and Boaz.

PILLAR OF CLOUD/FIRE. Manifestation of God's presence (Exod. 33:9) during the Exodus, instructing Israel when to move (Exod. 13:21) or acting as a shield (Exod. 14:19–20).

PILLAR OF SALT. The fate of Lot's wife, overcome by sulphur fumes when she hung back at the destruction of Sodom and Gomorrah (Gen. 19:26; Luke 17:32).

PINNACLE. Highest point of the Temple's outer court, dizzily overlooking the deep Kidron valley (Matt. 4:5, AV/KJV).

PIRAM. Amorite king of Jarmuth, who unwisely joined the attack on Gibeon (Josh. 10:3).

PIRATHON. Ephraimite hill town, SW of Shechem (Judg. 12:13; 2 Sam. 23:30).

PISGAH. Moabite ridge, NE of Dead Sea (Num. 23:14; Josh. 13:20). Moses' viewpoint of the Promised Land (Deut. 3:27; 34:1).

PISHON. One of Eden's four rivers (Gen. 2:11). Unidentified.

PISIDIA. Mountainous region of S Asia Minor, in the Roman province of Galatia from 25 BC (Acts 13:14; 14:24).

PISIDIAN ANTIOCH. *See* Antioch 1.

PIT. Cistern for catching rainwater, a trap for the unwary (Exod. 21:33–34; 2 Sam. 23:20; Matt. 12:11). Applied figuratively to evil plots (Ps. 9:15), spiritually dead (Matt. 15:14), abode of the dead (Ps. 28:1) and doom of fallen angels (2 Pet. 2:4). *See* Abyss; Winepress.

PITCH. Bitumen (Gen. 6:14; Exod. 2:3; Isa. 34:9), occurring naturally in the Dead Sea area.

PITCHER. *See* Domestic life p. 53.

PITHOM. Store city built by Hebrew slaves in the E delta of Egypt (Exod. 1:11). Location unidentified.

PITY. Divine characteristic (2 Chron. 36:15). More than sorrow; involves active help (1 John 3:17).

PLAGUE. The Hebrew term usually means bubonic infection (2 Kings 19:35), not always followed by translators.

PLAGUES OF EGYPT. Ten divine judgments to compel Pharaoh to release the Hebrews (Exod. 7—11), culminating in the death of the

Plants

Briers. Planted to protect vineyards (Ps. 80:13). Growing wild, a sign of neglected land (Isa. 5:6) or degenerate society (Isa. 32:13). Their removal a sign of Messiah's kingdom (Isa. 55:13; Ezek. 28:24).

Gall. Bitter-tasting plant and its fruit. Included in the stupefying drink offered to Jesus on the cross (Matt. 27:34). Metaphorically describes a bitter experience (Acts 8:23).

Hyssop. Not the present-day herb but either Syrian marjoram or common caper (1 Kings 4:33). Used for sprinkling blood (Exod. 12:22) and in ritual cleansing (Lev. 14:4). Stem strong enough to support a wet sponge (John 19:29).

Lily. Botanical identifications rarely assured. The 'lilies of the field' (Matt. 6:28) may be poppy anemones or crown marguerites. Song of Sol. 2:1-2 could refer to hyacinth and 'lips' in Song of Sol. 5:13 to scarlet tulip. A moist habitat suggests yellow flag for Hos. 14:5. Lily-work in Solomon's Temple (1 Kings 7:19) probably refers to carvings of the Egyptian lotus, popular in Near Eastern art.

Mustard. Its tiny seeds used as the point of Jesus' parables: great growth from insignificant beginnings, for the kingdom of God (Matt. 13:31) and individual faith (Matt. 17:2).

Myrtle. Hillside shrub, with fragrant leaves and white flowers. Branches used at the Feast of Tabernacles (Neh. 8:15). Symbolises God's transforming touch (Isa. 41:19; 55:13) and his peace (Zech. 1:8-11).

Lilies of the field

Anemone

Poppy

Chrysanthemum

Nettles. Grow vigorously in Palestine, to 2 metres (6 ft), on wasteland (Isa. 34:13; Hos. 9:6). Wild brushwood is meant in AV/KJV of Job 30:7; Prov. 24:31; Zeph. 2:9.

Papyrus (whence 'paper'). Water-loving sedge (Exod. 2:3; Isa. 18:2; 35:7), abundant in Egypt and growing to 3-6 metres (10-20 ft). For writing material (2 John 12), strips of the pithy stem were laid vertically then horizontally to form a sheet, which was pressed, dried, rubbed smooth and beaten hard. Long lasting if kept dry, as in the sands of Egypt, where vast quantities of ancient papyrus documents have been recovered. Used in

Egypt from 3000 BC. Papyri inscribed in everyday Greek have thrown light on many NT words; for example, '*earnest* of the Spirit' (2 Cor. 5:5, AV/KJV) means 'down payment, deposit'. *See* Scroll.

Reed. Water-loving plant (Isa. 35:7). Figure of speech for unsafe support (Isa. 36:6), threat of judgment (1 Kings 14:15), or a weak character (Isa. 42:3; Matt. 12:20).

Rose of Sharon. The Hebrew implies a bulbous plant (Song of Sol. 2:1), probably the dazzling red *Tulipa montana,* still prolific in the area.

Thistle. Evidence of divine judgment (Gen. 3:18; Hos. 10:8). Its uselessness was proverbial (Matt. 7:16; Heb. 6:8). Appears in the fable of Jehoash (2 Kings 14:9).

Thornbush. Soon overruns neglected fields (Prov. 24:31) and smothers cultivated seedlings (Matt. 13:22). Useful as hedging (Hos. 2:6), and as fuel (Ps. 58:9; Eccles.7:6) quick burning (Judg. 9:14-15). Symbol of worthlessness (Heb. 6:7-8), judgment (Gen. 3:18), fruitlessness (Matt. 7:16), desolation (Isa. 5:6). Mocking symbol of kingship (Matt. 27:29). To be transformed in the messianic age (Isa. 55:13).

Trees

Acacia. Tree of the Sinai desert. Its hard timber used for the ark of the covenant and the Tabernacle (Exod. 25).

Algum. Lebanon tree (2 Chron. 2:8) providing prized timber (2 Chron. 9:11).

Almond (*Watched for*). Earliest fruit tree to blossom (Jer. 1:11–12). Shapeliness inspired ornamental work (Exod. 25:33). Kernels a welcome food (Gen. 43:11).

Almugwood. Red sandalwood, imported by Solomon for the Temple (1 Kings 10:11–12).

Broom. Common Palestinian shrub, affording welcome shade in the desert (1 Kings 19:4). Charcoal made from roots used for incendiary arrows (Ps. 120:4) and as fuel (Job 30:4).

Cedar. Once abundant in Lebanon (1 Kings 4:33) and valued for building (2 Sam. 5:11; 1 Kings 6:15; Ezra 3:7). Figuratively applied to greatness (Ezek. 31:3), height (Amos 2:9), vigorous growth (Ps. 92:12), and strength (2 Kings 14:9).

Acacia

Cypress. Tall densely-growing tree, valued for its timber (Isa. 41:19; Ezek. 27:6).

Palms

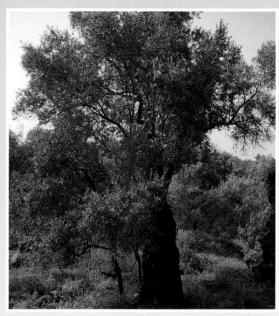

Olive

Poplar. Prized for its shade and blossom; thrives near water (Job 40:22; Isa. 44:4).

Sycamine. Mulberry tree (Luke 17:6, AV/KJV).

Sycamore. Easy to climb (Luke 19:4). Dressing sycamore trees (Amos 7:14) involved laboriously cutting each small fig with a long-handled knife. In three days the fig is tenfold the size. The cut releases ethylene gas, now wellknown as a fruit ripener.

Terebinth. Large deciduous tree (Isa. 6:13; Hos. 4:13). Appearance similar to an oak, hence translations in Gen. 35:4; 2 Sam. 18:9-10; 1 Kings 13:14; Ezek. 6:13.

Willow. Its need to grow by water (Ezek. 17:5) alluded to in Isa. 44:4 ('poplar', NIV). The tree on which Hebrew exiles hung their harps (Ps. 137:1-2, AV/KJV) was the Euphrates poplar; the weeping willow is a modern cultivation from China. The 'plaited container' (so the Greek) in which Paul escaped from Damascus (Acts 9:25; 2 Cor. 11:33) was probably of willow, as still used in Syrian basketry.

Ebony. Valued for fine furniture and carvings (Ezek. 27:15). Not the tree so called today (imported much later from tropical Africa).

Mulberry. Aspen is meant in 2 Sam. 5:23-24 and 1 Chron. 14:14-15 (AV/KJV); its leaves stir noisily in a breeze. The tree of Luke 17:6 is the sycamine.

Oak. Famous in Bashan (Isa. 2:13) but widespread. Useful as landmark (Gen. 35:8; Josh. 24:26) and hard timber (Ezek. 27:6). Symbolises strength (Amos 2:9).

Olive. *See* Foods p. 77.

Palm tree. Dates provide valuable food, eaten fresh or dried, or made into wine. Symbol of victory (Rev. 7:9), rejoicing (Lev. 23:40; John 12:13), and grace, elegance, dignity and usefulness, even to old age (Ps. 92:12).

Plane tree. Massive deciduous tree, growing in rocky stream beds in N Palestine (Gen. 30:37; Ezek. 31:8). Not 'chesnut' (AV/KJV); chestnut is not indigenous to Palestine.

firstborn (Exod. 12:12). The first nine plagues natural sequence, from July to March (Hebrew month of Abib; Exod. 13:4).

First plague (Exod. 7:14–25). Excessive Nile flooding brought down vastly more red soil than usual, killing fish.

Second plague (Exod. 8:1–15). Decomposing fish drove frogs out of the Nile into houses, where they died for lack of moisture.

Third plague (Exod. 8:16–19). The unusually high Nile encouraged mosquitoes to multiply.

Fourth plague (Exod. 8:20–32). The 'fly' was probably *Stomoxys calcitrans,* carrier of skin anthrax, the sixth plague.

Fifth and sixth plagues (Exod. 9:1–12). Anthrax carried by frogs to cattle in fields and by 'flies' to humans.

Seventh plague (Exod. 9:13–35). Severe hailstorms, common in early February in Upper Egypt, ruined barley and flax, but not the later wheat. Goshen, where the Hebrews were, benefited from the better Mediterranean climate.

Eighth plague (Exod. 10:1–20). The unusually high Nile earlier would by March have generated swarms of locusts.

Ninth plague (Exod. 10:21–29). The 'thick darkness' would be a *khamsin* dust storm, made many times worse by the dried-out red soil brought down by the earlier flooding.

Tenth plague (Exod. 12). After using natural forces, God finally acts directly, in slaying the Egyptians' firstborn and, for Israel, establishing the Passover.

PLANE TREE. *See* Trees p. 173.

PLASTER. Slaked lime for coating walls (Lev. 14:42; Dan. 5:5).

PLATTER. Capacious plate at a banquet (Matt. 14:8) ('charged' with meat, hence 'charger' in AV/KJV).

PLEDGE. *See* Money p. 146.

PLEIADES. Cluster of seven stars in the constellation Taurus (Job 9:9; Amos 5:8). Their rising and setting marked the seasons (Job 38:31).

PLOUGHING. *See* Farming p. 71.

PLUMBLINE. Essential tool for builders (Amos 7:7), but usually mentioned figuratively of assessing moral uprightness (2 Kings 21:13; Isa. 28:17; 34:11).

PODS. *See* Foods p. 77.

POETRY. Hebrew poetry still little understood, although it occupies over one-third of the OT (RSV in 1952 the first English translation to indent lines). Metre, as we understand it, and rhyme are absent, but much use is made of parallelism: restating a first line in the second (Ps. 2:8) or offering a contrast (Ps. 1:6).

POISON. The Hebrew word refers to the burning sensation that results from snake bite (Num. 21:6), contaminated water (Exod. 15:23) or the effect of certain plants (2 Kings 4:39–40). Figuratively, applied to distress (Job 6:4; Jer. 8:14), idolatry (Deut. 29:18), godlessness (Job 20:12–16), venomous speech (Ps. 140:3; James 3:8), injustice (Amos 6:12), lawsuits (Hos. 10:4).

POLLUTION. The effect of idolatry (Ezra 9:11; Acts 15:20), bloodshed (Num. 35:33), sexual immorality (Jude 8), worldliness (James 1:27). *See* Clean and unclean.

POLLUX *See* Castor.

POLYGAMY. Recognised in OT (Gen. 4:19; 30:26; Deut. 21:15–17, but for economic reasons usually confined to the better off (2 Sam. 5:13; 2 Chron. 24:3). Leads to conflict (1 Sam. 1; 2 Sam. 11) and turning away from God (Deut. 17:17; 1 Kings 11:1–8).

POMEGRANATE. *See* Foods p. 77.

PONTUS. Roman province (from 65 BC) in N Asia Minor. Local Jews were in Jerusalem for Pentecost (Acts 2:9). Christian communities established, possibly as a result (1 Pet. 1:1). Home of Aquila (Acts 18:2).

POOR. God's special concern for them (Isa. 41:17) must be shared by his people (Deut. 15:7–8; 24:12–14, 17–22; Rom. 12:13). *See* Poverty; Year of Jubilee.

POPLAR. *See* Trees p. 173.

PORPHYRY. Fine-grained variegated purple rock, used as a tesselated pavement in Xerxes' Susa palace (Esther 1:6).

PORTENT. Warning of imminent divine action (Isa. 20:3).

PORTICO. Porch of pillars in Solomon's palace and in the Temple (1 Kings 7:6, 12).

PORTION. Share of land (Josh. 19:49), food (Gen. 43:34) or spoils of war (Num. 31:27). A double portion was the eldest son's inheritance, to cover the expense of household responsibilities on the father's death. Divine confirmation that Elisha was to succeed Elijah (2 Kings 2:9).

Ironically, the inheritance of the wicked city (Rev. 18:6).

PORTION OF JACOB. Divine title, the culmination of Jeremiah's scathing demolition of impotent idols (Jer. 10:16; 51:19). To God alone is worship due, for it is he who provides for his people.

PORTION, MEMORIAL. Cereal burned on the altar (Lev. 2:1–3). *See* Grain offering.

POSSESSION. *See* Demon possession.

POSSESSIONS. All things belong to God (Lev. 25:23; 1 Chron. 29:14; Ps. 24:1; Ezek. 18:4; Hag. 2:8), but are his gifts for human benefit (Eccles. 5:19; Acts 14:17) and stewardship (Matt. 25:14–30). The temptation to amass is futile (Ps. 39:6; Luke 12:20; 1 Tim. 6:7) and leads to worry (Matt. 6:25–34) and spiritual danger (Prov. 30:8–9; 1 Tim. 6:9–10).

POST (AV/KJV). *See* Couriers.

POTIPHAR. Egyptian officer who bought Joseph as a slave and put him in charge of his household (Gen. 37:26; 39:1–23).

POTIPHERA. Joseph's father-in-law (Gen. 41:45), named after the Egyptian sun god Re. His title 'priest of On' (Heliopolis) indicates he was in charge of the national centre of sun worship.

POTSHERD. Piece of broken pottery (Isa. 45:9), often used as writing material. Sherds (ostraca) are invaluable for dating archaeological sites. Figuratively, of the crocodile's sharp-pointed underbelly (Job 41:30).

POTTAGE. *See* Foods p. 77.

POTTER. His work (Jer. 18:1–6) symbolised God's right as Creator (Isa. 29:16; Rom. 9:20–21).

POTTER'S FIELD. *See* Akeldama.

POVERTY, MATERIAL. Not God's will (Deut. 15:4–5), but inevitable (Matt. 26:11). Can be due to disobedience (Deut. 28:47–48), idleness (Prov. 6:10–11), debt (2 Kings 4:1–2), enemies (Judg. 6:6), injustice (Isa. 10:1–2; Matt. 23:14), neglect of God's work (Hag. 1:9), famine (Gen. 45:11). Need not turn one away from God (Mark 12:43–44), but lead to blessing (2 Cor. 8:2, 9). *See* Poor.

POVERTY, SPIRITUAL. Needs to be realised (Rev. 3:17) for it keeps one from God as much as paganism (Eph. 2:12). But once realised, can prove a spiritual path to God (Ps. 63:1; Matt. 5:3, 6).

POWERS THAT BE. Civil authorities, appointed by God (John 19:11) as his agents (Rom. 13:1–7) to govern (1 Pet. 2:13–14). To be obeyed, so long as they act lawfully in God's sight (Acts 4:19).

PRAETORIUM. Governor's official residence (Matt. 27:27; Acts 23:35; Phil. 1:13).

PRAISE. Adoring response to God in word and music (1 Chron. 16:25; Ps. 68:32; 1 Pet. 2:9). A door to God's presence (Ps. 100:4) and a practical expression of faith (2 Chron. 20:22). Believers are warned against looking for human praise (John 12:43; Gal. 1:10; 1 Thess. 2:4–6).

PRAYER. Communion with God (Heb. 11:6), based on his revealed character (Ps. 9:10). Expressed in adoration (Deut. 6:5), praise (Ps. 150), thanksgiving (Ps. 100:4), intercession (Eph. 6:18; Heb. 7:25), petition (Phil. 4:6), confession (1 John 1:9), claiming divine promises (Matt. 7:7–11; John 14:13–14), honouring God (Matt. 6:9) and seeking his will (1 John 5:14–15). Requires faith (Matt. 21:22; Heb. 11:6), persistence (Luke 18:1–8; Eph. 6:18), obedience (1 John 3:21), humility (Luke 18:13).

PRAYERLESSNESS. Caused by unbelief (Ps. 53:4), presumptuousness (Jer. 17:5), idolatry (Deut. 32:17–18), tiredness (Matt. 26:40–41), nominal religion (James 1:6–7), sin (Heb. 3:12), disobedience (Zech. 7:13).

PREACHER. Self-description of author of Ecclesiastes (Eccles. 1:1).

PRECIOUS STONES. About 30 mentioned, mainly associated with the high priest (Exod. 28:17–20) and New Jerusalem (Rev. 21:18–21). Identification uncertain, as the ancients named gems according to external qualities (brilliance, toughness, not colour or mineral content).

PREDESTINATION. Divine foreordaining of events (Ps. 33:11), for God's glory (John 9:33) and his people's blessing (Rom. 8:28). It cannot be thwarted (Prov. 19:21; Dan. 4:35).

PREDICTION. Foretelling future events, with certainty only by God (Isa. 44:7–8). Revealed through prophets (1 Sam. 15:28; Heb. 3:5) or dreams (Gen. 41:25; Dan. 2:28; Matt. 2:13), and through Jesus (Matt. 16:21; Mark 13:1–2) and Christians (Acts 11:28; Jude 18).

PRE-EMINENCE. Descriptive of Jesus Christ (Col. 1:18, AV/KJV), as excelling over all (Matt. 11:27; John 3:31; Rev. 17:14), whether human beings (John 17:2) or spiritual powers (Col. 2:10, 15), on account of his divinity (John 1:1–2; 10:30; Phil. 2:9).

PRE-EXISTENCE. Mark of the divinity of Jesus (John 8:58; 17:5; Heb. 7:24; Rev. 1:17).

PRESENCE OF GOD. The privilege of angels (Luke 1:19) and of believers (Isa. 41:10), especially in trouble (Ps. 27:1–4; Isa. 43:2), in dying (Ps. 23:4) and in the next life (Jude 24). Promised to those praying together (Matt. 18:20).

PRETENCE. Deception for the sake of self-interest (Gen. 27; Josh. 9; Prov. 12:9), useless before God (Jer. 3:10; Matt. 15:8–9). Exposed by the gospel (2 Cor. 10:5).

PREVENT. Archaic term for 'precede' (1 Thess. 4:15, AV/KJV).

PRICKS IN THE EYES. Figure of speech to warn against socialising with pagans (Num. 33:55; Josh. 23:13).

PRIDE. Condemned (1 Pet. 5:5) as godlessness (Deut. 8:14; 1 John 2:16). Perilous (1 Kings 20:11; Prov. 16:18; James 3:5), for it leads to spiritual blindness (Luke 18:11; Rev. 3:17).

PRIESTHOOD. Aaron and his descendants chosen by God as religious leaders (Exod. 28—29) with specific duties (Num. 18). Those despising the privilege were condemned (Num. 3:3–4). The priesthood of all believers, foreshadowed in Exod. 19:6, is fulfilled in Jesus (Heb. 5; 1 Pet. 2:5, 9). *See* Melchizedek.

PRIESTS. Men set apart to offer sacrifice (Lev. 21—22) and administer the sanctuary (Num. 18—19). Continued to function in NT times, until the Temple's destruction in AD 70. *See* Dress, p. 55; High Priest; Sadducees.

PRINCE. One in power and authority, not necessarily royal (Gen. 23:6; Deut. 33:16; Ps. 68:27). Applied to the archangel Gabriel (Dan. 10:21) and to evil powers (Dan. 10:13).

PRINCE OF PEACE. Messianic king (Isa. 9:6) in his ability to establish peace (Rom. 5:1; Eph. 2:14–17).

PRINCE OF THIS WORLD. Identified with Beelzebub (Matt. 12:24) and Satan (Matt. 9:34; John 12:31; 2 Cor. 4:4).

PRINCIPALITIES AND POWERS. Human governments (Titus 3:1), but more usually cosmic powers (Rom. 8:38; Col. 1:16), often in a bad sense (Eph. 6:12). All alike are subject to Christ (1 Pet. 3:22).

PRISCILLA (*Prisca*) and **AQUILA.** Jewish-Christian leather workers from Pontus, expelled from Rome by the edict of Claudius against Jews in AD 49 (Acts 18:1–3). Used their home for worship (1 Cor. 16:19). Praised by Paul (Rom. 16:3). Helped Apollos to a deeper faith (Acts 18:18–28).

PRIZE. Goal of Christian life, likened to a race (2 Tim. 4:7–8) requiring discipline (1 Cor. 9:24–27) and perseverance to the end (Phil. 3:14), conscious of the perils of sin (Heb. 12:1) and false teaching (Gal. 5:7).

PROCESSION. Paul likens suffering for Christ to the lot of those condemned to the arena

(1 Cor. 4:9). Christ's triumph over the powers of evil alludes to a Roman general's victory parade of prisoners of war (2 Cor. 2:14).

PROCONSUL. Roman official authorised to govern a district outside Rome, usually for twelve months (Acts 13:7).

PROCORUS. One of the Seven, appointed to dispense relief to needy Greek-speaking believers (Acts 6:5).

PROCURATOR. Appointed by the emperor to look after his interests in a province (Matt. 27:2; Acts 23:24; 24:27).

PROMISE. Not to be made rashly (Matt. 14:9), but once given must be kept, whether to God (Eccles. 5:4) or to people (Josh. 9:21). Divine promises are unbreakable (Num. 23:19; 1 Kings 8:56; Rom. 4:21; 2 Pet. 3:9).

PROMISED LAND. Canaanite territory entrusted by God to Abraham and his descendants (Gen. 15:18–21). Israel's occupation depended upon obeying God (Num. 20:12; Josh. 5:6), for the land still belonged to him (Lev. 25:23). Prophets warned in vain that straying from God's ways would lead to exile (Isa. 5:13; Jer. 25:8–11; Amos 7:17), though eventually the people would be allowed to return (Jer. 30:3).

PROPHECY. Making God's will and purposes known through those inspired (2 Pet. 1:19–21), orally (Jer. 1:7) or in writing (1 Chron. 29:29). Spiritual gift for all believers (Joel 2:28; Acts 2:17; 1 Cor. 14:5).

PROPHET. God's agent to speak (Amos 3:8), act (Jer. 43:8–9) or write (Hab. 2:1–3; Rev. 1:3)

divine messages of warning (Ezek. 3:17), instruction (Deut. 4:2) or guidance (Isa. 30:21), and concerning future events (1 Kings 11:29–32) and Messiah (Acts 2:30–35).

PROPHET, FALSE. Denounced for leading people astray (Deut. 18:20; Jer. 23:13–40; Matt. 7:15). A sign of the last days (Matt. 24:24; Rev. 19:20).

PROPHETESS. Those mentioned include Deborah (Judg. 4:4), Huldah (2 Kings 22:14), Miriam (Exod. 15:20), Noadiah (Neh. 6:14), Isaiah's wife (Isa. 8:3), Anna (Luke 2:36), Jezebel (Rev. 2:20), Philip's daughters (Acts 21:9) and others unnamed (Acts 2:17; 1 Cor. 11:5).

PROPITIATION. *See* Atonement.

PROSELYTE. Convert from another religion; especially used of pagans turning to Judaism (Matt. 23:15; Acts 2:10).

PROSPERITY. Divine gift (Gen. 32:9), on condition of obedience (Deut. 30).

PROSTITUTION. Ancient practice (Gen. 38:15), for gain (Gen. 38:17) or for pagan worship (Deut. 23:17). Figuratively, applied to spiritual infidelity (Jer. 3:1–3; Ezek. 23; 1 Cor. 6:15–20). Its practitioners not beyond responding to God (Matt. 21:31; Heb. 11:31).

PROVERBS (book). Collection of popular sayings expressing some truth or moral lesson, attributed to Solomon (Prov. 1—29) and the otherwise unknown Agur (30) and Lemuel (31:1–9). Concludes by describing the ideal wife (31:10–31).

PROVIDENCE. God's activity, sustaining creation (Gen. 8:22; Neh. 9:6), providing needs (Job 38:41; Matt. 5:45; 2 Tim. 4:18), and working to fulfil his ultimate purposes (Gen. 28:15; Isa. 46:4; Matt. 25:34; Phil. 1:6).

PRUNING. Vine culture (Lev. 25:3), essential for fruiting, symbolises God's training of disciples (John 15:2).

PSALMS (book). Composed of 150 religious songs of prayer, praise and instruction; in five collections, each ending with a doxology (Ps. 41; 72; 89; 106; 150).

PSALMS (titles). Nearly half (73) ascribed to David; others to Solomon (Pss. 72; 127), Asaph (Pss. 50; 73—83), Heman (Ps. 88), Etham (Ps. 89), Moses (Ps. 90). The meaning of the technical terms Maskil, Miktam, Selah and Shiggaion is lost in antiquity.

PTOLEMAIS. Only natural harbour S of Phoenicia (Acts 21:7). Acco in OT times (Judg. 1:31).

PUAH. 1. Hebrew midwife (Exod. 1:15) who courageously defied Pharaoh's order to kill infant boys.

2. Son of Issachar (Gen. 46:13; Num. 26:23); father of the judge Tola (Judg. 10:1).

PUBLICANS. *See* Tax collectors.

PUBLIUS. 'Chief man' of Malta, who welcomed Paul's shipwrecked company. The apostle healed his father of dysentery (Acts 28:7–8).

PUL. Tiglath-Pileser III, king of Assyria (2 Kings 15:19;1 Chron. 5:26).

PUR (*Lot*). Haman's means of choosing a suitable day for his plot against the Jews (Esther 3:7; 9:24, 26). *See* Feasts and festivals, p. 250 (Purim).

PURITY. Moral and spiritual cleanness in the sight of God (Ps. 24:3–4). Required of his people (Lev. 19:2; 1 Pet. 1:22), but achieved only by divine action (John 15:3; Eph. 5:26). Symbolised by whiteness (Isa. 1:18), light (1 John 1:7) and snow (Ps. 51:7).

PURPLE. Valuable fabric, used in the Tabernacle (Exod. 25:4). Denoted high honour (Dan. 5:7), royalty (John 19:2) or wealth (Luke 16:19). Dye obtained from a sea mollusc.

PURSE. *See* Dress p. 54.

PUTEOLI (*Sulphur Springs*). Trading port, near Naples (Acts 28:13). Named after local volcano.

Q

QUAIL. *See* Birds p. 104.

QUARRY. Figuratively, of descent from Abraham (Isa. 51:1).

QUATERNION. Military term for squad of four soldiers (Acts 12:4, AV/KJV).

QUEEN. Chief wife of a king's harem, not usually concerned with state affairs (Esther 2:17). Infrequently sole sovereign (Athaliah, 2 Kings 11:3), but Sheba (1 Kings 10) had ruling queens for many centuries, according to inscriptions.

QUEEN OF HEAVEN. Babylonian goddess Ishtar (Phoenician Astarte), worshipped by Jewish women in Judah (Jer. 7:18) and Egypt (Jer. 44:17), despite God's warning (Deut. 4:19).

QUEEN OF SHEBA. Unnamed queen from Yemen who undertook the long journey to visit the new king Solomon (1 Kings 10), probably to agree a commercial treaty for her caravan luxury trade.

QUEEN OF THE SOUTH. Queen of Sheba (Matt. 12:42).

QUEEN MOTHER. The king's widow could wield great influence (1 Kings 2:19; 15:13).

QUICKSANDS. Treacherous sandbank (Syrtis, Acts 27:17), off the N African coast.

QUIRINIUS. Roman imperial legate of Syria-Cilicia, AD 6–9 (Acts 5:37, a census in AD 6 mentioned also by Josephus).

QUIVER. Arrow case, in hunting (Gen. 27:3) or battle (Isa. 22:6). Figuratively, of military power (Jer. 5:16), large families (Ps. 127:5), God's hiding place (Isa. 49:2).

QUOTATIONS. Some 250 clear OT quotations appear in the NT, many cited more than once, plus over 2500 allusions. The most quoted verse is Ps. 110:1 (18 times). Chain quotation in rabbinic fashion also occurs (e.g. 1 Pet. 2:6), linking a verse each from Pentateuch, Prophets and Writings (*see* Bible 2), to demonstrate how Scripture emphasises a lesson by reiteration.

R

RABBAH (*Great*). Ammonite capital (Josh. 13:25); Joab tactfully invited David to complete its capture (2 Sam. 11:1; 12:26–31). Modern Amman, capital of Jordan.

RABBI (*My Great One*). Honorific title for teachers of Jewish law; applied to Jesus (John 1:38) and the Baptist (John 3:26).

RABBONI. Aramaic form of 'Rabbi' (John 20:16).

RABMAG. Rank of Nergal-Sharezer, Babylonian officer at the sack of Jerusalem in 586 BC (Jer. 39:3).

RABSARIS. Rank of Assyrian officers: one (unnamed) who demanded the surrender of Jerusalem in 701 BC (2 Kings 18:17); Sarsechim, Babylonian judge after Jerusalem's capture in 587 BC (Jer. 39:3); the Babylonian Nabushazban, who liberated Jeremiah (Jer. 39:13).

RABSHAKEH. Assyrian rank; not a personal name (2 Kings 18:17).

RACA (*Empty-headed*). Aramaic insult (Matt. 5:22), illustrating Jesus' point that anger can lead to violence.

RACE. Athletics figure applied to the Christian life. Both demand singlemindedness (Acts 20:24) and perseverance (Heb. 12:1), but with the supreme prize at the end (2 Tim. 4:7–8).

RACHEL. Jacob's second wife (Gen. 29) and mother of Joseph (Gen. 30:25). Died giving birth to Benjamin (Gen. 35:16–19).

RAHAB. 1. Prostitute in Jericho who shielded Joshua's spies (Josh. 2); spared when the city fell (Josh. 6:22–25). Praised for her faith (Heb. 11:31) and hospitality (James 2:25). Ancestor of Jesus (Matt. 1:5).
2. Mythical personification of chaos (Job 9:13).
3. Symbol of Egypt (Ps. 87:4; Isa. 30:7).

RAIN. At most, from October ('former rains') to April ('latter rains'), but sometimes not beginning until January. Often erratic (Amos 4:7); clouds may disappoint (Prov. 25:14) or produce an unexpected downpour (in May, 1 Sam. 12:16–18).

RAINBOW. Sign of God's covenant with Noah after the Flood (Gen. 9:12–17). Symbol of divine glory (Ezek. 1:28; Rev. 4:3) or of God's messenger (Rev. 10:1).

RAISINS. *See* Foods p. 77.

RAM. *See* Domesticated animals p. 15.

RAM'S HORN. *See* Music p. 150.

RAMAH (*Height*). 1. Benjamite town (Josh. 18:25) between Bethel and Gibeon (Judg. 4:5; Jer. 40:1).
2. Samuel's home (1 Sam. 1:19; 7:17). Scene

of Israel's demand for a king (1 Sam. 8:4). Location uncertain.

RAMATH LEHI. *See* Jawbone.

RAMESES. Pharaoh's store city in NE Nile Delta (Exod. 1:11).

RAMOTH GILEAD. City of refuge (Deut. 4:43). Ahab killed trying to dislodge occupying Aramaeans (1 Kings 22). Ahab's son Jehoram wounded recapturing the town (2 Kings 8:28).

RAMP. *See* War p. 241.

RAMPART. *See* War p. 241.

RANSOM. Price paid to redeem a person or thing from obligation (Lev. 27), captivity (Isa. 35:10) or misfortune (Lev. 25:25–28). In NT, applied only to Jesus redeeming people from sin (Matt. 20:28; 1 Tim. 2:6; Heb. 9:15) and so claiming them as his property (1 Cor. 6:19–20). *See* Redeemer.

RAT. *See* Wild animals p. 17.

RAVEN. *See* Birds p. 104.

READING. Augustine (AD 380) surprised that Ambrose of Milan read silently, for ancient practice was to read aloud (Acts 8:30). Meditation involves reading Scripture, hence the reference to 'mouth' in Josh. 1:8 and Ps. 19:14.

REAPING. Figuratively of unburied corpses (Jer. 9:22), divine judgment (Rev. 14:15), consequences (Job 4:8; Ps. 126:5; 2 Cor. 9:6).

REARGUARD. Symbolic of God's defence (Isa. 52:12, alluding to Exod. 14:19).

REBEKAH. Isaac's wife and mother of Jacob and Esau (Gen. 22:23; 24—27). Buried at Machpelah (Gen. 49:31).

REBELLION. Refusing to accept God's authority a major OT theme (Deut. 9:7; Heb. 3:8), despite warnings (1 Sam. 12:15) that disobedience ends in death (Isa. 66:24) unless there is repentance (Neh. 9:26–28). Israel's rebellion a warning to Christians (Heb. 3:7–4:2). Defying delegated divine authority (Exod. 23:21; Deut. 21:18–21; Rom. 13:1–7) is likewise condemned.

REBUKE. Justified rebuke encouraged (Lev. 19:17; Luke 17:3), especially by the use of Scripture (2 Tim. 3:16). The wise will respond (Prov. 9:8).

RECHAB. 1. Army officer who with Baanah assassinated Ish-Bosheth, vainly thinking to ingratiate themselves with David (2 Sam. 4).
2. Ancestor of Rechabites (Jer. 35:6).

RECHABITES. Their religious lifestyle highly commended (Jer. 35). As nomads, they were a reminder of Israel's pilgrim life and a rebuke against materialism.

RECLINING AT TABLE. Lounging on couches around low tables at meals once considered a decadent luxury for the idle rich (Amos 6:4). By NT times it was established practice in better-off homes for diners to lean on the left arm and eat with the right hand (Matt. 26:7; Luke 7:36).

RECONCILIATION. Restoring relationships, primarily between God and people, leading to renewed human relationships. Alienation caused by sin (Isa. 59:2) has been resolved by Christ's work on the cross (Rom. 5:10; Col. 1:22), bringing peace with God (Rom. 5:1–2) and adoption into his family (Rom. 8:15–16), a ministry committed to believers (Matt. 5:24; 2 Cor. 5:18–20).

RECORDER. High-ranking official (2 Sam. 8:16; 2 Kings 18:18), who kept the king informed, gave advice, and communicated the royal commands.

RED. Dye for cloth (Exod. 25:5) obtained from the cochineal insect. Lead or iron oxide yielded a pigment for wall painting (Jer. 22:14; Ezek. 23:14). Stain irremovable, humanly speaking (Isa. 1:18).

RED HEIFER. *See* Heifer.

RED SEA (*Sea of Reeds*). Term covers Gulf of Suez (Exod. 10:19), Gulf of Aqaba (Num. 14:25) and the waterway miraculously crossed by escaping Hebrews (Exod. 15:4).

REDEEMER. Divine title (Isa. 54:8), otherwise Rock (Ps. 19:14), God Most High (Ps. 78:35), Holy One of Israel (Isa. 41:14), King (Isa. 44:6), Creator (Isa. 44:24), Lord Almighty (Isa. 47:4),

Saviour (Isa. 49:26). God's ability to redeem demonstrated by the Exodus (Deut. 13:5), his love (Deut. 7:8), power (Deut. 9:26), forgiveness (Ps. 130:8), deliverance from death (Ps. 49:15), and supremely from sin through the work of Jesus Christ (Col. 1:13–14).

REDEMPTION. Payment to recover property (Lev. 25:24–32), animals (Exod. 13:13), firstborn sons (Exod. 34:20), Israel (Exod. 6:6) and obtain release from slavery (Lev. 25:47–54), sin (Isa. 44:22; 1 Pet. 1:18) and the curse of the law (Gal. 3:13). Final redemption of all creation is awaited (Rom. 8:19–23).

REED. 1. Measuring rod (Ezek. 40:5; Rev. 11:1) of 3 metres (9 ft).

2. *See* Plants p. 171.

REFINING. Removing impurities from metals by heating (Ps. 12:6; 1 Pet. 1:7). Figure applied to purifying God's people (Zech. 13:9; Mal. 3:2–3).

REFUGE. Divine title (frequently in Psalms). False security offered by idolatry (Deut. 32:37), lying (Isa. 28:15), human defences (Jer. 21:13). *See* Cities of refuge.

Reclining at table

REFUSE. Paul deemed past achievements and family connections mere street sweepings (Phil. 3:8).

REGENERATION. God's action (John 1:12–13) through his love shown in Jesus (Eph. 2:4–5) to bring about spiritual birth (John 3:5–8) in response to faith (1 John 5:1). It makes believers members of God's family (Rom. 8:15–17).

REHOB. Northernmost Canaanite city observed by Joshua's spies (Num. 13:21). Beth Rehob in Judg. 18:28; 2 Sam. 10:6.

REHOBOAM. Son of Solomon and the Moabitess Naamah (1 Kings 14:21). King of Judah (931–913 BC). His obstinacy over taxes and forced labour led to the north (Israel /Samaria) breaking away (1 Kings 12:1–24). Having consolidated his position in Judah, he abandoned God's law, suffered attacks as a consequence, but repented (2 Chron. 12).

REHOBOTH (*Spaces*). 1. Well, between Gerar and Beersheba, dug by Isaac's servants without objection (Gen. 26:22).
2. Edomite royal city (Gen. 36:37; 1 Chron. 1:48; '*The* river' usually means Euphrates, which cannot apply here; probably the boundary wadi between Edom and Moab).

REHUM. Persian bureaucrat who opposed the rebuilding of Jerusalem's walls (Ezra 4:8–9, 17, 23).

REINS. Inner parts of the body, viewed as the centre of life; from Latin *renes*, kidneys (Ps. 139:13, AV/KJV).

REMNANT. Despite faithlessness around them, those remaining loyal to the Lord (Gen. 45:7; Neh. 1:2; Mic. 2:12; Mal. 3:16; Acts 15:17) will be heirs of God's new covenant (Jer. 31:31–33; Zech. 14:16; Rom. 11:1–5).

RENDING CLOTHES. Expressing intense grief at calamity (Gen. 37:29; 1 Sam. 4:12; 2 Sam. 13:31). More important is expressing grief for sin (Joel 2:13).

RENUNCIATION. Discipleship requires deliberate rejection of self (Matt. 16:24), sin (Prov. 28:13; 2 Cor. 4:2) and of all things for Christ (Luke 14:33; Phil. 3:8).

REPENTANCE. God's relenting from impending judgment (Jer. 26:3). Usually refers to human admission of sin (Lev. 5:5; Luke 15:18) and a sincere turning back to God (Isa. 30:15; Matt. 3:8; Acts 20:21).

REPHAIM, VALLEY OF. Named after its early inhabitants (Josh. 15:8). Near Jerusalem and scene of battle between Israelites and Philistines (2 Sam. 5:18).

REPHAITES, REPHAIM. Formidable warriors, known in Moab as Emim (Deut. 2:11) and in Ammon as Zamzummim (Deut. 2:20–21).

REPHAN. Babylonian god of the planet Saturn, whose cult was introduced into Samaria after the fall of the northern kingdom (Amos 5:26; Acts 7:43).

REPROACH. Cause for shame, such as childlessness for an eastern wife (Gen. 30:23; Luke 1:25) or slavery (Josh. 5:9). Believers must not invite such a charge against God's name (Neh. 5:9; Rom. 2:23–24; 1 Tim. 3:7), yet be prepared to suffer it undeservedly (Luke 6:22; Heb. 13:13; 1 Pet. 4:14).

REPROBATE. Person or thing rejected under test (Jer. 6:30; 2 Cor. 13:5).

REPTILES. Both Hebrew and Greek terms literally mean 'creeping things' (1 Kings 4:33; Rom. 1:23). In general, cold-blooded vertebrates, such as snakes and lizards; not to be eaten (Lev. 11:29).

REST. Needed physically (Ps. 23:2–3; Mark 6:31; John 4:6) and spiritually (Ps. 62:1–5; Matt. 11:28–30). Provided by the Sabbath (Exod. 34:21; Heb. 4:9), sleep (Ps. 4:8; 127:2), patient waiting upon God (Isa. 40:31), God's presence (1 John 3:19), heaven (Rev. 14:13); but not for the faithless (Isa. 28:12; Jer. 6:16; Heb. 3:18), wicked (Isa. 48:22), proud (Hab. 2:5), or evil spirits (Luke 11:24).

RESURRECTION. 1. The raising of Jesus from the dead, foreshadowed in Isaac (Heb. 11:19) and Jonah (Matt. 12:40), and predicted (Isa. 53:11; Hos. 6:2; Ps. 16:8–11; 1 Cor. 15:3–4). Jesus himself spoke of it (Matt. 16:21; 26:32; Mark 9:9; John 2:19–22; 11:25). Demonstrates God's power (Eph. 1:20) and Christ's divinity (Rom. 1:4). Foundation of preaching (Acts 17:18), justification (Rom. 4:25), the believer's faith (1 Cor. 15:14), hope (1 Pet. 1:3), own resurrection (John 14:19; 1 Thess. 4:14),

2. The raising of all people, good and bad alike, predicted (Dan. 12:2; John 5:28–29; Acts 24:15), despite denials (Matt. 22:23; 1 Cor. 15:12), ridicule (Acts 17:32) or disbelief (Acts 26:8).

RESURRECTION APPEARANCES. Jesus

Tomb with rolling stone door

appeared only to friends (never to score off enemies): disciples (John 20:26), Mary Magdalene (Mark 16:9), Emmaus travellers (Luke 24:31), Peter (Luke 24:34), Paul (Acts 9:5), 500 at once (1 Cor. 15:6), James, the Lord's brother (1 Cor. 15:7).

RESURRECTION BODY. One suited to conditions of the next life (1 Cor. 15:35–44). In some ways like the present physical body (Luke 24:39), yet subtly different. The risen Lord was not always immediately recognised (Luke 24:16) and could appear and disappear at will (Luke 24:31; John 20:19). The believer's resurrection body will be similar to Christ's (Phil. 3:21; 1 John 3:2).

RETRIBUTION. Recompense for evil done, the prerogative of God (Deut. 32:35) or of authorities ordained by him (1 Pet. 2:14), but not of individuals (Rom. 12:17–19). To be just (Gen. 18:25) and proportionate (Exod. 21:23–25).

REUBEN. Jacob and Leah's firstborn (Gen. 29:32) and ancestor of the tribe bearing his name. Defended Joseph against his brothers

(Gen. 37:21) and offered his own sons as hostage on behalf of Benjamin (Gen. 42:37); but pronounced an unstable character (Gen. 49:3) because of his incest (Gen. 35:22). Allocated territory E of Jordan (Josh. 4:12).

REUEL. Midianite father-in-law of Moses (Num. 10:29); also called Jethro (Exod. 2:21 with 3:1).

REVELATION. Truths about God's person and will, divinely made known and beyond human reasoning alone. In general, through creation (Rom. 1:19–21), but supremely through Jesus (Matt. 5:17–18; 11:25–27; Col. 1:25–27; Heb. 1).

REVELATION (book). Prophecy of the end-time, written about AD 95 to encourage believers in a hostile world. John tells of his seeing the glorified Christ (Rev. 1) and quotes letters to seven churches of Asia Minor (2—3). Visions follow: God's throne (4); the Lamb and the scroll (5); seven seals (6—7); seven trumpets (8—11); seven miscellaneous visions (12—14); seven last plagues (15—16); ruin of the city of Antichrist (17—18); wedding of the Lamb and Christ's return (19—21); millennium and last judgment (20); recreation of heaven, earth and Jerusalem (21—22).

REVENGE. Forbidden (Lev. 19:18; 1 Pet. 3:9). Attracts divine intervention (Ezek. 25:12, 15) and leads to a cycle of violence (Judg. 15). *See* Avenger of blood.

REVERENCE. Respectful awe of God (1 Sam. 12:24; Mal. 4:2), because of his holiness (Isa. 8:13), creation (Ps. 64:9), control of nations (Jer. 10:7), ability to forgive (Ps. 130:4). Issues in worship (Heb. 12:28), faithful service (1 Sam.

12:24), obedience (Deut. 8:6), joy (Neh. 1:11), witness to others (1 Pet. 3:2).

REWARD. Recompense for actions is a spiritual law (Luke 6:38): fulfilled by God (Eph. 6:8), in response to faith (Gen. 15:1), obedience (Ps. 19:11), godly living (Prov. 11:18), mercy (Prov. 25:21–22), loyalty (Matt. 5:12), prayer (Matt. 6:4), wholeheartedness (Col. 3:23–24), spiritual hunger (Matt. 5:6). *See* Wages.

REZEPH. Flourishing commercial town whose gods failed to withstand Assyrians (2 Kings 19:12).

REZIN. Aramaean king, allied with Pekah against Assyrians. When king Ahaz refused to join them, they invaded Judah (2 Kings 15:37; 16:5; 2 Chron. 28:5–8). Tiglath-Pileser III of Assyria responded to Ahab's appeal and Rezin was slain (2 Kings 16:7–9).

REZON. Leader of brigands based in Damascus; he caused chronic trouble for Solomon (1 Kings 11:23–25).

RHEGIUM. Port of S Italy, modern Reggio di Calabria (Acts 28:13).

RHODA (*Rose*). Servant girl of Mark's mother, too excited to open the door to Peter (Acts 12:13).

RHODES. Aegean island (Acts 21:1).

RIBLAH. Town on the river Orontes (Ezek. 6:14), scene of Jewish tragedies at the hands of Pharaoh Neco in 609 BC (2 Kings 23:33) and Nebuchadnezzar in 587 BC (2 Kings 25:6–7, 20–21).

RICHES, MATERIAL. God's gifts (Gen. 49:25; 1 Kings 3:13;1 Chron. 29:12), including wealth (Deut. 8:18), but as a trust (Luke 16:11) and not to be misused selfishly (James 2:6). Can be a spiritual peril (Matt. 19:23; 1 Tim. 6:5–10), give a false sense of security (Ps. 62:10; Jer. 48:7; Luke 12:16–21) and be too absorbing (Isa. 55:2).

RICHES, SPIRITUAL. True treasure (Matt. 6:19–21), beyond human realization (Rom. 11:33; Eph. 3:8). God's gift (Rom. 10:12; Eph. 3:16) and the believer's inheritance (Eph. 1:18; 1 Pet. 1:4). Provided through God's word (Col. 3:16), grace (Eph. 2:7), in Christ (Eph. 3:8).

RIDICULE. Derision of others betrays lovelessness (James 2:1–9), mindlessness (Prov. 11:12) and arrogance (Prov. 15:12); causes trouble (Prov. 22:10; 29:8) and invites divine retribution (Zeph. 2:10–11). To be expected by believers (Heb. 10:33), after Christ's experience (Luke 23:35); a sign of the last days (2 Pet. 3:3; Jude 18).

RIGHT HAND. Symbol of honour (1 Kings 2:19), power (Ps. 20:6), authority (Acts 5:31), status (Ps. 110:1). Considered more important than the left hand (Gen. 48:14; Matt. 25:33).

RIGHT HAND OF FELLOWSHIP. Sign of unity in the Lord (Gal. 2:9).

RIGHTEOUSNESS. Right relationship with God, to be sought (Matt. 6:33), though unobtainable (Eccles. 7:20; Rom. 3:10) apart from divine action (Phil. 3:9) through Christ (1 Cor. 1:30; 2 Cor. 5:21), repentance (Isa. 1:27), faith (Gen. 15:6; Rom. 3:21) and obedience (Rom. 6:16).

Rimmon, the Aramaean storm god

RIMMON (*Thunderer*). Aramaean storm god Hadad (2 Kings 5:18).

RIVER. Term includes wadis (dry in summer, raging torrents in the rainy season) as well as permanent waterways. Where unnamed, *'the'* river usually means Euphrates.

RIVER OF EGYPT. Not the Nile but the Wadi el-Arish, forming the boundary between Palestine and Egypt (Gen. 15:18).

RIZPAH. Daughter of Asiah, concubine of Saul and then of Abner (2 Sam. 3:7–8). Gibeonites murdered her sons (2 Sam. 21:8–11).

ROADS. *See* Travel p. 229.

ROBBERY. All too common (Hos. 4:2; Matt. 6:19), especially against the defenceless (Isa. 10:2; Ezek. 22:29) and even God (Mal. 3:9). Those caught must compensate victims (Exod. 22:1–4). *See* Stealing.

ROBE. *See* Dress p. 54.

ROCK. Divine title (Gen. 49:24; 1 Cor. 10:4), symbolic of strength and stability; the only sure foundation for the believer (Matt. 7:24–25; 16:18).

ROCK BADGER. *See* Wild animals p. 17.

ROD. The familiar rod of Ps. 23:4 was a heavy knobbed club which the shepherd beat against the rocky sides of a narrow defile to frighten off wild animals as he led his flock. Symbol of authority (Isa. 14:5). See Sceptre; Staff.

ROGELIM. Home of David's wealthy old patron Barzillai (2 Sam. 17:27). Location unknown.

ROMAN CITIZEN. Freeborn inhabitant of Rome with power to vote and hold office. Citizenship could be awarded for services rendered to the Roman state, or sometimes purchased (Acts 22:28). Paul's citizenship a birthright, since his father already had that status. Magistrates could not execute, flog, chain or torture a Roman citizen (Acts 16:37–38; 22:25; 23:27) or prevent him from appealing to the emperor's tribunal in Rome (Acts 25:11).

ROMAN COLONY. Rome settled army veterans in strategic cities, to safeguard its interests in outposts of empire. Paul quickly realised the potential of such centres for spreading the gospel.

ROMAN EMPERORS. During NT times: Augustus (27 BC–AD 14); Tiberius (AD 14–37); Caligula (37–41); Claudius (41–54); Nero (54–68); Galba, Otho, Vitellius (68–69); Vespasian (69–79); Titus (79–81); Domitian (81–96); Nerva (96–98); Trajan (98–117).

ROMANS (letter). Written by Paul about AD 57. Describes the lost spiritual position of Gentiles before God (Rom. 1:18–32), Jews (2:1–3:8) and of the world in general (3:9–20); God's provision to restore relationship with him (3:21–8:39); Jews' special place in God's plan (9—11); practical consequences of Christian living (12—15); personal greetings to believers in Rome whom Paul had met on his travels (16).

ROME. By NT times the population numbered one million and included many Jews (Acts 2:10; 18:2) and Christians (Paul names 28 in Rom. 16). The emperor ruled from his capital by delegating authority to governors. Initially, the Roman peace and Roman roads facilitated the spread of the gospel, but later Rome was branded 'Babylon' (Rev. 18:10).

ROOF. *See* House p. 100.

ROOT OF DAVID. Expression alludes to

'stump of Jesse' (David's father), a reference to Jesus' family tree (Isa. 11:1–10; Rom. 15:12; Rev. 5:5; 22:16).

ROPE. Made from plant fibres (papyrus, flax, vine). Symbolised submission (1 Kings 20:31–32), capture (Isa. 3:24), bondage to sin (Isa. 5:18), personal calamity (Jer. 10:20).

ROSE OF SHARON. *See* Plants p. 171.

RUBY. Gem in the high priest's breastpiece (Exod. 28:17). Figuratively expresses the greater value of wisdom (Job 28:18) and of an exemplary wife (Prov. 31:10).

RUDDER. Applied figuratively to the tongue (James 3:4–5).

RUE. *See* Herbs and spices p. 93.

RULER OF THE SYNAGOGUE. Presiding official, responsible for synagogue services (Mark 5:35; Acts 18:8).

RUTH (*Companion*). Moabite woman (Ruth 1:4), whose attachment to her Jewish mother-in-law Naomi (1:6–22) led to her marrying Boaz (2:1—4:17) and becoming the ancestor of David (4:18–22) and of Jesus (Matt. 1:5). The anonymous book, set in the period of the Judges (Ruth 1:1), was probably compiled early in David's reign.

SABAOTH (*hosts, armies*). In AV/KJV for heavenly forces (Rom. 9:29; James 5:4). 'Sabaoth' simply transliterates the Hebrew word.

SABBATH. Rest day commanded by God (Exod. 20:8–11), following his own example (Gen. 2:3) and to be a mark of God's people (Exod. 31:13–17). Replaced in the early church by the resurrection day, Sunday (Rev. 1:10). *See* Lord's Day.

SABBATH DAY'S JOURNEY. *See* Day's journey.

SABBATICAL YEAR. *See* Year of Jubilee.

SABEANS. Traders of Sheba (Yemen), dealing in gold and precious stones (Ps. 72:10, 15) and perfumes (Isa. 45:14; Ezek. 23:42).

SACKCLOTH. *See* Dress p. 55.

SACRED GARMENTS. *See* Dress p. 55.

SACRIFICE. Only unblemished, 'clean' animals could be offered in OT sacrifice (Lev. 22:17–25). The disposal of the blood at the altar distinguished sacrifice from mere slaughter (Lev. 17). The animal's hard fat (on the entrails) had to be burnt on the altar (Lev. 3:15–16) by the priest (Lev. 3:5, 11). Bloodless offerings were of cereals, olive oil, wine and frankincense. All sacrifices must be salted (Lev. 2:13; Ezek. 43:24; *see* Salt). OT sacrifices were inadequate (Hos. 6:6; Matt. 9:13) and rendered obsolete by Jesus (Matt. 26:28; Heb. 4:14–5:5; 7:27). Christians are to offer themselves as living sacrifices (Rom. 12:1). *See* Lamb; Ram; Sheep; Tail, fat.

SACRIFICE, HUMAN. Pagan practice (Deut. 12:31; 2 Kings 3:27), denounced (Isa. 57:5; Jer. 19:5; Ezek. 16:20–21).

SACRIFICE, SPIRITUAL. Obedience (1 Sam. 15:22), mercy (Hos. 6:6; Matt. 9:13), just dealings (Amos 5:22–24), penitence (Ps. 51:17), humility (Mic. 6:6–8) and praise (Heb. 13:15–16) are far more acceptable to God than animal sacrifice.

SADDUCEES. Priestly aristocracy of Jerusalem, controlling the Temple and maintaining political power (Acts 5:17) by cooperating with the Romans. Denied the spiritual world and afterlife (Matt. 22:23–32; Acts 23:8). Denounced by John the Baptist (Matt. 3:7–10) and by Jesus (Matt. 16:6–12). Disappeared after the destruction of the Temple in AD 70.

SAINTS. Believers (Acts 9:13), who together form the people of God (Eph. 5:3) and the church (1 Cor. 1:2). The Greek word means those set apart for God ('holy ones').

SALAMIS. Commercial port of E Cyprus, with several Jewish synagogues (Acts 13:5).

SALECAH. City of E boundary of Og's kingdom of Bashan (Deut. 3:10), allocated to Transjordanian tribes (Josh. 13:11).

SALEM. Jerusalem (Gen. 14:18; Ps. 76:2; Heb. 7:1–2).

SALIM. Near where John baptised, W of Jordan (John 3:23, 26), S of Bethshan.

SALMONE. Promontory of E Crete (Acts 27:7), modern Cape Sidero.

SALOME. 1. Daughter of Herodias by her first husband, Herod Philip (unnamed in Matt. 14:6).

2. One of the women who saw Jesus crucified (Mark. 15:40) and then found his tomb empty (Mark 16:1).

SALT. Abundant around the Dead Sea (Ezek. 47:11), although, unlike rock salt, contains impurities which remain after the salt dissolves (Luke 14:34). Used to season (Job 6:6) or preserve food (Matt. 5:13). Rubbed on newborn infants (Ezek. 16:4) as an antiseptic, according to present-day Arab practice. Required on all sacrifices (Lev. 2:13), signifying the eternal covenant between God and his people (Num. 18:19) and of harmonious human relationships (Mark 9:50; Col. 4:6). Symbol of desolation (Deut. 29:23; Judg. 9:45).

SALT SEA. The Dead Sea (Num. 34:3).

SALVATION. Deliverance by God (Ps. 62:6; Rev. 7:10), from danger (Matt. 8:25), sickness (Acts 4:12), persecution (Acts 7:34), enemies (Exod. 14:13; 2 Sam. 22:4), fear (Ps. 27:1), trouble (Ps. 37:39), but especially from sin's power and penalty (Isa. 44:22; John 5:24; 1 John 1:9) through the atoning death of Jesus (1 Pet. 2:24).

SAMARIA. 1. Omri king of Israel bought the hill site from Shemer to build his capital, replacing

Tirzah (1 Kings 16:23–24); NW of Shechem, commanding trade routes over the Esdraelon plain.

2. The name also applies to the surrounding territory, 'the land of Samaria' (Jer. 31:5), i.e. the N kingdom of Israel, after the death of Solomon (1 Kings 22:51).

SAMARITANS. 1. Israelites of the N kingdom, named after Omri's capital Samaria. Many deported to Assyria (2 Kings 17:6) and replaced by other displaced peoples, who brought their gods with them (2 Kings 17:24–41).

2. Although rebuffed by some Samaritans (Luke 9:51–56), Jesus ignored traditional Jewish antagonism (Luke 17:16; John 4:39–41), an example followed by disciples (Acts 8:25), pointedly told his famous parable (Luke 10:25–37) and was abused for his attitude (John 8:48).

SAMOS. Mountainous Ionian island off Ephesus (Acts 20:15).

SAMOTHRACE. Small mountainous Aegean island (Acts 16:11).

SAMSON. Nazirite son of the Danite Manoah and one of the last Judges. Famous for his immense physical strength and, although subject to moral weaknesses (Judg. 13—16), among heroes of faith (Heb. 11:32).

SAMUEL. Son of Elkanah and Hannah (1 Sam. 1:20), called by God as a child (1 Sam. 3) and last of the Judges (1 Sam. 7:16–17). Reluctantly responds to Israel's demand for a king and anoints Saul (1 Sam. 8). Condemns Saul for disobedience (1 Sam. 13:13) and anoints David as Saul's successor (1 Sam. 16).

1 & 2 SAMUEL. Anonymous account of the life of Samuel (1 Sam. 1:1–25:1), the institution of the monarchy (8—12), Saul's failure (13—15) and the rise of David (16—31). 2 Samuel relates David's reign.

SANCTIFICATION. Being set apart for God, the Holy One (Lev. 11:44; Acts 20:32; 1 Pet. 1:15–16) to fulfil his will (1 Thess. 4:3). Brought about through Jesus (1 Cor. 1:30; Heb. 13:12), the Holy Spirit (Rom. 15:16; 1 Pet. 1:2), God's word (John 17:17), grace (2 Tim. 1:9), faith (Acts 26:18).

SANCTUARY. Place set apart for worship. In OT, mainly the Tabernacle (Exod. 25:8–9) and Temple (1 Chron. 28:10). *See* High place; Shekel.

SANDALS. *See* Dress p. 55.

SANHEDRIN. Jewish Supreme Court of 71 members, priestly and lay, the number traditionally derived from Moses and the 70 elders (Num. 11:16). Lesser sanhedrins (31 members) operated locally (Matt. 5:22; 10:17).

SAPPHIRE. Not the modern stone, but lapis lazuli; blue flecked with gold. Set in high priest's breastpiece (Exod. 28:18) and in the foundations of New Jerusalem (Isa. 54:11; Rev. 21:19).

SARAH (*Princess*). Beautiful wife (Gen. 12:11) and half-sister of Abraham (Gen. 20:12), who gave birth to Isaac in her old age (Gen. 21:3), after God's promise (Gen. 17:19). Dying at 127, she was buried at Machpelah (Gen. 23). Despite her disbelief (Gen. 18:12), included in the roll of faith (Heb. 11:11). As a freeborn woman, contrasted with Hagar's servitude, prefigures heav-

Remains of the great ancient synagogue, Sardis

enly Jerusalem (Gal. 4:22–31). Considered a model wife (1 Pet. 3:6).

SARAI (*Princess*). Earlier form of 'Sarah' (Gen. 17:15).

SARDINE STONE. Deep red or brown variety of chalcedon quartz (Rev. 4:3, AV/KJV).

SARDIS. Capital of ancient Lydia, E of Smyrna. Rebuilt by the Romans after an earthquake in AD 17. Gold mined from the local river Pactolus minted the world's first coinage. Contains the largest synagogue yet excavated. Hosted many pagan cults. The city's acropolis was never captured by force, but twice betrayed. The local history gives colour to Christ's admonitory letter (Rev. 3:1–6).

SARDIUS. Red quartz gem on the high priest's breastpiece (Exod. 28:17, AV/KJV). Symbolised one foundation of New Jerusalem's wall (Rev. 21:20).

SARDONYX. Brown and white striped chalcedony (Rev. 21:20, AV/KJV).

SAREPTA. *See* Zarephath.

SARGON II. Assyrian king after Shalmaneser. He died shortly after capturing Samaria in 722 BC (2 Kings 17:6). Sargon's records claim to have deported 30,000 captives from Samaria (Isa. 20:1). Succeeded by Sennacherib.

SATAN. Not strictly a personal name, but a legal term: 'adversary', i.e. prosecuting counsel

Sargon II

(Rev. 12:10). Spiritual enemy of God and his people (1 Chron. 21:1; Matt. 4:10; Luke 13:16; Acts 5:3; 2 Cor. 12:7). In character, evil (Matt. 6:13) and devious (2 Cor. 11:14). He lies (John 8:44), schemes (Eph. 6:11), slanders (1 Tim. 5:14), deceives (1 Tim. 2:14), blinds (2 Cor. 4:4), incites to evil (Gen. 3:1–5; Luke 22:3); yet his power is limited (Job 1:12;1 Cor. 10:13).

SATAN, SYNAGOGUE OF. Jewish adversaries of Christians in Smyrna and Philadelphia (Rev. 2:9; 3:9).

SATRAP. Persian provincial governor (Ezra 8:36; Esther 9:3; Dan. 6:1).

SATYR (*Hairy One*). The Hebrew word usually refers to goats (Lev. 4:23), but evil spirits behind goat-shaped idols are sometimes meant (Lev. 17:7; 2 Chron. 11:15).

SAUL (*Small*). 1. Benjamite son of Kish (1 Sam. 9:2) and first king of Israel (1 Sam. 10:17–25), in response to public demand (1 Sam. 8). Jealous of David's successes (1 Sam.

18), he hounded him in vain (1 Sam. 19–24; 26). Threefold disobedience (1 Sam. 13:7–10; 15; 28) led to his deposition (1 Sam. 15:23) and death (1 Sam. 31).

2. The apostle Paul's Jewish name (Acts 13:9).

SAVIOUR. One who delivers another from evil (Neh. 9:27, AV/KJV). Title usually reserved for God (2 Sam. 22:3) and Jesus (Luke 2:11).

SAWN ASUNDER. According to Jewish tradition, Isaiah's fate at the hands of king Manasseh (Heb. 11:37).

SCALES. 1. Distinguished marine animals allowed for food (Lev. 11:9–12).

2. For weighing, *see* Balance.

SCAPEGOAT. Goat driven into the wilderness, symbolising the banishment of Israel's sins (Lev. 16:7–10, 20–22). Prefigures Jesus' perfect atoning work (2 Cor. 5:21; Heb. 9:11–14).

SCARLET. Expensive dye obtained from crushed cochineal insects. Used on fabric for the Tabernacle (Exod. 25:4), priestly dress (Exod. 28:6) and some sacrifices (Lev. 14:4). Colour associated with great luxury (2 Sam. 1:24; Rev. 18:12) and sin (Isa. 1:18, where God's forgiveness is contrasted with the virtual impossibility of removing scarlet stain).

SCARLET BEAST. The beast's colour (Rev. 17:3) alludes to sin (Isa. 1:18) and demonic power (Rev. 12:3).

SCARLET WOMAN. Expensively dressed harlot, symbolising Rome as 'Babylon' (Rev. 17:3–5), contrasted with the simple purity of the Bride of Christ (Rev. 19:8).

SCEPTRE. Staff of sovereignty of earthly rulers (Esther 4:11; Zech. 10:11), but most often symbolising divine authority (Ps. 45:6), especially of Christ's reign (Gen. 49:10; Ps. 2:9; Rev. 19:15).

SCEVA. Jewish high priest, whose itinerant exorcist sons in Ephesus invoked the name of Jesus, with painful results (Acts 9:14–16). No Jewish high priest of this (Latin) name is known. Probably a self-adopted title to impress.

SCORPION. *See* Insects p. 105.

SCOURGING. The only corporal punishment allowed in Israel, with a maximum of 40 stripes (Deut. 25:1–3); in practice 39, to avoid breaking the law (2 Cor. 11:24). Suffered by Jesus (John 19:1) and disciples (Matt. 23:34; Acts 5:40). Roman citizens exempt (Acts 23:25).

SCRIBES. Experts in Mosaic law, who came to prominence after the exile (Neh. 8:1). By NT times had become a political party, sat in the Sanhedrin (Matt. 16:21; 26:3) and expected deference (Matt. 23:5–7). Some open-minded towards Jesus (Mark 12:28–34), but most were antagonistic (Matt. 9:3; 12:38). Jesus condemned their hypocrisy (Matt. 23:13–33).

SCROLL. Early type of 'book' made from a roll of papyrus, leather or parchment. Could be secured with a seal to protect the contents from unauthorised eyes (Isa. 29:11; Rev. 5:2). For biblical scrolls, goatskin dried and thinned by scraping was fastened to a wooden spindle at each end, allowing the scroll to be rolled and unrolled sideways, not vertically as in some representations (Luke 4:20). *See* Papyrus.

SCYTHIANS. Considered uncouth, cruel and

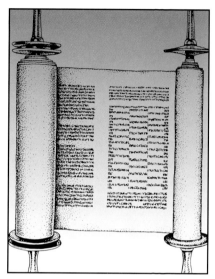
Scroll with two spindles

anti-Greek; consequently a byword for uncultured barbarians (Col. 3:11).

SEA. Created (Gen. 1:9–10) and controlled by God (Jer. 5:22). Figuratively applied to rebellious nations (Isa. 17:12), terrifying noise (Jer. 6:23), relentlessness (Ezek. 26:3), limitlessness (Job 11:9), immense power (Ps. 93:4), lack of trust (James 1:6). Due to disappear at the new creation (Rev. 21:1). *See* Dead Sea; Great Sea; Red Sea.

SEA, BRONZE. Huge water-basin, a remarkable technological achievement, 5 metres (16 ft) in diameter, 2.5 metres (8 ft) high, with a capacity of 45,000 litres (10,000 gallons). Used in the Temple service (1 Kings 7:23–26; 2 Kings 25:13; Jer. 52:17).

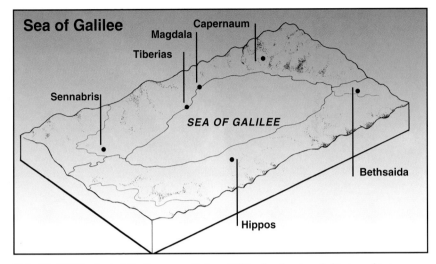

Sea of Galilee

Capernaum
Magdala
Tiberias
Sennabris
SEA OF GALILEE
Bethsaida
Hippos

SEA OF ADRIA. Central Mediterranean (Acts 27:27).

SEA OF GALILEE. Lovely pear-shaped lake (Matt. 4:18), 21 km (13 mi) long and 13 km (8 mi) wide, fed by the Jordan. Also called Sea of Chinnereth (Num. 34:11), Lake of Gennesaret (Luke 5:1) and Sea of Tiberias (John 21:1). The waters supported a flourishing fishing industry. Due to the surrounding mountains, contrasts in temperature give rise to sudden storms (Matt. 8:24; 14:24).

SEA OF GLASS. Figurative description applied to the heavenly scene (Rev. 4:6–7; 15:2), and reminiscent of Solomon's Temple (1 Kings 7:23).

SEA PEOPLES. Warriors from Aegean islands, especially Crete (Caphtor, Deut. 2:23), who settled on the coast of Canaan. *See* Philistines.

SEAL. Small engraved object, used to impress a personal mark. Signified ownership (Gen. 38:25; 2 Cor. 1:22; 2 Tim. 2:19), authenticity (1 Kings 21:8), authority (Esther 8:8) or witness (Neh. 9:38). Affixed to documents to prevent tampering. Jeremiah's purchase of a field (Jer. 32:10–14) illustrates common practice: one deed was enclosed in a sealed 'envelope' of clay, upon which was a summary of the contents. Used to prevent unauthorised entry (Deut. 32:34; Dan. 6:17; Matt. 27:66). A 'sealed prophecy' applied to some future date (Dan. 12:9); only an authorised person might break the seal and reveal the contents (Rev. 5:1–5).

SEAT. Sitting the posture of authority (Rev. 19:4), royalty (Neh. 2:6), judges (Ruth 4:1–4; Jer. 26:10), teachers (Matt. 5:1), one being honoured (James 2:3) or dignified (1 Kings 10:5), of one whose work is completed (Heb. 1:3). 'Best seats' (Matt. 23:6) were occupied by leading synagogue officials. *See* Judgment seat; Mercy seat; Moses' seat.

SEBA. Country of S Arabia (Isa. 43:3). Seba and Sheba (Ps. 72:10) are probably identical, one derived from Arabic, the other from Hebrew.

SECOND COMING. The glorified Christ's return to this earth (Mark 14:62; Rev. 1:7) as the climax and fulfilment of history (Rom. 8:19; 2 Pet. 3:13; Rev. 21:1). Brings about the final conquest of Satan and his forces (1 Cor. 15:23–24) and the world's judgment (1 Cor. 4:5); completes the redemption of believers (1 Thess. 4:16–17; Heb. 9:28; 1 John 3:2). The event delayed to give opportunity for repentance (2 Pet. 3:8–12). Foretold (Dan. 7:13–14; Acts 1:11;1 Thess. 5:2). Preceded by universal evangelism, persecution of believers, apostasy, nominal religion, wars, famines, earthquakes and cosmic changes (Matt. 24).

SECRET. Human secrets are open to God (Ps. 44:21; Matt. 6:4; Rom. 2:16) and he can expose them (Luke 8:17). Divine secrets (Deut. 29:29) will be made known only by God's decision (1 Cor. 2:7) and cannot be discovered by human beings (1 Cor. 4:1). *See* Mystery.

SECRET ARTS. Satanic practices (Exod. 7:11; Acts 19:19). *See* Sorcery.

SECURITY. Assured protection, to be found alone in God (Deut. 33:27; Heb. 13:6). Conditional upon obedience (Exod. 19:5; Jer. 22:21). False security based on wealth (Ps. 52:7; Luke 12:19; 1 Tim. 6:17), political alliances (Isa. 31:1), human support (Jer. 17:5), self-sufficiency (Jer. 49:4), self-confidence (Prov. 28:26; 1 Cor. 10:12). *See* Pledge.

SEED. Symbol of God's word (Isa. 55:10; Luke 8:11), Christ (Gal. 3:16), believers (Gal. 3:29), spiritual life (1 Pet. 1:23), evil influence (Prov. 22:8; Isa. 57:3). Illustrates the resurrection body (1 Cor. 15:35–38). *See* Mustard.

SEETHING. Israelites were banned from boiling a kid in its mother's milk (Exod. 23:19; Deut. 14:21) because, as Canaanite texts reveal, it was a rite of fertility magic.

SELA (*Rock*). Moabite city captured by Amaziah king of Judah and renamed Joktheel (2 Kings 14:7).

SELAH. Frequently in the Psalms. Probably a musical direction, but meaning uncertain.

SELEUCIA. Port of Antioch in Syria (Acts 13:4).

SELF-CONTROL. Mastery over one's desires (1 Thess. 4:4), words (Ps. 141:3), thoughts (Phil. 4:8) and actions (1 Sam. 24:18), especially when provoked (Luke 6:27) or tempted (1 Cor. 7:5). Spiritual gift (Gal. 5:23), exemplified by Christ (Isa. 53:7; 1 Pet. 2:23).

SELF-DENIAL. Willingness to forgo status (Phil. 3:7), freedom (Acts 21:13), sinful pleasures (Heb. 11:25), relationships (Matt. 10:37) and possessions (Matt. 19:29), or risk misunderstanding (Dan. 1:8), by putting God first (1 Sam. 2:30; Matt. 16:24).

SELF-INDULGENCE. Yielding to craving (Isa. 56:11–12), typical of the godless life (Eph. 2:3); revealed in selfish ambition (James 3:14–16), wanting one's own way (James 4:2), immorality (Gal. 5:19), gluttony and drunkenness (Prov.

23:20) or desire for riches (Josh. 7:21; 1 Tim. 6:10). Leads nowhere (Luke 12:19–20) but to ruin (Luke 15:13–14) and judgment (Phil. 3:19).

SELF–RIGHTEOUSNESS. Moral conceit, fostering illusions of sinlessness (Rom. 10:3), innocence (Prov. 16:2; Jer. 2:35) or superiority (Luke 18:9–12; John 9:24), issuing in separation from God (Gal. 5:4; 1 John 1:10).

SELFISHNESS. Characteristic of unbelievers (Rom. 8:5; 2 Cor. 5:15), especially in the last days (2 Pet. 3:3). Condemned (Isa. 5:8), for it never satisfies (Hab. 2:5), ignores others (Ezek. 34:18; Mark 10:37) and results in eternal loss (Rom. 2:8; Phil. 3:19).

SENATE OF ISRAEL. Sanhedrin (Acts 5:21, AV/KJV).

SENNACHERIB. Son and successor of Sargon II as king of Assyria and Babylonia (705–681 BC), and father of Esarhaddon. Invaded Judah (2 Kings 18:17—19:37).

SEPHARVAIM. Syrian city captured by Assyrians (2 Kings 17:24; 19:3); location uncertain.

SERAIAH. 1. Secretary of State at David's court (2 Sam. 8:17); also called Sheva (2 Sam. 20:25), Shisha (1 Kings 4:3) and Shavsha (1 Chron. 18:16).
2. Son of Azriel, sent in vain by king Jehoiakim to arrest Jeremiah and Baruch (Jer. 36:36).
3. Baruch's brother who took Jeremiah's prophecy of doom to Babylon, read it in public there, then sank it in the Euphrates to indicate the end of Babylon (Jer. 51:59–64).

SERAPHS/SERAPHIM. Spiritual beings around God's throne (Isa. 6:2, 6; the only references). The term comes from Hebrew for 'fire'.

SERGIUS PAULUS. Proconsul of Cyprus (AD 47–48), who responded to Paul's preaching (Acts 13:7–12).

SERMON ON THE MOUNT. Popular designation of teaching recorded in Matt. 5—7, Jesus' manifesto setting out the nature of discipleship.

SERMON ON THE PLAIN. Parallel version of some of Jesus' Sermon on the Mount (Luke 6:20–40).

SERPENT. *See* Wild animals p. 17.

SERVANT. Mosaic law distinguished between hired hands and slaves (Lev. 25:6). *See* Ear; Slavery.

SERVANT SONGS. Term applied to the messianic portrayal of God's Servant in Isaiah (42:1–4; 49:1–6; 50:4–9; 52:13—53:12).

SETH. Adam and Eve's third son (1 Chron. 1:1), born after Abel's murder and Cain's banishment (Gen. 4:25–26). Died aged 912 (Gen. 5:8).

SEVEN CHURCHES. Christian communities in Asia Minor (Rev. 1:4) to whom letters are addressed in Rev. 2—3.

SEVENTH DAY. Day of rest (Gen. 2:2–3; Exod. 20:10; Heb. 4:3–11), reflecting the notion that the number seven indicates completeness. *See* Day's journey; Sabbath.

SEVENTY. Conventional name for the band of

disciples sent out in pairs to prepare the way for Jesus' preaching (Luke 10:1–17), although many manuscripts speak of 72. Going in pairs provided the acceptable testimony of two witnesses (Deut. 17:6). The conventional 'Seventy' may allude to Jacob's family (Gen. 46:27) or to the number of nations listed in Gen. 10.

SEVENTY TIMES SEVEN. Jesus teaches (Matt. 18:22) forgiveness must go as far as that rogue Lamech was prepared to go in his thirst for revenge (Gen. 4:24).

SEXUAL RELATIONS. God's gift (Gen. 1:27) for husband and wife to complement one another (1 Cor. 11:11). Sexual activity ordained by God (Gen. 1:28) within the marriage union (Gen. 2:23–24; Matt. 19:4–6; Eph. 5:31–33). The gift is perverted in adultery (Exod. 20:14), promiscuity (Ezek. 16:25), lust (1 Pet. 4:3) and prostitution (Lev. 19:29), and leads to trouble (Gen. 38:15–26) and judgment (1 Cor. 6:9). *See* Homosexuality.

SHADOW. Shelter from midday sun (Job 40:22) and so symbolic of protection (Isa. 49:2). Figuratively of this life's brevity (1 Chron. 29:15) or approaching end (Ps. 23:4).

SHADRACH, MESHACH AND ABEDNEGO. Babylonian names given to Hebrew captives Hananiah, Mishael and Azariah on entering Nebuchadnezzar's service (Dan. 1:7).

SHAKE. To shake off the dust from feet (Matt. 10:14) or clothes (Acts 18:6) signified total rejection of the local inhabitants. To 'shake out the lap' (Neh. 5:13) was to tip out personal items carried in the folds of a garment normally kept secure with a belt (the ancient equivalent of pockets). The action symbolised God's jettisoning people who broke promises.

SHALLUM (*Recompense*). Popular name with parents. About 15 mentioned.
    1. Briefly king of Israel (2 Kings 15:10) whose accession then death by assassination was typical of Israel's last 25 years, before Samaria fell in 722 BC.
    2. Son and successor of Josiah king of Judah (1 Chron. 3:15; Jer. 22:11), usually called Jehoahaz (2 Chron. 3:15).
    3. Husband of the prophetess Huldah and keeper of state and Temple robes (2 Kings 22:14).

SHALMANESER V. Son and successor of the Assyrian king Tiglath-Pileser III (727–722 BC). Forced the last king of Israel, Hoshea, to pay an

Shalmaneser V

annual tribute, but when Hoshea rebelled and sought help from Egypt, Shalmaneser besieged Samaria, which fell three years later, in 722 BC (2 Kings 17:3–6).

SHAMGAR. His exploit against the Philistines (Judg. 3:31; 5:6) gave Israel relief. An ox goad was an unorthodox but effective weapon, being 3 metres (10 ft) long and tipped with metal.

SHAPHAN. Royal secretary who told king Hezekiah about the Book of the Law discovered during Temple repairs (2 Kings 22:3–14).

SHAREZER. *See* Adrammelech.

SHARON. Coastal pastureland (1 Chron. 5:16; 27:29; Isa. 65:10) between Carmel and Joppa. Evangelised by Peter (Acts 9:35). *See* Rose of Sharon.

SHAVEH. *See* King's Valley.

SHAVING. Shaving the head signified mourning (Isa. 15:2; Jer. 16:6; Ezek. 7:18; Amos 8:10; Mic. 1:16), though the pagan practice of shaving only the forehead was forbidden (Deut. 14:1). Signalled the conclusion of a vow (Num. 6:18; Acts 21:24) or a slave girl's proposed marriage to her captor (Deut. 21:12). Figuratively describes the destruction of Gaza (Jer. 47:5) and the disgrace brought upon backsliding Israel (Isa. 3:24). *See* Baldness; Hair.

SHEAF. *See* Farming p. 71.

SHEALTIEL. Eldest son of king Jeconiah (1 Chron. 3:17) and reputed father of Zerubbabel (Ezra 3:8).

SHEARING. Although secured for shearing, sheep remain quiet (Isa. 53:7; Acts 8:32). Laban's sheepshearing would have taken many days and given Jacob time to escape (Gen. 31:19). Time of festivity (1 Sam. 25:2–11). *See* Lamb; Ram; Sheep; Wool.

SHEBNA. Hezekiah's Secretary of State (2 Kings 18:18), denounced for egotism (Isa. 22:15).

SHECHEM. 1. Strategic highland city of Manasseh, E of Nablus. Site of altars erected by Abraham (Gen. 12:7) and Jacob (Gen. 33:20), Joseph's burial place (Josh. 24:32), and Joshua's covenant with the tribes (Josh. 24:1–27).

2. Son of Hamor the Hivite, who raped Dinah and provoked violent reaction from her brothers (Gen. 34).

SHEEP. *See* Domesticated animals p. 15.

SHEEP GATE. Gate in N wall of Jerusalem restored by Nehemiah (Neh. 3:1). That in John 5:2 was in the Herodian wall, N of Nehemiah's repair.

SHEEPFOLD. Simple enclosure of stones and thorns as a night shelter for the flock. The 'door' was a gap in the wall across which the shepherd lay down to sleep (John 10:1–16).

SHEKEL. *See* Money pp. 146-147.

SHEM. Noah's firstborn, brother of Ham and Japheth (Gen. 6:10), whose descendants (Gen. 10:21–31) lived N and E of Canaan.

SHEMAIAH. 1. Prophet who denounced Rehoboam's plan to make war against Jeroboam

(1 Kings 12:22–24), conveyed God's messages concerning Shishak's invasion (2 Chron. 12:1–8), and whose records were used by the Chronicler (2 Chron. 12:15).

2. Jew who wrote from Babylon falsely predicting a speedy return from exile and demanding Jeremiah's imprisonment (Jer. 29:24–32).

3. False prophet hired by Sanballat and Tobiah to intimidate Nehemiah (Neh. 6:10–14).

SHEPHATIAH. One of four powerful Judean ministers who demanded that the weak king Zedekiah should sentence Jeremiah to death for undermining morale (Jer. 38).

SHEPHELAH (*Lowland*). Tract of low hills between Philistian coast and Judean highlands (RSV of 1 Kings 10:27; 1 Chron. 27:28; 2 Chron. 26:10; Jer. 17:26; Obad. 19).

SHEPHERD. In the Bible, one caring for goats and cattle as well as sheep (Gen. 46:32). Considered a lowly task (1 Sam. 16:11), but involved responsibility for guiding (Exod. 3:1), providing pasture (Mic. 7:14), protecting (1 Sam. 17:34–35), searching for wanderers (Ezek. 34:16), checking numbers (Lev. 27:32). The ancient practice of going before (Ps. 23:2), not driving, sheep used as a metaphor for leaders with responsibility for caring: God (Gen. 48:15), Jesus (John 10; Heb. 13:30), kings (2 Sam. 5:2), church pastors (1 Pet. 5:2). *See* Rod.

SHERD. Broken piece of pottery (Isa. 30:14, AV/KJV). *See* Potsherd.

SHESHBAZZAR. Prince of Judah (Ezra 1:8), entrusted by the Persian king Cyrus with returning gold and silver vessels to the Temple (Ezra 5:14).

A shepherd leads his flock

SHETHAR-BOZENAI. Persian provincial official who protested to king Darius about Zerubbabel's right to rebuild the Temple. The decree of Cyrus was unearthed in the royal archives and Darius ordered harassment to cease and for the work to be funded (Ezra 5:3, 6; 6:6, 13).

SHEWBREAD. *See* Bread of the Presence.

SHIBBOLETH. Password demanded by Jephthah's sentries, which retreating Ephraimites were unable to pronounce (Judg. 12:6).

SHIELD. 1. *See* War p. 241.

2. Divine title (Gen. 15:1; Abram may have feared reprisals after Gen. 14:14–17). Symbolises

God's protection (Deut. 33:29) and faith (Eph. 6:16).

SHIHOR. Easternmost branch of the Nile (Josh. 13:3; Jer. 2:18).

SHILOAH. Aqueduct from the Gihon spring into Jerusalem (Isa. 8:6). Isaiah's remark alludes to David's royal line (associated with Gihon, 1 Kings 1:33) and to Jerusalem as God's city. Ahaz was despising God's ability to protect his own. *See* Siloam.

SHILOH. Highland town in Ephraim (Judg. 21:19), N of Jerusalem; religious and administrative centre from Joshua's day (Josh. 18:1, 8), until its destruction by Philistines about 1050 BC, when the local priests retreated to Nob (1 Sam. 21:1–6; 22:19). Sanctuary (1 Sam. 1:3) served by Eli's sons (1 Sam. 14:3), where Samuel spent his childhood (1 Sam. 3).

SHIMEI. Cursed David as he fled from Absalom for usurping the house of Saul (2 Sam. 16:5–13). Pardoned by David (2 Sam. 19:18–23), who on his deathbed, however, tells Solomon to deal with him (1 Kings 2:8–9). Executed after breaking his word not to leave Jerusalem (1 Kings 2:36–46).

SHINAR. Area of Babylonia including cities of Babel, Erech and Akkad (Gen. 10:10; 11:2). Source of the luxurious garment causing Achan's downfall (Josh. 7:21).

SHIPPING. *See* Travel p. 229.

SHIPWRECK. *See* Travel p. 229.

SHISHAK. Sheshonq I, Pharaoh of Egypt (reigned 945–924 BC), with whom Jeroboam sought refuge from Solomon (1 Kings 11:40). Invaded Judah in 925 and looted the Temple and Rehoboam's palace (1 Kings 14:25–26).

SHOBAL. Caleb's son, who founded Kiriath Jearim (1 Chron. 2:50). Descendants incorporated into Judah (1 Chron. 4:1).

SHRINE. Small local pagan sanctuary (1 Kings 12:31). Often on high ground (2 Kings 17:10). *See* High place. Term also applied to hand-sized representations of gods (Acts 19:24).

SHROUD. Linen wrapping for a corpse, indicating honourable burial (Matt. 27:59), even more so when a private tomb was used (Matt. 27:60). *See* Burial.

SHULAMMITE. Woman in Song of Sol. 6:13, who may be the beautiful Abishag who ministered to the aged David (1 Kings 1:3–4). The name can also be a feminine Hebrew form of 'Solomon' and mean his spouse.

SHUNAMMITE. Inhabitant of Shunem.
1. Abishag, who nursed David (1 Kings 1:15) and attracted Solomon's older brother Adonijah (1 Kings 2:13–22).
2. Elisha's unnamed benefactress (2 Kings 4), whose generosity was later rewarded (2 Kings 8:1–6).

SHUNEM. Canaanite town, captured by Joshua (Josh. 19:18). Philistines camped there before engaging Saul (1 Sam. 28:4). Frequently visited by Elisha (2 Kings 4:8–37). *See* Abishag; Shulammite; Shunammite.

SHUTTLE, WEAVER'S. Its rapid movement

likened to life's swift passing (Job 7:6). *See* Weaving.

SIBMAH. Moabite cattle town (Num. 32:38; Josh. 13:19). Later retaken by Moab, but the destruction of extensive local vineyards was foretold (Isa. 16:8; Jer.48:32).

SICKNESS. Sometimes the consequence of sin (Deut. 28:58–61; 1 Cor. 11:30); the popular view (John 9:2). Associated with Satan (Mark 1:32; Luke 13:16; Acts 10:38; 2 Cor. 12:7) and thus the object of many of Christ's miracles (Matt. 4:24; 8:16).

SIDDIM, VALLEY OF. Located SE of Dead Sea (now submerged) (Gen. 14).

SIDON. Phoenician seaport (modern Saida) and Canaanite stronghold (Gen. 10:19; Isa. 23:4), W of Mt. Hermon (Deut. 3:9). Famous for oarsmen (Ezek. 27:8), woodsmen (1 Kings 5:6), commerce (Isa. 23:2), worldly wisdom (Zech. 9:2), self-confidence (Judg. 18:7), its goddess Ashteroth (1 Kings 11:5). Captured by Sennacherib (Isa. 23:2–12), Esarheddon, then Nebuchadnezzar (587 BC; Jer. 25:22). Visited by Jesus (Matt. 11:21; 15:21–28) and Paul (Acts 27:3).

SIEGE. *See* War p. 241.

SIEVE. Mentioned symbolically of God's judgment (Judg. 7:4; Isa. 30:28; Amos 9:9) and of Satan's attack on Peter (Luke22:31).

SIGN. Event or action charged with meaning beyond itself: rainbow (Gen. 9:13), circumcision (Gen. 17:11), plagues of Egypt (Exod. 8:23), Passover blood (Exod. 12:13), Sabbath (Exod. 31:13–17; Ezek. 20:12), Aaron's rod (Num. 17:10). St John's preferred term for Jesus' miracles (John 2:11; 20:30).

SIGNS AND WONDERS. Unusual events witnessing to divine activity in redemption (Exod. 7:3; Acts 2:19–21; 4:30; 7:36). *See* Miracles.

SIHON. Powerful Amorite king of Heshbon. His failure to bar Israel from his territory (Deut. 2:26–34) frequently recalled (Deut. 31:4; Josh. 2:10; Judg. 11:19–21; Neh. 9:22; Ps. 135:11).

SILAS. Jewish Christian and Roman citizen (Acts 16:38). Delegated by the Council of Jerusalem to report to the church at Antioch on accepting Gentile converts (Acts 15:22). Accompanied Paul on the second missionary journey (Acts 15:40); shared his imprisonment at Philippi (Acts 16:19) and the troubles at Thessalonica (Acts 17:1–10).

SILENCE. Appropriate attitude before God (Hab. 2:20; Zeph. 1:7). Silence in heaven (Rev. 8:1) may be the dramatic pause before God acts (Gen. 24:21; Josh. 6:10). Euphemism for death (1 Sam. 2:9; Ps. 94:17).

SILOAM (*Conducted*). Original name of aqueduct (Isa. 8:6) that 'conducted' water from Gihon, E of Jerusalem, into the city's 'Pool of Siloam' (Neh. 3:15; John 9:7).

SILVANUS. Latin form of the name Silas.

SILVER. *See* Money, p. 146.

SIMEON. 1. Jacob's second son by Leah (Gen. 29:33). On Joseph's orders, a hostage in Egypt (Gen. 42:24). With Levi, took revenge against

Siloam tunnel

3. Brother of Jesus (Matt. 13:55).
4. Rude Pharisee (Luke 7:40).
5. Leper of Bethany (Matt. 26:6).
6. Passerby from Cyrene, conscripted to carry Jesus' cross (Matt. 27:32).
7. Father of Judas Iscariot (John 6:71).
8. Magician ('Magus') of Samaria (Acts 8:9).
9. Tanner of Joppa (Acts 9:43).

SIN (*desert*). Wilderness between Sinai and Elim (Exod. 16:1). Not to be confused with the Wilderness of Zin.

SIN. Main Hebrew and Greek terms both mean 'missing the mark'. Rebellion (Isa. 30:9) against God and his laws (Ps. 51:4); universal (John 8:7; Rom. 3:23; Gal. 3:22). Defined as wrongdoing (Gen. 4:7; 1 John 5:17), failing to do good (James 4:17), unbelief (John 16:9), not acting from faith (Rom. 14:23), transgressing God's law (1 John 3:4), wrong attitude towards others (Prov. 14:21), wrong motive (Prov. 21:4). Means separation from God (Ps. 66:18; Isa. 59:2; 2 Thess. 1:9). Apart from God's action in Christ, issues in death (Rom. 6:23; 2 Cor. 5:21; James 1:15). Deceitful (Rom. 7:11; Heb. 3:13; 1 John 1:8), Satan inspired (1 John 3:8), temporarily pleasurable (Heb. 11:25).

SIN, UNFORGIVABLE. Accusing Jesus of being inspired by an evil spirit and so doing the work of Satan (Matt. 12:24–32).

SIN OFFERING. In Mosaic law, atoning for sins committed in ignorance or inadvertently (Lev. 4:1–5:13). Inadequate (Heb. 1:4). Foreshadowed Jesus' sacrifice (Rom. 8:3; Heb. 13:11–12).

SINAI. Mountain (probably Jebel Musa), also

Shechem for raping their sister Dinah (Gen. 34:25–31). *See* Simeonites.
2. Elderly prophet of Jerusalem who recognised the infant Jesus as Messiah (Luke 2:25–35).
3. Peter's Hebrew name (Acts 15:14; 2 Pet. 1:1), usually spelled 'Simon'.
4. Christian prophet at Antioch (Acts 13:1).

SIMEONITES. The descendants of Jacob's son Simeon (Gen. 35:23; Josh. 19:8). Numbers fell rapidly (Num. 1:23; 26:14), as foretold in Jabob's final blessing (Gen. 49:5–7). The tribe was apparently absorbed by Judah (Josh. 19:1–9; not named by Moses in Deut. 33).

SIMON (*God Heard*). Popular name with parents (variant of 'Simeon').
1. Peter's first name (Matt. 16:17).
2. The apostle called a 'Cananaean', Aramaic for 'Zealot'; a different word from 'Canaanite' (Matt. 10:4; Acts 1:13).

called Horeb, where God revealed himself to Moses (Exod. 3:1–10) and the people (Exod. 19), published his laws (Exod. 20:1–23:19) and established his covenant with Israel (Exod. 24:4–18). In the NT, symbolises the old covenant (Gal. 4:24–31; Heb. 12:18–29). *See* Horeb.

SINFUL NATURE. Human impulses opposed to God (Gal. 5:16–21), a conflict described by rabbis as one between good and bad inclinations (Gen. 6:5). *See* Flesh.

SINIM. *See* Syene.

SINNERS. Often almost a technical term for those not keeping the Mosaic law (Matt. 9:10). In NT letters, human beings separated from God by sin (Rom. 5:8).

SIRA/SIRACH. *See* Ecclesiasticus.

SIRAH. Well near Hebron, to which Joab lured Abner to his death (2 Sam. 3:26–27).

SIRION. Phoenician name for Mt. Hermon (Deut. 3:9; Ps. 29:6).

SISERA. Canaanite general defeated by Deborah and Barak, treacherously killed by Jael (Judg. 4–5).

SITNAH (*Enmity*). Second well dug by Isaac's herdsmen, but opposed by locals (Gen. 26:21).

SKIFF. Speedy reed boat (Isa. 18:2), symbolising for Job (9:26) the swift passage of life.

SKIN. 1. Infectious skin diseases were taken very seriously (Lev. 13). *See* Boils; Leprosy.
  2. *See* Leather; Tanning.

Roman slave's badge

SKY. Simile for the colour of the heavenly 'pavement' (Exod. 24:10), alluding to blue sapphire, as used in Babylonian royal pavements. Figuratively, of great height (Deut. 1:28; Prov. 23:5) or power (Jer. 51:53; Matt. 11:23).

SLANDER. Malicious or false reports; condemned (Lev. 19:16) as sinful (Matt. 15:19), destructive (Prov. 11:9), foolish (Prov. 10:18), godless (Jer. 6:28), divisive (2 Cor. 12:20), Satanic (1 Tim. 5:14). When suffered by believers (Ps. 38:20; Rom. 3:8), to be dealt with positively (1 Cor. 4:13). *See* Flesh.

SLAUGHTER, VALLEY OF. New name for Topheth or Valley of Ben Hinnom, just S of Jerusalem, where God's judgment would fall because of Judah's pagan practice of human sacrifice (Jer. 7:32; 19:6).

SLAVERY. Subjection to unpaid compulsory labour, the consequence of war (Deut. 20:11), purchase (Lev. 25:44–45), debt (2 Kings 4:1), birth (Lev. 22:11), conscription (Josh. 9:23) or theft (Exod. 22:3). Slaves regarded as property (Lev. 25:46), yet in Israel had some rights: recompense for physical harm (Exod. 21:20, 26–27), participation in religious festivals (Exod. 23:12), ability to inherit (Gen. 15:3), asylum (Deut. 23:15), liberty after six years (Exod. 21:2–4). In the NT, slavery is recognised, not condoned, as part of the culture; but slave *trading* is condemned (1 Tim. 1:10). Christian slaves must regard their service as being to Christ (Eph. 6:5–8; Col. 3:22–23); but all believers have this status in relation to their Master, Christ (Rom. 1:1; 1 Pet. 2:16). *See* Servant; Year of Jubilee.

SLAVERY, SPIRITUAL. Negatively, in bondage (Rom. 6:16) to sin (Rom. 6:20), Satan (2 Tim. 2:26), Mosaic law (Gal. 4:24), depravity (2 Pet. 2:19) or fear (2 Tim. 1:7; Heb. 2:15). Positively, yielding one's life to Christ (Rom. 6:22) as his slave/servant (same Greek word), after his example (John 13:1–17), and thereby securing true liberty (John 8:31–36).

SLEEP. Divine gift (Ps. 127:2), bringing renewal (Jer. 31:26), peace of mind (Ps. 4:8), protection (Ps. 121:4; Ezek. 34:25). Metaphor for believer's physical death (1 Cor. 15:6), even death by violence (Acts 7:60); symbolises spiritual deadness (Isa. 56:10; Mark 13:35–36).

SLEEPLESSNESS. Due to anxiety (Eccles. 5:12), foolish action (Prov. 6:1–5), overwork (Eccles. 2:23), sickness (Job 7:4), evil deeds (Prov. 4:16; Isa. 48:22), concern for God's work (Ps. 132:4–5; Acts 12:12), some divine purpose (Esther 6:1; Dan. 6:18).

SLIME (AV/KJV). *See* Bitumen.

SLING. *See* War p. 241.

SMELL. Figuratively indicates divine acceptance of sacrifice (Gen. 8:21; Eph. 5:2). Idols helpless in this respect (Deut. 4:28; Ps. 115:6).

SMOKE. Symbolises human transitoriness (Ps. 102:3; Hos. 13:3) or, by contrast, the awesome divine presence (Exod. 19:18; Isa. 6:4) or wrath (Isa. 30:27), or the Day of the Lord (Joel 2:30; Acts 2:19).

SMYRNA. Great commercial port (modern Izmir, Turkey), founded before 2000 BC. One of

Remains of ancient Smyrna

two churches unconditionally praised by the glorified Christ (Rev. 2:8–11).

SNAKE. *See* Serpent.

SNARE, TRAP. Device for catching wild creatures (Job 18:9; Ps. 124:7). Applied figuratively to idols (Exod. 23:33), evil plots (Ps. 119:110), fear of people (Prov. 29:25), Satan (1 Tim. 3:7), lust for wealth (1 Tim. 6:9), foolish words (Prov. 18:7).

SNOW. Most references are symbolic: leprosy (Exod. 4:6), purity (Isa. 1:18), divine glory (Rev. 1:14).

SO. Pharaoh whom Hoshea, Israel's last king, asked to back his rebellion against Assyria (2 Kings 17:4). No help was forthcoming and Samaria fell in 722 BC, bringing Israel to an end.

SOAP. Lye, a crude detergent, derived from a vegetable alkali (Jer. 2:22; Mal. 3:2).

SOD, SODDEN. Archaic for 'seethe, boil' (AV/KJV of Gen. 25:29; Lev. 6:28; Lam. 4:10).

SODOM. Notorious for wickedness (Gen. 13:13). Its spectacular destruction (Gen. 19:1–11) frequently recalled.

SODOMITE. Homosexual (Deut. 23:17; 1 Cor. 6:9). Term derived from the story of Sodom (Gen. 19:1–11).

SOJOURNERS. Permanent residents in an alien country (Gen. 23:4). They could be numerous (2 Chron. 2:17), but because of Israel's own experience must be well treated (Exod. 23:9). Expected to observe certain laws (Exod. 12:19;

Lev. 17:10; 18:26; 20:2; 24:16). Christians are aliens in this world, with their true citizenship in heaven (1 Pet. 1:17). *See* Foreigners; Stranger.

SOLEMN ASSEMBLY. Special national gathering for worship (Lev. 23:36; Neh. 8:18). Jehu's stratagem lured Baal's followers to their death (2 Kings 10:20).

SOLOMON (*Peaceful*). David's successor as king (1 Kings 1). God promised him wisdom (1 Kings 3) and wealth (1 Kings 10). Built the Temple (2 Chron. 2-7), his palace (1 Kings 7:1–3) and many cities (1 Kings 9:17–21). But marrying many foreign wives led to idolatry and trouble (1 Kings 11).

SOLOMON'S PORCH/COLONNADE. On E side of Temple, popular with public speakers in winter for its shelter (John 10:23). Scene of early Christian preaching (Acts 3:11; 5:12).

SON OF. Apart from literal relationship, a Hebraism indicating destiny (as with Judas, 'son of perdition'; John 17:12, AV/KJV).

SON OF DAVID. Title applied especially to Messiah (1 Chron. 17:13; Matt. 12:23; 22:42–45; Rev. 22:16).

SON OF GOD. Term of special relationship to God, applied to angels (Job 1:6, AV/KJV), Israel (Exod. 4:22), the king (2 Sam. 7:14), Messiah (Ps. 2:7), peacemakers (Matt. 5:9), disciples (Matt. 5:45); but supremely to Jesus (Matt. 3:17; John 5:19–30; Rom. 1:4) and his followers by adoption (Rom. 8:14–17; 2 Pet. 1:4).

SON OF MAN. 1. Ezekiel so named over 90 times in his book, emphasising his human frailty before the awesome might of God.

2. Jesus' usual title for himself (only in Gospels and Acts 7:56), indicating his humanity (Matt. 8:20) and service (Matt. 20:28), yet hinting at his heavenly origin (Dan. 7:13; Luke 5:24; 6:5; 10:22; 12:40; John 3:13–14). Avoided being misunderstood as making a political claim.

SONG OF ASCENTS (degrees, AV/KJV). Title of Psalms 120—134 sung by pilgrims going up to Jerusalem for the festivals.

SONG OF THE LAMB. Praises the great deliverance brought about by Jesus, as foreshadowed in Israel's rescue at the Red Sea (Exod. 15; Rev. 15:3).

SONG OF MOSES. One celebrating God's deliverance of his people from Egypt (Exod. 15) and another recounting God's mercies (Deut. 32). Young Moses would have been schooled in the Egyptian practice of singing lessons as a memory aid (Deut. 31:19).

SONG OF SOLOMON (or Song of Songs). Intensely personal oriental poem, traditionally ascribed to Solomon, rejoicing in God's gift of human love.

SONG OF THE THREE YOUNG MEN (Apocrypha). Purports to describe the response of Shadrach, Meshach and Abednego in Nebuchadnezzar's fiery furnace (Dan. 3).

SONGS, SPIRITUAL. See Music p. 150.

SOOTHSAYER. One claiming to divine the future (Dan. 2:27; Acts 16:16). The practice condemned as pagan (Isa. 2:6; Mic. 5:12).

SOPATER. See Sosipater.

SORCERY. Divination with the help of evil spirits. Forbidden (Deut. 18:9–12), on pain of death (Lev. 20:27; 1 Chron. 10:13).

SOSIPATER. Hebrew Christian (Rom. 16:21). Probably the same as Sopater (Acts 20:4).

SOSTHENES. Successor to Crispus as president of the Corinth synagogue. Beaten up by the mob when the proconsul Gallio refused to hear their charge against Paul (Acts 18:17). May be Paul's colleague in 1 Cor. 1:1.

SOUL. Hebrew and Greek terms have a wide range of meaning: breath (Gen. 2:7), life (2 Sam. 1:9; Jer. 38:16), person (Prov. 1:11), spirit (Prov. 11:30; Rev. 18:13), whole being (Ps. 103:1; Luke 1:46), seat of emotions (Heb. 4:12).

SOUR GRAPES. Proverbial expression reflecting ancient belief in collective responsibility, rejected by the prophets in respect of individual wrongdoing (Jer. 31:29–30; Ezek. 18:2).

SOUTH (Negeb). Israelites faced the rising sun to fix directions; hence S was to the speaker's right hand (2 Sam. 24:5, AV/KJV).

SOUTH, QUEEN OF THE. Queen of Sheba (Matt. 12:42).

SOVEREIGN LORD. NIV translation of 'Lord God' in most other versions.

SOWING. 1. See Farming p. 71.

2. Proverbial for foolishly inviting dire consequences (Hos. 8:7), hard labour bringing reward (Ps. 126:5), faithfulness in work (Eccles. 11:6),

turning to God (Hos. 10:12), peacemaking leading to right relationships (James 3:18). Likened to preaching (1 Cor. 9:11) and the body (1 Cor. 15:42–44).

SPAN. Handbreadth (Exod. 28:16), between tip of little finger and end of extended thumb.

SPARROW. *See* Birds p. 104.

SPEAR. *See* War p. 241.

SPECKLED. Selective breeding and reliance on superstitition could not have continued Jacob's success with his animals after Laban altered the conditions. The outcome was due to divine overruling (Gen. 30—31).

SPELL. Employing magic formulae, condemned as an occult practice (Deut. 18:10–12; Isa. 47:9; Rev. 18:23).

SPELT. *See* Farming p. 71.

SPICES. *See* Herbs and spices pp. 92-93.

SPIKENARD. *See* Nard.

SPIRIT. Hebrew and Greek each have one word meaning breath (2 Sam. 22:16), wind (Gen. 8:1) or spirit (John 3:8). *See* Holy Spirit.

SPIRIT, FAMILIAR. Demon summoned by a medium for consulting the dead (Lev. 20:6).

SPIRITISM. Attempts to secure knowledge of the future from supernatural powers. Practised in Israel (2 Kings 21:6), though condemned by God (Lev. 20:27) as futile (Isa. 8:19) and dangerous (Lev. 19:31).

SPIRITS, evil. *See* Demons.

SPIRITS, SEVEN. Either the sevenfold messianic Spirit of Isa. 11:2, or the seven archangels (Tobit 12:15) around God's throne (Rev. 1:4; 3:1; 4:5; 5:6).

SPIRITUAL GIFTS. Special abilities bestowed for God's service (1 Cor. 12—14) to build up the church (1 Cor. 14:12). To be exercised in love (Rom. 12:6–9; 1 Cor. 13; Eph. 4:15–16).

SPITTING. Expression of disapproval (Num. 12:14; Deut. 25:9) or contempt (Isa. 50:6; Matt. 26:67). Jesus used the popular belief that spittle had healing properties to indicate what he was about to do (Mark 8:23; John 9:6). *See* Blindness; Mute.

SPOT. Skin diseases (Lev. 13) were examined by a priest. A period of quarantine determined whether a condition was contagious, benign or malignant.

SPRING. The many place-names beginning with *En-* (Hebrew, *Spring*) indicate the need to establish towns near a reliable water supply.

SPRINKLING. Sign of atonement or consecration. Blood sprinkled on door frames at Passover (Exod. 12:7), on the altar (Lev. 7:2) or on the mercy seat (Lev. 16:14). Symbolised forgiveness in Christ (1 Pet. 1:2). Oil signified consecration (Lev. 8:11) and water, cleansing (Num. 8:7).

SQUARE. Cities were usually incredibly congested, so some space inside the gate was kept as a so-called public square for people to gather for news and business (Job 29:7; Isa. 15:3). *See* Gate, city.

STADIA. Plural of Greek measure of distance (Rev. 14:20; 21:16), about 182 metres (610 ft). The singular (*stadion*) was a footrace course (1 Cor. 9:24), from which 'stadium' is derived.

STAFF. Walking-stick (Gen. 38:18), considered personal to its owner (Gen. 38:25; Exod. 7:10; Num. 17; 2 Kings 4:29). Figuratively, of readiness (Exod. 12:11); or of a covenant, useless when broken (Zech. 11:7–14).

STANDARD. 1. Ensign, as a rallying point (Num. 1:52).
2. Authorised unit of measurement (2 Sam. 14:26; Ezek. 45:11).
3. Accepted moral or cultural norms (Ezek. 11:12; John 8:15; 2 Cor. 10:2).

STAR OF BETHLEHEM. Heavenly body announcing Messiah's birth, sufficiently extraordinary to catch the attention of astrologers (Matt. 2:1–10). Explanations include a comet, the planetary conjunction of Jupiter, Saturn and Venus (in 7 BC), or a supernova (explosive flare-up of a star, visible for several months). *See* Dove's dung.

STAR OF JACOB. Prophecy of a king of Israel who would conquer neighbouring countries (Num. 24:17–19).

STARS. 1. Part of God's creation (Gen. 1:16–18); not to be worshipped (Deut. 4:19). Their immense number symbolic of Abraham's descendants (Gen. 22:17; Deut. 1:10). Their brightness suggests the world to come (Dan. 12:3) and their darkening and fall the last days (Isa. 13:10; Matt. 24:29; Rev. 6:13). Poetic language for God's ability to use 'natural' forces for his purposes (Judg. 5:20).

2. Seven stars symbolise the angels of the churches (Rev. 1:16, 20; 2:1; 3:1). *See* Seven churches.
3. Crown of twelve stars stands for the tribes of Israel (Rev. 12:1).

STATURE. Physical size (Num. 13:32; 1 Sam. 2:26; Luke 2:52; 19:3). The Greek word also means 'life-span' (Matt. 6:27) or maturity (Eph. 4:13).

STEALING. Depriving another of property by stealth. Prohibited (Exod. 20:15) as an act against God (Prov. 30:9). Simile of the thief often used for the unexpected hour of Christ's return (1 Thess. 5:2; 2 Pet. 3:10; Rev. 3:3; 16:15). *See* Robbery.

STEPHANAS. Baptised by Paul (1 Cor. 1:16), who greatly appreciated his services (1 Cor. 16:15–18).

STEPHEN. Hellenistic Jewish Christian, one of the Seven appointed to distribute charity to widows. His vigorous proclamation of the Christian message before the Sanhedrin resulted in martyrdom (Acts 6—7), the persecution of Hellenistic members of the Jerusalem church and the evangelisation of Samaria (Acts 8).

STEWARD. Overseer of a master's property and business affairs (Matt. 20:8; Luke 16:1). Metaphorically applied to Christian workers (1 Cor. 4:1; 1 Pet. 4:10).

STIFF-NECKED. Idiom derived from an obstinate farm animal refusing the yoke by stiffening its neck. Figuratively applied to Israel's disobedience (Exod. 32:9; Jer. 7:26; Acts 7:51).

STOICS. Emphasised the supremacy of reason and morality. Paul debated with a group in Athens (Acts 17:18).

STONE, LIVING. Figurative title for Jesus (1 Pet. 2:4, based on Isa. 28:16), which believers share (1 Pet. 2:5) because they belong to him.

STONE PAVEMENT. *See* Gabbatha.

STONING. Jewish ritual execution (Exod. 19:13), for blasphemy (Lev. 24:16), leading others into idolatry (Deut. 13:10), rebellion against authority (Deut. 21:18–21), adultery (Deut. 22:20–24). Could be an expression of mob rule (Num. 14:10; Luke 20:6; Acts 14:19). Witnesses were to throw the first stones (Deut. 13:9; John 8:7), but false witnesses were liable to the same penalty (Deut. 19:19).

STORE CITIES. Royal warehouses, constructed for Pharaoh (Exod. 1:11), Solomon (1 Kings 9:19) and Jehoshaphat (2 Chron.17:12). *See* Pithom; Rameses.

STORM GOD. *See* Hadad 1.

STRAIGHT STREET. Long E-W Damascus thoroughfare (Acts 9:11), still existing.

STRAIT. Constricted, narrowed by reason of obstacles on either side: applied to the gate leading to life (Matt. 7:13, AV/KJV).

STRANGE FIRE. Term applied to unauthorised action by Aaron's sons Nadab and Abihu, on the very day of their ordination. The sacrilege met with instant retribution (AV/KJV of Lev. 10:1; Num. 3:4; 26:61).

STRANGER. Outsider (Gen. 15:13); more particularly, a foreigner, someone not belonging to the community (Exod. 12:43). Judas' unclean money used for an unclean purpose, a cemetery for non-Jews (Matt. 27:7). *See* Foreigners; Sojourners.

STRAW. Applied figuratively to the wicked (Job 21:18), the messianic age (Isa. 11:7; 65:25), dreams (Jer. 23:28), evaluating Christian work (1 Cor. 3:12). *See* Brick; Chaff; Threshing.

STRENGTH. Human physical and spiritual strength has its source in God (Isa. 41:10; 2 Cor. 12:9; Eph. 6:10), a fact overlooked by the proud and self-sufficient (Deut. 8:17–18).

STRIFE. Contention (Hab. 1:3), quarrelling (Gen. 13:7), expression of ill will (Prov. 30:33), violence (Ps. 55:9–11). Issues from godlessness (Rom. 1:28–31) and conceit (1 Tim. 6:3–4). To be avoided (Prov. 20:3) by self-control (Prov. 15:18) and by keeping close to God (Ps. 31:20).

STROKE OF THE PEN. Matt. 5:18 and Luke 16:17 refer to the tiny differences between similar Hebrew letters. *See* Jot and tittle.

STUBBORNNESS. *See* Stiff-necked.

STUMBLING BLOCK. Obstacle causing someone to fall (Lev. 19:14; Ezek. 7:19; Rom. 14:13). Threatened for disobeying God (Jer. 6:21) or apostasy (Ezek. 3:20). Paul terms Christ a stumbling block to disbelieving Jews (1 Cor. 1:23) for dying as a criminal (Deut. 21:23; Gal. 3:13). Jesus associates Peter with Satan for suggesting the same temptation (Matt. 16:23), that is, seeking the kingdom without the cross (Matt. 4:9–10). Believers warned against upsetting another's faith (Rom. 14:3; 1 Cor. 8:9).

SUCCOTH. 1. Israelites' first campsite after leaving Egypt, between Rameses and Etham (Exod. 12:37).

2. Stage on Jacob's return to Canaan (Gen. 33:17) in the Jordan valley. Inhabitants unwisely refused to give food to Gideon and his men (Judg. 8:4–16).

SUCCOTH BENOTH. Babylonian goddess brought to Samaria by deportees (2 Kings 17:30).

SUFFERING. May result from sin (Num. 14:34; 1 Pet.2:21–24), but not always (John 9:3). Universal (Job 14:1) and the consequence of disobedience (Gen. 3:16–19; Deut. 28:15–68). May be allowed as remedial (Prov. 3:11–12), but can appear baffling (Ps. 22:1–2) or unjust (1 Sam. 20:1). Can issue in hardness of heart (Exod. 7:22), repentance (2 Chron. 33:12; Luke 15:17–19), or a deepening experience of God (Job 42:1–6; Isa. 38:17; Rom. 8:35–39).

SUICIDE. Taking one's own life: said of Saul and his armourbearer (1 Sam. 31:1–7), Ahithophel (2 Sam. 17:23), Zimri (1 Kings 16:18), Judas (Matt. 27:5).

SULPHUR. Yellow non-metallic substance, highly flammable, occurring in volcanic regions like the Dead Sea valley (Gen. 19:24; brimstone in AV/KJV). Symbolises agonising judgment (Isa. 34:8–10; Rev. 19:20).

SUMMER HOUSE. Opulent seasonal residence of the wealthy (Amos 3:15).

SUN. The 'great light' (compared with moon and stars as seen from earth), created by God to 'rule' the day, that is, as its sphere of influence (Gen. 1:16; Jer. 31:35). Indicator of time (Ps. 74:16–17) and direction (Josh. 1:4; *see* Lefthanded). Its light not needed in heaven (Rev. 22:5). Figuratively, of a just ruler (2 Sam. 23:4), a woman's beauty (Song of Sol. 6:10), and an angel's brilliance (Rev. 10:1). Divine title (Ps. 84:11; Mal. 4:2), implying the blessing of light and life.

SUN WORSHIP. Widespread in the ancient world. Forbidden (Deut. 4:19; 2 Kings 23:11), but place names including *shemesh* (Hebrew for *sun*) reflect the practice (Jer. 43:13). *See* Beth Shemesh; Heliopolis.

SUPERSCRIPTION. 1. Notice of charge against Jesus, affixed to the cross in Palestine's three languages, Hebrew, Greek and Latin. John 19:19 gives the full wording: 'This is Jesus of Nazareth, the King of the Jews'; other Gospels quote part (Matt. 27:37; Mark 15:26; Luke 23:38). The title implied Jesus was a lawbreaker (Deut. 21:23). Paul saw it as meaning that it was the Jews who were guilty, but Jesus had paid their penalty (Gal. 3:13; Col. 2:14).

2. Wording ('Tiberius Caesar Augustus, son of the divine Augustus') on the silver denarius; compulsory for paying Roman taxes, however much Jews resented the emperor's claim (Matt. 22:20).

SUSA (Shushan). Capital of Elam (SW Persia) and site of winter palace of Persian kings (Neh. 1:1; Esther 1:2; Dan. 8:2).

SUSANNA. 1. One of the women supporting Jesus and his disciples in Galilee (Luke 8:1–3).

2. Book of the Apocrypha, an addition to the canonical book of Daniel. Tells of the beautiful

and pious wife of Joakim, falsely accused of adultery by two elders who had failed to seduce her. Sentenced to death, she is vindicated through Daniel's skilful interrogation.

SWADDLING CLOTHES. Cloth strips wrapped tightly around a newborn infant (Luke 2:7), with the notion of keeping the limbs straight. Used metaphorically of earth's creation (Job 38:9).

SWEAT. 1. Alludes to hard labour being the consequence of disobeying God (Gen. 3:19).
2. Jesus' profuse sweating in Gethsemane (Luke 22:44) likened to blood pouring off him (the only ocasion in the NT where 'agony' occurs).

SWORD. *See* War p. 241.

SYCAMINE. *See* Trees p. 173.

SYCHAR. Town on E slope of Mt. Ebal (John 4:5).

SYCAMORE. *See* Trees p. 173.

SYENE. Modern Aswan, on S border of Egypt (Ezek. 29:10; Sinim in Isa. 49:12, AV/KJV).

SYMPATHY. More than mere words (lit. 'suffering with'). To be expressed to others (2 Sam. 10:2; Job 2:11), especially fellow believers (Heb. 10:34; 1 Pet. 3:8), following Christ's example (Heb. 4:15). Personal experience fits one to support others (2 Cor. 1:3–7).

SYNAGOGUE. Jewish place of worship (Matt. 12:9), probably originating during the exile (Ezek. 20:1) when Temple sacrifices were impossible. Widespread by the 1st century AD, wherev-

Cutaway illustration of an ancient synagogue

er Jews were living, provided there was a quorum of ten men. The building included a portable ark housing biblical scrolls (Luke 4:16–17), before which were the 'chief seats' (Matt. 23:6, AV/KJV). After prayers and readings from the Law and Prophets, officials could invite any qualified man to speak (Acts 13:15). Also used for instruction in the Mosaic law and for local government. Officials empowered to flog (2 Cor. 11:24) and excommunicate (John 16:2). *See* Moses' seat; Satan, Synagogue of; Seat.

SYNTYCHE *See* Euodia

SYRACUSE. Port on the E coast of Sicily (Acts 28:12). Extensive ruins include the temple of Apollo and Christian catacombs.

TABLE 213

SYRIA. Not the much smaller modern state, but the general area N and NE of Palestine bounded by the Taurus Mountains, river Euphrates and Dead Sea. *See* Damascus; Naaman.

SYROPHOENICIAN WOMAN. Greek-speaking mother from the district of Tyre and Sidon, whose persistence secured her daughter's healing (Mark 7:26). The older term 'Canaanite' is used in Matt. 15:22.

SYRTIS. Dangerous quicksands off Libya's N coast (Acts 27:17), today's Gulf of Sidra.

SYZYGUS (*Companion*). The Greek word may be a personal name (Phil. 4:3, JB), but most translators assume it is a common noun ('yoke-fellow', AV/KJV).

T

TAANACH. Canaanite town, S of Megiddo. Scene of Sisera's defeat by Barak (Judg. 5:19).

TABEEL (*God is Good*). 1. Father of the man proposed as puppet king of Judah in place of Ahaz during the Syro-Ephraimite war of 735–732 BC. The Hebrew name (Isa. 7:6) has been given different vowels, changing the meaning to '*Good for Nothing*'.

2. Samaritan official who tried to stop 'rebellious' Jews from rebuilding Jerusalem's wall (Ezra 4:7).

TABERAH (*Burning*). Campsite where Israelite grumbling caused God's anger to flare up (Num. 11:1–3; Deut. 9:22).

TABERNACLE. *See* pp. 214-215.

TABITHA. Aramaic version of the name Dorcas, industrious woman of Joppa restored to life by Peter (Acts 9:36–41).

TABLE. At banquets, position at table indicated relative importance of guests (Luke 14:7–10). Crumbs falling from the rich man's table (Luke 16:21) were from bread used for wiping greasy fingers (acting as a napkin). *See* Lord's table.

Tabernacle

Tabernacle. Prefabricated mobile sanctuary for use in the wilderness (Exod. 25-31; 35-40) before Solomon's Temple was built. Also called 'Tent of Meeting [*with God*]' (Exod. 27:21). The outer courtyard (Exod. 27:9-12) contained the altar of sacrifice and the laver (Exod. 38:1-8). The Holy Place housed incense altar, golden lampstand and shewbread table. The Holy of Holies, the inmost sanctuary, contained the ark of the covenant. Object lessons in divine truths for Christians (Heb. 8:5; 9:23-24; 10:1). *See* Altar of burnt offering; Altar of incense; Ark of the covenant; Bread of the Presence; Courtyard; Curtain; Holy of Holies; Holy Place; Laver.

Altar. Altars built of earth or unhewn stone (Exod. 20:24–25), or wood overlaid with bronze and thus rendered fireproof (Exod. 27:1). Unlawful altars condemned (1 Kings 12:32; Hos. 8:11; Amos 3:14).

Altar of incense. In the Tabernacle (Exod. 27:1–8), a square construction of acacia wood overlaid with gold, for burning the holy incense (Exod. 30:34–38). An incense altar was in the Temple (Luke 1:11) and appears in the heavenly scene (Rev. 8:3).

Altar of burnt offering. In the Tabernacle (Exod. 27:1–8), a hollow square construction of acacia wood overlaid with bronze, with four bronze horns at the corners (Ps. 118:27), placed in the outer court and thus accessible to all Israelites (Exod. 40:29). In the Temple, a larger all–bronze altar was used (1 Kings 8:64). The altar fire was kept permanently burning (Lev. 6:13).

Table of Shewbread. Special table of acacia wood overlaid with gold, set at the N side of the Holy Place in the Tabernacle for the holy bread (Exod. 25:23-30; Heb. 9:2). *See* Bread of the Presence (p. 215).

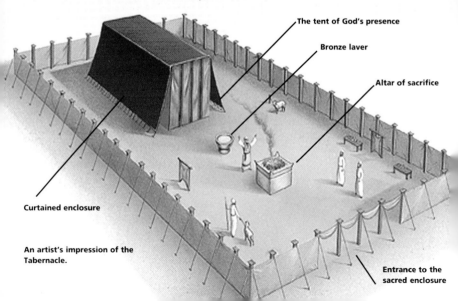

The tent of God's presence

Bronze laver

Altar of sacrifice

Curtained enclosure

An artist's impression of the Tabernacle.

Entrance to the sacred enclosure

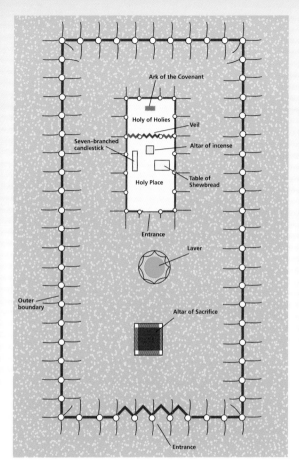

Ark of the Covenant

Holy of Holies

Veil

Seven-branched candlestick

Altar of incense

Holy Place

Table of Shewbread

Entrance

Laver

Outer boundary

Altar of Sacrifice

Entrance

Bread of the Presence.
Twelve loaves of unleavened bread placed in the Tabernacle (Exod. 25:30; Matt. 12:4).

Holy of Holies. Wyclif's literal rendering of Exod. 26:33, more usually translated 'Most Holy Place'. This inmost room of the Tabernacle was cube-shaped, each dimension 10 cubits (4.5 metres, 15 ft). The corresponding room in the Temple was twice the size. The high priest alone, and only on the annual Day of Atonement, was allowed access (Lev. 16; Heb. 9:3). *See* Ark of the covenant; Tabernacle.

Holy Place. Outer of the two sanctuaries in the Tabernacle and Temple, where priests performed daily routine duties. Separated from the inner sanctuary (Holy of Holies) by an elaborate curtain (Exod. 26:33; Matt. 27:51). In the Tabernacle the Holy Place measured 20 x 10 x 10 cubits (9 x 4.5 x 4.5 metres, 30 x 15 x 15 ft). That in the Temple was twice the size. *See* Tabernacle.

Laver. Bronze washbasin in the outer court of the Tabernacle for priests to wash before ministering (Exod. 30:18-21).

Ark of the covenant.
Rectangular wooden box covered with gold, its solid gold lid ('mercy seat') surmounted by two cherubim (Exod. 25; 37). Contained the Ten Commandments (1 Kings 8:9), a pot of manna and Aaron's staff (Heb. 9:4). The appointed meeting place with God in the Most Holy Place (Holy of Holies) of the Tabernacle, where God's will was revealed (Exod. 25:22). Lost when Babylonians destroyed Jerusalem in 587 BC. No ark in the second Temple.

TABLE OF SHEWBREAD.
See Tabernacle p. 214.

TABLETS. 1. Hewn stones (Exod. 24:12) inscribed with the Ten Commandments by God (Exod. 31:18). When Moses smashed the tablets, angered by the Israelites' idolatry (Exod. 32:19), the laws had to be rewritten (Exod. 34:1–4). The tablets were placed in the ark of the covenant as a permanent reminder of God's law (Deut. 10:5; 1 Kings 8:9; 2 Cor. 3:3; Heb. 9:4). *See* Ten Commandments.

2. Scribes' writing tablets were of wood covered with wax, which made alterations easy (Luke 1:63).

TABOR, MOUNT. Isolated dome-shaped mass of limestone, rising steeply from the Plain of Esdraelon (Ps. 89:12; Jer. 46:18). Possible site of the Transfiguration (Matt. 17:1).

Mount Tabor

TABOR, OAK OF. Where Saul received the second sign confirming his appointment as king (1 Sam. 10:3). Between Bethel and Rachel's tomb at Zelzah.

TADMOR. Oasis city of Syria (modern Palmyra), rebuilt by Solomon (1 Kings 9:18).

TAHPANHES. Egyptian frontier city, E of Nile delta. Jewish refugees took Jeremiah there (Jer. 43:5–7).

TAIL, FAT. In the main breed of Palestine sheep, an organ for storing fat, serving as the hump in camels. Sacrificed to God as the best portion (Exod. 29:22; Lev. 3:9).

TALENT. *See* Money p. 147.

TALITHA KOUM/CUMI. Aramaic words spoken by Jesus to Jairus's daughter: 'Little lamb, get up' (Mark 5:41). The variations *koum* and *cumi* (AV/KJV) reflect different dialects.

TALMAI. 1. Descendant of Anak, whose stature intimidated Moses' spies (Num. 13:33). Overcome by Caleb 40 years later when capturing his inheritance (Josh. 15:14).

2. Absalom took refuge with him for three years after murdering his half-brother Amnon (2 Sam. 3:3; 13:37).

TAMAR. 1. Judah's daughter-in-law, wife of Er, then of Onan. By a subterfuge, Tamar became mother of twins, Perez and Zerah, by Judah (Gen. 38:6–30; Ruth 4:12).

2. David's daughter, raped by Amnon, her half-brother, and avenged by Absalom (2 Sam. 13).

TAMBOURINE. *See* Music p. 150.

TAMMUZ. Babylonian fertility god of vegetation. 'Weeping for Tammuz' (Ezek. 8:14), a cult lamentation for his death with the vegetation under the fierce summer sun, was being practised by Jewish women at the very door of God's house.

TANNING. Treating animal skins was an evil-smelling trade, practised outside towns; needed an abundant water supply. *See* Leather.

TAR. *See* Bitumen.

TARSHISH. Port (or land) apparently distant from Palestine (Isa. 66:19; Jon. 1:3), famous for shipping (Isa. 60:9; Ezek. 27:25); 'ships of Tarshish' (1 Kings 22:48; Ezek. 38:13) may refer to a type of large oceangoing trading vessel.

TARSUS. Cilician birthplace of Paul (Acts 21:39). Roman citizenship for some local Jews (Acts 22:25–28) probably dates from Pompey's settlement.

TARTAN (*Second*). Not a personal name (AV/KJV of 2 Kings 18:17; Isa. 20:1), but a high Assyrian military rank.

TASSEL. Knotted cord or fringe on a garment, originating in the Mosaic law (Num. 15:38). Jesus rebuked scribes and Pharisees for wearing unnecessarily large tassels to impress (Matt. 23:5).

TAX. *See* Money pp. 146-147.

TAX COLLECTORS. Contemptuously associated with 'sinners' (Matt. 9:10) and 'prostitutes' (Matt. 21:31) for working for the Roman occupying power. Profits came from extortion (Luke 3:13; 19:8). *See* Zacchaeus.

TEACHER. Supremely, applies to God himself (Jer. 31:33; 1 Thess. 4:9), the Holy Spirit (John 14:26) and Jesus (Matt. 7:29). Disciples commissioned to continue the work (Matt. 28:19–20; Acts 5:42; Eph. 4:11).

TEACHERS OF THE LAW. *See* Scribes.

TEACHING. Instruction, especially in God's law, a duty laid upon priests, Levites (2 Chron. 17:7–9; Mal. 2:7) and parents (Deut. 4:9–10; Eph. 6:4). Major feature of Christ's ministry (Matt. 7:28; 26:55); carried on by disciples, orally (Acts 4:2), through writing (Luke 1:3—4; 2 Thess. 3:14; Jude 3) and by example (Phil. 3:17; 1 Pet. 2:21) and mutual edification (Col. 3:16).

TEARING CLOTHES. Expression of mourning (Gen. 37:34) or anguish (Gen. 44:13), forbidden to the high priest (Lev. 21:10) except on hearing blasphemy (Matt. 26:65).

TEKOA. Highland city, S of Jerusalem, home of a quick–witted woman who acted a parable before David (2 Sam. 14:1–4), and of a prophet (Amos 1:1). Near scene of Jehoshaphat's remarkable victory (2 Chron. 20:20–25).

TEL AVIV. Not the modern Israeli city, but an unidentified place in Babylonia, allocated to Jewish exiles in 597 BC (Ezek. 3:15).

TEMAN. Edomite city; inhabitants renowned for wisdom (Job 2:11; Jer. 49:7), but threatened with God's judgment (Ezek. 25:13; Amos 1:12).

TEMPERANCE. Self-control (Acts 24:25, AV/KJV).

The Temple

Temple (Jerusalem). National sanctuary built by Solomon (1 Kings 5-8) to replace the Tabernacle of wilderness days (2 Sam. 7). Treasures appropriated by later kings for political purposes: Asa (1 Kings 15:18-19), Joash (2 Kings 12:17-18), Ahaz (2 Kings 16:7-8), Hezekiah (2 Kings 18:14-15); looted by invaders: Shishak (1 Kings 14:25-26), Nebuchadnezzar (2 Kings 24:13). Renovated by Joash

The Temple Mount, Jerusalem, site of the Temple in Bible times

Cutaway illustration of Solomon's Temple

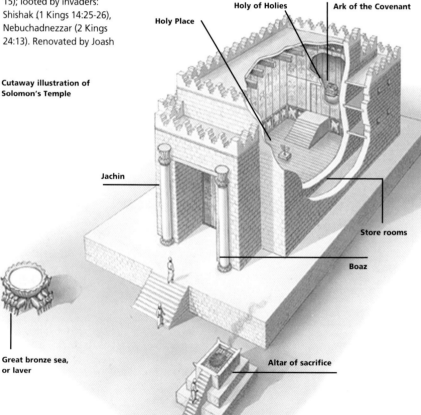

Holy of Holies

Ark of the Covenant

Holy Place

Jachin

Store rooms

Boaz

Great bronze sea, or laver

Altar of sacrifice

Ground Plan of Herod's Temple

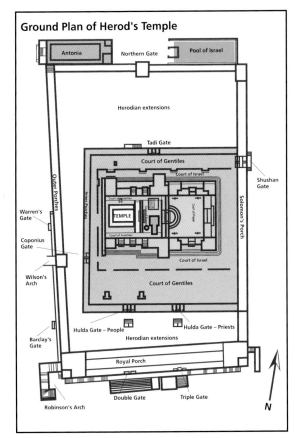

Antonia
Pool of Israel
Northern Gate
Herodian extensions
Tadi Gate
Court of Gentiles
Court of Israel
Shushan Gate
Court of the Gentiles
Inner Porches
Outer Porches
TEMPLE
Court of Israelites
Court of Prayer
Solomon's Porch
Warren's Gate
Coponius Gate
Wilson's Arch
Court of Israel
Court of Gentiles
Barclay's Gate
Hulda Gate – People
Hulda Gate – Priests
Herodian extensions
Royal Porch
Robinson's Arch
Double Gate
Triple Gate
N

Jews at Jerusalem's Wailing Wall,

(2 Kings 12:4-5), Jotham (2 Kings 15:35), Hezekiah (2 Chron. 29), Josiah (2 Kings 22:3-7). In 587 BC destroyed by Babylonians (2 Kings 25:13-15). The vision of a new Temple given to Ezekiel about 571 BC to encourage the exiles (Ezek. 40-43).

Second Temple built by Jeshua and Zerubbabel (Ezra 3) on orders from the Persian king Darius, about 537 BC (Ezra 6), encouraged by Haggai and Zechariah (Ezra 5:1-2; Zech. 6:12-15).

Herod the Great's Temple (in building 19 BC–AD 64), the one familiar in the Gospels, destroyed by the Romans in AD 70 (Matt. 24:2).

TEMPLE (Jerusalem). *See* pp. 218-219.

TEMPLE OF THE HOLY SPIRIT. The body of believers, individually (1 Cor. 6:19) and corporately (1 Cor. 3:16–17), made holy by God's presence, as were the Tabernacle in the wilderness and the Temple in Jerusalem, both now superseded (2 Cor. 6:16; 1 Pet. 2:5).

TEMPLE NOT MADE WITH HANDS. Jesus' resurrection body (John 2:19–22); here 'temple' means 'sanctuary' (Holy of Holies), the dwelling-place of deity.

TEMPTATION. 1. Testing character (Exod 17:2) or faith (Gen. 22:1).

2. Enticement to sin (1 Cor. 7:5), arising from human desires (James 1:13), which need examining (Gal. 6:1). God promises help to overcome (1 Cor. 10:13).

A tent, secured by ropes

TEMPTATIONS OF JESUS. By Satan, seeking to deflect Jesus from his divine programme (Matt. 4:1–11); and by Peter (Matt. 16:23), his own brothers (John 7:2–5) and the crowd (John 6:15). His experience enables him to strengthen his people (Heb. 2:18; 4:15–16).

TEMPTER. Satan (Matt. 4:3; 1 Thess. 3:5), using the ways of the world (Eph. 2:2), people (Prov. 5:3–6), human desires (1 Tim. 6:9), easier situations (Heb. 11:25), weakness (Matt. 26:41), pride (Prov. 16:18; 1 Cor. 4:6), pleasures (2 Tim. 3:4).

TEN COMMANDMENTS. Basic laws given to Israel (Exod. 20:1–17). Jesus summarised them as 'love to God' and 'love to others' (Matt. 22:37–40). *See* Tablets 1.

TENT. Made of cloth or skins (Exod. 26:7, 14), secured by ropes to stakes (Judg. 4:21). Figuratively, of creation (Ps. 104:2), pilgrim life (Heb. 11:8–10), David's line (Amos 9:11), temporary nature of life (Isa. 38:12), its dismantling, death (Job 4:21: 2 Cor. 5:1).

TENT OF MEETING. *See* Tabernacle p. 214.

TENTHS. *See* Tithe.

TENTMAKER. Occupation of Paul, Priscilla and Aquila (Acts 18:3). The term applies to leather work in general.

TERAPHIM. Household gods (Gen. 31:19), small idols kept at home and employed for divining (Judg. 18:14–20, AV/KJV). Their use condemned (1 Sam. 15:23; 2 Kings 23:24).

TEREBINTH. *See* Trees p. 173.

TERESH. Persian officer who joined a plot to assassinate Xerxes. Foiled by Mordecai (Esther 2:21–22; 6:2).

TERTIUS (*Third* [child]). Christian who penned Paul's letter to the Romans at his dictation (Rom. 16:22).

TERTULLUS. Advocate in the Sanhedrin delegation brought by the high priest Ananias to Caesarea to state the prosecution's case against Paul. The blatant flattery of Felix accorded with the rhetorical fashion of the time. Felix's administration was anything but a 'long period of peace' (Acts 24:1–9).

TEST. *See* Temptation 1.

TESTAMENT. 1. Farewell message. Many in Scripture: Jacob (Gen. 49); Moses (Deut.); Joshua (Josh. 23—24); David (1 Chron. 28—29); Jesus (John 13—17); Paul (Acts 20:17–38).
2. Agreement by which God promises, on certain conditions, to bless his people, as at Sinai (Exod. 19:5–8). *See* Covenant.

3. Commonly accepted term used by Christians for the Hebrew Bible (OT) and early Christian literature declared canonical by the church (NT). *See* Bible 2.

TESTIMONY. 1. Ark of the Covenant (Exod. 16:34) in the Tabernacle, also known as the Tent of the Testimony (Num. 9:15).
2. Tablets containing the Ten Commandments (Exod. 31:18).
3. Witness to God's revelation in Jesus (John 3:32; Acts 22:18).
4. Evidence in court of law (Exod. 23:2; Prov. 12:17). *See* Witness 1.

TETRARCH. Governor of Roman province (Luke 3:1).

THADDAEUS (*Warmhearted*). Apostle (Matt. 10:3; some manuscripts, followed by AV/KJV, have Lebbaeus), otherwise called Judas son of James (Luke 6:16).

THANKSGIVING. Fulfils God's will (1 Thess. 5:18). Helps us to recognise God's presence (Ps. 95:2; 100:4), as a habit prepares for emergency calls (Ps. 50:14–15), strengthens confidence in petition (Phil. 4:6), promotes spiritual life (Col. 2:7; 4:2), witnesses to unbelievers (Acts 27:35) and counteracts unpleasant talk (Eph. 5:4). Its absence a sign of godlessness (Rom. 1:21). Demands effort (not just being thankful but *giving* thanks), as with OT sacrifices (2 Chron. 29:31), especially in times of trouble (Dan. 6:10). *See* Freewill offerings.

THEATRE. Open-air place of assembly (Acts 19:29–31); that at Ephesus held 25,000 people.

THEBES. Greek version of the Hebrew name

No (used in AV/KJV) for the Egyptian capital, S of modern Cairo, from about 1570 BC). City of the national ram-god Amon (Jer. 46:25). Its destruction by Assyrians under Ashurbanipal (663 BC) foretold (Ezek. 30:14–16; Nah. 3:8–9).

THEBEZ. Town NE of Shechem, where a woman's millstone killed Abimelech (Judg. 9:50; 2 Sam. 11:21).

THEOPHILUS (*Loved by God*). Addressee of Luke's two volumes (Luke 1:3; Acts 1:1). 'Most excellent' suggests a man of standing.

1 & 2 THESSALONIANS. Probably the earliest of Paul's NT letters. Written from Corinth about AD 50 to the young church at Thessalonica. Opposition compelled Paul to leave (Acts 17:1–10), but he sent Timothy back to see how the new converts were faring (Acts 19:22; 1 Thess. 3:2). His encouraging report spurred Paul to write, emphasising the hope of Christ's return. The second letter was to correct certain misunderstandings of the first letter, taken to mean the Lord's return was imminent.

THESSALONICA. Major port and commercial and military centre on the Egnatian Way. Although Paul's visit was short-lived, he left behind a lively new community of Christians, despite Jewish antagonism (Acts 17:1–10).

THEUDAS. Leader of an unsuccessful uprising against the Romans (Acts 5:36).

THIGH. Symbolic of strength (Dan. 2:32) and so a prime sacrifice (Exod. 29:22). Euphemism for procreative organs, thus making some oaths specially solemn since they involved descendants (Gen. 24:2; 47:29).

THIRD DAY. The idea of national resurrection (Hos. 6:2–3) is applied to Jesus' rising (Matt. 16:21). Although Mark 8:31 has '*after* three days', the terms are idiomatically equivalent and can even simply mean 'a short time' (Gen. 22:4).

THIRST. Ever-present possibility in Palestine's climate (Deut. 8:15), and could be God's judgment upon disobedience (Deut. 28:48; Isa. 5:13; Ezek. 19:13; Hos. 2:3). Its removal a messianic promise (Isa. 49:10; John 7:37; Rev. 21:6). Spiritual thirst will be satisfied (Isa. 41:17–18; Matt. 5:6; John 4:14; 7:37; Rev. 7:16).

THIRTY. Age for entering life's work (Gen. 41:46; Num. 4:3; 2 Sam. 5:4; Luke 3:23).

THISTLE. *See* Plants p. 171.

THOMAS. Paired in lists of apostles with Matthew (Matt. 10:3) or Philip (Acts 1:13). Called Didymus (*Twin*) in John 11:16. Prepared to admit lack of comprehension (John 14:5). Only the evidence of the senses could persuade him of Christ's resurrection (John 20:24–28).

THORN IN THE FLESH. Paul's unspecified suffering (2 Cor. 12:7) not necessarily physical but may allude to continuing troubles, to restrain spiritual pride (Num. 33:55; Josh. 23:13; Judg. 2:3; Ezek. 28:24).

THORNBUSH. *See* Plants p. 171.

THOUGHT. 1. Human thought always exposed to God (1 Chron. 28:9; Matt. 9:4) and infinitely inferior to his (Isa. 55:8–9). Not a foundation or substitute for faith (1 Cor. 3:19–20; 2 Cor. 10:5).
2. Obsolete meaning of 'anxiety' used in AV/KJV (1 Sam. 9:5; Matt. 6:25; 10:19).

THREE TAVERNS. Stopping place well-known to travellers (Acts 28:15); on the Appian Way, SE of Rome.

THRESHING. *See* Farming pp. 71-72.

THRESHOLD. Stone sill at entrance. Considered specially sacred (1 Chron. 9:19), hence the significance of Dagon's fall (1 Sam. 5:4–5) and the pagan practice of stepping over the threshold being condemned (Zeph. 1:9).

THRONE OF DAVID. David's dynasty (Jer. 22:2) and pointing ahead to Messiah (Isa. 9:7; Luke 1:32; Acts 2:30; Rev. 3:7).

THRONE OF GOD. Concept borrowing images from earthly kings (1 Kings 22:19; Isa. 6:1). Founded upon righteousness (Ps. 97:2), justice (Ps. 9:7–8), love (Rev. 7:15–17) and holiness (Ps. 47:8).

THRONE OF SATAN. The Pergamum letter (Rev. 2:13) may allude to the throne-shaped hill on which the city was built; or to the local great throne-altar of Zeus. Worshippers of Asklepios, god of healing, used the snake as an emblem (the symbol of medicine to this day), as did the followers of Zeus; for both Jews and Christians the snake denoted Satan. This background adds point to the most likely explanation of 'Satan's throne': the recent order to worship the Roman emperor Domitian as 'saviour' and 'lord and god'.

THUMB. With ear and great toe, symbolises the whole body and all its faculties, to be consecrated to God (Lev. 8:23; 14:14). Mutilating thumbs and great toes incapacitated prisoners (Judg. 1:6–7).

Coin of Tiberius Caesar

THUMMIN. *See* Urim.

THUNDER. Often ascribed to divine activity (Exod. 9:23; 1 Sam. 12:18; John 12:29; Rev. 4:5). The nickname 'Sons of thunder' given to James and John reflected their stormy characters (Mark 3:17; Luke 9:54).

THYATIRA. City of W Asia Minor. Home of Lydia, Paul's first European convert (Acts 16:14) and dealer in Thyatira's famed purple cloth. Local Christians formed one of the 'seven churches of Asia' (Rev. 2:18–29).

TIBERIAS. Busy port on the W shore of the Sea of Galilee. No record of its being visited by Jesus, although near his base at Capernaum (John 6:23).

TIBERIAS, SEA OF. *See* Sea of Galilee.

TIBERIUS CAESAR. Succeeded Augustus as emperor in AD 14, retired to Capri in AD 26 and died 11 years later, aged 79 (Luke 3:1).

Tiglath-Pileser III

TIBNI. Unsuccessful rival to Omri to become king of Israel (1 Kings 16:21–22).

TIDAL. With three other rulers raided Sodom and carried off Lot among their prisoners. Pursued and defeated by Abram (Gen. 14:1–16).

TIDINGS. The angel's message (Luke 2:10, AV/KJV) echoes prophecies of Isaiah (Isa. 40:9; 41:27; 52:7).

TIGLATH-PILESER III. Powerful Assyrian king (745–727 BC), called Pul (his throne name) in 2 Kings 15:29. His records mention 'Menahem of Samaria' among those paying him tribute in 738 BC (2 Kings 15:19–20). Invaded Israel and deported many inhabitants to Assyria (2 Kings 15:29). In return for support against the Syro-Phoenician alliance, Ahaz became his vassal, with pagan consequences (2 Kings 16:5–10).

TIGRIS. One of four rivers associated with Eden (Gen. 2:14; Hiddekel, AV/KJV). Rises in Armenia and flows SE across Babylonia (Dan. 10:4) before joining Euphrates, N of the Persian Gulf.

TILING. *See* House pp. 100-101.

TIMBREL. *See* Music p. 150.

TIMNAH. 1. Highland town (Josh. 15:57), W of Beth Shemesh, where Judah was accosted by his disguised daughter-in-law Tamar (Gen. 38:12–14).
2. Town of Dan (Josh. 19:43) on Judah's border (Josh. 15:10), where Samson found a Philistine woman (Judg. 14:1).

TIMNATH SERAH. Ephraimite town where Joshua was buried (Josh. 19:50; 24:30).

TIMNITE. Inhabitant of Timnah of Dan (Judg. 15:6).

TIMON. One of the Seven, appointed to dispense charity to Jerusalem believers (Acts 6:5).

TIMOTHY. Born at Lystra in Lycaonia, son of a Greek father and Hebrew-Christian mother, Eunice (Acts 16:1). Her faith, and that of his grandmother Lois (2 Tim. 1:5; 3:14–15), gave him a Christian upbringing. Local Christians thought highly of him (Acts 16:2). Served Paul for 15 years as a colleague (Acts 16:3; 19:22; 20:4) and often fulfilled his commissions (1 Cor. 4:17; 16:10; Phil. 2:19; 1 Thess. 3:2). His presence mentioned in nearly all Paul's letters.

1 & 2 TIMOTHY. Addressed to his close associate by Paul towards the end of his life (2 Tim. 4:6–8). Urges Timothy to refute false teaching at Ephesus (1 Tim. 1) and gives instructions about church worship and order (1 Tim. 2–4). The second letter implies a worsening situation (2 Tim. 1:15). Paul exhorts Timothy to persevere faithfully (2 Tim. 1:13–14; 2:1–7, 15; 4:5), despite persecution outside the church (2 Tim. 3:11–12) and false teaching within (2 Tim. 2:16–18; 3:1–9).

TIN. Important as a constituent, with copper, of bronze. Symbolic of Jerusalem's spiritual dross (Ezek. 22:18–22).

TIRE. Archaic AV/KJV term for a woman's headband (2 Kings 9:30; Isa. 3:18; Ezek. 24:17, 23).

TIRHAKAH. King of Egypt and Cush (690–664 BC). In 701 went to Judah's relief against Assyrian threats (2 Kings 19:9).

TIRZAH. NE of Shechem (Josh. 12:24). Capital of Jeroboam I (1 Kings 14:17) and of his successors, until Omri built the city of Samaria (1 Kings 16:24).

TISHBITE. Inhabitant of Tishbe in Gilead (1 Kings 21:17; 2 Kings 1:3).

TITHE. Thank-offering to God of one tenth of harvests and livestock (Mal. 3:10), his due for being the true owner of land and produce (Lev. 27:30–33). Delegated to Levites for serving God's sanctuary (Num. 18:20–29). Practised prior to the Mosaic law (Gen. 14:20; Heb. 7:1–9). By NT times, scribes and Pharisees were meticulously tithing the smallest garden crops, while neglecting more important issues (Matt. 23:23).

TITIUS JUSTUS. Corinthian Christian who offered Paul a base for a house-church (Acts 18:7).

TITUS. Gentile believer and colleague of Paul (Gal. 2:1, 3; 2 Cor. 2:13) who sent him on several commissions (2 Cor. 7:6–15; 8:6, 16–23; 2 Tim. 4:10; Titus 1:5). Surprisingly unnamed in Acts, suggesting he may have been Luke's brother (2 Cor. 8:18).

TITUS (letter). Written by Paul to his coworker entrusted with a mission to Crete (Titus 1:5) to counteract error in the church (1:10–16; 3:9–11) and to instruct believers (2—3).

TOB. Small Aramaean principality, between Bozra and Edrei. Refuge of Jephthah when an outlaw (Judg. 11:3). Allied with Ammonites against David (2 Sam. 10:6; Ish-tob in AV/KJV).

TOBIAH. 1. Family of returned exiles, unable to prove their genealogy (Ezra 2:60; Neh. 7:62).

2. Ammonite official persistently opposing Nehemiah's work (Neh. 2:10; 4:3, 6:12, 17; 13:4).

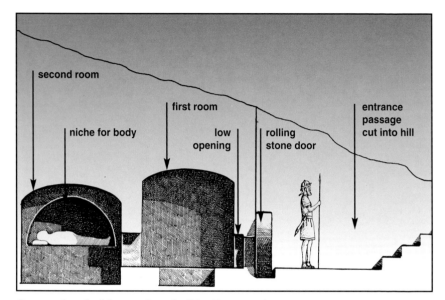

Cross section of a rich person's tomb of New Testament times

TOBIT (Apocrypha). Pious fiction set in the days of Israel's exile, illustrating God's care for individuals in spite of calamities. Blind Tobit sends his son Tobias to Media to collect a debt. Prompted by an angel, Tobias marries a widow whose seven husbands have all been killed on their wedding nights by an evil spirit, puts the demon to flight and heals his father's eyes.

TOE. *See* Thumb.

TOLA. 1. Son of Issachar (Gen. 46:13), whose descendants formed the leading clan of Tolaites (Num. 26:23) and provided soldiers for David (1 Chron. 7:2).

2. Judge of Israel for 23 years (Judg. 10:1–2).

TOMB. Royal tombs of David and his line (2 Chron. 32:33; Acts 2:29) were near the King's Garden in Jerusalem (2 Kings 21:18). Other rich people could afford such interment, usually a space cut in rock. Shebna's was denounced as ostentatious (Isa. 22:15–19). Family tombs in the ancestral inheritance used when possible (Judg. 8:32; 2 Sam. 17:23). The site of Joseph's tomb lent to Jesus (Matt. 27:60) is uncertain, despite fervent claims. Contact with death rendered one ceremonially unclean (Num. 19:11–16). *See* Burial; Grave.

TONGUE. Divine gift (Exod. 4:11), to be used wisely (Prov. 10:19; James 3:5–9). Needs control (James 1:26), for it has power for good or ill

(Prov. 15:1–4; 18:21). Figuratively, of divine judgment (Isa. 30:27; Rev. 16:10), hatred (Prov. 26:28), flattery (Prov. 28:23), deceit (Jer. 9:8; Rom. 3:13), slander (Ps. 15:3), joy (Ps. 16:9), praise (Ps. 66:17), witness (Ps. 71:24). *See* Mute.

TONGUES, speaking in. Spiritual gift (Mark 16:17; Acts 2:4; 10:44–46; 19:6; 1 Cor. 12:10); foretold (Isa. 28:11). Primarily for private use (1 Cor. 14:2, 14–15). In public, needs the gifts of interpretation (1 Cor. 14:27–28) and love (1 Cor. 13:1).

TOOTH FOR TOOTH. The law of retribution (Exod. 21:24) was to limit retaliation to the same amount; Jesus overrode it altogether (Matt. 5:38).

TOPAZ. Precious yellow stone; used in the high priest's breastpiece (Exod. 28:17) and as a foundation of the wall of New Jerusalem (Rev. 21:20).

TOPHETH *(Place of Burning).* In the Valley of Hinnom, where children were burned in sacrifice to the Ammonite god Molech (Lev. 18:21), copied by some Israelites (Jer. 7:31), despite Josiah's destruction of the site (2 Kings 23:10).

TORCH. Blazing stick (wrapped in oily rags), normally for giving light (Judg. 7:16); Samson had another use (Judg. 15:5).

TORRENT. *See* Wadi.

TOWN. Distinction from village or city not always maintained. Bethlehem called a village (John 7:42), town (Luke 2:4) and city (Judg. 17:8, AV/KJV).

TOWN CLERK. Executive officer liaising between the civic government and the Roman provincial authority (Acts 19:35).

TRACHONITIS. Part of Philip's tetrarchy, in N Transjordan (Luke 3:1).

TRADITION. Beliefs or practices *handed down* (the meaning of the Greek word) from earlier generations. Israelites told to teach their children God's ways (Deut. 4:9–10; 6:6–9; Ps. 78:3–7). By NT times, rabbis had added oral tradition to clarify the written law in changed circumstances, the 'tradition of the elders'. Jesus criticised scribes and Pharisees for not practising what they preached (Matt. 23). God's law always had priority (Matt. 15:1–9; Col. 2:6–23). Christian tradition included stories of Jesus' ministry (Luke 1:1–2; 1 Cor. 11:23–25; 15:1–8; Eph. 2:20; 1 Thess. 4:15).

TRANS-EUPHRATES. Persian province, sometimes translated 'Beyond the River', covering the whole of Syria-Palestine.

TRANSFIGURATION. Brief appearance of Jesus, dazzling in his divine majesty, to Peter, James and John (Matt. 17:1—8; 2 Pet. 1:16–18). Talking with Jesus about his coming death were Moses and Elijah, representative of Law and Prophets (that is, the whole OT order). Both men saw God on a mountain (Exod. 24:15; 1 Kings 19:9–13) and left no known grave (Deut. 34:6; 2 Kings 2:11). Some identify them with the two at the empty tomb (Luke 24:4; John 20:12; 'angel' in Greek can mean 'messenger') and Ascension (Acts 1:10) and with the two witnesses of Rev. 11:3. The heavenly voice indicated Jesus as God's Son (Mark 9:7) and the expected Prophet (Deut. 18:15). The cloud signifies God's

Travel

Travel. Mostly on foot (Exod. 15:22; Acts 9:32); otherwise by animal (Exod. 4:20; Luke 10:34), chariot (2 Sam. 15:1; Acts 8:28) or ship (Acts 13:4; Rev. 18:17). Limited in times of unrest (2 Chron. 15:5) and could be dangerous (Luke 10:30; Acts 27:9). Travelling overland by night was cooler (Luke 11:5-6). *See* Day's journey; Grain ship; Roads; Shipping.

Chariot. Light two-wheeled cart of wood and leather, sometimes with iron fittings (Judg. 4:3), pulled by two horses. Solomon the first Israelite king to make much use of them (1 Kings 9:19; 10:26). Only the well-to-do used chariots in peacetime (Acts 8:28).

Couriers. Royal messengers, literally 'runners', though usually mounted (2 Chron. 30:6; Esther 3:13). Travelled 40-140 km (25-90 mi) a day, according to urgency. 'Posts' in AV/KJV.

Day's journey. Distance covered by a loaded mule, around 40 km (25 mi). On the Sabbath (Acts 1:12) must not exceed 2000 cubits, about 900 metres (3000 ft).

Feet washing. Needful after walking along dusty roads and an obligatory welcome to visitors (Gen. 18:4; Luke 7:44). Usually a slave's task (1 Sam. 25:41); undertaken by Jesus as an example (John 13:4-15; 1 Tim. 5:10).

Greetings. Can be oral, without physical contact: 'Rejoice' (Luke 1:28) or 'Peace' (John 20:21). Or by a formal kiss on both cheeks (1 Sam. 10:1; 2 Cor. 13:12), rudely omitted by the Pharisee entertaining Jesus (Luke 7:45). Not to be given on urgent journeys (2 Kings 4:29; Luke 10:4): greeting another was a lengthy business requiring innumerable personal exchanges. Christian letters turned the opening greeting into a prayer for the recipient (Phil. 1:1-2). *See* Kiss.

Rich Romans travelled by sedan chair

Highway. Land routes were mostly just tracks until the Romans laid out their great road system, primarily for military purposes. *See* King's Highway; Roads.

Hospitality. Due to strangers (Gen. 18:2-9), after God's example (Deut. 10:18-19). Even more important among Christians, to demonstrate practical love (Heb. 13:2; 1 Pet. 4:8-9; 3 John 5-8).

Inn. Public khan or caravanserai (Luke 10:34). Another word used in Luke 2:7 may indicate a private guest room, normally available for entertaining strangers but already occupied.

A Roman merchant ship

Roads. Usually mere tracks, needing urgent attention before an important personage travelled (Isa. 40:3; 62:10), and dangerous (Isa. 33:8; Luke 10:30). Main highways, greatly improved by the Romans, were timely for spreading the gospel (Acts 11:19; 13:3, 49; 14:6-7, 21). *See* King's Highway.

SEA TRAVEL

Shipping. Israelites preferred dry land (Ps. 107:23-30). Their naval inexperience (1 Kings 22:48) usually meant depending on foreign seafarers (1 Kings 9:27) for overseas trade (Ezek. 27:25). Christians like Paul made much use of sea travel to spread the gospel (Acts 13:13; 16:11; 18:18). *See* Anchor; Skiff.

Anchor. Metaphor for vibrant Christian hope (Heb. 6:19) which, moored upon the sure promises of God, counteracts the tendency to drift (Heb. 2:1). *See* Hope.

Grain ship. Egyptian grain ships from Alexandria offered the quickest sea passage to Rome (Acts 27:6, 38). Prevailing winds meant the journey took about eight weeks (only 9-12 days for the return).

Shipwreck. Paul's fate three times (2 Cor. 11:25) even before his last voyage to Rome (Acts 27:44). Metaphorically, of believers backsliding (1 Tim. 1:19).

Below: There was a variety of means of road transport in New Testament times

presence (Exod. 24:15–18; Acts 1:9; 1 Thess. 4:17; Rev. 1:7). *See* Tabor, Mount.

TRANSGRESSION. The English word literally means 'overstepping' God's law; translates the more robust Hebrew term 'rebellion', particularly against God (Exod.34:7; Ps. 32:1–5).

TRAVEL. *See* pp. 109; 228-229.

TREASURE. Often buried for safekeeping, so might be unearthed by others (Job 3:21; Prov. 2:4). Jesus stressed the superlative value of spiritual treasure (Matt. 13:44; alluded to in Isa. 45:3).

TREASURER. In charge of official funds (Ezra 1:8; 2 Kings 12:5). *See* Erastus.

TREATY. *See* Covenant.

TREE. Symbolic of Nebuchadnezzar's widespread power (Dan. 4:10–26). Metaphor for Jesus' cross (Luke 23:31; Acts 5:30; 10:39; 1 Pet. 2:24), alluding to Deut. 21:23 (Gal. 3:13).

TREE OF KNOWLEDGE. Set in the Garden of Eden (Gen. 2:9, 17). The 'knowledge of good and evil' is more than 'becoming morally responsible' (Adam and Eve already were: Gen. 2:16; 3:6). Solomon's prayer for a 'hearing' heart to distinguish between right and wrong (1 Kings 3:9) may point to the meaning: would Adam and Eve heed God or determine on independent self-sufficiency?

TREE OF LIFE. In the midst of Eden (which appropriately means 'Delight'), guarded by cherubim (Gen. 2:8–17; 3:22–24). Figuratively, of the source of life and blissful well-being (Prov. 3:18; Rev. 2:7; 22:2).

TRIAL BY ORDEAL. *See* Jealousy.

TRIBES OF ISRAEL. Descendants of the 12 sons of Jacob, renamed Israel by God (Gen. 32:28). The Promised Land was divided among the tribes (Num. 32:33–42; 34), with special arrangements made for Levites (Num. 35:1–8). The books of Joshua and Judges reveal how far the tribes succeeded in occupying their allocation.

TRIBULATION, GREAT. Period of intense suffering for God's people before the end of the age (Dan. 12:1; Matt. 24:21; Rev. 7:14).

TRIBUNAL. *See* Judgment seat.

TRIBUNE. The Greek term literally means 'leader of 1000', but by NT times meant, more vaguely, 'high-ranking officer'; applied to Claudius Lysias (Acts 24:22).

TRIBUTE. 1. Payment by vassals, in forced labour (Josh. 16:10, AV/KJV) or in valuables (2 Kings 23:33–35; Isa. 16:1).
2. God's share of spoils taken in war (Num. 31:28–29).

TRIUMPHAL PROCESSION. Suggested by the splendour of a Roman general's victory procession, parading his prisoners of war. Believers, formerly enemies of God (Rom. 5:10), are those taken captive by the triumphant Christ and now joyfully displayed to the world as trophies of grace (2 Cor. 2:14). 'Fragrance' alludes to the practice of burning sweet spices along the route of the procession in Rome.

TROAS. Seaport of Mysia, on NE coast of Aegean Sea. Scene of Paul's call to evangelise

Part of a Roman triumphal procession

TRUTH. Moral attribute of total reliability, attributed to God (Ps. 31:5; Isa. 45:19; Rom. 1:25), Jesus (John 1:14), especially in his familiar 'Verily, verily' (John 3:3, AV/KJV), the Holy Spirit (Acts 28:25) and God's word (Col. 1:5). Should apply to humans (Ps. 15:2; Prov. 16:13), especially Christians (Eph. 4:15; 1 John 1:6–8).

TRYPHENA and **TRYPHOSA.** Christian women of Rome, probably sisters (Rom. 16:12).

TUBAL-CAIN. Descendant of Cain and son of Lamech and Zillah; pioneered metallurgy (Gen. 4:22).

TUMORS. Sympton of bubonic plague (Deut. 28:27; 1 Sam. 5:10–12), spread by rats (1 Sam. 5:6; 6:4).

TUNIC. *See* Dress pp. 54-55 (Robe).

TURBAN. *See* Dress p. 55.

Macedonia (Acts 16:8–11) and where he restored Eutychus to life (Acts 20:5–12). Made other visits (2 Cor. 2:12–13; 2 Tim. 4:13).

TROPHIMUS. Paul's Ephesian companion from Macedonia to Jerusalem (Acts 20:4; 21:29) and later at Miletus (2 Tim. 4:20).

TRUMPET. *See* Music p. 150.

TRUST. Dependence on God frequently encouraged (Exod. 14:31; John 14:1). Brought about by awareness of his revealed character (Ps. 9:10), love (Ps. 13:5), power to save (Isa. 12:2), holiness (Ps. 33:21), word (Ps. 119:42). Encourages the faith of others (Ps. 40:3) and expels fear (Ps. 56:3). Misplaced, if in human beings (Ps. 41:9), however exalted (Ps. 146:3), or in strongholds (Prov. 21:22), weapons (Ps. 44:6), false gods (Isa. 42:17) or deeds and riches (Jer. 48:7). *See* Faith.

TWELVE. 1. Number associated with God's elective purposes: tribes of Israel (Gen. 49:28), apostles (Mark 4:10; 1 Cor. 15:5); frequently used in Revelation (12:1; 21:12, 14, 21; 22:2).

2. Jewish term for the Minor Prophets (Hosea to Malachi).

TYCHICUS. Paul's travelling companion from Macedonia to Jerusalem (Acts 20:4), at Ephesus (Eph. 6:21; 2 Tim. 4:12) and Colosse (Col. 4:7). He may also have gone to Crete (Titus 3:12).

TYPOLOGY. Term derived from Greek for 'figure, model, example' to refer to people or events in biblical history foreshadowing the future (Rom. 5:14; 1 Cor. 10:6; Heb. 9:24; 1 Pet. 3:21).

TYRANNUS. Founder or owner of lecture hall used by Paul at Ephesus (Acts 19:9–10).

TYRE. Fortified commercial port, partly built on an island (Ezek. 26:4–5; 27:32). Ahab's marriage to the Tyrian princess Jezebel (1 Kings 16:31) ensnared Israel in pagan practices (Isa. 23; Ezek. 26—28). Paul visited the local Christians (Acts 21:3–7).

U

ULAI. Irrigation canal near Susa (SW Iran), where Daniel received visions (Dan. 8:2, 16).

UMPIRE. Arbiter (Job 9:33, RSV; 'daysman' in AV/KJV). His hand upon both parties implies evenhanded authority to adjudicate.

UNBELIEF. Inability to comprehend spiritual truths (Mark 9:24; 1 Tim. 1:13) or a deliberate refusal to accept them (Rom. 11:20; Heb. 3:19).

UNCIRCUMCISION. Men literally uncircumcised (Philistines, 1 Sam. 17:26), or the spiritually obtuse (Jer. 9:26; Acts 7:51).

UNCLEANNESS. *See* Clean and unclean.

UNCLOTHED. Figuratively, of the soul's disembodiment at physical death, desirable to Greek philosophers, but not to Christian Paul, expecting a resurrection body (2 Cor. 5:4).

UNEDUCATED. Untrained under a recognised rabbi (Acts 4:13, RSV).

UNFADING. Laurel garlands presented to victors at Greek games soon withered, unlike the believer's inheritance (1 Pet. 1:4; 5:4).

UNFAITHFULNESS. Usually refers to disloyalty to God (Deut. 32:20); cheating other people is viewed in the same light (Lev. 6:2; Num. 5:5–8). Leads to judgment (Num. 14:33; Ps. 73:27). Suspected marital unfaithfulness was subjected to trial by ordeal (Num. 5:11–31; *see* Jealousy).

UNICORN. *See* Wild animals, p. 17 (Wild ox).

UNITY. Characteristic of God (Deut. 6:4) and of his will for his people (John 17:22–23; Eph. 1:10; 2:13–19). Disrupted by sin (Isa. 59:2; James 4:1–4). *See* Reconciliation.

UNKNOWN GOD. Dedication noticed by Paul among the multitude of pagan shrines in Athens (Acts 17:23). Evidently an insurance against one god being overlooked.

UNLEAVENED BREAD. *See* Bread; Feast of Unleavened Bread.

UNSEARCHABLE. Beyond human comprehension and defying description; applied to God's judgments (Rom. 11:33), greatness (Ps. 145:3, AV/KJV), wonders (Job 5:9) and Christ's grace (Eph. 3:8).

UNWASHED HANDS. Ceremonially unclean (Mark 7:1–5). Ritual washing of hands before eating, scrupulously observed by Pharisees, was not an OT law. There were much more important matters (Matt. 15:1–20).

UPHAZ. Source of gold (Jer. 10:9; Dan. 10:5). More probably, not a place name but meaning 'refined'.

UPPER ROOM. Chosen by Jesus for the Last Supper, evidently at the home of a wealthy supporter, courageous enough to risk trouble from the authorities (Mark 14:15). 'Furnished' refers to cushions and carpets.

UR. Abraham's native place (Gen. 15:7), on the Euphrates.

URIAH (*The Lord is my Light*). 1. Outstanding soldier, one of David's Thirty (2 Sam. 23:39). Married to Bathsheba, whom the king seduced and then plotted her husband's death (2 Sam. 11).

2. Leading priest in Jerusalem, witness to Isaiah's significant naming of a yet unborn son (Isa. 8:2). Ordered by king Ahaz to erect a pagan altar in Jerusalem (2 Kings 16:10–16).

3. Son of Shemaiah from Kiriath Jearim. His oracles of impending judgment incensed king Jehoiakim who had him executed (Jer. 26:20–23).

URIM AND THUMMIM. Means by which the high priest (Deut. 33:8) obtained answers from God (Exod. 28:30; Num. 27:21;1 Sam. 28:6; Ezra 2:63). No details are given and even the terms themselves have never been satisfactorily explained.

UZ. Job's land (Job 1:1), in the Arabian desert E of Edom (Jer. 25:20; Lam. 4:21).

UZZA. 1. Owner of garden where kings Manasseh and Amon were buried (2 Kings 21:18, 26).

2. Descendant of Ehud (1 Chron. 8:7), expelled from Geba with other Benjamites, apparently because of intertribal quarrels, to Manahath, SW of Jerusalem.

UZZAH. Son of Abinadab, who died attempting to save the ark from toppling when oxen pulling the cart stumbled (1 Chron. 13). The ark should have been carried by Levites (Num. 4:15; 1 Chron. 15:12–15).

UZZIAH (*The Lord is my Strength*). Son and successor of Amaziah as king of Judah; also called Azariah (*The Lord is my Help*). Co-regent from 791 BC when Amaziah was imprisoned (2 Kings 14:13, 21), making for a long reign of 52 years, until his death in 739 BC. Struck with leprosy for usurping priestly privileges (2 Chron. 26; Isa. 6:1). A violent earthquake in his reign was long remembered (Amos 1:1; Zech. 14:5).

UZZIEL (*God is my Strength*). Youngest of four sons of Kohath and grandson of Levi (Exod. 6:18). His descendants (Num. 3:27) helped to transfer the ark of the covenant (1 Chron. 15:10) and served in the Temple (1 Chron. 23:12).

VALLEY OF DECISION. Scene of God's final judicial verdict on the war crimes of the Assyrian invaders of Judah; otherwise called the Valley of Jehoshaphat (Joel 3:2).

VALLEY OF HINNOM. *See* Topheth.

VALLEY OF LEBANON. High valley between the Lebanon and Antilebanon ranges (Josh. 11:17; 12:7). Today's Beqa'a Valley.

VALLEY OF SALT. Battlefield S of the Dead Sea (2 Sam. 8:13; 2 Kings 14:7).

VANITY. Literally the Hebrew means 'breath' (Ps. 144:4), but no one English word captures the meaning, which includes lack of substance (Ps. 62:9; Eccles. 2:11), unreliability (Job 15:31; Isa. 57:13), frailty (Ps. 39:11), brevity (Ps. 39:5; Eccles. 3:19), lack of purpose (Eccles. 2:11), dissatisaction (Eccles. 5:10), paganism (2 Kings 17:15; Jer. 10:15).

VASHTI (*Most Desirable*). Wife of the Persian king Ahasuerus (Xerxes), deposed for defying a drunken royal command (Esther 1:9—2:17).

VASSAL. Defeated ruler allowed to continue in office in return for an oath of allegiance to the conqueror and paying him tribute (2 Kings 17:3–4).

VEIL. *See* Dress p. 55.

VEIL, TEMPLE. *See* Curtain.

VENGEANCE. Retribution reserved to God (Deut. 32:35; Rom. 12:19). *See* Avenger of blood.

VERILY. *See* Amen; Truth.

VESSELS. Metaphorically, of times, events and people used by God for his purposes (Rom. 9:22–23, AV/KJV).

VINE. *See* Grapes and wine pp. 236-237.

VINE OF SODOM. Probably the poisonous colocynth (Deut. 32:32), symbolising Israel's venomous enemies.

VINEDRESSER. *See* Grapes and wine p. 236.

VINEGAR. Sour wine, forbidden to Nazirites (Num. 6:3); an acceptable seasoning (Ruth 2:14) and a refreshing drink (Matt. 27:48).

VINEYARD. *See* Grapes and wine p. 236.

VINTAGE FESTIVAL.
See Grapes and wine p. 237.

VIOLENCE. A consequence of the Fall (Gen. 4:8, 23) and resulting in the Flood (Gen. 6:13). Due to individual greed (Ps. 73:6), covetousness (James 4:2), hatred (Ps. 25:19) or war (Jer. 51:35). Forbidden to God's people (Jer. 22:3; Eph. 4:31), as exemplified by Messiah (Isa. 53:9; Matt. 11:29; Luke 22:50–51).

VIPER. *See* Wild animals p. 17.

VIRGIN. The Hebrew term means 'girl of marriagable age' (Gen. 24:16), though includes one sexually chaste (Exod. 22:16). Figuratively, of Christ's bride the church (2 Cor. 11:2; Eph. 5:25–27; Rev. 19:7–8).

VIRGIN BIRTH. The doctrine that Jesus was conceived by Mary through the direct action of the Holy Spirit (Matt. 1:18–25; Luke 1:26–56; 2:1–7), as foreshadowed by Isa. 7:14. *See* Mary 1.

VIRGIN DAUGHTER OF ZION. Jerusalem (2 Kings 19:21; Lam. 2:13).

VISITATION. Usually a reference to divine intervention, in blessing (Gen. 21:1; Job 10:12; Luke 19:44) or, more often, in judgment (Jer. 48:44).

VOW. None was decreed, but if one were made, it must be kept (Deut. 23:21–23). *See* Nazirites; Promise.

VULTURE. *See* Birds p. 104 (Eagle).

Grapes and wine

Vine. Invaluable food source, cultivated from earliest times, especially around Hebron (Num. 13:24). Blossom fragrant (Song of Sol. 2:13) and only the wood is useless (Ezek. 15:2-8). Grapes eaten fresh (September; Isa. 65:21) or dried (1 Sam. 30:12; Song of Sol. 2:5; *see* Raisins). Juice boiled down into heavy syrup ('honey' often in translations). Unripe grapes (July) are sour (Jer. 31:29; Ezek. 18:2; *see* Sour grapes). Failure (Joel 1:11; Amos 4:9) or destruction (Isa. 16:8) viewed as divine judgments (Ps. 78:47; Jer. 8:13). The 'wild vine' of 2 Kings 4:39 is the bitter colocynth. Symbol of Israel as God's people (Gen. 49:22; Jer. 2:21; Zech. 3:10). Adopted by Jesus as a sacred title (John 15:1-5). *See* Vinedresser; Vineyard; Wine; Winepress.

Vinedresser. Vines need constant attention (2 Kings 25:12), reflected in Jesus' description of the Father (John 15:1). Occupation for women (Prov. 31:16; Song of Sol. 1:6) as well as men (Matt. 21:28). Work involved setting up supports, training vine-tendrils, summer hoeing between rows and winter pruning (Isa. 5:6), burning useless twigs (John 15:6), digging irrigation channels (Isa. 27:3; Ezek. 19:10) and keeping them clear.

Vineyard. The messianic parable Luke 20:1-19 (alluding to Isa. 5:1-7) was set against the social background of the NT period. Much of the Jordan Valley and Galilean uplands were owned by foreign absentee landlords, their

A Roman wine amphora

estates managed by landless Jewish peasants. Creating a vineyard involved the owner in considerable expense: making a boundary ('set a hedge'), digging a pit for the winepress and building a watchtower. Vines need time to get established. Only in the fifth year could a commercial profit be expected, though meanwhile vegetables were grown between rows (the 'fruit of the vineyard'). In the parable, servants came to collect the owner's annual tenths of the vegetables. Under Jewish law, sitting tenants could claim the

Vineyard in Israel today

Grapes trodden under foot in a winepress

The vintage ilustrated on a Roman lamp

Medicinal properties recognised (Luke 10:34; 1 Tim. 5:23). Token of blessing (Deut. 7:13); its absence, of judgment (Jer. 48:33). Figuratively, of God's wrath (Ps. 75:8), quenching spiritual thirst (Isa. 55:1), moral decadence and consequent judgment (Rev. 14:8-10).

vineyard if they could prove sole enjoyment of three successive harvests. The arrival of the son and heir at the time of the fourth harvest was critical for the tenants' plot. When finally the owner himself appeared, armed with the contract, he ruined (not 'killed') the tenants in the lawcourts. *See* Watchtower; Wine; Winepress.

Vintage festival.
Celebration on completing grape harvest (Judg. 9:27; 21:19-21). Its absence an indication of divine judgment (Isa. 16:10).

Wine. Common drink; less likely than water to be contaminated. Made from grapes, raisins, dates, apples, figs, pomegranates or grain.

Winepress. Grapes were trodden under foot in a cistern cut in the rock (Jer. 48:33). The juice flowed out through a hole into a vat, where skin, pips and sediment could collect; the clear juice was run off through a higher hole to be stored in wineskins or jars to ferment. Treading grapes a figure of God's judgment (Isa. 63:3).

WADI. Riverbed, filled with water only during the rainy season.

WADI OF EGYPT. *See* River of Egypt.

WAFERS. Thin cakes of wheat flour, baked unleavened and spread with olive oil. To accompany the thank-offering (Lev. 7:12), priestly ordination (Exod. 29:2) and a Nazirite's offering on completing a vow (Num. 6:15).

WAGES. Payment for work done, in cash (Zech. 11:12) or kind (Gen. 29:15). To be paid promptly (Deut. 24:15; James 5:4) and at a fair rate (Luke 10:7; 1 Tim. 5:18). Figuratively, the inevitable deserts of sin (Rom. 6:23).

WAITING ON GOD. Patient anticipation of divine instructions (Num. 9:8; Ps. 123:2; Hab. 2:1), the fulfilment of his promises (Acts 1:4; Heb. 6:15), the coming of God's kingdom (Luke 23:51), vindication (Pss. 17:1–2; 135:14), adoption into God's family (Rom. 8:23), Christ's return (1 Thess. 1:10).

WALK. Often a metaphor for 'way of life'.

WALL. Main defence of a city against enemy attack (Deut. 3:5). Figuratively, of God's protection (Isa. 26:1) or of misplaced trust in wealth (Prov. 18:11). The wall of New Jerusalem (Rev. 21:12–21) depicts the total peace and security of God's presence (Ezek. 48:35). *See* Middle wall of partition.

WAR. *See* pp. 240–241.

WARDROBE KEEPER. Official in charge of Temple and state garments (2 Kings 10:22; 22:14).

WARFARE. Usually due to unfulfilled desire and envy (2 Chron. 18:1–3), and characteristic of a fallen world (Gen. 4:8; James 4:1–2). Israel's invasion of Canaan undertaken on God's instructions to provide his people with a homeland by expelling idolatrous nations (Deut. 7:1–6). Sometimes commanded as a punishment (1 Sam. 15:2; 2 Kings 24:2–4). Israel's victories or defeats ascribed to their attitude towards God (Deut. 28). One indication of the last days (Matt. 24:6–7); but the messianic age will bring peace (Ps. 46:9; Isa. 2:4).

WARFARE, SPIRITUAL. The struggle against the forces of evil (2 Cor. 10:3; 1 Pet. 5:8–9), using the equipment provided (Eph. 6:10–20). Ultimate victory assured at Calvary (Col. 2:15) and made plain at Christ's return (2 Thess. 1:7–10).

WATCHES OF THE NIGHT. Three in OT times (Ps. 63:6): first watch (Lam. 2:19), middle or midnight watch (Judg. 7:19) and last or morning watch (Exod. 14:24). The Roman practice of four watches was being followed in NT times: evening or first watch; midnight or second watch; cockcrow or third watch (Luke 12:38); morning or fourth watch (Matt. 14:25). *See* Hour.

WATCHTOWER. On city walls (2 Kings 17:9) or in fields and vineyards (Matt. 21:33) to watch for intruders.

WATER. All too scarce in Bible lands (Exod. 17:6; Num. 20:11), requiring settlements to be sited accordingly. (*See* Spring; Well.) Abundance a sign of divine blessing (Deut. 8:7), so symbolising salvation (Isa. 12:3) and spiritual life (John 4:14; Rev. 22:17).

WATER OF BITTERNESS. *See* Jealousy.

WAVE OFFERING. Expression derived from Hebrew meaning 'move to and fro'; in the case of the offering, towards the altar and back again, as a token of presenting the offering to God and his returning it to the priest (Exod. 29:26; Lev. 7:34; Num. 6:20).

Watchtower

WAY. 1. Used figuratively of God's actions (Deut. 8:2; Ps. 145:17) and of human conduct (Prov. 2:12–15; James 5:20).

2. Jesus' self-designation (John 14:6). His sacrifice has opened the true and living way into the Father's presence (Heb. 10:19–20).

3. Early name for the Christian manner of life (Acts 9:2; 24:22).

WAY OF CAIN. Wicked reaction to godliness (1 John 3:12; Jude 11), exemplified by Cain's conduct (Gen. 4:3–8).

WEANING. Lengthy process in ancient times (1 Sam. 1:22–24), up to three years (2 Macc. 7:27). The occasion for celebration (Gen. 21:8).

WEAPONS. Unreliable (1 Sam. 17:45; Ps. 20:7–8), compared with trust in God (Isa. 31:1; 2 Chron. 20:20–24). Used figuratively of verbal abuse (Ps. 64:3; Jer. 9:3, 8), spiritual warfare (2 Cor. 6:7; Eph. 6:11–17), divine words (Heb. 4:12; Rev. 1:16), protection (Gen. 15:1), judgment (Ps. 7:12–13; Isa. 13:5).

WEAVER'S BEAM. Heavy rod (1 Sam. 17:7; 2 Sam. 21:19) for raising and lowering vertical warp threads to allow the shuttle of horizontal woof threads to pass (Lev. 13:48).

WEAVING. *See* Loom; Shuttle. Figuratively, of life's brevity (Job 7:6; Isa. 38:12) and of evil plots being unprofitable (Isa. 59:5–6).

WEDDING GARMENT. Guests provided their own dress (Matt. 22:11); clean (preferably white); dirty clothes an insult.

WEEK. The Hebrew word means 'a seven'. Days are given numbers (Gen. 31:22; Matt. 28:1),

War

Archers. Essential for long–range attack. The tribes of Benjamin, Reuben, Gad and Manasseh noted for their skill (1 Chron. 5:18; 12:2; 2 Chron. 14:8).

Armour. Goliath's (1 Sam. 17:5) included helmet, greaves (shin protection) and a coat of mail. Figuratively describes spiritual protection (Isa. 59:17; Rom. 13:12). Eph. 6:13–17 reflects Roman equipment.

Army. Before the kings, armies in Israel were raised only in emergencies (Judg. 3:28; 4:6). First regular Israelite army organised by Saul (1 Sam. 13:2; 14:52) and developed by David (2 Sam. 23:8–39) and Solomon (1 Kings 4:26). The Roman army was based on the legion (nominally 6000 men) in ten cohorts each of six centuries.

Arrows. Metal-tipped reeds carried in leather quivers (1 Sam. 20:36; 2 Kings 9:24). Symbol of victory (2 Kings 13:18), God's word as a secret weapon (Isa. 49:2), unexpected trouble (Ps. 91:5), and the destructive power of evil words (Jer. 9:8).

Banner. Standard to rally troops (Ps. 60:4; Jer. 50:2). Figuratively to encourage faith (Exod. 17:15; Isa. 11:10).

Battering ram. Heavy wooden beam with iron head, swung on chains against the gate or wall of a besieged city to break open an entrance for troops (Isa. 22:5). An inclined ramp of local stones enabled attackers to assault the thinner upper wall (2 Sam. 20:15; Ezek. 4:2).

Bow. Made of tough springy wood, or of horn, sometimes strengthened with bronze (Ps. 18:34). The string was of twisted gut (Judg. 16:7).

Breastplate. Chest armour (1 Kings 22:34); metaphorically applied to righteousness (Isa. 59:17; Eph. 6:14) and faith and love (1 Thess. 5:8), as protective spiritual gifts.

Centurion. Roman officer in charge of 100 men, always well regarded in NT (Luke 7:3; Acts 10:1).

Warriors (*left to right*): Philistine, Assyrian, Babylonian, Greek and Israelite

Coat of mail. Scale armour (1 Sam. 17:5; Neh. 4:16). Weak point at sleeve joints (1 Kings 22:34). 'Brigandine' in AV/KJV.

Cohort. Basic unit of Roman legion, comprising 600-1000 men, commanded by a tribune (Acts 10:1). Roman citizens could enlist for 20 years (ages 17-37). Those who survived (about half) were well rewarded. Auxiliary cohorts of provincials gained Roman citizenship for their service.

Greaves (AV/KJV). Shin armour (1 Sam. 17:6).

Imperial Regiment. Title of honour ('Augustas', AV/KJV) bestowed on several Roman cohorts of auxiliary troops (Acts 27:1).

Italian Regiment. Auxiliary cohort of 1000 men, raised in Italy (Acts 10:1).

Legion. Basic Roman army unit of ten cohorts, nominally 10,000 men. Metaphorically, a powerful multitude (Matt. 26:53; Mark 5:15).

Military service. All male Israelites liable (Num. 1:3; 2 Chron. 25:5), except Levites (Num. 2:33), new property owners, newly married and fearful (Deut. 20:1-9). *See* Army.

Roman siege engine replica

Ramp. Artificial slope built with stones and rubble to enable attackers to scale city walls (2 Sam. 20:15).

Rampart. Second outer wall to reinforce city defences (Hab. 2:1). Figuratively applied to God's extra protection for his people (Ps. 48:13).

Shield. . Defensive armour (1 Chron. 12:8), full length (target; 1 Kings 10:16, AV/KJV), protected soldiers besieging a city wall; smaller (buckler; 1 Chron. 5:18, AV/KJV), used in hand-to-hand fighting. Both types also produced for ceremonial purposes (1 Kings 10:16-17). See Buckler.

Siege. Surrounding a city to enforce its surrender (Deut. 20:12). If intimidation failed (2 Kings 18:17–19:36), a ruse might succeed (Josh. 8:10-23) before attackers resorted to force. Jesus predicted the siege of Jerusalem (Luke 19:43-44).

Sling. Lethal long-range weapon, made from palm-fibre rope or leather. Employed in personal combat (1 Sam. 17:48-50), as artillery (Judg. 20:16; 2 Kings 3:25; 1 Chron. 12:2) or, by shepherds, to ward off wild animals (1 Sam. 17:40). Skilled slingers could hurl stones accurately at 160-240 km an hour (100-150 mph).

Spear. Goliath's huge weapon (1 Sam. 17:7) matched his strength. Symbol of royal authority (1 Sam. 18:10), but still effective (2 Kings 11:10).

Sword. Mentioned over 400 times, often to symbolise war (Lev. 26:6; Isa. 2:4). Figuratively, of God's word (Eph. 6:17; Heb. 4:12), wrath (Isa. 34:5-6) or judgment (Rev. 19:21); or of aggression (Jer. 2:30) or division (2 Sam. 2:26; Matt. 10:34).

not names, apart from the seventh, 'Sabbath', from a term meaning 'rest' (Gen. 2:2;Exod. 20:10–11). *See* Calendar; Feast of Weeks.

WEEPING. Expression of grief (Gen. 23:2; Matt. 2:18), remorse (Matt. 26:75; Heb. 12:17), sorrow for sin (Luke 7:38), joy (Gen. 29:11). Jesus' tears a sharing of grief with others (John 11:35) and his own grieving over Jerusalem's spiritual blindness (Luke 19:41). Banished from the age to come (Isa. 30:19; Rev. 21:4).

WEIGHTS AND MEASURES. Honesty demanded in their use (Deut. 25:13–16).

1. The weights themselves were stones, often in animal shapes for quickness in identifying. Only very rough relative values are possible. One talent (30 kg, 66 lbs) = 60 minas = 3000 shekels = 4500 pims = 6000 bekas = 60,000 gerahs.

2. In dry and liquid measures, one homer or kor (220 litres, 48 gals) = 10 ephahs or baths = 30 seahs = 60 hins = 100 omers = 180 kabs = 720 logs.

3. Linear measures were related to the human body: cubit = elbow to fingertip; span = thumb to little finger of open hand; palm = handbreadth at base of four fingers; reed or cane = 6 cubits; mile = 3000 cubits. *See* Day's journey; Mile.

WELL. The vital need for water is reflected in the many place names including *Beer*, Hebrew for '*well*' (Beeroth, Beersheba). Its importance could lead to disputes (Gen. 26:18–22). *See* Cistern; Jacob's Well.

WHALE. The critics' favourite animal (Jon. 1:17, AV/KJV). Some unidentifiable great marine creature is meant (the Hebrew means '*sea monster*').

WHEAT. *See* Farming p. 72.

WHEELS. Early wheels were solid wooden discs; replaced about 1500 BC by lighter, spoked wheels. Used on chariots (Exod. 14:25), by potters (Jer. 18:3), in threshing (Prov. 20:26), and in drawing water from wells (Eccles. 12:6). In visions, God's chariot-throne described as having wheels enabling it to turn in any direction (Ezek. 1:15–21; Dan. 7:9).

WHIRLWIND. Atmospheric vortex, liable to spring up in deserts as a dust devil, lifting even carts and trees by its violent swirling. Biblical references often relate to the glory and presence of God (Job 38:1; 40:6; Ezek. 1:4; Nah. 1:3; Zech. 7:14). Elijah was swept up to heaven on one such occasion (2 Kings 2:11).

WHITE. Symbolises holiness (Dan. 7:9), purity (Ps. 51:7), forgiveness (Isa. 1:18), enjoyment (Eccles. 9:8), victory (Rev. 3:4–5), superficial righteousness (Matt. 23:27–28). The white stone (Rev. 2:17) signified acquittal (jurors had black stones to vote 'guilty'). For the 'white fields' of John 4:35 (AV/KJV), *see* Colours.

WHITEWASH. Application of lime and water to make objects look more attractive than they were (Ezek. 13:10–16; Matt. 23:27; Acts 23:3).

WICK. Twisted flax fibres to draw up a steady supply of oil for the lamp's flame (Exod. 23:38). Applies figuratively to Jesus as Messiah, gently comforting those worn down by life's difficulties (Isa. 42:3; Matt. 12:20).

WICKEDNESS. Defined as malice (Exod. 23:1), godlessness (1 Sam. 2:12), murder (2 Sam. 4:11), oppression (2 Sam. 7:10), rape (2 Sam.

13:12), idolatry (2 Kings 17:11), sacrilege (2 Chron. 24:7), victimisation (Ps. 82:4), ill-gotten gains (Mic. 6:10–12). Examples listed in Rom. 1:29–32. *See* Evil.

WIDOW. Vulnerable, bereft of her legal protector. By remarrying (Deut. 25:5–6; 1 Sam. 25:39; 1 Cor. 7:39) or by returning to her father's home (Gen. 38:11; Ruth 1:8) she could avoid being exploited (Exod. 22:22; Isa. 10:2). Mark 12:40 refers to milking widows' assets by legal fees. God's concern (Ps. 68:5; Jer. 49:11) reflected in provisions to be made (Deut. 14:29; Isa. 1:17; 1 Tim. 5:3–16).

WIDOW'S MITE. *See* Coinage.

WIFE. Husband's helper and companion (Gen. 2:18; Prov. 31:10–31). Applied figuratively to Israel and God (Isa. 54:5) and to the church and Christ (Eph. 5:23–33; Rev. 21:2). *See* Barrenness; Helpmeet; Marriage; Polygamy.

WILD DONKEY. *See* Wild animals p. 17.

WILD GOAT. *See* Wild animals p. 17.

WILD OX. *See* Wild animals p. 17.

WILDERNESS. General term covering desolate areas with minimal rainfall, such as the Arabah (Deut. 1:1), and steppeland supporting flocks (1 Sam. 17:28; Luke 15:4). Scene of Israel's wanderings after the exodus (Num. 32:13), of John the Baptist's ministry (Mark 1:3), and of Jesus' temptations (Matt. 4:1), praying (Mark 1:35) and retreat (John 11:54). *See* Arabah.

WILL OF GOD. God's purpose, as revealed (Deut. 29:29) in Scripture (2 Sam. 7:21; Col.

1:25–26) and in Jesus (Eph. 1:9–10; Heb. 10:5–10). Fulfilled through divine resources (Heb. 13:20–21), by obedience (Phil. 2:13), sanctification (1 Thess. 4:3), thanksgiving (1 Thess. 5:18), persistence (Heb. 10:36), overcoming (Rev. 2:26) and supremely through love (Matt. 22:37–40).

WILLOW. *See* Trees p. 173.

WIMPLE. Veil worn round the face, head and neck (Isa. 3:22, AV/KJV).

WIND. 1. Rarely absent due to the closeness of sea, highlands and lowlands causing frequent temperature changes. More dependable in summer: farmers expect afternoon breezes for winnowing. Spring can bring *khamsin*, scorching E wind (Exod. 14:21).
2. Figuratively, of the Holy Spirit (John 3:8; *see* Spirit), God's control (Ps. 148:8), his chariot (2 Sam. 22:11) and judgmental power (Jer. 49:32); also used of brevity of life (Ps. 103:16), upsetting people (Prov. 11:29), empty boasts (Prov. 25:14), slipperiness (Prov. 27:16), useless effort (Eccles. 2:11), idolatry (Isa. 41:29), false prophets (Jer. 5:13), vain policies (Hos. 12:1). *See* Whirlwind.

WINDOW. *See* House p. 100.

WINDOWS OF HEAVEN. Picture language for openings in the sky for rain (Gen. 7:11), and divine deliverance (2 Kings 7:2) or provision (Mal. 3:10).

WINE. *See* Grapes and wine p. 237.

WINEBIBBER. *See* Drunkenness.

WINEPRESS. *See* Grapes and wine p. 237.

WINESKIN. Container made from animal hide (1 Sam. 1:24). New skins needed for new wine in order to absorb expansion upon fermentation; old skins lose their elasticity (Josh. 9:13; Matt. 9:17).

WINGS. Apart from literal references, signifies escape (Ps. 55:6), protection (Ps. 91:4), fleeting wealth (Prov. 23:5), invasion (Isa. 8:8), strength (Isa. 40:31). The 'wings of the morning' (Ps. 139:9–10) refers to brief feathery clouds seen in Palestine at dawn on the E skyline; the 'sea' is the Mediterranean, to the W. Whether E or W, no situation is beyond God's reach.

WINNOWING. *See* Farming p. 72.

WISDOM. Divine attribute (Prov. 8:22–31; Isa. 11:2), in degree shared with human beings by God's gift (1 Kings 4:29; Eph. 1:17; James 1:5). Philosophy seeks God as the *goal*; biblical wisdom *begins* with God and teaches practical skills in the business of living by divine principles (Prov. 4:11–13; Luke 7:35) and supremely in the knowledge of God himself (Eph. 1:17). Human wisdom is at best unreliable and insufficient (Isa. 47:10; 1 Cor. 1:18–25; 3:18–20).

WISDOM LITERATURE. Term applied to the OT books of Job, Proverbs and Ecclesiastes, and in the Apocrypha to the books of Ecclesiasticus and the Wisdom of Solomon.

WISDOM OF JESUS BEN SIRA. *See* Ecclesiasticus (Apocrypha).

WISDOM OF SOLOMON (Apocrypha). Although attributed to Solomon, composed in the last century BC by a Jew well educated in Greek thought. Encourages Jewish zeal for God and his law (chapters 1—5); praises divine Wisdom as a guide for life (6—9); illustrates how Wisdom has helped Jews and confounded their enemies (10—19).

WISE MEN. *See* Magi.

WITCHCRAFT. *See* Sorcery.

WITNESS. 1. Testimony in legal matters, needing support (Deut. 19:15; Ruth 4:1–9). Giving false witness attracted the penalty the accused might have suffered (Deut. 19:16–19).
2. Stone pile marking an agreement (Gen. 31:44; Josh. 22:27).
3. In the NT, one present during Jesus' life and ministry (Luke 24:48; Acts 1:22); or someone testifying to the truth about God and Christ (John 8:18; Rev. 1:5).

WOE. Expression of deep distress (1 Sam. 4:8; Matt. 23:13; Rev. 8:13).

WOLF. *See* Wild animals p. 17.

WOMAN. Created in the image of God, complementing man (Gen. 1:27) and interdependent with him (Gen. 2:18, 20–24). The fall disrupted the woman-man relationship (Gen. 3:16), but in Christ spiritual equality is restored (1 Cor. 11:11–12; Gal. 3:26–29). Of 150 named disciples in the NT, 30 are women (*see* Junias). Jesus' address of his mother (John 2:4; 19:26) was respectful, not cold as to modern ears. *See* Deaconess; Helpmeet; Prophetess; Widow; Wife; Zelophehad.

WOMB. In recognition that birth was under

Weaving wool on an upright loom.

God's control (Gen. 29:31), the firstborn male child or animal was deemed to be his: the animal was to be sacrificed and the child ransomed (Exod. 13:2, 12–16). *See* Barrenness.

WOOL. Invaluable (2 Kings 3:4) for soft clothing (Job 31:20; Prov. 31:13; Ezek. 34:3). Not worn by priests in the Temple, to avoid perspiration (Ezek. 44:17). In acknowledgment of God's gift (Hos. 2:9), the first clippings were to be offered to him (Deut. 18:4). Mixing wool and linen (banned, Lev. 22:11) creates static electricity, causing discomfort to the wearer. Its destruction by moths a figure of judgment (Isa. 51:8). *See* Shearing; Sheep.

WORD. 1. Divine title for the pre-existent Christ (John 1:1, 14; 1 John 1:1; Rev. 19:13), appropriate as God's self-revelation (Heb. 1:1–2).

2. Scripture (Matt. 15:6), especially the gospel (2 Tim. 4:2).

3. Preaching (Heb. 13:7).

4. God's word is creative (Ps. 33:6; Isa. 55:10–11; 2 Pet. 3:5), recreative (1 Pet. 1:23), sustaining (Heb. 1:3), life imparting (Phil. 2:16; 1 John 2:14), sanctifying (John 17:17), associated with faith (Rom. 10:8), the Spirit's instrument (Eph. 6:17).

WORK. 1. God's activity, to create (Gen. 1:1–2:3), to fulfill his purposes (John 5:17), to supply creation's needs (Ps. 104:10–17; Acts 14:17), to control nations (Ps. 22:28; Acts 17:26), to call out a people for himself (Exod. 6:6–8; 1 Pet. 2:9).

2. Human labour ordained by God (Gen. 1:26–28) and a moral duty (2 Thess. 3:7–12), yet futile without divine enabling (Ps. 127:1; John 15:5; 1 Pet. 4:11).

WORKMANSHIP. The Greek word is behind the English 'poem', suggesting that believers (Eph. 2:10, AV/KJV) are intended to be divine creations of beauty, rhythm and meaning.

WORKS, DEAD. Conduct belonging to the pre-conversion life (Heb. 6:1), which can lead only to spiritual death (Rom. 8:6–8).

WORKS, GOOD. Expected of believers by Christ (Matt. 5:16) and by Christian leaders (1 Tim. 6:18; Heb. 10:24) as an expression of living faith (James 2:17–18; 1 Pet. 2:12), although not faith's foundation (Eph. 2:8–9; Titus 3:5).

WORKS OF DARKNESS. Expression echoing Jewish teaching on light and darkness as a contrast between good and evil (Rom. 13:12; Eph. 5:11).

WORKS OF THE FLESH. The outworking of life without God (Gal. 5:19–21).

WORKS OF THE LAW. Religious acts prescribed by the law of Moses; of themselves unable to bring about a right relationship with God (Rom. 9:32; Gal. 2:16).

WORLD. Term usually restricted to mean 'inhabited earth' (Gen. 11:1; Matt. 18:7). The object of Jesus' mission (John 3:16) against Satan (Matt. 4:8–9; John 12:31) and its own evil spirit (John 7:7; Gal. 1:4). Through Christ's work, humanity (2 Cor. 5:18–19; 1 John 2:2), the natural creation (Rom. 8:19–22; Col. 1:20) and the present earth (Rev. 21:1–4) will be redeemed and renewed.

WORLDLINESS. Conforming to the culture, attitudes and practices of those opposed to God (Rom. 12:2; Titus 2:12; 1 Pet. 4:3–4).

WORMWOOD. Star whose fall upon the earth contaminates fresh water (Rev. 8:11), alluding to Amos 5:7 (obscured in NIV.) Although the plant of this name is not poisonous, its bitter taste suggests death.

WORRY. Forbidden (Ps. 37:1), as useless (Eccles. 2:22–23; Luke 12:25–26), burdensome (Prov. 12:25), destructive of faith (Matt. 13:22), betraying lack of trust in God (Matt. 6:26–32).

Countered by turning to God (Isa. 26:3; Phil. 4:6–7; 1 Pet. 5:7).

WORSHIP. Due to God alone (Exod. 23:25; Ps. 95:6), never to Satan (Matt. 4:9–10), other beings (Rev. 22:8–9) or idols (Lev. 26:1; Dan. 3:18). To be expressed by God's people (1 Pet. 2:9) to acknowledge his greatness (Ps. 95:1–3), holiness (Ps. 96:9), concern (Exod. 4:31) and deeds (Matt. 9:7–8); in praise (Heb. 13:15), music (Eph. 5:19), prayer (Luke 2:37), thanksgiving (Dan. 6:10), adoration (Ps. 138:2), joy (Ps. 100:2), trust (Heb. 11:6), awe (Ps. 68:35), reverence (Ps. 5:7), wholeheartedness (Deut. 10:12).

WRATH OF GOD. Provoked by sin (1 Kings 8:46; Rom. 1:18), evil living (Rom. 2:8), disobedience (2 Kings 22:13; Eph. 5:6), impenitence (Rom. 2:5), apostasy (Num. 25:3), idolatry (Josh. 23:16; Col. 3:5–6), spiritual pride (Matt. 3:7–10), rejection of Christ (John 3:36). Issues in judgment (Isa. 13:5), punishment (Rom. 13:4), death (Job 4:9). Averted by intercession (Deut. 9:18–29), repentance (Joel 2:13) and because of his love (Eph. 2:3–7) and the work of Christ (Rom. 5:9; 1 Thess. 1:10).

WRITING TABLET. *See* Tablets 2.

XYZ

XERXES I. King of Persia (485–465 BC); Ahasuerus in AV/KJV. In the book of Esther, he divorces Vashti (1:10–22) and makes Esther queen (2:17). He rewards Esther's uncle Mordecai for his loyalty (6) and hangs Haman (7:9) for plotting against the Jews (3).

YEAR OF JUBILEE. Every fiftieth year, trumpets throughout Israel proclaimed liberty for Hebrew slaves and restoration of hereditary property; fields were to lie fallow (Lev. 25).

YEAST. Fermenting agent (leaven, AV/KJV) used in bread making. Readily a symbol of contamination, hence God's insistence on unleavened bread to mark the Exodus deliverance (Exod. 12:15); also of pervasiveness, for good (Matt. 13:33) or ill (Matt. 16:6; 1 Cor. 5:5–8).

YOKE. 1. *See* Farming p. 72.
2. Amount of land a pair of oxen could plough in one day (1 Sam. 14:14).

YOKEFELLOW. *See* Syzygus.

YOUTH. The Hebrew word covers an age range from Moses as a babe (Exod. 2:2) to Joseph at 17 years (Gen. 37:2). The term implies inexperience (Judg. 8:20; 1 Kings 3:7).

ZABAD. Assassin of king Joash, in revenge for his murdering Zechariah, son of Jehoiada the priest (2 Chron. 24:20–26).

ZABDI. Judahite ancestor of Achan (Josh. 7:1, 17–18, AV/KJV), called Zimri in 1 Chron. 2:6, probably because of easily confused Hebrew letters.

ZACCHAEUS. Responsible for tolls on merchandise passing through Jericho (Luke 19:1–10). *See* Tax collectors.

ZACHARIAS. *See* Zechariah (NT).

ZADOK (*Righteous*). High priest who supported David during Absalom's rebellion (2 Sam. 15:24–29) and Solomon in his securing the succession (1 Kings 1).

ZAHAR. Wool district (Ezek. 27:18), N of Damascus.

ZALMUNNA. *See* Zebah.

ZAMZUMMIM, ZAMZUMMITES. Ammonite nickname for the Rephaim they expelled (Deut. 2:20). The word means '*Gibberish*' (their speech was not understood); the people are unknown apart from this verse.

ZAPHENATH-PANEAH. Egyptian name bestowed upon Joseph by Pharaoh when appointing him vizier (Gen. 41:45). Giving a new name to mark a promotion was common in Egypt.

ZAREPHATH. Commercial city-state, on the coast between Tyre and Sidon, where God sent Elijah to lodge with a destitute widow during a severe drought (1 Kings 17:9–24; Obad. 20; Luke 4:26; 'Sarepta', the Greek equivalent, in AV/KJV).

ZARETHAN. On E bank of Jordan, N of Succoth (Josh. 3:16;1 Kings 4:12; 7:46).

ZEAL. Single-minded enthusiasm, towards God (1 Kings 19:10), his house (Ps. 69:9), service (Rom. 12:11), law (Acts 21:20). Often used of God's intense desire, for his people (Num. 25:11; 'jealousy' in AV/KJV), to punish sin (Deut. 29:20), to send Messiah (Isa. 9:7). *See* Jealousy.

ZEALOTS. Political party founded by Judas the Galilean, leader of the revolt against the Romans in AD 6 in protest against paying tribute to pagans (Acts 5:37). See Simon 2.

ZEBADIAH (*Gift of the Lord*). Favourite name with parents.

ZEBAH AND ZALMUNNA. Midianite chiefs, captured and executed by Gideon (Judg. 8:4–21; Ps. 83:11).

ZEBEDEE (*Gift of the Lord*). Father of the apostles James and John (Matt. 4:21) and head of a thriving fishing firm (Mark 1:20).

ZEBOIIM. One of the five cities of the valley (Gen. 10:19) suffering fiery judgment (Gen. 14:2; Deut. 29:23; Hos. 11:8).

ZEBUL. Abimelech's deputy at Shechem (Judg. 9:28), who lured rebel troops into a trap (Judg. 9:26–41). *See* Gaal.

ZEBULUN. Name of Jacob's 10th son (Gen. 30:20), the tribe formed by his descendants (Gen. 49:13) and their territory in the Promised Land (Josh. 19:10–16). References to the sea in Gen. 49:13 and Deut. 33:19 may mean that Zebulunites worked with fellow Israelites on the coast; their own domain was landlocked.

ZECHARIAH (*The Lord Remembers*). Over 30 mentioned. 1. Son of Jeroboam II (2 Kings 14:29) and briefly king of Israel (2 Kings 15:8–12).

2. Son of the priest Jehoiada, stoned on the orders of king Joash for condemning apostasy (2 Chron. 24:20–26). Considered the last OT martyr (Matt. 23:35), 2 Chron. being placed last in the Hebrew OT.

3. Post-exilic priest-prophet (Ezra 5:1; Zech. 1:1), whose prophecies are recorded in the OT book of Zechariah.

ZECHARIAH (book). Ascribed to the son of Berekiah (Zech. 1:1), a contemporary of Haggai (Ezra 5:1). Chapters 1—8 cover vision-prophecies, dated 520–518 BC, to urge former exiles to rebuild the Temple. Chapters 9—14 record two oracles concerning Messiah's coming, rejection and acceptance. The NT includes over 70 quotations and allusions to the book, notably references to Christ's entry into Jerusalem (Zech. 9:9; Matt. 21:5), his betrayal price (Zech. 11:12–13; Matt. 26:15; 27:3–7), arrest and desertion (Zech. 13:7; Matt. 26:31), crucifixion (Zech. 12:10; John 19:37), second coming (Zech. 14:5; Matt. 25:31).

ZECHARIAH (NT). Zacharias in AV/KJV. Elderly father of John the Baptist. Priests drew lots for the privilege of offering incense (Exod. 30:1–10; Luke 1:9). Zechariah and Elizabeth had long ceased to pray for a child (Luke 1:7), but their prayers had not been lost (Luke 1:13).

ZEDEKIAH. 1. Leader of 400 false prophets who advised Ahab and Jehoshaphat to attack Ramoth Gilead and ridiculed Micaiah's warning of disaster (1 Kings 22).

2. Last king of Judah, originally called Mattaniah but renamed Zedekiah by Nebuchadnezzar as a sign of vassalage (2 Kings 24:17). Considered an evil and weak ruler (Jer. 37:1–39:7).

ZELOPHEHAD. Manassite who died in the wilderness, leaving no male heir (Num. 26:33). His five daughters appealed to Moses and Eleazar and won the right to succeed to the family inheritance, bringing about a change in the law (Num. 27:1–8; Josh. 17:3–4).

ZENAS. Jurist of Roman (not Mosaic) law, visiting Crete with Apollos on Paul's behalf (Titus 3:13).

ZEPHANIAH. 1. Priestly son of Maaseiah (2 Kings 25:18), twice sent by king Zedekiah to Jeremiah (Jer. 21:1; 37:3). Sympathetic to Jeremiah and refused to put him in the stocks (Jer. 29:25–29). Captured when Jerusalem fell to the Babylonians and executed at Riblah (Jer. 52:24–27).

2. Prophet during Josiah's reign; unusually his genealogy is given to four generations (Zeph. 1:1). One of the 'Minor' Prophets. *See* next entry.

ZEPHANIAH (book). Following the evil reigns of Manasseh and Amon, the prophet announces the imminent judgment of the Day of the Lord (Zeph. 1:1-2:4) falling upon unbelieving nations: Philistines to the W (2:5–7), Moab and Ammon to the E (2:8–11), Egypt to the S (2:12) and Assyria to the N (2:13–14); but also upon Jerusalem (3:1–8). Ultimately a faithful remnant in Jerusalem will lead to God's kingdom being established (3:9–17).

ZERAH. Cushite general, whose huge army was remarkably defeated by king Asa at Mareshah (2 Chron. 14:9–15).

ZERED. Last wadi on the Israelites' wanderings before reaching the river Arnon (Num. 21:12–13; Deut. 2:14).

ZERESH. Haman's wife, a member of his advisory council (Esther 5:10; 6:13).

ZERUBBABEL (*Seed of Babylon*). Born in exile (hence his name). With Jeshua led the refounding of the Temple after the exile (Ezra 3; 5—6; Hag. 1—2).

ZERUIAH. Mother of David's three generals, Joab, Abishai and Asahel (2 Sam. 2:18). The unusual mention of mother and omission of father suggests the latter died early (2 Sam. 2:32).

ZEUS. Greek version of the Roman supreme god Jupiter, credited to Barnabas by Lystrans amazed at a cripple's healing (Acts 14:12).

ZIBA. Appointed by David to manage Saul's estates on behalf of Jonathan's crippled son Mephibosheth (2 Sam. 9). During Absalom's revolt, Ziba claimed Mephibosheth was remaining in Jerusalem to seize the kingdom, which Mephibosheth later denied. Not knowing whom to believe, David divided the property between them (2 Sam. 16:1–4; 19:17, 24–29).

ZIKLAG. Negeb town, SE of Gaza, allocated to

Feasts and festivals

Feast of Dedication (Hanukkah). Instituted by Judas Maccabaeus in 165 BC, to celebrate the purification of the Temple, after its desecration by Antiochus Epiphanes (1 Macc. 4:36-59; John 10:22).

Feast of Passover (14 Abib, later Nisan, Mar.-Apr.). Marks Israel's deliverance from Egyptian slavery (Exod. 12), so called because the angel of death 'passed over' the blood-sprinkled houses of the Israelites.

Feast of Purim, or Lots (Adar, Feb.-Mar.). Celebrates the Jews' deliverance from Haman's plot (Esther 3:7; 9:15-32).

Feast of Tabernacles (Tishri, Sept.-Oct.). Or Feast of Booths, from the practice of camping out for the week under rough shelters, recalling the wilderness wanderings (Lev. 23:42-43). Autumn thanksgiving for harvest (Num. 29:12-38), culminating on the 8th day with a liturgical prayer for rains (Zech. 14:17) with a ritual drawing of water from the pool of Siloam for spiritual renewal. Jesus offered himself on that day as the satisfier of spiritual thirst (John 7:37). His claim at the same season to be the Light of the World (John 8:12) may allude to the evening lights ritual at the feast. Of the three major Jewish festivals, Passover was

fulfilled by Jesus on Good Friday (1 Cor. 5:7) and Pentecost by the coming of the Holy Spirit (Acts 2). The harvest festival of Tabernacles remains to be fulfilled, presumably at Christ's second coming (Matt. 13:24-30).

Feast of Unleavened Bread. Seven days commemorating the Israelites' hasty meal before escaping from Egypt (Lev. 23:6-8).

Feast of Weeks (Sivan, May-June). So called because it fell a week of weeks (7 weeks, 50 days inclusive) after Passover. From 2nd century BC called Pentecost (from the Greek word for 'fifty').

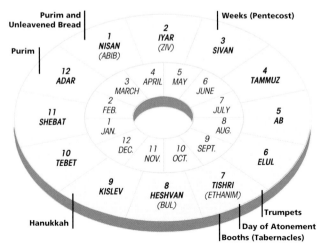

Simeon (Josh. 19:5), but later in Philistine hands. While a fugitive from Saul, David was given it by the Philistine king of Gath as a fief (1 Sam. 27:6–7). Burned by Amalekites during David's absence, but avenged by him after a strenuous campaign (1 Sam. 30). Rallying point for David's supporters before he became king.

ZILPAH. Leah's maid, given to Jacob as a concubine; mother of Gad and Asher (Gen. 29:24; 30:9–13).

ZIMRI. Meaning uncertain, but an ill-fated name.

1. Simeonite elder (Num. 25:8–14), among those who brought down a heavy plague upon Israel for liaising with foreign women (Num. 25:9; 1 Cor. 10:8).

2. King of Israel for one week after assassinating Elah. Committed suicide at Tirzah when facing Omri's certain victory (1 Kings 16:8–20; 2 Kings 9:31).

3. Descendant of Judah and Tamar's illicit union (1 Chron. 2:6); also called Zabdi, grandfather of the notorious Achan (Josh. 7:1, 17–18).

4. Descendant of king Saul (1 Chron. 8:36).

ZIN. Wilderness S of the Promised Land (Num. 13:21; Josh. 15:1); not to be confused with the Wilderness of Sin. *See* Kadesh Barnea.

ZION. Strictly, the Jebusite fortress captured by David and made his palace (2 Sam. 5:6–9). Situated below the peak upon which Solomon built the Temple (1 Kings 8:1). By extension, the name was applied to the whole city of Jerusalem (Isa. 10:24).

ZION, DAUGHTER OF. Poetic term for Jerusalem (Ps. 9:14; Isa. 1:8) or its inhabitants (Song of Sol. 3:11; Zech. 9:9).

ZIPH. 1. Town of S Judah, near the Edom border (Josh. 15:24).

2. Hill town of Judah (Josh. 15:55), fortified by Rehoboam (2 Chron. 11:7). The neighbourhood, the Wilderness of Ziph, a refuge for David (1 Sam. 23:14–19; 26:1–2).

ZIPPORAH. Wife of Moses and mother of Gershom (Exod. 2:16–22) and of Eliezer (Exod. 18:2–4). Aaron and Miriam's derision at Moses' marriage earned the Lord's rebuke (Num. 12:1–15). The obscure incident of Exod. 4:24–26 baffled even early Jewish commentators; evidently intended to stress the importance of circumcision as a covenant sign.

ZOAN. City in the Nile's E Delta, effectively the capital of Egypt, 1100–660 BC (Isa. 19:11; 30:4; Ezek. 30:14).

ZOAR (*Small*). Lot's preferred, if temporary, refuge from the overthrow of the cities of the plain (Gen. 19:18–23, 30).

ZOBAH. Aramaean city-state between Hamath and Damascus, overcome by David (2 Sam. 8:3).

ZOPHAR. One of Job's would-be comforters (Job 2:11; 11:1; 20:1; 42:9); a man of common sense but of set opinions.

ZOPHIM. Vantage point on Pisgah to which Balak took Balaam to curse Israel (Num. 23:14).

ZORAH. Home town of Manoah, Samson's father (Judg. 13:2), N of the Valley of Sorek.

ZUPH. Region where Saul searched for his

father's asses and first met Samuel (1 Sam. 9:5–14).

ZUR. Midianite chief, killed in Israel's campaign against the Ammonite king Sihon (Num. 31:8; Josh. 13:21). His daughter Cozbi was slain by Phineas (Num. 25:15).